Nina's Journey

Nina's Journey

A Memoir of Stalin's Russia and the Second World War

NINA MARKOVNA

REGNERY GATEWAY

Washington, D.C.

Library of Congress Cataloging-in-Publication Data
Markovna, Nina.
    Nina's journey : a memoir of Stalin's Russia and the Second World
    War / Nina Markovna.
        p.   cm.
    ISBN 0-89526-550-8
    1. Markovna, Nina. 2. Crimean—History—1921–1944—Biography.
    3. Crimean—Biography.   4. Soviet Union—History—1925–1953.
    5. World War, 1939–1945—Personal narratives, Russian.   I. Title.
    DK508.835.M37A3   1989
    947'.710842'092—dc20   89-36926
                                                            CIP

Published in the United States by
Regnery Gateway
1130 17th Street, NW
Washington, DC 20036

Distributed to the trade by
National Book Network
4720-A Boston Way
Lanham, MD 20706

Manufactured in the United States of America

10 9 8 7 6 5 4 3 2 1

To My Dear Father.

Acknowledgments

Regnery Gateway was my first choice among publishers to whom I might send my manuscript. I had followed for years its splendid record in selecting an exceptional catalogue of books to be presented to the reading public. And, having for years silently admired its founder, Mr. Henry Regnery, I am happy now to be able to express publicly this deep admiration. Regnery Gateway, Inc., may be regarded by some as a small publisher, but to me they are a giant.

Henry Regnery's son, Alfred, now president and publisher, I shall forever thank for reading, liking, and accepting my story and, in this period of ostensible *glasnost* or openness, for providing me with a platform for my personal *glasnost*, that is, for bringing *Nina's Journey* to the American public.

It should be noted that *glasnost*, to a Russian, does not literally mean "openness," for which there is a specific word, *otkritost*. Rather, it means "voice-giving," its root being an ancient Russian word, *glas* (voice). In the past, when most people could not read, a man would walk from house to house, from street to street, shouting into a long horn, and in this way would *"glasit"* the current news and information to the populace, hence the word *glasnost*. Alfred Regnery did, indeed, provide me with a platform, this opportunity for my written *glasnost*.

I also sincerely thank my editor, Harry Crocker, who led me patiently through the revisions (and excisions!) that my original manuscript has undergone in assuming its finished form as *Nina's Journey*. His earnest desire to help me, I greatly appreciate. He persuaded me to leave out many chapters dealing with the history of old Russia, and certain episodes of World War II in which I was not involved personally. Painful as it was at first, in the end I came to agree fully with the rightness of his judgement.

My dear husband helped me immeasurably in every way during those three years that I spent day in and day out at my writing table. The most difficult decision I had to make at the very start was whether to write in my native Russian—a language so infinitely expressive and natural to me—or in English, which I have learned in my later life. To write in Russian would have been easier, but in translation something of the original *dushà* (soul) dies, no matter how well it is done. So, I took courage and began to write in English, my husband being at various times my dictionary, my thesaurus, my orthographer. I could never fully express my thanks to him in words, Russian or English, printed or spoken.

Contents

FACTS DO NOT CEASE TO EXIST
BECAUSE THEY ARE IGNORED.

Aldous Huxley

Part One

Within Soviet Borders

". . . the devout Russian people no longer needed priests to pray thto heaven. On earth they were building a kingdom more bright than any heaven had to offer. . . ."

JOHN REED—Greeting the
October revolution of 1917.

CHAPTER ONE

The ship was gliding steadily toward the shore. Only hours separated me from American soil. And the baby I was carrying within
me—it was destined to be born on that blessed soil—an American!

How many routes I had taken—tortuous, unforeseen routes—
before Fate finally brought me to the land of so much promise and
light.

I was only ten when the journey began. . . .

A large copper samovar stood majestically on our kitchen table, glowing under the light of a hanging kerosene lamp. Snug, warm, I sat at the
small double window, hypnotized by the eerie stillness of the outdoors.
Not a branch moved, not a sound disturbed nature's spell. The sun,
after trying in vain all through the day to warm up the snow-blanketed
earth, finally retired. The earth sank under the huge, down-like snow
comforter; the roofs of buildings, too, disappeared under a layer of
white, and only the upper parts of puffing chimneys remained spared.
Even fences decided to sink into the ground, only here and there
exposing the round tops of supporting wooden posts—a warning to
pedestrians. The snow behaved as if its sole duty was to try to cleanse
everything in its path before turning into wild torrents and muddy
rivulets with the approaching thaw of spring. And with the calendar
marking the eighth day of March, the spring thaw was not far off.

In the samovar's gleaming surface I saw a reflection of my 46-year-
old father—a handsome man with a dark moustache and a soft, but
determined, clean-shaven chin. His full mouth was partially hidden

under the moustache, as if trying to disguise his true nature—that of a man of overwhelming kindness. To me, Father's eyes mattered most; the color of overripe sweet cherries, those eyes were not able to hide anything—neither silent laughter nor tearless sorrow.

Next to Father sat twelve-year-old Slava, my only sibling—a slender, small boy with golden curls falling over his extraordinarily high forehead. That forehead prompted many people to predict great intellectual achievements for Slava, noting that nature herself endowed the boy with double the ordinary amount of brain.

Although two years younger, I was already taller than my brother, taking after Father's side of the family where even seven-footers were known to grace this earth. Actually, the family name itself, which could be translated as "Huge," was derived from its ability to produce exceptionally tall offspring.

Not only would I have gladly swapped my height with Slava, but also my straight brown hair for his golden locks. Even our neighbors saw some injustice in nature being so blind as to endow a girl with great height and straight hair, while giving a boy the most beautiful curls but no height. On seeing Slava and me together, they shook their heads in mock sadness and good-naturedly reproached Mother:

"Natasha, dear, you and your Mark made a mistake. Ninochka should have been a boy, and Slava a girl." And they clicked their tongues in a disapproving manner, while smiling encouragingly at my brother and me.

Mother was not with us at the table. She was away celebrating a day dedicated to her particularly—Woman's Day—when from one end of the country to the other, Soviet females dutifully marked equality with men. In truth, Mother was more than equal with Father on that special day, turning into a superwoman of sorts. After completing an eight hour shift on Woman's Day at the office manager's "request" (with double pay!) she hurried home on foot. No public transportation existed between our neighborhood and the Dulovo porcelain factory two kilometers away, where she worked as a typist and Father worked as an accountant.

At home, she quickly threw together a supper for the three of us, warming up some cabbage soup called *shchi*. Then, having transformed cold, leftover buckwheat *kasha* into tasty, hot pancakes to accompany the *shchi*, Mother expertly fixed a samovar and began to change out of her ordinary work clothes into more festive attire. Out of the storage chest appeared an embroidered peasant-type blouse, followed by a woolen skirt of navy blue. Over cherished high-heeled pumps she put on a pair of felt boots, and throwing an imitation fur coat over her shoulders, while still trying to find the sleeve holes, she kissed us a hasty goodbye. Opening the heavy door to the frosty world outside, Mother half-shouted, half-sang, "Wait for me, everybody! I won't return empty-handed!"

We remained at the table, slowly sipping the fragrant tea, while holding a coarse, brownish lump of raw sugar between our teeth, sucking on it very gently so as to make it last longer. Those parting words of Mother—"I won't return empty-handed"—kept me and Slava in blissful suspense. What will she bring from the Woman's Day party? Candy? Fruit? Cookies? If only the samovar would remain hot, I wished, to greet her with a glass of steaming tea.

Peculiar, that the liquid so highly cherished by the Russians, the liquid that the samovar offered, was nothing more than plain, ordinary, boiled water. To the non-Russian, any container—tea kettle or simple pot—could serve to boil the tea water satisfactorily. But not to the Russian. The word *samovar* itself always intrigued me, filling me with the question of why this name should have been applied to such a cumbersome water container. The word *samo* means self, and *var* means cooking, which implies that a samovar provides a labor-free procedure for boiling water for tea, but it provides nothing of the sort! In actual practice, twenty minutes minimum were necessary to force this awkward, stubborn, giant pot to produce results.

As a rule, women attended to the preparation of the samovar; men only rarely helped. The container had to be first filled with water, while the metal tube in the middle of it initially required some crumpled newspaper, then a few dozen sticks of dry, thin wood, then charcoal. After the paper was lit, wooden sticks were added and watched closely to encourage the flame, not allowing it to expire. While kneeling, with one's face almost touching the ground, one puffed and puffed. Once the sticks caught fire, one carefully—holding one's breath from sheer anticipation—added the coals. And this step was crucial. If the coals refused to glow with the heat available from the sticks and paper, one had to concede defeat and start from scratch. No matter how strong or how long one blew to try to promote the flame, it would already be choked by the cold, heavy coals. The procedure had to be repeated from the beginning: paper, wood, coals.

When the routine was successful and water reached the boiling point, the samovar was carried to the table and placed on a metal tray, protecting the table from sparks and ashes of red hot charcoal. This step was called *postavit*—to stand. And the whole procedure of preparing the temperamental superpot was called neither to boil, nor to fix, nor to prepare, but to *postavit*. Once the samovar stood proudly on the table, steaming, puffing, singing to the surrounding company, inviting all to partake of its generosity, previous labors were forgotten and the samovar remained the darling of the traditional Russian table.

Our friends and neighbors cherished an invitation to Mother's standing samovar, but not to Father's. Men seemed not to possess the magical touch, the natural rhythm women had, to succeed with the samovar. While men blew and puffed fiercely, yet shallowly, impatiently, women blew quietly at first, taking their time, turning more energetic later. They knew instinctively when to puff and when to just be still, observing the flame. They knew when to whisper, implore, and shame the samovar into cooperation.

Mother's stream of words directed at the samovar during the *postavit* ritual was heard daily. "Glow, little sticks, glow. Don't let me down! I count on you. Go on, go on. Give me fire, and warm up the coal!" And a bit later, more sternly, "See how I am trying? Cooperate! Don't be lazy!" And with the coals starting to glow, Mother would exclaim enthusiastically, "Good boy! Good boy!"—a samovar being of masculine gender. Rising from her knees, she would shake off the dust, and rosy-cheeked, eyes glowing with accomplishment, call out gaily, "Mark! Children! Samovar is standing!"

And in no way would a samovar tolerate its replacement with some other form of container. Once, when Mother was preoccupied with something outside our home, she asked Father to fix the samovar. After half an hour of exasperated labor, he sat on the ground next to the still-cold machine and holding his head in both palms, whispered, "What a stubborn, good-for-nothing monstrosity."

"Papa," I tried to offer some advice, "why can't we boil the water in a pot and fill the samovar with it?"

"That would be cheating. Mother would know."

"How?" I persisted.

"The water wouldn't taste the same. The tea wouldn't be worth drinking. Ninochka, let's try once more. While I stuff the pipe with the sticks, you just put your head to the ground and blow. But try to blow with . . . with a certain magic—like your mother."

No magic was forthcoming from me, so Slava had to be called, and while all three of us were hovering over the utterly indifferent samovar, Mother returned and took charge.

Very soon, her clear, bell-like call rang through the house.

"Mark! Children! March to the table! Samovar is sta-a-n-di-i-ng!"

CHAPTER TWO

The snow drifted high around our log house, but inside it was warm and secure. During the long wait for Mother's return from the Woman's Day celebration, Slava and I dozed off from time to time, our heads drooping low, touching the top of the kitchen table. Yet, when Father suggested it was bedtime, we immediately came to life, insisting that Mother "asked" us to wait for her.

Despite the low temperature outside, our dwelling—constructed from smooth, round logs—stayed comfortable because of a stove-hearth called *pechka,* a creation borrowed in the distant past by the Russians from our Finnish neighbors, and turned into a pure *russkaya pechka,* Finns conveniently forgotten.

The warmth did not come without cost, however, since the *pechka* robbed us of one-third of our entire living space. Yet we could not face winter without it, for while its lower part—the hearth—performed the duties of boiling, baking, broiling, even barbecuing, filling the house at the same time with much-needed warmth, the flat brick top, accessible by a short ladder, served as a toasty bed for up to six or eight people. In large families, the top space was given wholly to the children.

During the hot, dusty summer months this elephant of a *pechka* was regarded with much irritation for robbing us of so much precious living space. But in the stormy winter months, when hurricane-like winds pierced through the double windows and the tiny cracks in the log walls, spraying icy air inside our home—then the *pechka* again became one's best friend.

We lived in the small town of Dulovo, about ninety kilometers east of Moscow. The town was dedicated exclusively to the operation of a porcelain factory, formerly owned by a super-rich merchant, Savva Kuznetsov. Since the October revolution, his seven factories, including the one in Dulovo, belonged "to the people."

Dulovo's factory was famous for producing high quality porcelain, concentrating on magnificent tea sets and trays, and artificial porcelain eyes, much in demand by Italian toy-makers. Mother, employed as a typist in this factory, often took dictation addressed to such Party big shots as Kaganovich, Kalinin, Jagoda, Molotov, and once even to Comrade Stalin himself, informing him that the tea set of the "Suliko" design was on its way and would he please in his unending kindness and wisdom accept the set as a gift from the workers of the Dulovo porcelain factory.

While six of the seven Kuznetsov factories were situated in Russia proper, one was in Riga, capital of Latvia. Riga's location on the western Dvina River, which flows into the Baltic Sea, was for centuries admired and sought after by the rulers of Russia. Peter the Great, in the year 1700 ordered his army to march into Swedish occupied Riga, starting the "Great Northern War" that lasted almost twenty years. The Czar took much from the Swedes, including a marshy piece of land at the mouth of the Neva River. On this side Peter dreamed of building a city with his name, which he spelled in the Dutch fashion: "Now, by God's help, the foundations of Sankt Piter Bourkh are securely laid for all time." Riga, too, became his a bit later and a route to the West was opened via the Baltic Sea.

The Czar, in order to populate Riga with Russian subjects, lured Muscovites and other Great Russians, to settle in this newly acquired land. Mother's ancestors were among the pioneers in "Russianized" Riga, and for the following two centuries it was there that they made their home.

World War I erupted in 1914, and by the following year the victorious German armies were bursting into Riga, at which point the porcelain king, Kuznetsov, offered all his Russian employees and their relatives the chance to move to the six factories inside Russia proper. Mother found herself in the town of Dulovo with about 2,000 other Rigavites, waiting for the outcome of the war. The Germans were expected to be beaten soon, with Riga again welcoming the temporary exiles back to the part of town called *Moskovsky Forstadt* ("a suburb of Moscow") inhabited mostly by people of Russian descent.

Moscow itself, in the Rigavite-Dulovans' opinion, would never fall to the Germans. And Moscow did not. Yet much bigger upheavals came her way. In February of 1917 the first, the truly democratic, revolution embraced Muscovy and much of the country. The monarchy was dislodged, giving way to a republican type of government. Then, only eight months later came the October revolution, or, more precisely, counter-revolution, led by Lenin and Trotsky. It swept away the original true democracy, melting it in foams of passion as if it never existed. Then came the all-engulfing civil war. So much hate and anger poured forth that the word "brother" seemed to have disappeared from the people's vocabulary.

Even as those volcano-like eruptions gripped all of Russia, Riga was spared much of this upheaval. Latvia regained its much cherished national independence and Riga, its capital, blossomed into a vibrant European city-port, glad to be rid of its Slavic "brethren."

After the smoke cleared and the fighting ended, Mother tried to leave the cold, gray, poverty-stricken half-village, half-city called Dulovo, and return to her lovely Riga. But she did not succeed, for although just a few years earlier no borders existed between Dulovo and Riga, now one place belonged to the newly formed Soviet Union, while Mother's birthplace belonged to the newly independent country of Latvia. Many war-displaced Latvians were allowed to leave the Soviet Union in the early 1920s, but by then my mother met another obstacle to her return—my father. Her fate was sealed since my father, a Muscovite, was not allowed to leave his country and accompany his wife to Riga.

Looking at my parents, I could not escape some wonderment at the difference in their physical appearance. While Father was very tall, slim, strikingly handsome, Mother at first glance looked drab, uninteresting. She was quite short, hardly reaching Father's armpit, stocky, with generous hips, yet narrowish shoulders. Her square face was pale, with small brown eyes hidden behind metal-rimmed glasses. At the age of forty her forehead was already deeply and permanently marked by horizontal wrinkles, while a web of small wrinkles surrounded her seldom smiling mouth.

Yet in the family album, photographs of Mother in her teens and twenties revealed a fetching girl, ravishing in her early blossom. Father fell head over heels in love with that girl in the album. He called her "the mermaid," because then Mother possessed a head of wavy, golden hair that almost touched the floor when unbraided, covering her whole body as if with a long, silky gown.

The album photo also showed a small, exceptionally well-defined mouth, a mouth that knew how to burst open in contagious, rolling laughter, or to lead in a pleasant contralto into a lusty folk melody. And those brown eyes, when not hidden behind the glasses, were alight with a calm, steady glow.

At the age of four, Mother and her two brothers—Shura and Vanya—were orphaned and brought up by nuns. Riga's monastery-run orphanage was not the warmest, most responsive place for a four-year-old child, robbed first of a mother's tenderness, then of her father, then separated from her brothers (who were brought up in a monastery run by monks). Yet the orphanage was not a cruel, unfeeling place. Only once was Mother beaten. She was caught reading the sensuous, forbidden works of the French author Guy de Maupassant, and whipped so severely that her back took a month to heal.

The nuns helped Mother receive a fairly well-rounded education. She finished Riga's highly acclaimed gymnasium and enrolled immediately after in a newly established business-oriented school, dedicated to courses for women in many fields, with the goal of making them more self-reliant. The most popular course was typing, because in the first quarter of the 20th century this skill was highly sought after in eastern Europe and in Russia particularly. The American method of typing—"blind" and with all ten fingers, the "touch typing" method—was so appreciated that Mother received pay equal to university professors or medical doctors. At the time of the Soviet takeover, there were in Russia about two thousand typists trained in the American method—out of a population of nearly one hundred million. Consequently Mother was able to avoid starvation much better than many others, and often was the main—and at times, the only—source of our support.

CHAPTER THREE

*M*y *father's* background was very different from Mother's. While she had lived at the very window to the West, and was of necessity trilingual, Father's family never left Muscovy.

He had come from a tribe of Slavs who were by nature very peaceful, unaggressive, self-sufficient people. Before turning to Christianity, those pagans worshiped the Sun, Earth, Wind, Frost, but they had no gods to represent War. They were a "forest" people, finding in the ever-alive woods everything necessary for survival. The forest floor was covered with a variety of berries and mushrooms from summer to fall, and brimming with animal life all year round. This natural abundance—of vegetation and meat to fill one's stomach, skins and furs to cover and warm one's body, wood to build shelter—made the Muscovite woodsman a happy and secure individual. Somewhat phlegmatic in his security, the Muscovite's motto was "live and let live."

And the Muscovites did live quite peacefully, turning in the 10th century to Christianity. Then the Mongols galloped into Russia, subjecting its populace to a dreadful ordeal. After the Mongols were expelled, the neighboring Poles began periodically to attack weakened Muscovy, aiming to take over the Kremlin, and to install their own ruler. In 1550, Czar Ivan the Terrible, in order to protect himself from the palace intrigues of his boyars and Poles, originated a Praetorian Guard unit called *Streltsy* (the sharp-shooters). One had to be tall, strong, and "brave in battle," and one was expected to be devoted to the "God-annointed Czar-Batushka." From that time forward, Father's family was connected to this body of warriors. During the reign of

Peter the Great's father and under Peter himself, the Streltsy suffered political and religious persecution, and were destined never again to serve the Czars. Father's family turned to agriculture and commerce, prospering greatly in the 18th and 19th centuries. Then, turmoil engulfed all of Russia.

In 1919, during the height of the civil war, Father's family attended Easter services with other relatives at a church in the town of Vladimir, neighboring Moscow. The Orthodox meet the "rising of Christ" at midnight in a church brightly lighted by hundreds of candles. They kiss each other three times, forgiving all the hurts and wrongs that they might have inflicted upon one another during the past year.

This midnight was different. No time to kiss, to embrace, to forgive and be forgiven. Two peasants burst into the overcrowded church a few minutes before midnight, and shouted to the congregation, "Run! Run! We spotted the Reds! Commissars! They're coming here with machine guns!"

No one had time to do anything. The machine gun bullets started to pelt the faithful, killing the message carriers, killing the priest, killing my grandmother and grandfather. Father's two oldest brothers died. Because Father was in the choir loft, upstairs, the bullets did not find him.

The surviving brothers—my father and his youngest sibling Ivan—left their ancient home, trying to lose themselves in the vastness of Russia, but ended up settling in Dulovo.

Father soon met my mother, and the two of them, as man and wife, taking the reins of life in their young, energetic hands, entered a newly created country, with its own laws and rules, its own rewards and punishments—a country to be known as the Soviet Union. And the moment the Soviet Union came into being, Russia officially died.

CHAPTER FOUR

Nineteen years had passed since the Easter massacre of Father's family, and now it was Woman's Day, 1938. On this 8th of March, the cafeteria in Dulovo's porcelain factory was turned into a festive banquet hall, all tables pushed together in long rows and covered with brand new oil cloth. Chairs and tabourets stood like soldiers on parade, waiting to receive the command to relax. On the tables, very deliberately and proportionally arranged, stood a row of various bottles with sweet liqueurs, some sporting labels of "Slivianka" (the plum brandy much favored by women), along with Curaçao and Port. A few bottles of vodka peeked through, hiding between the sweet wines. Vodka was despised by many women because of what it did to their men—especially on pay days.

There were also plates of food, and a mass of various-sized meat pies that lay in small mountains waiting to be tasted. No festive Russian table could get away without having in a prominent place salted herring, marinated in sour cream or in oil, accompanied by beet and potato salad—called vinaigrette—and, of course, thickly sliced rye bread. There were bowls with marinated mushrooms, a great specialty of Muscovites, next to plates of thinly sliced smoked ham with horseradish. Yet, the table on that special day also had something that appeared in profusion only at Woman's Day parties—sweets! Candies, some wrapped in pretty paper, some unwrapped, lay like round, multi-colored balls, asking to be popped into one's mouth immediately. A variety of cookies and small cakes were piled on top of one another in tempting disarray. And those plates with sweets were the object of most interest for every woman present, because all had promised their children to bring some sweets home.

It was still early when Mother reached the factory cafeteria. She took off her artificial fur coat and the felt boots, handing them to the check girl—an old woman who, although retired, came out at festivals, earning extra money to supplement her pension.

No one was in a hurry to march toward the tables as yet, because they were off limits until the manager of the factory, a jolly little fellow by the name of Igor Ivanovich, invited the women to be seated. The women stood, first in small groups seeking out their friends and relatives, and then in one tightly packed mass.

While waiting for her in-laws, Mother recollected the previous Woman's Day celebration held in the same hall. Igor Ivanovich arrived a bit late that evening, already quite intoxicated, and in an enthusiastic voice he shouted from the raised wooden platform, "Comrade women! Our Soviet flower of motherhood! Greetings! Greetings to you from our highest Soviet leadership!" While the women clapped dutifully in gratitude at being remembered, Igor Ivanovich pulled out of his breast pocket a telegram, and holding it as if it were an icon, he lowered the boom, which, by the way, the women half expected, for it was always lowered on their holiday, for some reason.

"Our dear, wise leader, Josef Vissarionovich Stalin is honoring us, the Dulovans—honoring our porcelain factory, honoring everyone of us, by ordering a magnificent tea set for 48 persons. 'Suliko' it will be called. Imagine! Our very own, dearly beloved leader and us, the workers of Dulovo's factory—the little, unnoticed people! But, no! Comrade Stalin noticed us, honored us! We shall all be closer to Comrade Stalin in spirit through this set of dishes that our hands will create, our thoughts, our very life's energies poured into!"

While Igor Ivanovich was whipping himself into a frenzy of delight and unending gratitude, the women remained still, their faces blank, with only one thought disturbing them—how much this time? How many rubles were to be deducted from their pay, since the managing director surely was planning to send the set as a present. And he did.

"We must prove to our beloved leader how much we appreciate being chosen by him! Us! Dulovans! To honor us with such an order! Therefore, I propose that we send our Comrade Stalin this set as a present!"

Silence. He continued, "We shall willingly, joyously give up two day's pay from our monthly salary to achieve this patriotic goal!"

There was a sigh of relief. It could have been worse.

Igor Ivanovich shouted, "All who are for my proposition, remain still! Those who disagree, raise their hands!"

And not really looking for any hands to be raised, the director started to descend from the platform, ready to lead the famished women to the tables. Suddenly he stopped, jerking his whole body in a spasm-like movement, staring at one offending hand, raised in protest.

"Comrade Director," a creaky, female voice timidly addressed Igor Ivanovich. It belonged to Pelagea Kulina, a woman in her late sixties who had a slightly surprised, wondering look permanently settled on her deeply wrinkled face.

She had worked since her teens as a cleaning woman under the original owner, Kuznetsov, later doubling as a message carrier or cafeteria helper, and also as a check girl on festive occasions. After a full half century of work Pelagea retired, believing that at this point her dues were paid to society. The time had come for society to take care of her. Her aging, worn-out body was not responding readily to her commands anymore; it demanded some rest. Not lacking in native intelligence, Pelagea figured that because the Soviet Union's new constitution supported the humane principle of "from each according to one's ability, to each according to one's need," help was due her. She had heard that slogan many, many times—during the revolution, during the civil war, and in all the years since. Every source of information combined to drum into her head those noble words. She knew them by heart. Now her "need" was to receive that help promised by the constitution itself, by Comrade Stalin's constitution.

But then, to her utter surprise, Pelagea learned that the Soviet constitution was established not on the principle that had been quoted to her, but on a new, drastically changed principle: "From each according to one's ability, to each according to one's *toil*."

The 1936 constitution, named in honor of Stalin, also stated that "he who does not toil, neither shall he eat," implying that as long as one toiled, well and good. If one stopped toiling, one was more or less dismissed from society. One was useless, a burden to the rest. Pelagea's pension was 27 rubles a month, forcing her only a few weeks after going into retirement to knock on the director's door, asking for her job back, because 27 rubles carried her no more than a week. So she continued to force her aging body to keep toiling, to keep contributing to society as a producer, earning another 55 rubles a month. To Pelagea, a ruble was very precious, as was even a kopek. That was why she raised her gnarled hand, and hurried to explain to Igor Ivanovich, bowing to him from her waist, "Might you be blessed by all the

Orthodox saints, Comrade Director! But, I don't approve. Two days pay out of my pocket into. . . ."

"Keep your Orthodox saints out of it, Pelagea." The director tried to appear authoritative. It was expected of him to maintain discipline. "Your single voice doesn't count. The decision is *unanimous!* Unanimous! And you, old crow," he leaned toward the old woman, tapping her on the forehead with his index finger, "you wouldn't last out this evening if we didn't know that you're short on nuts and bolts."

"Nuts!" Pelagea exploded. "I am not a bit short on nuts, Comrade Director! Not a bit! I can still count! What do you earn, Comrade Director? 800 rubles? More? I make 80. You take out of my miserable 80 rubles a share for United Bonds. You take ten percent of my money to buy government bonds. You take a *subbotnik* once a month, so I work one day for nothing. And today! That table isn't free, eh? One day of my salary is soaked in those *piroshki* and liqueurs!"

Igor Ivanovich could not allow this mad woman to continue. He saw that the rest of the women, who earlier appeared utterly uninterested in Pelagea's outburst—their faces blank, careful not even to cross glances with the old rebel—now were staring at the flushed director with ironic, laughing eyes, as if to say, "Now get out of this one." Igor Ivanovich gave in.

"Pelagea! This is your last warning! Any more trouble from you and you're finished! Now, as you are half retired we won't deduct money out of your pay for the tea set. All right, females! March to the tables!"

That was a year ago. Another Woman's Day party was about to start. Igor Ivanovich appeared in the cafeteria exactly on time, followed by a bayan player named Zikin.

Zikin was a shadowy figure. No one knew much about this thirty-year-old fellow, who came and went, sometimes disappearing from Dulovo for months, then, as suddenly, reappearing. Some, reportedly, had observed Zikin escorting NKVD men, unfamiliar with the locale, to the homes of people they wanted to arrest.

The women, on seeing Zikin, stopped chatting, and a hush fell over the hall. The little director climbed onto the platform, unusually subdued, and somewhat distracted. He reached the long, narrow table reserved especially for him and other officials, and to the surprise of his audience, gulped down a huge tumbler full of red wine. Still no opening speeches came, no proclamations of gratitude to anyone. It looked as if Igor Ivanovich would invite his female flock to the feast tables immediately, when a tall, gawky fellow with dark, wavy hair and thick-rimmed glasses entered the hall, marching with deliberate steps to the place where Igor Ivanovich stood.

"Dear comrade women, I am your new 'partorg,' " the man announced in a guttural, un-Muscovy accent.

Mother felt that if a fly had appeared at that moment, its buzz would have been taken for thunder. "Part org" is the shortened version of two words—party organizer. Where was the old partorg? And why should the new one introduce himself at the Woman's Day party?

He turned to a visibly shaken Igor Ivanovich. Mother, standing close to the platform, caught a few words.

"Bring the prepared list. It must be ready by now."

And the director obediently, with hurried step, left the hall, while the new partorg addressed his audience.

"Soviet women! Count your blessings!" he demanded, in a resonant, upbeat voice. "Before the October revolution you were nothing but sex objects to your male counterparts. As though with chains, you were tied to monotonous, unrewarding housework; to the kitchen; to whimpering infants! You had to pay with sleepless nights and soiled diapers. That's all you knew in those old, rotten days!"

"That's what you think!" a muffled female voice reached Mother's ear. Who? Mother could not tell, since every face was blank, every mouth tightly shut.

"Now, Soviet women, you are free! Free to stand shoulder to shoulder with your men as equal partners in your daily toil! Now you toil diligently to please your Soviet state! Continue!"

A strong nudge in Mother's back almost threw her off balance. Pelagea Kulina was standing behind her, grinning apologetically, in mischievous silence, as the partorg went on.

"On this Woman's Day you must thank the Soviet government, because it takes care of your children now; it provides you with day nurseries, with kindergartens, pre-school care. It is educating your offspring in Soviet patriotism, turning them into dedicated Soviet citizens while you, Soviet mothers, are free to pursue your worthwhile careers, to be fulfilled, proud mates to your Soviet men! You are no different from men when it comes to productivity! You are doctors! You are teachers! You are miners! You are loggers! You are no longer just women—you are *toilers!* Let us continue to toil diligently, whole-heartedly, earning the respect of our beloved Comrade Stalin! Earning the respect of our beloved Communist Party! Hurrah!"

A somewhat mocking hurrah rang back in answer, tinged with relief because, finally, the women could march to the waiting tables.

Mother spotted her favorite sister-in-law, Liza, wife of Mother's older brother, Shura. She liked hazel-eyed, blond Liza for her unhurried, unruffled manner—a woman who always managed to find enough time and patience for her troubled friends or relatives. Their only child, Inna, was five years my junior, preventing us two from finding much in common; but still I enjoyed being invited to their tiny, two room apartment where dancing and singing needed no special imploring. Uncle Shura led his guests in song—first slow, moody melodies, progressing steadily into a medley of folk songs that led inevitably into a dance.

"Mama, dance! Dance *gopak!*" little Inna would shout during the party. Imitating her father's movements, she—like a rubber ball—bounced across the floor in the *gopak* manner. Her slender, long-legged mother, not able to withstand the daughter's adorable teasing, would take a snow-white handkerchief and begin to slide on the floor like a swan on the water—smooth, graceful, proud. Uncle Shura chased his wife, as the folk dance directed, but since their apartment was very tiny, he had to do his part almost immobile, standing on one spot, while Aunt Liza teased and teased, with her kerchief swirling around him, until he exploded into acrobatic feats—first raking the floor with his heels, then his knees, then turning a few somersaults, ending with a leap so high, as though to reach the ceiling. To bring the dance to a climax, Aunt Liza would throw her kerchief to him in a sign of submission. Uncle Shura, catching it expertly, would fall on one knee in front of his wife—in triumph. The whole company, as one, would burst into laughter and applause.

Mother and Liza found two chairs next to each other, while the other sister-in-law Olga, wife of Father's brother Vanya, sat directly opposite. She was very pale, with sky-blue eyes and black hair, tall but delicately built, with a worried, preoccupied look on her prematurely aging face. The worry was mainly over Uncle Vanya who was very ill, suffering from tuberculosis of the lungs. He had contracted it several years earlier, and everybody knew that his time was running out. Aunt Olga would have liked to remain home that night with Vanya, but attendance at such organized celebrations was mandatory, the names of those present being carefully checked. Although Olga's nine-year-old son, Alesha, was looking after his father, her mind was not quite at peace.

As soon as all were seated, the new partorg began to propose the various toasts that were standard, and repeated yearly, monthly, hourly, at every festive or political gathering in the Soviet empire, proclaiming the utter devotion of the Soviet people to all the dead and living leaders. Some women's throats after a while began to feel irritated, hoarse, but one could not remain silent, mouths could not remain closed, for the offenders would be immediately spotted. Women reached repeatedly for the bottles of sweet, soothing liqueurs.

The partorg and the bayanist downed a few shots at the beginning, but when Igor Ivanovich returned with a folder containing some papers, the partorg, glancing at them, whistled softly, and after that neither he nor Zikin took another drink. But Igor Ivanovich, as if in desperation, began to accompany his toasts with straight vodka, and very quickly became intoxicated.

"Females! Beloved!" he shouted from the platform, "Might the mad dog American capitalist-imperialists rot on piles of their own offal! Hurrah!"

"Hurrah!" the slightly tipsy women echoed.

"Might the earthworms grow fat on that American President Roosevelt! Hurrah!"

"Hurrah-h-h!" and more throat-cooling wine.

During and after repeating declarations of eternal devotion to the Communist Party and its leaders, and utter revulsion toward America and the capitalist world in general, the women fell upon the remaining herring with salad, and ham with mushrooms, washing it down with some wine. While those items were replenished from time to time, the plates of sweets appeared only once, and in only a few blinking moments after the women reached the tables, plates with sweets were completely empty. The women grabbed the candies and cookies, filling their pockets, brassieres, and boots with the sweets. Some came prepared, with sleeves that had elastic at the wrists so as to hold the candy, or utilized the elastic at their waists.

After the toasts came to an end, and some herring and vinaigrette had found its way into Zikin's mouth, the bayanist began to fill the room with the sounds of Red Army marches and Soviet hymns, switching soon to more enjoyable folk melodies, even romances. Mother, with her rich, strong contralto, began to add her voice to a growing chorus, and soon Liza, too, joined the slightly tipsy females who were belting out the songs at the top of their voices. Even Aunt Olga could not refrain from singing.

Once the women had sung, teary-eyed, all the sad romances they could think of, there was not much left to do but for the dancing to start. Zikin played several tangos, then some fox trots, while the females swirled about with each other, but the best dancing had to come not from Europe in the figures of society steps and twirls. No. The gopak had to be performed.

Everyone knew that Aunt Liza was a good dancer, and more and more eyes turned to her until finally a whole chorus of voices exploded. "Liza, dear! Get your rear end off that chair and dance for us!"

Tradition required that Liza would withstand a certain amount of pressure before succumbing.

"*Pava!* Our *pava!*" The women decided to flatter Liza's ego by calling her a peahen.

"Like a peahen our Lizochka floats on the dance floor! No one can compare with Liza—the *pava!*"

What was left to do? Aunt Liza, seemingly half-hearted, with an almost bored expression, slowly raised herself from the chair and, more or less turning into a peahen, slid toward the middle of the dance floor, not moving her hips, or shoulders, or neck, or even her eyes. She seemed to separate, to cut herself off from everyone in the room— proud, erect, almost arrogant—no eye contact with anyone.

There was again a chorus of voices shouting, "Manya! Manya! Go after Liza!" Half in command, half pleading, the chorus was addressed to a young woman who was almost six feet tall, with broad shoulders, slender in the hips, with a rosy glow to her round face. And she danced the gopak as well as any Dulovo man.

There was no prodding Manya, since tradition demanded that the dancer of the male part should immediately consent. She jumped up from her chair, and with a few leaps, found herself next to Liza, chasing her dancing partner—at first, quite slowly. Then, with the quickening tempo of the music, her steps quickened too, and she began to display such acrobatic feats that were it not for the wide, brightly colored skirt, one could have taken her for a lad.

Everyone was watching the dancers, clapping hands in unison, shouting out encouraging phrases, exhorting the dancers to excel even more in their performance. Aunt Olga moved next to Mother, occupying Liza's chair, and said quietly, "Natasha . . . something isn't quite right. The partorg and Zikin aren't drinking."

Startled by Olga's voice, Mother took her eyes off the dancing women and looked toward Olga. At the same time she observed the partorg reading something in front of him, pencil in hand, pointing right at her. Mother froze, sensing doom.

"Olga," she managed to whisper, "they're looking at me and pointing. They're talking about something. Maybe Igor Ivanovich is getting ready to fire me."

"I don't think so, Natasha," Olga mused. "You're the only 'American' typist in Dulovo. They need you. It scares me that they're not drinking. Only the director is getting loaded. Look at him! Our Igor Ivanovich is acting like a serf—bowing and scraping and smiling, wanting to please. But he looks scared."

Mother did not worry over the fact that the partorg and Zikin did not drink themselves into a stupor. What worried her was the impersonal gesture of that hand holding a pencil, pointing at her. She so desperately wanted to know, what were the men on the platform talking about?

She forced herself to appear calm, once more watching the young women on the dance floor. Liza was still moving like a peahen, but not as passive any longer, rather more sensual, while Manya was perspiring slightly, her nose losing its dull powdered look. The dance was almost at the end.

"I wish we could go home now," Mother whispered.

"Can't," Olga whispered back. "Not until the director dismisses us. Ah! How I want to be with Vanya! My sick angel. Not long until. . . ."

Mother took Olga's hand in hers. It must be so hard, waiting for one's own husband to die, to become a widow, Mother thought, not letting Olga's hand out of her grip.

Suddenly, a side door behind Mother's chair opened unceremoniously, and a man in NKVD uniform shouted, "Zikin!"

The bayanist was so entranced in what he was doing, knowing the dance was only a few seconds from the finale, that he did not hear the call.

"Zikin!" The shout rang out again. The bayanist heard and, as if in panic, he ran toward the NKVD man, bayan dangling on his chest, still producing discordant sounds. The partorg, very alert, followed Zikin, holding in both hands the pages he had been examining throughout the whole evening.

A grave silence fell upon the celebrating women. The director, as if on the verge of becoming sick, waved his hand in dismissal.

"Go, females. Go home," he said weakly, and on his unsteady legs tried to catch up with the Party officials.

Liza and Manya, arm in arm, returned to their chairs, suddenly aged, exhausted, mere shadows of what they had been only moments earlier.

CHAPTER FIVE

*M*idnight arrived. Slava and I, our stamina exhausted, had moved earlier from the kitchen table to our beds, dozing, yet ears still alert. And then we heard it—crunching in the snow, hurrying steps, steps that sent our blankets onto the floor and us back to the kitchen table. Father cleared away the pile of papers he was working on, papers connected with his bookkeeping that he often had to bring home in order to catch up with an overload of work. The samovar was still warm to the touch, so Mother could have a cup of decent-tasting tea after that long walk. Tea with what? Honey cookies, perhaps, or sugar cookies, or a gorgeous candy, maybe, with strawberry flavoring?

Mother tried to come in quietly, not wishing to awaken us if we were asleep, but seeing our not-at-all sleepy eyes riveted on her with a beaming question mark, she all at once began to empty her pockets.

"Ho! Ho! Ho!" she mocked in a masculine voice, imitating Father Frost. "I am loaded with sweets! Look!" And hard sugar candies began to fall out of her mittens like marbles out of a sack. She reached behind the collar of her loose, full blouse and produced several cookies.

To my delight, honey cookies—my favorite—appeared out of Mother's bosom. She reached into her snow boot and produced a pack of cigarettes called *Kasbek,* one of the more expensive Russian *papirosy.* Seeing Father's pleasure, she laughed. "What a rewarding Woman's Day party it was!" She looked at us two and said: "Now, let's get ready to hop into our beds. Dawn is not far off. School is waiting!"

Slava and I returned to our still warm beds, pleased beyond words with our presents. One hard candy was in my mouth, lying between cheek and gum, melting slowly. I was in bliss, preparing to fall asleep as soon as the candy completely melted.

After a few minutes at the samovar, our parents, too, went to bed, and sleep's rhythmic, soft breathing was soon the only sound in the house. When there was no more sweet liquid to extract in my mouth, I, too, began to fall asleep.

Then, thunder! Thunder? To my half-sleeping brain the noise of an approaching motor car sounded like roaring thunder. The noise burst into our room, alerting us to danger. No one in all of Dulovo owned a car privately. It could only be a "black crow"—a long, official vehicle, the function of which was to carry arrested individuals to the cellars of the NKVD. It sputtered to a stop, directly outside our house.

Father leaped out of bed and began to dress. He did not have far to reach. By his side of the bed stood a chair with his warmest clothes. A quilted long jacket, called *tolstovka*—in honor of Count Leo Tolstoy who, in his later years, so liked to dress as a peasant—was on the chair together with a pair of quilted, dark gray overalls. A fur hat with ear flaps, mittens, a woolen scarf and socks—all were waiting to be used in emergency. Even in the summer months, when the temperature approached 90 degrees Fahrenheit, those articles remained permanently on the bedside chair, becoming a familiar, even comforting feature in our home. Father's internal passport, cigarettes, reading glasses, and a small bottle of vodka—to calm the nerves—all lay on top of the *tolstovka*. Under the chair stood a pair of very long felt boots and a large sack of *suhary*—dried pieces of bread.

Watching Father dress, Slava and I started to shiver. That chair with Father's clothes, with its felt boots and bundle—it had stood there for more than a year, undisturbed. It was our security blanket of a sort. We were not frightened by this chair when "clothed," since it meant Father was home, safe, with us. But seeing it emptying, exposing its seat and back and legs, we felt as if some ugly skeleton had entered our home.

Mother's face, only a bit earlier laughing, dividing the sweets, became distorted by anguish.

"Darling, darling husband," she began to chant in that peculiar, sing-song way that Russian women often do, when faced with great unhappiness. "I didn't want to worry you earlier. Zikin was at the party. My falcon, my Mark. Try to hold on to your warm clothing. Don't smoke away your rations. Mark, my wedded husband, my one and only. Try to preserve yourself. Try to return to us, Mark, darling. For what? . . . Why? . . ."

Father was dressing quickly, as if he had rehearsed the procedure many times before. His nose became very prominent, thin and pale, and his eyes almost black, severe, yet very sad.

The steps of heavy, official, leather boots, crunching the snow path, were nearing our entrance. We, all four, stood staring at the door, all four separated from one another, as if to touch, to embrace would somehow kill us all.

"Open up! NKVD!" The solid door danced under the barrage of boots and fists. Father reached for Mother and, pressing her to his chest, he repeated over and over, as if convincing himself, "I'll survive, wifie. I'll survive. I won't give in. Streltsy, you know." He tried to smile. "You don't give in either, Natashinka—for the children's sake."

The violent knocks resumed. Father crushed Slava and me in his farewell embrace and, as if in a hurry to get away from us, from the heavy sorrow of parting, he shouted to those outside, "I am ready!"

Unbolting the door, he faced the officials with a bundle in one hand, and the other holding his passport. An out-of-town NKVDist burst into our home with Zikin, the bayanist, who sprang at once toward Father.

He pushed away Father's hand that was holding the passport, which a Soviet citizen had to surrender during an arrest, and barked in a shrill voice, "Go to hell with your f------ passport, you old whore's bastard! A tool! We need a tool! A hammer! We've got car trouble! Can't you move, you son of a much laid mother?"

Father remained standing, uncomprehending, as if he was being addressed in some foreign tongue, rather than the everyday, profanity-filled language of Soviet officialdom.

Zikin, losing patience, swung his huge fist at Father's jaw. "Move, son of a bitch! Hammer!" he roared.

Only then did Father realize that it was not to arrest him, to tear him away from his family, that those people had come. He hurried toward the corner where he kept his tools, and returned with a hammer. The intruders retreated to their limousine without another word.

Zikin, hammer in hand, crawled underneath the car, while from the windowless rear seat, a man's voice trying to shout something was stifled quickly into silence. We four clung to one another at the still wide-open entrance door, not believing that we could close it, bolt it. After what seemed to us endless hammering, grunting, and cursing, we heard the car's motor start to murmur, then with a great roar, the much-dreaded "crow" jumped forward and raced away from our house. Only then the tears came.

The kitchen table welcomed us once more, with its cookies, candies, expensive cigarettes—those rewards that had come Mother's way just a few hours earlier—rewards for being a woman. There in the kitchen, Mother, Slava, and I, all at once noticing Father's legs, began to giggle through the stubborn tears. He could not understand our sudden change of mood, puzzled by our half-crying, half-smiling faces, until Mother pointed to his long, lean legs—clad only in his dark gray underwear! The *tolstovka* jacket covered him to the lower hips, while the felt boots came almost to the knees; in between—just underwear.

"So, you were ready to face godforsaken Kolyma." Mother's lips parted in a slight smile, prompting me to want to break out laughing. Instead, I threw myself at Father's felt boots, and holding on to his bony knees, I cried out in a high voice, unfamiliar even to myself.

"Papa! I don't understand! I don't understand! Papochka, why were those men so brutal? What did you do wrong, Papa? What? Why should you be afraid? I am afraid, too. I don't want to go to sleep."

Father lifted me from the floor. I shivered so that my teeth began to make a clicking noise. Slava, too, could not stop shivering.

"Let us all climb on top of the *pechka*," Mother proposed, and quickly arranged our beds in a warm, cozy corner, where it seemed neither Zikin nor the NKVD could possibly reach us.

Deep, restful sleep did not come to me that night. The thought that the warm, comforting bodies of my parents might disappear and leave Slava and me *besprizhorniks,* frightened me. *Besprizhornik* means, literally, "one without supervision." Our town—and every town in the country—swarmed with children who found themselves practically overnight without parental care or love. In many cases they were not truly orphans; rather, their parents were separated from them by force, and the state expressed not the slightest interest in the welfare of the children of "enemies of the people." The revolution and civil war produced a wave of *besprizhorniks,* as always happens in every country's internal upheavals. But in Russia, since 1921, even after the civil war ended, with the Communists consolidating their power, the homeless, abandoned children continued to fill the ranks of *besprizhorniks.* Those numbers were swelled in 1927, when the clergy and intelligentsia were punished with exile or death for their "anti-government activities." Another wave of *besprizhorniks* resulted from the kulak and peasant persecution, when many parents were "eliminated," leaving behind such a mass of *besprizhorniks* that it could not even be called a tidal wave.

An ocean of fatherless, motherless children of all ages left to fend for themselves, covered the Russian soil from one corner to another.

A new campaign, that of 1934–35, wiped out one-quarter of the population of Leningrad, punishing it for the murder of a Party big shot—Kirov. More *besprizhorniks*. And then, a wave of terror swept across the land, a wave that started to swell a year earlier, and had just knocked on our door.

When a man was arrested, his wife was often fired from her job, because she was considered an "undesirable." Family belongings were confiscated, frequently to the last piece of clothing, to the last cooking pot. The family was thrown out of its lodgings and, in the end, the wife, too, disappeared.

Children in such cases had, literally, to live on the streets or, as in Dulovo, run into the forest. To help a *besprizhornik,* to scrub his lice-infested scalp and bathe him, or to boil and mend his rags crawling with vermin, to give him some dried bread, *suhary,* was officially prohibited. No religious or other charitable organizations were allowed, under Soviet rule, to help *besprizhorniks*. These outcasts, although trying at first to remain decent—remembering their family upbringing—in the end had no alternative but to turn to crime.

I had had a personal encounter only a year earlier with one of the boys who had taken that road. I was walking home from school with a classmate, when a fourteen-year-old *besprizhornik*, Kolka, decided to attack me. When the 1934–35 wave of Kirov reprisals reached our town, his parents, both high school teachers, were arrested on the trumped-up charge of being foreign spies, because they had relatives in Finland. Kolka, for a while, was clandestinely taken care of by many Dulovans who knew his highly esteemed parents and felt terribly sorry for the boy. Then the boy, on his own account, came out of the forest less and less often for food and other help. Instead, he fell in with a gang of much older *besprizhorniks* who were turning to crime.

On that late spring day, Kolka hid behind a thick clump of Persian lilacs in a park near the school I attended, waiting. He chose to attack me despite the fact that my father personally had given Kolka some good felt boots, warm overalls, and an old rabbit fur-lined jacket. He often brought out a bowl of hot cabbage soup and stood by the gate while Kolka gulped it down, guarding the boy from possible arrest by the always snooping militiamen. One day Kolka asked Father for a knife, saying that he needed it to skin rabbits and foxes he was trapping. Father, although reluctant, gave the boy a knife, warning, "Don't use it for bad deeds, Kolka."

Remembering all the good Kolka had found in our house, I was utterly surprised that he would single me out for an attack. But attack he did. Pushing me to the ground, he began to tear off my baggy, thick bloomers, struggling with the tight cotton cord. My classmate ran back toward school, and spotting our 35-year-old mathematics teacher heading home on his bicycle, beseeched him to hurry to my rescue. Kolka, seeing the teacher, stopped struggling with my bloomers, and pulled a knife out of his boot—our knife!—threatening to kill the teacher if he were to come one step closer. The teacher did not doubt that Kolka would do just that, and he raced back to the school to recruit more men.

Kolka, breathing heavily, face distorted by anger, picked up a flat rock the size of his palm, aiming at my face. I instinctively turned my head to the right, trying to protect my nose and mouth from the rock. Kolka then began to hit my exposed left ear, after each blow saying, "That's for your mother! That's for your father!" And again, "That's for your mother! That's for your father!" He chanted as if in a trance. My ears began to ring with a heavy, dull sound. Those booming, penetrating sounds seemed to reach all the way to my stomach. The tree tops, the clouds in the sky above, all started to wave—far to the left, far to the right. I started to drift into unconsciousness. But before that merciful state could overtake me, Kolka's face swam into view, and I could not understand why he was crying. After all, it was I who was being hurt. Kolka was sobbing violently, while repeating his monotonous chant, "For your mother! For your father!"

He fled into the thick forest when more people ran toward us, and vanished.

One other encounter took place with a *besprizhornik* a few months later, when Father was accompanying me to the dispensary 12 kilometers away, at Orehovo-Zuevo, for a weekly treatment of my left ear which was discharging pus and blood since the beating. In order to save time, we went through a thickly wooded area. Walking briskly along the narrow path, we heard the rustle of leaves, and abruptly stopped. Father, expecting to face an animal of some sort, became tense, alert. Instead, a pale, scrawny girl about eight or nine years old crawled from under a layer of thick shrubs and stood there, facing us in silence. Her long, matted hair fell over forehead and cheeks, her eyes huge and dull, skin covered with open sores. She was shivering under her skimpy, soiled rags.

Ignoring me as if I was not present, staring at Father, she lifted her clothing above her naked hips, exposing a bloated belly, and said in a voice devoid of all emotion, *"Dyadenka* [Little uncle], if you feed me, you may f--- me."

While lying on the warm *pechka* with both parents near me, I could not erase the memory of that girl—the young recruit to the army of *besprizhorniks*. What name had been given her, I wondered. Anya? Luba? Perhaps Katya? Or Nina? Could I be next? And who would help me then, help me to survive? That day, Father said to the girl to wait for us to return with some hot soup and *suhary*, but the girl was afraid we would bring the militia, and asked for money. The five rubles we gave her, how long would it feed her? And that offer of her body, so casual, so matter of fact. How many girls were there in Dulovo's forests, girls like her? How many Kolkas were there, angry, swallowed by despair, who wept for the loss of their own parents while beating and raping the more fortunate ones?

And so I met the coming of dawn, eyes burning from lack of sleep, body heavy, stiff, unresponsive, as though I had spent all those pre-dawn hours toiling at some exhausting physical task. Over breakfast of tea and *suhary* Mother at one point caressed Father's hand with hers and said, "That poem by Akhmatova. . . . She wrote it for us, it seems." And, almost in a whisper, Mother proceeded to quote one of Russia's most beloved poets:

> "They led you away at dawn
> And I followed you, like a mourner
> In their room children cried, curtains drawn
> While the candle went dark in the holy corner.
> Your lips retain the icon's chill
> I cannot forget your death-sweat brow
> As the Streltsy wives, so I, too, will
> Under the Kremlin towers howl."

After breakfast tea, our parents hurried to the factory, while Slava and I stumped listlessly toward school. I silently kept repeating Akhmatova's poem, visualizing mother howling at the Kremlin wall as the Streltsy wives howled two and a half centuries earlier, begging the young Czar Peter to spare the lives of their menfolk. Those men tried physically to remove Peter from the throne; to kill him if need be. But my dear father—the bookkeeper—whom was he threatening? Why must he fear arrest and banishment to Siberia?

The three-story, modern school building met us from afar with a huge red placard on its wall. There was the image of Josef Vissarionovich Stalin, bigger than life, holding a child in his arms, a Burat girl whose name was Mamlakat; a mass of field poppies were in the girl's hands, as bright as Mamlakat's smile, as bright as her laughing eyes. Flowers for the *Vozhd*—the leader. Under their images was printed a direct quotation from Josef Vissarionovich himself:

"LIFE HAS BECOME BETTER!
LIFE HAS BECOME MORE JOYOUS!"

CHAPTER SIX

*O*n *the* night of the party, Aunt Olga, after separating from
Mother at the factory, hurriedly walked home, anxious to bring
her nine-year-old Alesha some sweets, and to see him to bed, for the
school day began in only a few hours. One could not easily miss
attending school, because parents were held strictly accountable. Olga
was planning to fix some weak tea with a lot of honey in it for her
Vanya. This seemed to soothe and relax the sick man into a restful
sleep. The thought that her husband might not see the next summer
never left Aunt Olga. That cursed *chahotka* (meaning "withering
away") attacked Dulovans like the common cold. Tuberculosis of the
lungs was feared more than cancer, heart ailments, or the various
children's diseases. And how to fight it? Doctors prescribed milk, eggs,
preferably raw, a lot of butter. They also prescribed isolating the sick
member of the family in a separate room. Further, they recommended
sunshine, and bathing in the warm sea. Not many could follow this
advice, and *chahotka* spread like wildfire.

One of the greatest promoters of its spread was a lack of living space.
Aunt Olga had an apartment in one of the numerous barracks surrounding the factory. The buildings were called just that—*baraki*. In
pre-revolutionary times they had been occupied exclusively by bache-
lors employed by Kuznetsov; of late, large families were quartered
there. Olga's family shared—with five other families—an indoor toilet
room, a washroom with a small, barrel-like tub to bathe in, and a
kitchen—a tiny, square cubicle with a sink and a four-burner stove that
had to take care of meal preparations for six families.

The one room apartment with electricity and running water was considered quite spacious—15 feet by 15 feet, with a window facing the highway. The largest part of the room by the window was given to Uncle Vanya. There he would lie, or sit on his cot, propped up with big pillows. An arm chair and a dining table doubling as a writing table completed the furnishings of his corner, which was separated from the rest of the room by a sheet secured to the ceiling. This sheet was intended to provide the required isolation.

The rest of the space in the room was taken up by two more cots and a small table standing between them. Nothing else could fit in, not even a closet, so that all clothing hung on the walls and doors.

The doctors in Uncle Vanya's case could really do nothing, only recommend what should be done. When Aunt Olga begged them for help, they looked at her patiently, compassionately, and then threw their arms out in a helpless gesture, as if to say: "Nothing we can do. We are powerless." The best they could do was to provide Aunt Olga with a new prescription for cod liver oil.

Reaching the apartment on the night of the party, Aunt Olga was surprised to see bright lights in her window, instead of the customary dimly lit bulb. She ran in the entrance door, and with relief observed that her husband had not taken a turn for the worse, as she had feared, but rather, was sitting up in his bed, partially dressed, with Alesha clutching his father's sleeve. Her relief turned to alarm when she realized that her husband and her son were unusually stiff in their posture, alert. Alesha seemed to lead her glance toward the bottom of the hanging sheet. There, Aunt Olga with sinking heart, saw two pairs of shiny black boots that belonged to no one in her family.

"We have visitors, Olinka. I must finish dressing now," Uncle Vanya said softly. All pretense aside, the NKVDists tore the sheet down, and commanded, "Hurry! Dress!"

Olga remembered Mother's words earlier that evening: "Look, Olga, the partorg is pointing at me." Now Olga realized that the partorg must have been pointing at *her*. *Her* Vanya was on the list of people to be arrested that night.

Recovering a little from the initial shock, she tried to approach the NKVDists. "But my husband has *chahotka*," she whispered. "What good is he to you? It must be some mistake! My husband is innocent! Innocent! And sick!"

"No mistake! We make no mistakes! Dress!"

Like a sleepwalker, Aunt Olga began to help her husband into a *tolstovka,* while Alesha was struggling to pull the warm felt snow boots on his father's feet. Then, awkwardly, he threw himself at the black leather boots of the officers, and started to wail, overcome by panic.

"Uncles! Please! I beg you! Be kind! Leave my father home!" Seeing the utter indifference on the official's faces, Alesha yelled at the top of his voice, "I heard the doctor tell Mother that Father will soon die! Let him die at home! With us! Uncles!" The boy hung on to the men's trousers, to their long leather jackets. He tried to catch their hands, tried to kiss those hands, to soften their hearts.

"Let loose, *sukin shenok!*" barked one, calling heartbroken Alesha a "bitch's pup."

Aunt Olga, in her very last gesture, took from the wall her oversized woolen shawl, and carefully, lovingly wrapped her husband's head and chest in it.

"*Poká, poká,* Vanichka," she murmured almost in a whisper, with this word implying that they would only be parted for a few hours or days.

No matter how hard she tried, Aunt Olga could not learn the whereabouts of her arrested husband. Then a note came, an official note, stating that her husband had been sentenced with no right to receive visitors, correspondence, or packages. To the Soviet citizen, this all-explaining notice meant that the person had ceased to exist.

Alesha, after his father's arrest, began to be called by his peers: "son of an enemy of the people." He at first fought back, insisting that his father was a good, decent man, not an enemy of the people. The boy's grades deteriorated, and the most important grade—that of citizenship—was unsatisfactory. After a while, Alesha stopped defending his father or himself, withdrawing from adults and from his peers. One day, in a tar-filled pond near the railroad tracks Alesha's body was found. No one knew if his death was accidental.

After that, Aunt Olga began to suffer from severe headaches. Sitting quietly, very pale, she would suddenly shout, "Help! Thunder! Thunder is coming! It is deafening me! It'll slaughter me!"

One day while at the communal well fetching water, I overheard one of our neighbors saying to her friend, next in line, while pulling up the rope with a full bucket, "Have you heard? Olga hanged herself."

The other woman clicked her tongue sadly. "Poor, poor Olga. Poor soul. Her Vanya is no more. Her boy's gone, too. She'll join them now. Might God have mercy on all of them, sinners."

The first woman whirled, retorting as if in anger, "May God have mercy on us, neighbor! We need His mercy. Olga and Vanya and their boy are safe. But what will you do tonight, I ask? I know what you'll do. You'll shake as if in St. Vitus's dance! That's what I am doing every night. Waiting, scared out of my wits for my little ones turning into *besprizhorniks*. I shake like a tarantula bit me, when I hear steps at night, or a car. God? No help from Him. Not even for our young ones—the blameless ones. Even they don't get His help. God is deaf and dumb. He has turned His back on us."

"Or we on Him," her friend mused, taking her turn at the well.

After filling the pails and balancing the yoke on my shoulders, trying not to bend under the weight of the full pails, not to break down under the weight of my sorrow over Aunt Olga's death, I walked home to pass the news to my family.

CHAPTER SEVEN

Nights were creeping by, taking along with them the remainder of the month of March. We waited with dread for the car to stop by our door again, and not depart empty-handed this time. Only at dawn sleep overtook us, leaving little time to rejuvenate, and forcing us to meet the new day pale, fatigued, depressed. Another chair joined Father's by the bedside, holding Mother's warm clothing, because Dulovo was losing women to the "black crow" too.

One day Father took Slava aside and had a man to man talk with the boy, door shut. I stood on the other side of the door, feeling offended at being excluded, and listened.

"Slavochka . . . don't be afraid of what you'll hear from me," Father began, haltingly. "It might never be necessary to do. . . . I hope it won't be necessary."

Neither Father nor Slava uttered a sound for a moment. Then, Slava's voice reached my ear.

"I know, papa. Arrests . . . *besprizhorniks,* isn't it?"

"Slavochka, on top of the *pechka* there is a loose brick. I'll show you tonight. Mother and I are putting spare rubles there—for an emergency. And perhaps that emergency is near. If they arrest us both, take that money, Slava, and sew part of it in your underclothes, part in Nina's. Try to get to Crimea—the town of Feodosia. Now, remember that name."

Slava sounded resolute, adult-like. "Of course I'll remember Feodosia. It's a famous place, anyway. The Black Plague spread from there. Besides, weren't we there on vacation long ago?"

"Well, I suppose five years would be long in your life," Father said, understandingly. "An older couple lives in Feodosia. Do you remember them? Praskovia Ivanovna and Dmitry Antonovich? No? Well, they are friends from way back. They'll help you. And above all else, son, don't join up with the *besprizhorniks*. Just tell everyone that you two are orphans. Understand? Orphans. Both your parents died of *chahotka*."

Father heard me sniffling, for I was visualizing Slava and me becoming real-life orphans. He opened the door, admitting me into his confidence, and very matter-of-factly continued to instruct us.

"The main thing, children, is to stay away from the older *besprizhorniks*—the *blatnoy*. They'll rob you of your last ruble and rip the warm clothing off your backs. Stick with older people. They'll protect you. Above all, children, get out of Dulovo, out of Muscovy. Get to Crimea. No one will know you. You'll just be plain orphans, and not 'enemies of the people.'"

This time Slava, too, could not refrain from the sniffles. We sat at our father's side—living, warm, loving Father, who was telling us how to become orphans!

"Finish school, both of you. That's very important. Don't fall into despair, like Kolka or that little girl in the woods. Slava, try to protect your sister from . . . from. . . ."

I got up and left the two of them, running outside. Before the door banged behind me, I heard Slava say briskly, "Yeah, yeah, Papa. She'll protect herself. I showed her where to hit Kolka if he tries it again. She just has to kick him right in here and, boom, he'll be out."

March 27th was never to be forgotten by many Dulovans. On that night, not a limousine, but a van stopped on the left of us, on the right, and across from us. All arrested were, like my parents, non-Party members.

At the evening meal, in early April, Mother said, addressing no one in particular, "One more chair is empty in my office. I keep looking at the emptying chairs around me and want to run someplace. Any place! To run out of their reach."

At Father's place on the table stood a little, stubby vodka glass, filled to the brim. He gulped it down, and immediately put to his nostrils a crust of rye bread, sniffing at it several times in a row, the way Russians do to "get the aroma" of the bread. That, supposedly, helped one to remain sober. He finally lifted his head and facing Mother, asked, "Where? Where can we run, Natasha? There is no escape. Like an octopus, they reach out in all directions. . . ."

Father drank more and more. While before, especially on evenings in the winter, he had a shot of vodka "to warm up," of late a whole bottle was emptied on some nights. Still, Mother was considered to be a lucky woman for having found a "non-drinking" man for a husband, since many Russian men drank heavily, stopping almost daily on the way home from work in one of the bar-package stores called *sheltok* (egg yolk) because their walls sported egg-yolk yellow paint, easily spotted from afar, and to a thirsty man as teasing as a red flag to a bull.

When thrown out of the *sheltok,* all money spent, the drunk would stagger home, at times not reaching it, but dropping somewhere in a ditch. Young children would go out on a scouting trip, looking for their father. Finding him, they dragged the half-unconscious fellow home, calling out to him pleadingly, "Papochka! Papochka! Let's go home. Help us some. You're so heavy. Mama is waiting for you."

His wife would undress him, sponge off the soil and dirt, and tuck him into a soft down bed. "The old pickle has to have a good night's rest. He'll be as good as new tomorrow," she would announce, good-humored.

Russian women had an unending patience with their drinking husbands, but when a wife, on the brink of abandoning this patience, reproached her man for losing all self-restraint toward the blasted bottle—asking repeatedly, "Why? Why to drink?"—he as a rule answered that he drank to *sabytsa* (to forget himself). This *sabytsa* seemed to express so much, to explain it all. And the soft-hearted wife repeated to herself, to her children, to the neighbors, that her husband must be forgiven since he drank to forget himself—to *sabytsa*—as if this *sabytsa* were some sort of self-sacrificing, noble act.

In our home the word *sabytsa* began to ring out more and more often. That April evening, when our parents were talking about wanting to move out of Dulovo, Father once more reached to refill his vodka glass, but stopped at hearing a moan escape Mother's lips.

"Natashinka, dear, I need to *sabytsa*," he uttered self-pityingly.

Quite liberal toward an occasional drink, Mother became very irritated this time. She refilled Father's soup bowl with thick, hot stew and said sharply, "Eat quickly, husband, so you won't get soft in the brain. We need sharp brains now. And don't feed me that *sabytsa* business! You might want to forget yourself. I might want to forget myself. But let's not forget our young. They have no one but us to help them."

Slava and I, after finishing supper, retired to our corner, concentrating on homework, while our parents remained at the samovar, deciding about our future. And the future seemed to lead to one place—Feodosia, the Crimea, the Black Sea, Paradise!

When I was five years old, we spent a vacation in Feodosia on the invitation of old friends—a childless couple of Greek and Italian descent. I remembered neither the old people nor the surroundings. And yet, something connected either with our hosts or with the sea, or with my old, one-eyed teddy bear, Mischka, periodically entered my mind's eye, disturbing and frustrating me. The mental picture was always the same. It was of a body of water and my cherished Mischka, who still stared at me with his one laughing eye from the top of the blanket chest. Mischka was old by now, fur missing here and there, getting bald, but still appreciated, if only from a distance. Yet, in my memory he appeared wet, dripping, floating away from me. And I, too, was floating. Then—the abyss, darkness.

This uneasiness, however, was not about to stop me from wishing desperately to move away from Dulovo, from the all-dominating porcelain factory with its early morning whistle, calling people to toil, its smoking chimneys punctuating the sky, smearing it with a gray, lead-like shroud.

Dulovo's summers could be unbearably hot and dry, sparking yearly forest fires that at times engulfed several neighboring villages at once. Then there were weeks of oppressive stillness, when not one leaf, not one blade of grass moved, with temperatures climbing above 90 degrees Fahrenheit. Winters, on the other hand, were so severe that only the *pechka* could provide the much-needed warmth. But this oven-hearth demanded in return a lot of fuel, and the only practical fuel was turf. During the summer months we sank thigh-deep in the surrounding peat bogs, doing strenuous acrobatics, pulling first one leg out of the gluey, heavy, wet peat, then the other. With bent backs, hands and arms plastered to our shoulders in blackish-brown stuff, we strained at extracting the heavy mass and pouring it into the waiting brick forms. And all the time we fought off the persistent, blood-thirsty mosquitoes who valiantly protected their ancient home, knowing that the peat bogs belonged rightfully to them and not to those invading human giants.

Yet even the turf in the *pechka* was not enough to protect our home from the ravaging cold. So people devised a structure about three feet wide and three feet high, encircling the whole house with a sort of earthen bench called *zavalinka*. We—the young—were convinced that the *zavalinka* was constructed specifically with us in mind, since it was the coziest bench devised by man. On it, we often lay outstretched, dozing, catching the rays of a warming sun or just sat, half reclined, backs supported by the wall of the house, spitting sunflower shells. The *zavalinka*'s intended role was not at all to accommodate children, of course, but rather to protect the lower part of the building in winter from icy layers of snow, keeping the floors warm. In spring, when seemingly overnight, all that snow turned into torrents of mud, *zavalinka* did its duty in protecting the dwelling from this menace, too.

At first glance, it would appear that to live in the apartments near the factory the way our relatives did, would be more convenient, less burdensome than to live in a house. But when Father was given the choice to live in a house two kilometers walking distance from the factory, with no electricity, no running water, and no indoor toilet, or to live in an apartment five minutes walk from one's job, with electricity, running water, and indoor toilet and bathroom, Father chose the house. We burned kerosene to light our way in the dark; we stumped the turf bogs to feed our *pechka;* we marched to the communal well to fetch water. Also we trotted in all kinds of weather—with an umbrella during the pouring rain, and in felt boots and *tolstovkas* in the deep, deep snow—to the outhouse.

All those inconveniences, the chores, extra activities, and the lack of comfort became superficial, unimportant when compared to what we got in return. Land! A tiny, L-shaped strip of land that we were allowed to turn into a kitchen garden. That giving, rewarding, feeding scrap of Russian soil! While the long strip was given over to potato plants, beets, cabbages, radishes, carrots, cucumbers, and dill, the short part of the L—parallel to the road—was taken up with a profusion of sunflowers, providing us not only with nourishing seed, but with an effective hedge that hid all the trucks, the horse-drawn wagons, and curious pedestrians from our front windows.

The kitchen garden received a lot of tender, loving care from Father. None from Mother. She readily admitted that she was not a gardener. Her passion was the typewriter. In front of this machine, Mother was transformed from a drab, unexciting person into a fiery virtuoso. Her back instantly achieved the disciplined posture of a concert pianist, her strong neck leaning slightly forward, proudly bearing her involved, alert face toward the blank paper waiting in the machine, soon to be covered with letters, words, phrases. Very seldom, as if accidentally, she brushed the keys with her eyes, dismissing them right away, concentrating intently on the text to be copied.

Leaving Mother to her natural calling, Father turned to his—gardening. I, according to him, began to till the soil at the age of three.

When I was five, I was given two small water pails with a light-weight yoke, and began training in the art of water carrying from the communal well, about 200 meters from our house. The pails grew slowly in size as my bodily strength increased. While carrying water for washing laundry or any other housework was a chore, it was a joy to carry water for the garden. Seeing plants drooping in the 80 to 90 degree temperatures on a late summer afternoon, I hurried to the well, drawing pail after pail of refreshing water, pouring the cooling, life-saving liquid on the withering potato plants or the shriveling dill and drooping scallions, watching with pleasure the grateful plants perk up and become vigorous once again. And all the time I was in verbal contact with my wards, half-singing to them, "There, little potato, take some water. Don't droop, don't cry anymore. And don't forget to grow big for me—juicy, tasty." I stepped toward the sunflower plants, their heads always turning, following the sun, addressing them a bit more sternly than the potato plants. "Don't try to fool me, clever little sunflower. You don't need that much water. So here—just enough for a drink. To carry pails isn't easy, you know. Take what you need, and not a sip more, hear?" I would lift my face to that of the sunflower—so much taller than I was—daring to imagine that the plant was smiling at me, even winking.

The food that our cherished kitchen garden provided was of immeasurable help to us. In all Dulovo there were a couple of bakeries, a store where dairy products were sold, and a meat market. The shelves in all of them were empty most of the time since those stores were just not geared to provide enough food for the thousands of inhabitants of the area.

Dulovo also had two large grocery stores, pretentiously called "pavilions." One pavilion was located across from the factory, its revolving glass door spoke of modernity and progress. But it, too, could not sufficiently accommodate the populace, the store's door remaining most of the time unused. Still, the pavilion's glass display window was forever beckoning, promising, seducing one's eye with the chunks of hanging smoked hams, various types of sausages, carcasses of plump chickens, geese, and ducks; or with glistening loaves of bread, from black rye to white French loaves, and heaps of piled up *baranky* (bagels), some plain, some covered with poppy seeds.

And the vegetables! The fruit! What mouth-watering torment it was to stand by that glass store window, waiting for my parents to appear at the factory gate, and trying to persuade myself that those articles, those fairy tale articles, were just that—a fairy tale—all made of clay and porcelain.

The real items were seldom obtainable. On those rare days when trucks with food supplies arrived, the alert went out by word of mouth, spreading rapidly from one dwelling to another. Hundreds of food-seekers lined up for several blocks around the pavilion, praying silently, as my mother did, for something to be left when their turn came. Something! Anything! No one, with the exception of the very few who were first in line, expressed a preference for any specific item. Were it a chicken or a bunch of grapes, a pound of precious butter or eggs—all were gratefully accepted.

The second pavilion, located near our home, was a much smaller store than the one near the factory. Mostly bread and soy-based candy, dipped in artificial chocolate, were sold in this trailer-shaped pavilion. The candy lay in decorative piles in the store windows, sometimes for months, undisturbed, due to its mediocre taste and exorbitant price. Vodka, too, was occasionally dropped off in this store, together with wines and sweet liqueurs. From time to time the arrival of herring or cheese surprised the shoppers.

Because the store was near our home, Slava and I paid close attention to its activities. If merchandise arrived, we were to find the rubles left under the tablecloth for that particular purpose, grab a plate, pot, or shopping bag—since the stores did not provide anything in the way of packaging—and run to stand in line.

One late summer afternoon, while walking by the pavilion, I noticed a truck stopping at the store's back entrance, and ran to investigate. The saleswoman informed me that a shipment of cottage cheese had arrived. Delectable, not often seen cottage cheese! To spread it thick on a slice of bread, preferably white—black would do—to sprinkle some sugar on it—the best breakfast in the world! Being very perishable, it was available rarely, as were all items requiring refrigeration.

I was aflame, yet I had neither money nor the dish. I knew that in a matter of minutes the place would be buzzing with shoppers, and the cottage cheese would be gone.

"Auntie," I said to the sales clerk, "I am Nina, Mark Illarionovich's daughter. Please, auntie, reserve some cottage cheese for me. Be so kind."

"All right, kid. Four in the family? You'll get one kilo, one quarter per person."

Wow! Two pounds of that gorgeous stuff! I shot like a deer toward home, grabbed the dish, found the rubles, and with the same speed, approached the pavilion once more. Too late! People ran in droves toward the store, especially the ones who were on their way home from work. On top of that, it was pay day, when practically every man made it his duty to stop in the pavilion for a liter of vodka. He was not deeply interested in the arrival of cottage cheese, leaving it up to his wife to worry about such matters. But he was interested in his liter. Those men had to enter through the same door as the people who came to buy cheese. Tired, hungry, impatient for a relaxing drink, men were pushing, cursing, spitting, and smoking their ever-present coarse Russian tobacco—*mahorka*.

When I reached the line, I tried to sneak between the standing men, sort of torpedoing myself through the ocean of human bodies, moving steadily toward the store entrance.

Some men swore violently, others good-heartedly shouted, "Hey! You! *Glista!*" calling me the affectionate, but unappetizing nickname for a skinny child—a tapeworm. "Where do you think you're squeezing yourself to? Wait your turn! Aha! Aren't you Mark's little *glista?*" and they propelled me forward.

I finally reached the cheese counter, but I did not receive my purchase. Instead, I was given a ticket.

"There, girlie," the saleswoman pointed to the corner where a cashier sat. "Go pay the cashier. Come back to that counter, there. See?" and she pointed to still another clerk. "That girl will give you the cottage cheese." The procedure in all the stores of the Soviet Union was devised by the government in such a manner that a shopper had to stand not only once in line, not only twice, but three times in order to collect the purchased item.

I took the ticket given me, and started to squeeze toward the cashier. There was no breathing space between the shoppers, so that I could do nothing but follow the human flow, being hemmed in on all sides by the sweaty, *mahorka*-permeated men.

The cashier was not far from me any longer, when the manager barked out, "No more vodka! Finished!"

The men began to curse, push women aside, and hurry to the exit door, not wanting to waste any more time in trying to find a fresh vodka supply. At one point I received such a jolt that the all-important numbered ticket and money I was holding, fell out of my grasp to the floor. Without those two things there would be no cottage cheese! I began to lower myself toward the floor to salvage the lost items when another wave of pushing men threw me completely off balance and under their stampeding feet. Heavy boots started to hit my shoulders, my buttocks, my head, pressing my face into the filth-covered floor. I wanted to scream, to let the stomping boots know that I, Nina, was under their feet! Yet, no air came to my throat to help me utter a sound. After several people kicked me, unconcerned about what it was that they were stumbling over, one man decided to inspect what was under his feet. I, by then, had become extremely weak, dazed by what was happening to me, my body growing numb.

"It's Mark's girl!" my savior shouted. "Fellows! What the hell are we doing? Killing Mark's little tapeworm!" He and a couple of his buddies lifted me up and prepared to carry me home.

"Cottage cheese," I managed to squeak out weakly. One of the men ran to the cashier, paid for my purchase, and brought it out triumphantly. "A present," he said, smiling.

Neither Slava nor my parents were home yet. The men placed me on the sun-warmed *zavalinka,* and with apologies, left to pursue their hunt for spirits.

That evening Mother bathed my body in hot, then ice-cold, water, massaging it with sunflower oil.

"Don't scream, little one," she commanded, "I must massage all that blue out and make the blood circulate."

She wrapped me later in a soft flannel sheet and tucked me into a mountainous down comforter. Then she brought me a glass of hot tea with home-brewed raspberry brandy in it, and sticking a thick lump of raw sugar between my teeth, said sternly, "No more pavilion shopping, girlie. Not on paydays!"

CHAPTER EIGHT

My parents came to a firm decision to move to Feodosia. But to move required herculean efforts, because a Soviet citizen had no right to change his place of residence without a special permit from the regional party office. What to do?

Our greatest hope was pinned on the town physician, Moisey Grigorevich, to provide us with a medical certificate attesting to the poor health of one of us that would necessitate a move south. Whose health? Mother was quite robust. Slava and I, although very thin, were otherwise healthy. Father was our only hope. Six feet three inches tall, he weighed only 70 kilograms, or about 154 pounds. Because his brother, Vanya, had tuberculosis, it could be emphasized that Father, too, was in danger of contracting this lung disease, since it had a tendency to run in the family.

Father asked for a day off from his job to go to the local dispensary for a physical examination. I trotted along, wanting to help in some way.

The dispensary was a one story square structure, painted dark green, with a row of small windows that let very little light into the building. In days gone by, it served as a mercantile warehouse, but due to an acute shortage of clinics and dispensaries, it was remodeled slightly, and put to its present use.

A middle-aged female, her thinning, sandy hair pulled back in a bun, huge bosom adding to her domineering posture, sat at a desk, right at the entrance door. On seeing us enter, she commanded in a loud, no-

nonsense voice, "Come! Name! Certificate from place of employment! Fill in this questionnaire, then sit and wait."

We looked around the long, narrow corridor, called a waiting room, and asked, "Where to sit?" since there was not a single free spot that we could occupy. The woman, as if insulted, lifted her pale, cold eyes and said, "I don't give a damn where."

There were long wooden benches along both sides of the corridor, all spaces taken. The waiting room was swarming with many out-of-towners, peasants from neighboring *sovkhozes*. But women with ailing children predominated, waiting patiently for their turn. One old, toothless peasant sat on the floor Hindu fashion, rolling a *mahorka* cigarette. Some men were already inhaling the crude smoke, then, choking in response to its always unexpected harsh strength, spat on the floor in obvious disgust. There were several middle-aged men and women who, like my father, sat with certificates in their hands from their place of employment, excusing them temporarily from work.

Suddenly, a coarse, short-legged woman in a nurse's uniform and a long, white oil cloth apron, came out into the corridor, and shouted for all to hear, "Who has a fever over 38 degrees?" This was the temperature—38 degrees Celsius, 100 degrees Fahrenheit—at which a Soviet citizen could legally lay claim to medical attention and qualify for examination by a doctor.

Several women responded to the nurse's question, promptly raising their hands. "My boy is very hot, comrade sister," one young, tired-looking woman said, addressing the nurse in the Russian fashion, calling her "sister." "He's very hot to touch, poor child. Feel for yourself, comrade sister."

The nurse declined to touch the boy's forehead. "Well, what good to feel him? Means nothing. What's his temperature?"

"I don't know, comrade sister. I have no thermometer at home. You know how hard it is to get a thermometer."

"Yeah, yeah! No need for tirades. Take the kid's shirt off."

The nurse stuck a thermometer under the armpit of the pale, listless child, and left it there for a couple of minutes. Then she announced with cold finality that the child's temperature was below the minimum requirement to be considered sick.

The mother howled in despair, "Sister! Darling sister! Help! Give me something! He doesn't sleep nights! I don't sleep, and then I can't toil well on the *sovkhoz* farm. Give me something!"

The nurse, trying perhaps, to live up to her professional title of "sister of compassion" or "sister of mercy and kind heart," ended up giving several aspirin tablets to the young woman.

"See if that helps, and come only if his temperature gets to 38 degrees, understand?" The dismissed mother went out, holding on to the hard-to-get aspirin as if some unearthly magic was locked up in those tablets.

The nurse turned next to the old man sitting on the floor, kicking him lightly with her shoe, trying to make him rise to his feet. "So, Petr, you're back," she snapped. "What are you going to say? Your ulcers hurt? How many times do I have to tell you? Doctor can't help you! He can't help you, you stubborn peasant! Get out of here!" Seeing the old man not moving, she said—knowing from past experience what would chase this patient away—"You want me to give you another enema?"

Old Petr raised himself with surprising agility and, quite dignified, he marched toward the exit, muttering with his toothless mouth, "Enema! That's all they're good for. I pain inside and all they promise is a god-forsaken enema."

Father maneuvered me to the seat vacated by the now-departed woman with the fever-free child.

"I'll sit outside on the step and smoke," he said. "Here, put some newspaper on the bench."

While he arranged some newspaper for himself, I, too, spread several pages, automatically dismissing the very familiar bench carvings. Quite artistically, the male and female reproductive organs were permanently cut in the seat, surrounded by the vilest words that the Russian language can offer. People became immune to such carved graffiti, since benches in militia stations, in school cafeterias, in buses and trains, all were, not just crudely, but painstakingly carved in similar fashion. Who did these carvings? When? No one seemed to know. And not only benches, or tables, or stair rails, or fences were decorated, but bodies were too. That day in the dispensary several younger men, when told to remove their tops for the purpose of taking their temperature, exposed without the slightest embarrassment their chests and arms and backs tattooed in the same fashion as the benches.

Why such exhibitionism? Father, once, when our fence needed some repair, hired a young fellow to help him prop up the sagging structure. Warming up from the beaming sun and energetic labor, the youth removed his top shirt, exposing his upper torso—all tattooed. Father was curious to know why the fellow chose to violate his skin in such a way.

"Protesting," the yound man said. Only one word—protesting.

Time crawled slowly, while we waited for Father to be seen by the doctor. On the bench across from me, a man in his late thirties was bent over, holding on with both arms to his lower abdomen, and obviously in pain. The nurse came out again into the corridor and taking this man's temperature, said in an almost joyous voice, "Well, well! Over 38 degrees! Good. Wait now. I'll be right back."

She returned with a good-looking, soft-spoken female doctor, who observed the patient with kind, compassionate eyes, touching his abdomen in several spots, asking him what he ate that day, and the day previous. Then the doctor retreated, followed by the nurse.

Several minutes passed. The nurse reappeared and said to the sick man, "Come, citizen. I'll give you an enema."

Getting up with effort and still holding on to his abdomen, the man said weakly, "What good will it do, sister? The pain is persistent. For days now it's been growing."

The nurse cut him off sternly. "Don't give yourself airs to question the doctor's judgment, citizen! We'll give you an enema and clean your system of poison. Your pain should vanish."

"And if not?" the man persisted.

"Then Maria Pavlovna [the doctor's name] might send you to Orehovo-Zuevo, to the clinic there."

That enema was supposed to have the ingredients to cure all ills, but seldom did. When at home, it was done with much consideration to the comfort of the recipient. But in any public medical facility, one tried to avoid receiving an enema, because it was given in a crude, unfeeling, hurried manner. The medical staff was not overly concerned with the rules of sanitation, using the same insert on all patients who were found to need an enema, with only a quick rinse between.

Our dispensary building had only one lavatory with an oval hole carved out of a wooden plank, and a pull chain to release the flush water that often refused to appear. On the wall of this cubicle was a long, thick nail, with dozens of newspaper pieces serving as toilet paper, Stalin's images carefully clipped out beforehand. The patients who were not getting enemas, were required to use an outdoor toilet in back of the building, where there was no running water. In this way, the indoor toilet could be left for the use of patients with more urgent needs. Those more needy ones, holding on to their trousers or skirts, popped out of the room where the nurse had attended to them a few minutes earlier, and aimed toward the lavatory room, often not being able to reach it in time.

In the event of such an accident, an old pensioner woman, like Pelagea at the porcelain factory, appeared with a mop and pail, trying half-heartedly to clean up the mess, grumbling, "They miss it by a step. On purpose. So I would have something to do to earn my rations."

By no means was the lavatory in the Dulovo dispensary an exception. When I went for ear treatment in neighboring Orehovo-Zuevo, where there was a three-story clinic, I had to walk on a feces-splashed lavatory floor, trying to put one foot, then the other on any small spot on the floor still unsoiled.

Moscow hospitals offered lavatories that were not much cleaner. Father, who was treated at one time for a heart disorder in the very famous Botkin Hospital, encountered the same filth in its lavatories. As a rule, people tried to go to doctors *na toshak* (on an empty stomach and an empty bladder) in order to avoid the necessity of using the unsanitary facilities.

We spent about three hours waiting for Father's name to be called. Maria Pavlovna departed, leaving another doctor, Moisey Grigorevich, to take care of the remaining patients. This fact left Father visibly pleased, since Moisey Grigorevich was everybody's favorite physician.

Soon the bosomy, pale-eyed clerk called out Father's name, "You'll be next—the last patient." She promptly departed, throwing over her arm a large canvas shopping bag known familiarly as an "in case case." On the way home, she might be lucky enough to stumble over something eatable in one of the stores, or the "in case case" could be filled with small branches and pine cones that would come in handy when fixing the samovar.

Moisey Grigorevich popped out of his cabinet and said in a friendly energetic voice, "Come! Come, Mark. And you, *glista,* you can come in, too."

The cabinet-examination room was spartan. By one wall stood a cheap veneer desk, almost empty of any papers, or any reference books, with only an ink well, pen, and writing pad. The various drawers held meager supplies of iodine, cotton, aspirin, gauze, and very little else. By the opposite wall was a cot-type examining table with a soiled sheet covering its wood base—a sheet that had served several dozen patients that day. On the wall, over the cot, hung a large portrait of our two leaders—Lenin and Stalin—in profile.

Moisey Grigorevich was in his late forties, broad-chested, of medium height, with strong, Semitic features, his brown hair thick and wavy, with a high forehead above a prominent nose. His clean-shaven face was dominated by a full, generous mouth, and when he smiled, one felt, as the Russian saying goes, as if one had been given a ruble. Moisey Grigorevich had known our whole family and our relatives for years. It was he who gave me the very first treatment for my injured ear, sending me immediately to the clinic in Orehovo-Zuevo, concerned that without special treatment I would develop an infection that would lead to a loss of hearing. Uncle Vanya, too, was his patient.

"So, so, Mark," the doctor said, after inspecting the corridor and shutting the door behind him. "I heard about your brother. Devastating. Such a shame. Utter tragedy, not allowing a sick man to die at home. How much could Vanya give them toil-wise?" Moisey Grigorevich wondered.

Father, in a tight, choking voice said, "What if they meant to arrest me, the healthy one—and just mixed up the first names? I torture myself thinking about it."

There was the bang of a pail dropped sharply on the floor in the next room. The old pensioner was in the process of mopping the floors before retiring herself.

"That's why I am here, Moisey Grigorevich," Father went on. "Vanya first—could I be next? I need a certificate from you to allow me to move south, to *escape*. . . ."

The doctor put a finger to his lips, eyes pointing to the thin wall separating the two rooms. At the same time, he helped Father to take off his shirt, tapping on the exposed back, on the chest, holding his ear to Father's chest, listening to his heart beat. Then Father's eyes, ears, and mouth were inspected.

"You're too skinny, Mark, too skinny. Not good. Try to smoke less. I sincerely hope you won't follow Vanya's example . . . with *chahotka*," the doctor said pointedly, both men exchanging meaningful, mutually understood glances. And the charade continued after the doctor took Father's temperature.

"So . . . you worry that you might get *chahotka*, since it is running in your family?" Moisey Grigorevich was speaking louder, as if to address not only Father, but someone beyond his vision.

"You're right, Mark, the warm climate would be an *escape* in a way. Dulovo will miss you. But we need healthy, productive citizens."

There appeared an outrageously funny wink on the doctor's conspiratorial face, before he pronounced his diagnosis.

"I find that your constitution, your general health, would be beneficially served in the Crimean climate. You are qualified to receive my certificate. Go south." And then, in a barely audible whisper, he added, "And stay there, Mark."

CHAPTER NINE

I was longing to leave dreary Dulovo for warm, friendly Feodosia. Perhaps there—in faraway Crimea—my parents would not need to have their winter clothes laid out year round on chairs at their bedside, snow boots standing as if on alert even in the stifling heat of summer. Those chairs became a source of nightmares to me. I often woke up in the middle of the night, my eyes instantly settling on the chairs. Were they full of clothes? Were the snow boots still there? Good! That meant my parents were still at home. They had to be, because their special clothing was still home. Or were my eyes deceiving me? Were the chairs empty? Screaming, I would wake up, calling to my parents.

"Ninochka, hush, hush, darling child. Our chairs aren't empty, see?" Their voices lulled me back to sleep.

Besides the fervent hope of escaping this ever-present fear of being torn from my parents, I also desperately wished to escape witnessing the almost daily funeral processions. Pulmonary tuberculosis, that devastating "withering away," had no mercy on Dulovans, the victims being carried past our house to their final resting place amidst the frightful din and clamor of the accompanying brass band. The musicians blasted their way through Chopin's Funeral March, with bass drum booming, horns bleating, joined periodically by a horrendous crash of cymbals. No priests followed the catafalque, since no religious rites were permitted.

As the procession approached, people stood by their dwellings, on the sidewalks, or at the side of the road, waiting for the horse-drawn wagon, or in the case of a Party member, an open truck carrying the coffin. If it was a truck, then no use or need to come any closer, but if horses drew the coffin, people came near the catafalque, bowing low to the passing corpse, and in some instances touching or kissing a hand or forehead.

Some shouted a final farewell of *"Proschaiy!"* ("Forgive and be forgiven!") The very old, the brave ones, crossed the corpse and themselves.

"Again death," a neighbor would sigh, clicking her tongue sadly.

"Yes," another agreed. "No end to this plague. Poor Milova. She was so young. That greedy *chahotka* . . . always on the prowl."

The next day or even a few hours later, the same Chopin Funeral March blaring, the same horses stamping—a different corpse.

"Who is it this time?" people asked each other.

"Sarapin, that rooster! Six children he left behind. Now what? Who will provide for them?"

And although roundly disgusted with Sarapin's productivity, people sighed and wiped their eyes at the sight of the new widow with her young ones.

Lack of proper nourishment and, even more importantly, lack of the required isolation prescribed by physicians, were the main causes for the spread of tuberculosis. Yet, one other cause existed in Dulovo—a department in the porcelain factory where gold was processed for application on the dishes. This gold, in the form of dust almost imperceptible to the naked eye, settled in unprotected lungs, resulting in various ailments. The original owner, Kuznetsov, allowed only young, unmarried men to work in this department, and only for six months at a stretch. The workers were then transferred to other jobs, minimizing their chances of contracting a lung disorder. The Soviets put aside these precautions, and even employed women in this gold dust department. The results were quick and disastrous. The incidence of tuberculosis and other respiratory problems shot up sharply among Dulovo's female population. What was even more disturbing, the women employed in this department began to have miscarriages, or give birth to premature, often physically and mentally retarded children.

In old Russia, every village and town seemed to harbor one or two "touched by God" creatures, as people called the afflicted ones. Those "special souls," by some unwritten law springing from a deep pity for them, enjoyed a certain privileged status among the population, being clothed, fed, and given alms. In the Dulovo of my day, so many physically and mentally deficient people appeared, that they became a burden and annoyance to the rest. Instead of calling them "touched by

God," or "special souls," more often people began to chase them away, armed with brooms or shovels, yelling, "Out! Out of my property, *durak!* I've got nothing to give you! One *durak* after another! I'm sick of you all!"

And the poor *durak* (the halfwit) dragged himself away, meeting the same response wherever he went.

Those "unproductive" ones had nothing else to try but to beg. The same applied to people injured in industrial mishaps, and to disabled military men who, in order to get a crust of bread or a bowl of soup, knocked on doors, offering to trade their medals—badges of former glory. Some, without an arm, or missing a leg, hopping on crutches, begged to be allowed to fall into a pile of hay or rubbish in a shed, and spend the night there. Some pleaded for just one precious slice of dried, long-lasting *suhar*. Begging was outlawed by the Soviet government, but it continued to exist clandestinely, with the giver and taker forced to look in all directions before proceeding—to avoid being fined by the ever-vigilant militia.

There was one person in Dulovo with whom I truly hated to part—my girlfriend Lida. She was a pretty, delicate girl with short, unbraided hair the color of corn, and large, round, dark blue eyes—a girl quick to laugh, quick to forget an insult or hurt.

She came from a family that seemed destined to be doomed by a series of tragedies. After the forced collectivization, her father, a young, robust farmer, left his devastated village and came to the town of Dulovo, hoping for a better future there. In a nearby *sovkhoz* he found employment as a tractor operator. With his seemingly inexhaustible energy, he succeeded in providing his family with better living conditions than most of the white collar workers on our block. Many Dulovans considered him a peasant. But in his good-natured way he continued to plod along, to truly toil—at the work place and at home. His house, next door to ours, was a show place of sturdiness and neatness, fence never sagging, roof never leaking, and with an ample supply of turf and wood logs. In the winter months, his yard was the favorite playground for us children, because he was an expert in building a snow mountain, and by throwing buckets of water on it, he turned it into a mountain of ice. We spent hours sliding down this ice *gorka* on our sleds, or snowboots, or on our bellies.

Lida's mother was not of peasant descent, but came from a merchant family with good schooling and manners. She bore three children. Lida was my age. Her sister, Katya, was in appearance a twin to Lida, but five years older. Then came a long-awaited son, Boria, one year younger than Lida, and a copy in looks and temperament of his enterprising, resolute father.

All was well with Lida's family until her mother contracted *chahotka* after working for a time in the "gold dust" department of the porcelain factory. The disease spread to the oldest daughter, sparing the boy, but Lida began to look and act quite listless.

When the mother died, the three children were left more or less on their own during the day. But then, few Soviet children received much supervision after the age of seven or eight, because in the Soviet Union the occupation of housewife or home maker did not exist legally. It was classed as "parasitical." Only if a woman was disabled by disease, such as *chahotka,* or by injury, could she stay at home and give at least minimal supervision to her children. Soviet law also allowed a woman with eight children to become a full-time *domashniaya hosiayka* (housewife). She was at the same time awarded a title of "Mother-heroine of the Soviet Union."

Although the wives of Party members were excused from the necessity of toiling, many hiring nannies and housekeepers, to the average citizen such help was out of the question. If there were no grandmothers or great aunts, a family was in trouble.

This chronic lack of adult supervision led one day to a dreadful tragedy involving Lida's brother, Boria. It was early fall, the beginning of a new school year. Having eaten lunch on returning home from classes, Slava and I decided to hit a few balls of *lapta*—a children's game resembling a primitive form of tennis in which a small, heavy ball was batted back and forth with flat wooden paddles, using no net. We played right on the highway—a paved road two lanes wide, stretching in front of our house. Lida and Boria joined us soon, and all four of us started to scurry back and forth, taking up the whole highway, secure in the knowledge that our road was usually deserted at this time of day. When, infrequently, a horse-drawn wagon approached, we got out of the way, impatiently waiting to return to the game. Our heated, competitive shouts were the only noise in the otherwise silent neighborhood. After running and jumping for some time, Lida, having little stamina, withdrew to the sidewalk and leaned against the fence, resting. I soon joined her, watching the two boys truly getting into the spirit of the play without us two hampering their efforts.

Then, abruptly, we all four became quiet for a moment, listening in surprise to the noise of a motor truck. This truck came by daily to pick up filled porcelain orders, but in the morning hours, when we were at school. To watch a truck speed past our house was to us an excitement, an adventure. After all, those round, huge wheels—how many thousands of kilometers they covered! How many different towns, cities they went through!

Competing fiercely, the boys began to run with more vigor after the ball, while the truck was still blocks away. Then Slava stopped, retreating from the road, waving his paddle at Boria in command for the younger boy to retreat too.

"Come on, Slavka! Let's play to the very last!" Boria shouted, black curls sticking to his damp forehead, dark eyes laughing, teasing, shaming Slava into joining him.

My brother barked out an urgent command. "No, Boria! Stop! I mean it! I am older here! I give orders!"

The younger boy just laughed. "Oh, you're a regular sissy, Slavka! Worse than your sister! I bet my legs are faster than yours! Let's run and see!

Slava ran after Boria, trying to catch the deerlike boy and by force to remove him from the highway. The truck was approaching steadily. We saw the driver's suntanned face, prominent nose, moustache, pipe hanging out of a corner of his mouth, eyebrows drawn into a stern wrinkle. He must have seen youngsters playing *lapta* in all the villages and towns he passed through. So what? The kids were street-wise, they knew when to jump to the side.

Boria, as if possessed, refused to join us three on the sidewalk, shouting to him to get off the road. He hit the ball once more, and dashed after it.

"Stop!" Lida's panicky, high pitched scream pierced the air. "Stop!" she repeated.

Boria seemed to be deaf to her pleading, perhaps not truly believing that the driver would not put on the brakes, slow down at least. The boy dashed after the ball, but the driver did not put on the brakes, did not slow down. All at once, Boria was no longer upright, on his feet, but pinned down by the truck's front wheel.

The driver cursed violently, pipe falling from his mouth as he screeched to a stop, then backed up, wheels retreating. I looked at the spot where the wheel was a moment earlier, half expecting for Boria to rise, to shake his sweat-dampened curls, straighten out his trousers, and walk toward us with a guilty, apologetic smile.

Instead, my eyes saw Boria's motionless body, eyes closed, pink frothy foam at the corners of his mouth, and then, lower, where his

loose shirt hung over his belly—now the shirt was torn open . . . and
. . . and Boria's belly, naked . . . and like the shirt, his belly, too, was
torn! Gray and pink intestines spilling out of the opening, steaming,
crawling out of Boria's body, slowly, steadily, as if an unseen hand
inside Boria's belly was pushing the intestines out.

"He is dead, dead. Boria is dead." Who was chanting? All three of us?
Then, to our utter horror, Boria's right hand moved toward his face.
Our eyes followed his hand to his eyes—dull, perhaps already unseeing
eyes, but now open wide.

"Thirsty." His voice seemed far, far away. Boria did not repeat his
plea; he died with it on his lips.

The coarse, agitated voice of the truck driver brought us out of our
stupor. "You miserable bastards! Hooligans! To cause me this trouble!
Now I have to report this to the militia! You rob me of my time! You
waste my time!" The driver climbed back to his seat, looking for his
pipe. Then he sped off, still cursing us.

Lida, Slava, and I sat on the ground, surrounding Boria, weeping.
Weeping for Boria, for ourselves. We felt so terribly lonely, so utterly
helpless. We so needed a caring adult to help us, but all adults were
away, toiling.

Lida held Boria's hand in hers for a long time, chanting, "What will
Papa do? What will he do without you? Boria, Borinka! Mama died . . .
and now you."

I kept Lida company, weeping uncontrollably. Slava still choking
with tears, got up finally, and went in our house, bringing back a
blanket. We covered Boria, leaving his face open, and sat there on the
side of the empty highway, guarding his ripped body. Until his father
returned from the *sovkhoz* a couple of hours later, not one car, or truck
passed, not even a horse-drawn wagon.

It was only a few months later that I encountered Lida's older sister,
Katya. I was standing by the factory gates, waiting for the whistle
signaling my mother's appearance with her daily portion of cafeteria
soup. Katya came out of the rear exit by the Party administration
building and, spotting me, hurried over. Eagerly, she asked in a
hushed, out-of-breath voice if it were true that we were planning to
move to Crimea. I nodded.

"Where? What city, Nina? Is it Evpatoria?" When I named Feodosia,
Katya was visibly disappointed. We saw Pelagea Kulina at the factory's
gates, then Mother appeared. A female guard frisked her body, inspect-

ing even the soup canister, to make sure that no saucer or cup, no porcelain dish of any kind was carried off the premises by the employees.

Seeing Mother cleared, Katya hurried to her, not restraining sudden tears. "Natalia Alexandrovna, I need help!"

Mother embraced the girl's waist and, leading her away from the check booth, asked how she could help. Katya reached into her dress pocket and produced a thin, gray booklet.

"Look, Natalia Alexandrovna," the girl said, pushing the booklet toward Mother's hand. "It's my passport! I just now received it! I am sixteen today!"

"Well, congratulations, Katinka," Mother said, noting aloud how nicely dressed the girl was for the occasion.

Katya seemed to be indifferent to the compliments. "So, I am an adult now, with a passport," she said to Mother, who still could not understand the reason for Katya's extreme agitation. "What good is the passport to me, Natalia Alexandrovna, if my lungs, if *chahotka* . . . like Mother. . . ." The girl could not bring herself to utter the word "death." She caressed with her palm the brand new identification document, and when one of the tears dropped on the passport cover, she quickly wiped it off with her sleeve. "You know where I was today, Natalia Alexandrovna? Before receiving the passport? At the dispensary to see Moisey Grigorevich. He gave me this certificate, see? He wrote here that I am real sick, and need a warm climate. That's all he could do. So I went to the Party representative." Katya burst into a new wave of sobs. "He asked me how many months I had worked, Natalia Alexandrovna! I didn't finish school yet! I told him so. I said, 'Comrade, I am only 16, I have two more years of schooling.' Then he said that one must have six months of 'useful employment' before one could be entitled to a bed in a sanatorium. 'Come back when you get six months of fruitful toil to your credit,' he said."

Katya seemed all at once drained of energy, and leaning on Mother's arm, for a while she walked in silence.

"And then what, Katinka?" Mother asked.

"Well, when the partorg told me to return in six months, I said to him, 'Comrade, I won't be among the living in six months if . . . if you don't help me now.' He shrugged his shoulders. Then he wanted to know who my father was. I said, a tractor operator. Mother? I said, she died—*chahotka*. Anyone belonging to the Party? No."

We were walking slowly toward home, crushed by Katya's predicament. Those sanatoriums! Those fantastic places! Pictures in magazines, in school books, in newspapers—so beautiful! Clean beds, doctors, nurses, plentiful food for the sick, medications—and the sea! Children go home rejuvenated, feeling well again. And there was our little Katinka, our neighbor, an honor student, unable to open any door that would lead her to a sanatorium. No one in her family belonged to the Party.

It was soon after, that Katya, denied any hope of medical help, began to give up her grip on life. One day when I came to fetch Lida for our weekly visit to the *banya* (steam bath), Katya, in bed, implored her younger sister not to leave home.

"Lidochka," she begged, "don't go to *banya*. Don't leave me today. I am afraid to be alone. Death is," Katya halted and with her eyes open wide, she pointed toward the bolted back door, "death is after me . . . knocking. I hear it." Her sunken eyes shone brightly, her cheeks looked as if carelessly smeared with rouge, dried specks of blood on her bluish lips.

I left Lida home with her sister, and ran toward the steam baths where one could cleanse oneself thoroughly, using as much hot and cold water as desired, while at home no such bathing conveniences existed. In the middle of my bathing, Lida appeared, and spotting me through the thick blanket of steam, she joined me on the wooden bench.

"Poor Katya," she said, starting hurriedly to scrub herself with a harsh sponge. "I waited for her to fall asleep. Now I'll catch a quick bath and run back."

Briskly, we completed the bath ritual that at other times could take hours, and ran back, bursting into Lida's front entrance. To our dismay, the front door was partially opened. Katya lay on the floor, half blocking the door, as if she had tried to call out, to get help, to get someone's, anyone's, attention.

"Katinka!" Lida screamed, in the same piercing child's voice as she had when Boria ran under the wheels of the truck. "Answer! Answer me! Move! Katya, breathe!" Lida tried to lift her sister back into bed. She banged her fists on Katya's stilled chest, as if this frantic pounding could instill life back into the already lifeless girl.

I stood at the threshold, heavy with self-reproach, feeling that in some way I had contributed to this devastating scene of grief. Perhaps if I had not stopped by on my way to *banya*, Katya would have died peacefully in her sister's arms.

And so I stood and stared at the two sisters. One was now calm, indifferent, no longer struggling with death. The other was frightened, full of despair, just starting to walk the road her sister had already completed.

CHAPTER TEN

Summer was coming to an end. We were sitting on pins and needles, waiting for the Party officials to approve our move to Crimea. One needed a lot of patience and emotional endurance in order to make such a move to another state, as we chose to do. So far, we had only completed one step—that of acquiring the health certificate from Moisey Grigorevich, without which the wheels of bureaucracy would not move.

Yet, two more steps had to be completed. We needed one more certificate from the city of Feodosia, attesting that we would not be a burden to the city and would not expect it to provide us with living quarters. In other words, friends or relatives had to certify their willingness to share their quarters with us. On receiving this extremely important certificate from our old friends in Feodosia, stamped and signed by several officials, we were still tied to Dulovo because a third requirement, the most important one, had to be fulfilled and another certificate—actually two separate certificates—one in Mother's name and another in Father's, had to be in our possession, proving that both parents had guaranteed employment waiting for them in the Crimean town.

What was continuing to hold us up, was the lack of proof that Father, the head of a family, could be certain of a job in Feodosia. Mother soon received a document from the state railway, located in Feodosia's outskirts, at Sarigol. It stated that Natalia Alexandrovna was accepted as an "American style" typist at the monthly salary of 200 rubles, plus coal and bread rations, with free rail tickets once a year to any place in the Soviet Union!

One slight inconvenience was tied to this proposition: Mother's internal passport would be confiscated. No one could live in any town of the Soviet Union without having to produce this apartheid-type internal passport. Many farmers were tied to their collective farms by this means. In Mother's case, the railroad officials were afraid that if passports were not impounded, employees, on receiving the free train tickets, would just disappear. Without a passport Mother would be more or less tied to Feodosia. But who cared! Only to receive the opportunity to be tied to Feodosia!

On the arrival of this certificate, we immediately started to raise the money for the move. Our burgundy leather sofa which, like the samovar, had seen better days in my paternal grandfather's study, brought us a whopping 1500 rubles. All the mattresses, beds, tables, chairs, tools, were sold for another 500 rubles, but remained ours to use until the time of the move. Father and Slava carried several small pictures and cushions, together with our tall indoor rubber plant to Lida's place, beautifying the girl's room a bit, while informing her that healthy ozones were concentrated in the tree's leaves.

Then we resumed the wait for Father's notice of guaranteed book-keeping employment in Feodosia. While the country seemed to be still in short supply of good typists, there was a surplus of people who were extremely efficient on an abacus. It was rumored that many well-educated men and women, including members of the nobility, in order to hide their background, joined the ranks of bookkeepers.

Father's preference was to be employed by one of the *sovkhozes*.

A *sovkhoz* (state farm) differed from a *kolkhoz* (collective farm) in two respects. While *kolkhozniks* were by law permanently tied to their collective farms with no right to be absent for more than 72 hours, the *sovkhozniks* were free to come and go, their internal passports not having been confiscated, as was done with *kolkhozniks*. Many *sovkhozniks* lived in nearby villages and towns, and even in big industrial cities, traveling to and from work by train.

The other all important difference was that *sovkhozniks* were allowed, after meeting a required quota of produce delivered to the government, to sell their surplus on the free market, setting their own price. *Kolkhozniks,* on the other hand, even after meeting the government's quota, still were obligated to sell their surplus to the same government at prices dictated by the government. The fruit *sovkhoz* was Father's most desired place of new employment, but any place connected with food would be welcomed, for it would hold out the hope of putting a bit extra on our table.

And then it came! That precious, much stamped, much signed certificate, promising Father a job as head bookkeeper at Feodosia's fish preserving *sovkhoz*. No fruit, yet fish, too, was welcomed, since it was an excellent substitute for the seldom available protein of chicken, veal, or pork, or utterly unavailable beef.

Father's salary was set at 250 rubles a month, giving us altogether 450 rubles for a family of four. By standards of Party members, that would be considered living in poverty—in deep poverty. Not by ours. True, a man's woolen suit cost around 1400 rubles—six month's of Father's salary. Yet, with extreme economy, Father could perhaps in two to three years scrape up enough to reward himself with such a suit. A woolen jacket-sweater for Mother cost about 300 rubles, requiring one and a half month's of her salary. A cotton, unlined "between seasons" coat for me cost 96 rubles—half of Mother's monthly salary. A silk-type adult dress was 200 rubles, so that Mother had to work a whole month for it. Leather shoes, very seldom found, would take Father's entire pay for two months. Grocery prices were quite exorbitant if compared to the average salary. Butter, for instance, cost 16.50 rubles a kilogram, sugar cost 5 rubles. Bread was 1 ruble per kilo. Separate prices existed for Party and non-Party employees. Zoya, a nineteen-year-old typist at the Dulovo factory, who often ran to Mother's desk to ask her about spelling and who typed with two fingers to Mother's ten, nevertheless received 500 rubles a month to Mother's 200. Zoya was a Komsomol, married to a Communist. Her salary was automatically higher—by 150 percent. Yet this comparison was quite misleading when one took into account what Zoya could buy in the stores specially designated for Party members. There, for a woolen sweater jacket that would cost Mother 300 rubles in an ordinary store, Zoya paid only 75 rubles, one-fourth Mother's price. Her husband could buy a suit for 350 rubles that would cost Father 1400. And this disparity held true on everything, be it clothing, furniture, or, most of all, food. So Zoya's salary of 500 rubles would stretch to 2,000 rubles if given to my mother to live on and shop with in ordinary stores. Thus Zoya was receiving ten times, proportionally, the salary of my mother. And Party members paid no taxes.

In the last days of August we took our departure from our remaining relatives, good neighbors, and my friend, Lida, and proceeded toward the railroad station.

Slava and I each dragged a ballooning bundle made up of down pillows and comforters—Mother's highly treasured items, her wedding presents. Religiously, once a week we aired the down in the sun, or even on frosty days outside on the laundry line, so as not to let it rot. Good down disappeared with the shortage of poultry, so that those pillows and comforters became more or less priceless. Father lugged the pride and joy of his long-gone-by university days, a massive maroon suitcase of genuine leather—an item that, too, of late had become unavailable. Zoya's husband, who paid so well for our tufted leather sofa, offered us enough money for the suitcase to buy Father two woolen suits, but we knew that if we parted with it, never would we be able to replace it. It was the one and only suitcase we possessed, and was filled mostly with our family album, cutlery, and a good set of porcelain dishes, each one wrapped in a towel, pillowcase, or item of underwear. Besides the heavy suitcase, Father carried on his back a large bundle of clothing, stuffed in a salmon pink, square pillow cover. On Mother's back was an identical pillow cover, tied with a string, and filled with the remainder of our winter clothing, mainly *valenky*, tolstoy jackets, fur hats with ear flaps—articles that helped to keep us warm in Dulovo's winters. At first, they were meant to be sold, but somehow my parents could not bring themselves to part with those items. What if warm clothing would still be needed in Crimea—to dress the chairs?

Reaching Moscow, we stepped from one slow-moving train and boarded another slow-moving train that would drop us off in Feodosia on the third morning, after covering 1,435 kilometers.

The railway coach, with its wooden benches carved in the mode of Dulovo's dispensary and its small, grimy windows, was packed solidly. We four were all together in one corner, occupying two short benches facing one another, and with a window all to ourselves. There was very little room to stretch one's legs so that Father's long frame soon began to suffer in confinement. He often jumped up and attempted to take a stroll through the coach, which was a feat of acrobatics in itself. Slava and I, in order to give Father more room to stretch on the bench, sat much of the time on the comforters and pillows, between the two benches on the floor of the car. The salmon pink casings on those down articles were soon turned charcoal gray, to Mother's consternation, but we did not lack in comfort. Mother, too, arranged herself comfortably with the help of the *tolstovka* jackets' padded softness, but her mind was not totally relaxed—she worried over the safety of our samovar. The machine quickly caught the eye of many passengers, for the samovar was a handsome creature, calling attention to itself. Big, arrogant in its handsomeness, this hardy witness to February and October revolutions followed by a devastating civil war, displayed a few bumps and dents, as if to remind us of all the tossing and dragging it had received during past upheavals—yet survived!

"Oh, my," a woman—our next bench neighbor—said in genuine awe, soon after we settled down, "that samovar is 'before,' isn't it?" "Before" meaning pre-revolutionary. "All that ivory inlay! And silver! More silver than copper, isn't it?" she persisted.

Mother had reason to worry about our samovar, because theft was all prevailing. Women's bags, if worn over the shoulder or over one's wrist, were sliced from their straps, and so "light-handedly" that often one would not notice right away. Women could not wear fur skins around their necks. They would be cut or snatched off. A good fur hat was often not safe on one's head.

We took turns holding on to our belongings, especially the samovar, and taking naps. Mother periodically took off her left shoe, dusted it, inspected its sole, then did the same with the right shoe. One was inclined to think that she took extra good care of her brand-new, rubber-soled shoes, but what she really did was to inspect them periodically to convince herself that the 500 rubles in one shoe and the 500 rubles in the other were still safely tucked away under the heel and toe of the insole. Another 500 rubles were sewn into my skirt, and 500 more in Slava's trousers. Father had about 200 rubles for trip expenses in his wallet, safety-pinned inside his jacket.

After only a few minutes of travel, our coach began to fill with the thick, sweetish smoke of *mahorka,* burning our eyes, tickling our throats. Coughing, Slava and I shook the small window, banged on it demandingly, until it gave way and opened. The blue *mahorka* smoke began to crawl out of the window and, somewhat relieved, we reached into our coat pockets filled with toasted sunflower seeds and began expertly to separate those tasty, nourishing seeds from their shells, competing in spitting the shells the longest distance out of the window.

Slowly, lazily, we crawled along the Russian landscape, forced to give way to express trains, military trains, and the maroon-colored prison trains that were transporting people who in Russian jargon were "sitting"—that is, imprisoned. Mother, staring at one of the coaches unblinking, sad, whispered to Father, "You could have been there . . . among the sitting. Maybe Vanya died in one of them."

Our coach quieted down when encountering those special trains. Affected by the somber mood of the whole coach, Slava and I stopped spitting the sunflower seeds when we met up with those Stolypin cars, as if it was disrespectful somehow, to enjoy chewing on the fat seed.

Muscovy was passing us slowly by, with its thickly wooded stretches, its low hills and small lakes, with muddy roads twisting through the towns and villages, showing here and there a wooden church, its cupola leaning to the right or to the left, rotting, unattended. The squatty, small *izbas* (log houses) lined the roads, some surrounded by drunken-looking, decaying wood fences. By some deserted *izbas*, skinny, neglected dogs were pacing, howling like wolves, calling for human attention and getting none. Gray, monotonous landscape accompanied us the entire first day of our journey. As darkness set in, Slava and I retreated from the window, curled up in our down bundles, and left the passing Muscovy countryside for a long night's sleep, while our parents took turns protecting our belongings—our entire worldly possessions.

The next day the Ukraine's steppes and fields replaced the woods of the northeast. The log *izbas* were succeeded by neat clay dwellings, well kept, some surrounded by kitchen gardens. The womenfolk attending those gardens were shorter and heavier than their northern sisters, broad-faced and fair, and their clothes were brighter. Their dialect was very different, softer to the ear, with hard Muscovy Ks turning into soft Hs. Because of this, Ukrainians earned a derogatory nickname of *Hohol*, emphasizing the letter H. On the other hand we, the Muscovites, were called *Kazap* by the Ukrainians, because of our hard Ks and hard Zs. At the train stops, Slava and I tried to talk to the Ukrainians through the window, and were often not able to understand many words. The moment they realized we did not understand them, the Ukrainians good-humoredly said, "Ah! Kazap! Kazap!" and switched into good Russian. Yet we, the Great Russians, could not switch into Ukrainian dialect.

The closer we came to the Crimean border, the more colorful were the new passengers. Armenians began to appear, many Jews, and in even greater numbers the slender, proud-looking Crimean Tatars. All, among themselves, communicated in their ancient tongues, yet to be understood by others, almost all could speak Russian.

One of the new occupants to squat near our corner on a huge bundle wrapped in a thin Oriental carpet, was a middle-aged Caraim with olive skin, thick, black hair and moustache, stocky but agile. He spotted our gleaming samovar and immediately approached Mother.

"Comrade citizen, this beautiful machine is of old times?!" he more proclaimed than asked. "I'll pay you good money, comrade." Not discouraged by lack of any kind of response, he persisted, "You go to Zhankoy? That's where I go, too. Or maybe you go to Crimea?"

Father decided to put a stop to the unwelcome conversation. Aiming his long-lashed dark eyes at the fellow, he more or less hissed, *"Krim!"* (Crimea). He tried to roll the letter "r" in *Krim,* so as to sound cutting, menacing, but without success.

The agile round ball exploded in a joyous leap. "Krim! My place of birth! My forefathers came from Krim! Good place, good opportunities, trade! Well, not of late, of course. . . . Madame. . . ." The Caraim dropped the customary "comrade" or "citizen" in addressing Mother, and leaning low over her small hand, he proceeded to bring it to his crimson lips in the outmoded—downright outlawed—gesture of the bourgeois hand-kiss. Mother quickly withdrew her hand, hiding it under a pillow on her lap.

"I implore you, madame! Consider! I can give you a bag of rubles for it!" The born tradesman emphasized the word "bag," leaving to one's imagination and wishful thinking what the size of the money bag might be. "Or, perhaps, if not rubles," he leaned toward Mother's face speaking very softly, as if imparting secrets, "we can swap, perhaps, an old Caucasian runner. I have a magnificent Chichi rug—like your samovar, a museum piece. No? Perhaps a shawl, a silk and gold shawl from a former noblewoman?" The Caraim seemed to want to offer the world for our samovar.

Father, bored by the whole procedure, whispered to us all, "Ignore him," and closed his eyes, snoring softly.

The Caraim retreated. When the conductor shouted "Zhankoy! Zhankoy!" he, loaded like a camel under the staggering weight of his wares, threw one last, longing glance at our samovar, and left.

A new wave of passengers was pushing into our car. The coach, by this time, was filthy, smoke and sweat permeating its very walls, floors covered with a thick layer of sunflower shells.

A high school girl in a white blouse and navy skirt, with a red Pioneer kerchief on her neck, entered our car. Her pretty, oval face was framed by wavy, blond hair, scooped back into one thick braid. She took the seat across the narrow aisle from our benches. The girl's arms and legs were covered with multiple sores, some angry red, others pussy, resembling the sores of chicken pox. Withered, raw cabbage leaves were tied with thin string around some exceptionally ugly sores, almost wounds, and giving off such a stench that Slava and I unceremoniously covered our nostrils, and leaned out of the coach window practically to our waists, to emphasize to the newcomer our disgust.

The young girl, in a good-natured, although slightly sarcastic voice, called out to us, "Don't worry, I don't have leprosy. It's just *moskitka!*"

Moskitka, a disease similar to yellow fever, reportedly reached Crimean shores many years earlier through visiting Spanish sailors. If bitten by a mosquito carrying the disease, a person developed a devastating high fever that responded well to treatment with quinine; or one developed ugly, pus-oozing, long-lasting sores. Interestingly, many girls between ten and fourteen seemed to suffer from this latter form of *moskitka,* making doctors ponder over the possible connection between the disease and the beginnings of puberty in the female body. There was a medicinal cream, very inexpensive, that did wonders in helping to heal the sores. Yet the Crimean drug stores were sparsely stocked with supplies of this cream, while drug stores in Moscow carried it in over-abundance.

Mother sat closer to the affected youngster, sympathizing with the girl's predicament, and the girl, in turn, disarmed by the older woman's kindness, at once broke out in tears.

"You know, auntie," she sobbed, hiding her tear-stained face on Mother's sleeve, "I beg the doctors to give me more cream. They say, 'We've run out of cream. Moscow has it. Ask your friends or relatives to send you some!' I have no friends there, auntie, no relatives. And the train ticket to Moscow! I can't afford it! So, the doctors said to put some raw onion or cabbage leaves on the sores. There are vitamins in those things. They'll help close the wounds. No, no help. I am so afraid it'll last forever."

Mother tried to comfort the girl, predicting that soon the sores would heal by themselves.

"Wishful thinking, auntie," the girl snapped. "The cream costs just three rubles. But it's not available here. Why must Muscovites have this cream? They get no *moskitka!* Only Crimeans get it."

The girl got off in another hour, and the oppressive smell left with her. Fewer people entered our coach. Not many vacationers traveled by this slow, uncomfortable train, and others seemed not to be too anxious to go to Feodosia—a place primarily dedicated to the well-being of those on holiday.

CHAPTER ELEVEN

*C*rimea was opening to us, with its mild, agreeable climate and the friendly, bountiful Black Sea that teemed with fish of all kinds. Dolphins—three different types—found a home in this sea, jumping up and down, in and out, as if only to delight the human eye. Herring, very fat and juicy, abounded. Anchovies were plentiful as well, along with sprat, horse-mackerel, tunny, and lufar. And there were colonies of purple medusa that looked like adorable toy parachutes decorating the waves. The beaches were lavishly strewn with shiny pebbles and shells.

The mountains and hills on the approach to Feodosia came right to the seashore on one side, while the other was reserved for seemingly endless steppes and given to grazing, mainly by sheep. The rest of the land was cultivated in the production of tobacco, grapes, exotic eggplants, red and green peppers, and field after field of round, dark green, saffron-yellow-striped watermelons, the sweetest in the world! And honeydews, cantaloupes, pumpkins! And wild pear trees, cherry trees, and apple trees with fruit bright red on one half and bright yellow on the other. There were almond trees, whole forests of almond trees! And wheat! Crimea was the breadbasket of the ancient Greeks! Very few potatoes? No matter.

"Feodosia! Get ready to move! No dilly-dallying!" the train conductor shouted, and, for emphasis, spat on the floor that had a two-day accumulation of cigarette butts and a carpet of empty sunflower shells.

"Feodosia," Mother echoed joyously. "Ah! We are here! Golden Feodosia. Quick! Mark! Children! You know what you're supposed to carry. Grab it! I'll carry the samovar. Pick up the feather beds. Shake them a bit. My! All black. Not a speck of pink left! Oh! How will I get that grime out of the cases? And the suitcase. . . . Mark, look! Someone poked a hole in it! They tried to slice it open while we slept. Thieves! Crooks!"

While Mother grumbled and organized, Slava and I hung out of the window, trying to catch a first glimpse of the sea. So far, only low, rocky, half-naked hills were opened to our view, a grim-looking desert-like steppe, in spots almost black, covered by sun-baked foliage. Then, without warning, the train shook in convulsions while making an abrupt turn on the sharply curving rails, and suddenly, dramatically, we were right at the shore of the magnificent sea—a very long, crescent-shaped shore, stretching spectacularly in front of our almost disbelieving, delighted eyes. The edge of the sea ran parallel with the rails, and so near that the breezes blew flecks of foam from the waves into our faces. Slava and I, giggling, stretched out our hands to the sea. While in Dulovo we were catching snow flakes in the same manner, now we tried to catch wind-blown mists from that gorgeous, friendly Black Sea. Black? It was not black at all, but sparkling in shades of turquoise, turning to bright, rich emerald, then farther, to the horizon, changing to pale violet.

Slava put his moist palm to my face and said, "Smell, Nina. The sea smell! It's like the freshest fish right off the hook! Fantastic! Look, sis! All those white fishing boats! Father, maybe it's your *sovkhoz* people fishing there! Wow! Sure would like to start fishing." Slava was excited. But Father mercilessly brought reality into my brother's world.

"No one can fish here, Slava. That is, no individual is allowed to fish in the sea, or on the shore. There is only organized fishing, like the *sovkhoz*. Private fishing is outlawed." Seeing Slava's crestfallen expression, Father embraced the boy's slender shoulders and promised to find a spot somewhere, away from the militia's observing eyes, where the two of them could hide and fish.

Feodosia's shoreline was divided in three adjacent strips. Right next to the sandy beach and parallel to it, ran a dark, narrow double line all along the fifteen kilometers of the natural curve of the shore—the railroad tracks. Surprisingly, the rail line was laid in the best part of the town's real estate. The town fathers, back in the 1890s, during the all-consuming enthusiasm for constructing a railway that would connect Crimea with the rest of Russia, decided to follow the crescent shore line with the tracks, reasoning it would benefit the welfare of Feodosia, because the trains were to be devoted mainly to bringing in vacationers from the frigid north and east. How attractive it would be! The newcomers could step off the train and, if they wished, dip into the sea immediately.

And that is what Slava and I wanted to do—just jump off the train, and run into the cooling waves, clothes and all, throw ourselves on the lullabying, murmuring waves, and just lie there, outstretched, staring at the sky. And what sky! Not Dulovo's dusty, gray sky, but azure, with fluffy, curly, snow white clouds, as if a flock of sheep had shed their wool, and decorated the sky with it.

After the sandy shore and the railroad tracks, came the third strip— the paved boulevard called by the natives *Naberezhnaya* (shore line) but officially named "Lenin's Prospect." Alongside it stood magnificent hotels, museums, and villas built by very wealthy Jewish and Caraim merchants in pre-revolutionary times. Those once private villas were now serving as sanatoriums.

And behind the villas, museums, hotels, and office buildings, the town began slowly, imperceptibly to climb up the hill. Neat, clay buildings clinging to the mountains, spread high up, some hanging in the fashion of beehives, when one building's roof served as a patio for the building above. One mountain, called "Fete Obas," the highest at 916 feet, dipped dramatically into the sea, while neighboring hills, already much lower, surrounded Feodosia paralleling the sea. This protective ring ended with Bald Mountain—so called because nothing, but nothing wanted to grow on this hill. There, the hills sort of gave up, as in disgust, leaving the town exposed to dull, desert-like fields abruptly becoming steppes stretching beyond the horizon, allowing sheep to graze, while yielding little and promising nothing.

Loaded with the feather beds, in my heavy Dulovo coat and thick stockings, I stood at the train window, soaked in my own perspiration, agape at the wonders before my eyes, staring at the sea that seemed to have no end. The whole horizon was flooded with its magnificence.

And beyond the horizon were unfamiliar countries, unfamiliar peoples, strange customs, strange languages! There was Turkey— Byzantium of the past, with its Constantinople—and Italy and Greece. People of all those countries at one time or another walked the soil I was now preparing to walk on, some leaving their imprint forever, others vanishing without a trace.

Six centuries before Jesus was to walk this earth, the Mileta Greeks discovered a town on the Black Sea, and established a colony there, calling it Theodosia—"God's given." Over the centuries many peoples tried their hand at colonizing Theodosia, including the Romans, who booted out the Greeks, and were themselves booted out eventually.

The Goths came, then the Huns, and later the Khazars. In the year 1260 Genoese Italians became the new masters, calling the town Kafa (or Kaffa). Ottoman Turks drove the Genoese out in 1475, and all that the Christian masters had erected and created was destroyed in the name of Allah. Soon, though, on the graveyard of one culture, another sprang up. Magnificent minarets, mosques, palaces, Turkish baths, fountains—all even more splendid than under Genoa—adorned the town. Great, sprawling, oriental-style bazaars mushroomed, and at this time the town had 80,000 inhabitants.

In the year 1771, the whole Crimean peninsula fell into the hands of the Russians, who were then ruled by Catherine the Great. On her famous "Potemkin village" tour, the Czaritsa visited Kafa (Kefe under the Turks) and soon gave the town back its Greek name, Russianizing it to Feodosia.

When Soviet rule came on November 14, 1920, and private enterprise was outlawed, many merchants including those of Jewish, Armenian, and Syrian descent deserted Feodosia. The harbor became devoid of bustling merchant ships, of free wheeling and dealing. The import shops closed, bazaars emptied of eager bargain hunters.

Now, as our train was coming to a stop, Feodosia gave permanent residence to only 19,000 inhabitants, one-fourth the population of 300 years earlier.

CHAPTER TWELVE

A *slight jolt,* and our train stopped. Slava and I jumped onto the platform, catching small items Mother was tossing to us out of the window, including pillows. The down comforter protested, refusing to be squeezed into an undersized ball, and had to be carried down by Mother with a certain care. She returned for the samovar, this time leaving the coach permanently, and was followed by Father, dragging the bulging, slightly wounded suitcase.

The militiamen were vigorously chasing the new arrivals off the platform. One fellow came up to us and shouted at Father, "Get your junk out of here in a hurry! No cluttering up Lenin's Prospect! Why the hell did this train stop here in the first place! Only express trains should stop here! Now move!"

We were ready to accommodate the militiaman, only we did not know where to move. Our parents looked around hoping to find a place where we could wait unharassed.

"Comrade militiaman, our friends should be here any minute to fetch us," Father explained.

"Ten minutes! That's all you get from us! Then you'd better be gone!" the official ordered.

The train shook like a long caterpillar and puffed away, out of sight. Now the other side of the railroad tracks was open to our view, showing us the Lenin Prospect and the most renowned of local hotels, the Astoria. In the old days, well-to-do travelers had only to cross the boulevard from the railway station and enter the hotel's waiting luxury.

To the right of the Astoria were villa-sanatoriums, occupied by hundreds of vacationers, who were lining the streets and sidewalks. In pairs, in groups, they chatted in unrestrained fashion, shouting at the top of their voices when recognizing a friend hundreds of feet away. They proudly sported their striped, cotton, pajama-like suits—a mark of privilege. Suits were striped in yellow, maroon, or blue—the color connecting the wearer to a specific sanatorium. Some vacationers resembled circus clowns, arms and legs too short or too long for their pajama suits. Others looked quite sharp in well-fitting crisply starched stripes, with a gleaming star or an order of some sort dangling on their breasts— a Party award for an outstanding deed. But no matter in what condition the striped pajamas were, all the wearers looked as proud as peacocks.

Feodosia's street traffic was to my eye and ear absolutely horrendous. Every few minutes a black official limousine carrying high-ranking passengers hurried by, blowing its horn and scattering the pedestrians to the sides of the road, or back to the crowded sidewalks. The foot traffic spilled out on the road again, people walking arm in arm, when another limousine, bus, or motorcycle would blow its horn, demanding the right of way. From time to time, as if to compete with the machines, a two-wheeled cart drawn by a small steppe horse galloped by, with a Crimean Tatar standing in the cart and plying his obedient horse with an unnecessary whip.

And how many humans with different shades of skin passed by us! While the visitors were mainly light-skinned, many natives were golden and olive-skinned descendants of Tatars, Gypsies, Turks, Greeks, Italians, Armenians, Crimean Jews—all having varying degrees of dark tint in their smooth, pigment-rich skin, and all openly envied by the pasty northerners.

Those lobster-red vacationers, in their striped pajamas, often stopped at the Hotel Astoria's impressive glass facade, debating whether to enter or not and then, having decided, pushed the revolving door, disappearing into the hotel's lobby. And what a lobby! My young, eagle-like eyes were dazzled by the luxurious setting, separated from me only by the width of the Lenin Prospect. There were giant palm trees potted in Chinese fish bowls, ornately framed mirrors, leather divans and arm chairs strategically positioned for maximum comfort, complemented by small and large marble tables. Oriental and Caucasian rugs lay on parquet floors. The old Czechoslovakian crystal chandeliers sparkled even without being lighted, chiming softly in the sea breezes.

While devouring with my eyes the Astoria's rich facade, I suddenly became still, almost not breathing, lips falling open, eyes unblinking.

"Slavka, look." I poked my brother in the ribs with my elbow. "Is it real?" I pointed to a small, narrow display window, hardly noticeable at first, just a few feet away from the Astoria's grand entrance. It proclaimed in large, fat letters—PEKARNIYA—a bakery. Shelves, almost from floor to ceiling, were neatly, solidly stacked with glossy loaves of bread—round, oval, square, high, flat—and all shades from black to white. And my favorite: *baranky* (bagels), so named after the curved horn of the ram, *baran*. In overwhelming profusion, *baranky* hung on strings like necklaces—some blackened with poppy seeds, some golden with onions, others with caraway seeds or plain. I turned to my tired, preoccupied mother, and tried to speak nonchalantly.

"Mama, look at that bakery! It's . . . it's not like Dulovo's pavilion?" A stutter unexpectedly gripped me, "It's real? The *baranky* . . . are they real?"

Father dug out a couple of rubles from his hidden wallet, and allowed Slava and me to cross the street to find out for ourselves if our eyes were deceiving us. Minutes later we were skipping back to our baggage, strings of bagels dangling and dancing on our chests. We hardly had time to express our joy at the purchases, when the pair of militiamen returned, and harshly, with foul words, kicked our feather beds with their boots, ordering us to disperse.

"Get! Get!" they shouted. "More of you parasites from the north! Look at those bastards, already stuffing their mouths with our bread!" They looked at Slava and me swallowing the marvelous tasting bagels practically unchewed, the way a snake would swallow its prey, as if afraid of being robbed of it, yet almost choking, because our throats refused to stretch to accept the size of the bagel chunks. The militiamen aimed their boots at our samovar, but Mother, suddenly agile and young, grabbed the tea maker in her caring arms, and lifting our bundles, we all marched away from the station.

The entire length of Lenin's Prospect was lined on both sides with tall, slender, century-old southern poplar trees that provided shade for wooden benches, spaced a few feet apart. All the benches were occupied with people gazing at the lively sea and spitting sunflower seeds, or chewing on toasted pumpkin seeds. One amorous couple, seeing us approach their bench, and not wishing to share their world with anyone, left abruptly, opening the whole bench to us.

When we had settled down, Mother said very quietly to Father, with a ring of obvious uneasiness, "Praskovia Ivanovna isn't coming. We must disappear from here by dusk. The militia will definitely kick us out."

Father, listening to Mother's worries, was rolling a cigarette and after a few puffs, visibly calmed by the tobacco's magic, declared convincingly, "Praskovia Ivanovna or Dmitry Antonovich will soon arrive. Now, don't forget, Natasha, we never told our friends what day we'd arrive, since we didn't know ourselves. We only knew we wouldn't be coming on the express. Don't worry, dear," and lifting his head toward a clear, tender blue sky, with rosy and lavender clouds intruding here and there, Father said blissfully, "I could stay here forever."

And, I thought, so could I remain forever on that spot where the bench stood. If only some magic could turn this bench into a small cabin, just big enough to quarter four of us, and we could be forever lullabied to sleep by the gently breaking sea waves, inhaling the sea's aroma, only steps away from the sandy shore.

Barefoot by now, chewing on a sweet-tasting poppy seed bagel, I watched a middle-aged Tatar woman with long, black hair piled high, coming near us, her bright harem pants practically hidden under a long tunic.

"Beautiful lady. . . . Please, precious lady," she said in broken Russian, pushing toward Mother a small glass of dark, fat sunflower seeds. "Very good sunflower seeds. Crimean seeds—better than northern. Very juicy, very cheap. One ruble. Only for you, fair-haired lady. Please buy."

We bought. Slava immediately pronounced, after tasting the seeds, that they were no different from the Dulovo's. While we two tried to compare the taste of the sunflower seeds, a prune-faced, old Gypsy fortuneteller approached us. She wore several layers of brightly colored skirts, reaching to the ground, a blouse decorated with row upon row of gaudy glass beads, and long, dangling earrings to match. After observing us for a while from afar, the Gypsy came to our bench, grabbed Mother's hand unceremoniously, and proceeded, after a quick glance at the palm, to forecast in a hurried, but authoritative, voice.

"Madame! You think you will be happy here! Yes?" she half-asked, half-pronounced. Her hoarse, tobacco-permeated voice had a mocking tone. At Mother's positive nod, the Gypsy sputtered, "No, madame! No happiness. Very bad troubles. Lose your man. . . . Lose him."

Father, so relaxed only a few minutes earlier, frowned, pulling Mother's hand out of the Gypsy's grip. But he could do nothing to dispel the curiosity and apprehension the Gypsy had aroused in Mother. Russians, from time immemorial, have held a certain respect for the art of fortunetelling. In Dulovo too, there were Gypsy fortunetellers, and Mother, with her female friends, often, at lunch break outside the factory walls, listened for a few kopeks to the forecasts of some all-knowing seeress. No Gypsy in Dulovo had predicted Father's disappearance. And here, a world away, only minutes after putting our feet on Feodosia's soil, this old, wrinkled hag already had found her way into our future. The Gypsy, not even bothering to retrieve Mother's palm, continued to address her, but staring all the while with burning, yet strangely vacant eyes at tobacco puffing Father.

"Nice man, madame, but you lose him."

"Why?" Mother challenged the Gypsy.

The shriveled face, abruptly moving her stare from Father, looked unblinkingly in Mother's eyes, as if trying to read thoughts, and said with a dismissing gesture, "No worry. No other woman." Seeing Mother's deep, guilty blush, and Father's forgiving smile, the Gypsy said, "No other woman . . . but much misfortune. For you both." Then, glancing at Slava's and my curiosity-filled eyes, she repeated, "Misfortunes for all of you."

Father jumped up from the bench and said in an irritated, impatient voice, "Stop your mindless crowing, old hag! It's not enough you frighten my wife. Now you drag in the young ones. Go away!"

But Mother, by then thoroughly involved, stretched her palm once more toward the Gypsy, and implored, "Don't you see anything good?"

Encouraged, the Gypsy gratefully proceeded, speaking more slowly, deliberately. "You live long, long time, lady. Maybe half century." Mother smiled contentedly, glad to hear of another fifty years allotted her to walk this earth. The Gypsy was solemn. "But, alone," she croaked. "No man with you—no husband."

"And where will I be?" Father demanded.

The Gypsy seemed to take those words for an invitation. She brusquely, determinedly snatched Father's left hand and immediately crowed, "You, sir, not in your grave, your wife no widow, but you two never see each other."

Mother, in a quiet, tight voice said imploringly, "Enough, enough. Might it not be so, Gypsy?" She turned to Father and whispered, "Again arrests, even here."

The sharp, alert Gypsy, who was not supposed to hear those words, caught them nevertheless, and quickly interjected, "No arrests . . . no Siberia. Farther. Over the great sea. An ocean! Ocean separate you."

I interrupted instructively, "You mean this sea? Sea and ocean are different. There's no ocean here."

The Gypsy, not tolerating any instructions, snapped haughtily,

"Ocean! Only first, much trouble. Much travel . . . much running. Like us Gypsies you travel here . . . there. You run, run. You never know about him." She pointed her brown finger at Father. "Never!" the Gypsy spat out, almost defiantly, trying to stare down Father's angry look. Over Mother's futile protests, he chased the old woman away from our bench, while sticking a ruble in her hand. "Go! Go! Lying wench! Not one good word came out of your mouth! To upset people like that."

The Gypsy took the ruble and hid it in her bosom. While already moving toward another prospect, she chanted, still defiant, "You see, you see. No lies."

I began to wish for someone to come and lead us somewhere, where a roof would be over our heads as night approached. Father became restless as well. He finally leaped off the bench, stamping the cigarette stub into the asphalt, and began to instruct us all to hold tightly to our belongings, even if the militia were to chase us away. He was going to try to locate Praskovia Ivanovna and her husband, Dmitry Antonovich.

I wanted to remember and visualize Praskovia Ivanovna and Dmitry Antonovich, but I could not, because I had last seen them when I was only five years old. Slava remembered a tall, skinny person, always in black, and with a booming voice, but he could not remember whether it was a man's voice or a woman's.

From our parents' conversations, we knew that Praskovia Ivanovna's family was acquainted from pre-revolutionary times with Father's family, continuing the friendship to the present day. While Praskovia Ivanovna had descended from a well-to-do merchant family of Greek ancestry, her husband, Dmitry Antonovich, was a descendant of Genoese Italians.

Dmitry Antonovich was an artist, a painter drawn to the sea, and Feodosia to him was God's chosen spot on earth, as it was to so many painters, including Russia's most prolific 19th century painter of water—Aivasovsky. Aivasovsky's sea lived, it moved on canvas. His sea refused to be placid, but played and teased, inviting, smiling in its calmness. Then in a storm, the sea frightened, forbade, chased, and mercilessly killed at times. A two-story building of massive proportions, the former residence of Aivasovsky's family, was turned into a memorial by the town council, dedicated to their native son's extraordinary talent and energy, its many walls covered with canvas after canvas of the Black Sea.

Dmitry Antonovich was so utterly devoted to his birthplace that when the civil war was ending in favor of the Reds, he was urged to pack the jewelry and gold of his ancestors, along with other precious items, and flee with the Whites. Instead, he planted his easel not far from the harbor, and recorded on canvas events never again repeated in his lifetime.

Thousands of officers and soldiers in Czarist uniform, unable to stop the flow of history, leaped in panic and disarray aboard the waiting ships, and sailed off to distant, unfamiliar lands. Constantinople (Istanbul) was the nearest destination, leading later to France, Germany, Yugoslavia, England—to any country that would take those defeated warriors. Near the end of 1920, the victorious Reds on their heels, the Whites could not retreat fast enough. Dmitry Antonovich observed and caught on canvas scenes of wounded Czarist soldiers being taken off the ships a few moments before departure, while rich merchants or members of the nobility were pressing a diamond necklace or a bag of gold coins in the captain's hands, and taking the place of the discarded wounded, dooming those men to certain death.

After the Soviet takeover in November 1920, Dmitry Antonovich lost his whole inheritance but, perhaps due to his paintings of the civil war—showing the Whites and nobility as he saw them—and perhaps because Dmitry Antonovich was a genuinely apolitical creature, wholly preoccupied with his art, the new rulers allowed him and Praskovia Ivanovna to live, not exterminating them as they did so many others belonging to the class of "rotten bourgeoisie." The couple was allowed to retain one room of their previous huge residence—a library room measuring 20 feet by 40 feet—a palace by Soviet standards. This room-palace the childless couple was willing to share with us four.

CHAPTER THIRTEEN

*F*ather *disappeared* around the corner of the stately building housing the Aivasovsky gallery, while Mother, Slava, and I, turning
away from the sea, were now tensely watching this corner, waiting for
Father to re-enter our vision at the same spot.

His tall, thin figure reappeared a few minutes later, highly agitated,
his long arms stretching pleadingly toward another thin, tall figure
harnessed in some sort of a strap arrangement that was connected to a
two-wheeled wagon resembling a chariot. Only this wagon was much
smaller, and not a horse, but an obviously elderly woman was pulling it.

Mother sprang up from the bench and shouted to us, "Look! Look!
Praskovia Ivanovna is coming! Children, get ready! Now everything'll
be all right!"

The individual in harness stopped for a moment, looking in the
direction of Mother's loud, resonant voice, and began literally to trot
toward us, while Father still tried to intercede and change places with
the woman, whose old-fashioned, long, black dress was flapping
wildly, riding up between her legs, and not allowing her to proceed as
swiftly as she would have liked. Visibly annoyed, she lifted the skirt to
her knees, revealing black, lace-trimmed pantaloons, reaching to slender, well-chiseled ankles. The woman's head was covered with a small,
lacy scarf which kept her white hair gathered in a bun, in perfect array.

We were hypnotized by Praskovia Ivanovna's rapidly approaching
silhouette, by her girlish waist clutched in a wide, silver belt made of
several intricately carved individual links. Two turquoise silk tassels

hung and danced from the massive belt buckle—the only color that was not black.

And there she was, in Mother's embrace, her large, hazel eyes moist, listening to Mother intoning, "Dearest, dearest Praskovia Ivanovna. Again we meet. So much has happened." Mother started to weep. Praskovia Ivanovna seemed to be one of those people who did not tolerate seeing anyone weep.

She freed herself from Mother's arms and boomed pitilessly in a strong, low voice, "Turtles! That's all you are!" Allowing Father finally to take the leather harness off her chest, she persisted. "Every day for the past week I am at the station . . . waiting. Even turtles would arrive quicker from Moscow than you people did!" she complained loudly in mock accusation. She then proceeded to greet Mother officially according to Russian custom, by planting a kiss on one cheek, then on the other, then on the mouth. She kissed Father in the same fashion, shaking her head in open disapproval. "Skinny, Mark, skinny. Might get *chahotka*." And she banged on Father's chest to emphasize the location in the human body that *chahotka* favored most. "How much do you weigh? 70 kilos! Dangerous!" Again embracing Mother with her large eyes, Praskovia Ivanovna boomed, "Now, Natashinka, five years were definitely not kind to you." She clicked her tongue, while shaking her head from side to side. "Look at your mouth. So many wrinkles around it. And you are too young for so much gray in your hair."

While Praskovia Ivanovna's mouth was uttering seemingly harsh, critical words, her eyes, her hands were caressing Mother as if she were a child. "Now, now, Natashinka, dear. We'll change all that. Fatten up Mark a bit and make your mouth smile more."

Then, as if remembering she was greeting four people, not two, she looked at Slava and, embracing him, planted three kisses on his face, adding a fourth on the boy's forehead.

"So, so. Our Slavochka, the philosopher! Didn't change too much. I would know you anywhere by that forehead of yours. Welcome, *sinok* [little son], welcome."

She then turned her eyes on me and, instead of the thunderous outburst that had greeted each member of my family, a hardly audible sound left her lips.

"Ninochka? The little one? Natasha, is this Ninochka?"

I eagerly tried to reassure Praskovia Ivanovna, and, remembering her earlier gesture of banging Father's chest, I too, thumped my chest, insisting, "It's me! I am Nina!"

Praskovia Ivanovna burst out laughing. "Yes! Yes! Big gray eyes with a question mark in them. Even then a question mark was there. And your hair . . . braided! Then you had short hair. But . . . so tall! Slava should be tall." After reflecting briefly, she seemed to decide that it was beyond our power to change the situation, and putting her slender, long fingers on my cheeks, she suddenly became tender, mischievous, years younger. Bending closer over my face, she chuckled, "Remember, child, how you tried to rescue your one-eyed Mischka— the teddy bear? Right there, see? On the public beach. You what? You remember something? Well, you were playing on the sand. A wave came and took Mischka away. You went tip-tip-tip after him. Another wave came and took *you* away! And your parents were there next to you, dozing, roasting in the sun. Good thing my Dmitry Antonovich saw your little bottom floating. He ran and got you out! He slapped your back, and turned you upside down till you gave all that water back. Close call that day, girlie. Well?" Praskovia Ivanovna looked at my wide open, tear-filled eyes. "Now what is it? I didn't mean to upset you, Ninochka." She pulled me closer to her.

But I was not at all upset. I cried with relief that the recurring mental pictures of Mischka, of water, of that frightening abyss, were part of my real life experience, and not some unexplainable, haunting nightmare, a product of my imagination.

After the exchange of greetings, we loaded the capacious two-wheeler with most of our belongings, leaving only our unruly down comforter out, and harnessing Father to the overflowing carryall, we were ready to leave the shoreline. Praskovia Ivanovna produced a large, linen handkerchief out of her dress sleeve and, waving it over her head like a scoutmaster, she commanded, "Let's march! Follow me! Dimochka is waiting!"

I said a silent "so long" to the glorious beach and sea, and followed Father's bent figure as we started to climb slowly up the hill. The dwelling we had to reach was on Karl Marx Street, situated between two major arteries—Kerch highway, which led straight as an arrow to a spot even older and richer in Crimean history than 2500-year-old Feodosia, and Simferopol highway, so named as the route to the Crimean capital. We left behind Lenin Prospect, along with Italian Street, a reminder of the Genoese presence. We passed the Aivasovsky Gallery and the street named for it, continuing to move away from the show places on the shore. Now poorly paved streets began to greet us with gloomy, peeling public buildings and foul-smelling cafeterias, where every patron had to provide his own fork and spoon—standard procedure in most Soviet eating places of this type. More Tatars began to appear, more barefoot, unkempt children, naked below the waist. We continued for another ten minutes or so, knees slightly bent, climbing toward the shadows of Bald Mountain. Slava, loaded down with the comforter, stopped at one point and said, "All right, sis, your turn," lifting the light-weight, but cumbersome down bundle on my back.

As we passed a small nearby hill, Praskovia Ivanovna commanded us to stop, and, pointing to a water well atop this mound, announced proudly, "Our water well. Only one in this neighborhood. It's hard to get good drinking water in Feodosia. Ours is very clear—tasty. I presume, Slava, it's your chore to provide the family with water?" the old lady inquired, as she once again began to march us forward.

"No, I do!" I interrupted eagerly, trying to extricate myself from under the fluffy down cover. "I like to carry the pails. Slava doesn't. Besides, I try to develop a good posture under the yoke. Like African women. They walk like dancers carrying things on their heads. Like this, see? No swaying hips." I proceeded to demonstrate what I thought was a dancer's posture, but Praskovia Ivanovna was not impressed.

"Yes, yes. Trying to dance with water pails—and look at your body! Your left shoulder is higher than the right, belly sticking forward!"

"I know!" I quickly agreed. "It's to make me shorter. When I get up from a chair and a boy doesn't know how tall I am ... he starts laughing or runs away. So, if I bend my knees a bit, curve my back, see? That throws my belly forward and I get a bit shorter."

We resumed walking, while Praskovia Ivanovna was comforting me with a promise that in the not too distant future, boys would not be laughing. Then her voice boomed, "Stop! Here we are." She pointed to a gate marked "7." "Our fence." She waved toward a tall wooden wall, completely hiding a courtyard and the dwelling itself, exposing nothing to the street and curious passersby.

I dropped the comforter next to the gate and, sitting on it, gave the neighborhood a quick, all-embracing look. Not bad, I thought. The water well was certainly closer than in Dulovo, although—as in Dulovo—it was open, and one had to lift the heavy pail by the rope. I had hoped for a pump well. A bakery was on the corner of the next block, its large sign visible all the way—easy to watch for the lines that meant bread was in stock. A kerosene store was on the opposite highway—just a one minute walk. In other words, I felt that all the most important essentials of life were more or less right there—in those two blocks. Perfect!

The whole length of Karl Marx Street was devoid of any greenery. The fences, gates, and walls of the houses lined the cobblestone sidewalk, leaving no space to plant a bush, a tree, or some grass. But facing Karl Marx Street, across from the highway, was a strip of land covered with perky green shrubs and several trees. "A park!" I thought to myself, quite pleased.

Then Praskovia Ivanovna, with an energetic gesture pushed the gate open, and my heart sank. A large cobblestone courtyard jumped out at me, naked, treeless, surrounded by half a dozen low, wooden, cabin-type dwellings. Children sprawled on thresholds, supervised by old, toothless men sitting nearby, sucking on their long, curved tobacco pipes. On my left by the fence, in the very first doorway, sat a gray-haired woman with strong semitic features. She was mending a shawl. A girl about my age, delicately built, pretty, snub-nosed with long, ashen braids was reading something in German to the old lady. Another woman, in her late thirties, lay on an outdoor cot, very pale, as if ill.

Across from the gate, almost directly in the middle of the courtyard stood a dark green wooden structure, on which was proclaimed in bold, brown letters, UBORNAYA, the outhouse, a strong smell of disinfectant drifting from its vicinity. So, I thought sadly, no privacy like we had in Dulovo. And Dulovo's garden. . . . There was no garden here. No growing dill, or scallions, no talking to blossoming potato plants or sunflowers. Nothing but cobblestones.

I counted the apartment cubicles, each marked by one window and a doorway. Seven cubicles, all connected, all bursting with the varied noise of men, women and children.

Praskovia Ivanovna's energetic voice announced, "All right. . . . We are home. This," she said, looking at Slava and me, and pointing to the courtyard with its seven tiny apartments, "this, earlier, was our stable, a very spacious courtyard. The horses went in a circle. All those doors, all seven of them, led into the stables." She made an all embracing, circular gesture with her left arm, ending the circle at the doorway of the young girl with the thick ashen braids. "Ah, Maya, dear, would you like to meet a Muscovite? Nina is your age. You two will probably go to the same school." Praskovia Ivanovna pushed me toward the girl, and we shook hands limply.

"My babushka," the girl said softly, introducing her grandmother and then the sickly looking woman, "my mother."

Praskovia Ivanovna, not allowing any more time to spend with my new acquaintance, directed us to turn right. "Come, come! Everybody to the right! Dimochka is waiting!"

Once more, I lifted the comforter, following with my eyes Praskovia Ivanovna's outstretched arm far to the right, and grinned in delight. A huge Crimean cherry tree, drooping under the weight of thousands of ripe cherries, stood majestically in the middle of a marble paved patio. The tree's top branches were scraping at the second story veranda windows, while the lower branches served as a vast umbrella for a round marble table on a tall pedestal. Several wooden folding chairs were arranged neatly, as if waiting for company. A samovar stood in the middle of a linen-covered table together with tea cups, plates, and a bowl of the same cherries that so profusely decorated the branches above. And to the side, all by itself, was a tall Napoleon-type torte, partially covered with a linen napkin.

Standing guard over the torte, with a rolled newspaper, chasing away the persistent flies was . . . a man? Or was it the skeleton of a man? Could any human who breathed, or moved his limbs, be so utterly emaciated, so that all the body's bones seemed to reveal themselves, and then, almost as an afterthought, out of decency, covered themselves with a parchment-like layer of skin? No flesh, it seemed, existed under the skin. And the dark shadows under the huge, sunken eyes. And nose! There is a Russian saying, "A nose that God intended for seven, but only one received it." Greek nose? No, Praskovia Ivanovna was Greek—Dmitry Antonovich was Italian. Well, perhaps Italians had such noses. Only, Dmitry Antonovich's nose was without flesh.

The first image of our host was devastating to my mind. And right after the joy of discovering the fantastically vibrant cherry tree! I wanted to run, to return to the bench at the shore so as not to be near this man-skeleton.

And then the skeleton, at our approach, cried a name. Not my brother's, not my mother's or father's, but mine—as if to prevent me from going through with my desire to flee.

"Ninochka!" His wide, still generously formed lips called out my name—not in a hollow or weak, invalid's voice, as I was sure the man would use, but in a resonant, booming bass. "Ninochka!" His almond-shaped, dark gray eyes laughed, the arrows of a young, contagious spark shooting out of them toward me. "Remember your one-eyed Mischka?" And peals of laughter followed.

"Yes, yes, Dmitry Antonovich, I do!" And confidently, no longer afraid, I sprang toward him, and taking his long, bony hand in mine, I raised it to my cheeks and to my lips.

Later that evening, while already in a bed that had been fixed for us on the veranda, I heard Praskovia Ivanovna, with a note of apology, explain in hushed tones, so as not to disturb the sleeping Dmitry Antonovich, why she did not inform us of her husband's illness.

I couldn't write you about it," she insisted. "You might've refused to share our lodgings, afraid you'd be in the way. Cancer, he has stomach cancer. Surgery? No, Mark. No surgery. Dimochka would have to leave Feodosia and go to Moscow. No. He wants to die here. Besides, the hospitals in Moscow are dreadful. He would die there sooner than under my care at home. What do I do for him? Well . . . I feed him a concoction an old Tatar woman taught me. It's made of crushed almonds, very fresh. Bitter? Of course almonds are bitter. But I put peach honey in with the almonds. Only peach honey works. Every morning on an empty stomach I feed Dimochka crushed almonds with honey. The Tatar woman's husband lived twelve years. Perhaps it'll help my Dimochka. . . ." And Praskovia Ivanovna, who was so stoic until then, all at once dissolved in tears under the weight of her sorrow.

A long, narrow veranda, serving also as a passage from the main room to the outdoors, became our sleeping quarters, with two narrow cots lining one wall, while two larger cots for our parents were against the wall opposite. Between, there were a couple of feet of empty space—just enough for a person to walk through. The veranda did not feel confining, due to the windowed wall where Slava's and my cot stood. This expanse of glass led one's eye to the patio with its cherry branches bending with fruit, more or less knocking at the panes, so that my brother and I had only to open one portion of the window, and load our cupped hands with the sweet cherries right from our beds.

Later, at times, we two deserted the veranda and spent many nights under the open skies in two old hammocks found in the storage shed. It was pure joy to spend September and even October's slightly chilly nights wrapped in Dulovo's down comforters, and for hours to gaze at the star-lighted heavens, thinking, wondering, yearning to learn what was beyond.

In the morning, fantasies aside, we joined the grownups in a spacious, to our eyes utterly palatial room that served in the past as a library. What had been the kitchen in the original house was turned into an apartment occupied by a young surgical nurse, Tanya, and her army doctor husband. The remainder of the old servant's quarters was divided among three more families, while the main part of the house, walled off solidly from the rest, was partitioned into apartments housing approximately forty people at the next address.

Our hosts' room had ten foot ceilings, immense French doors leading to the veranda, and a pale stained glass window opening onto the patio—to the same wonderful cherry tree. The apartment's parquet floors were generously strewn with old Caucasian rugs, while a couple of thin, Persian pastel silk rugs hung on the wall where the bed stood. That part of the room was separated from the rest with a tall, very old Chinese screen. The remaining space was furnished with a celadon-hued, raw silk upholstered divan, with a mass of overstuffed pillows piled into little mountains, giving the couch a definite Turkish flair, and in the evening transforming it instantly into a bed. In the middle of the room, flanked on one side by the divan, stood a round table covered with a persimmon velvet cloth reaching to the floor, with a Belgian lace top spread over the velvet. It served as a banquet table when opened up, or a table for two; also as a tea table, as well as a platform for chess and cards. It was the heart of the home, reflected in a huge, fabulously carved mirror that brightened and opened up the already spacious room, giving the illusion that it was double its true size. The mirror reflected also a space where originally a marble fireplace was located; but after the revolution it was ruthlessly knocked out and replaced with a two-burner black iron stove called, somewhat ironically, *burzhuyka* (bourgeois). Above the *burzhuyka,* covering the ugly gaping scar left by the fireplace removal, hung another tapestry-like rug, in front of which, suspended from a silk cord, was displayed a massive, curved, intricately carved ivory pipe, the monogram of the famous Garibaldi decorating it in one spot.

Bookshelves completely covered one wall opposite the window. Once probably spilling over with books, now most of the space was given to framed photographs, to bric-a-brac, to icons. The icons were arranged as photographs or pictures—individually, as if they were small paintings and not gathered in the left corner of the room as was the custom of old, a strictly religious tradition, not practiced of late. Many of the icons were very old, colors muted by age, some in gilded silver, others decorated with semi-precious stones.

Under Soviet rule, Dmitry Antonovich's talent gave him a certain privileged status—that of "Artist." He at first complied with the new regime's directives to produce paintings glorifying the victorious October revolution. It was not difficult for him to recollect and portray the disgraceful, greed-obsessed scenes that Feodosia witnessed during the panic of the White army's retreat. But after a while he began to long for peaceful subjects, depicting calm seas, calm human faces. The Party did not approve. Dmitry Antonovich was ordered to retain "revolutionary vigilance" in his art. When once he painted a young schoolgirl in a yellow dress, holding a daisy in her hand, plucking the flower's petals to see if her wish would come true or not, he was ordered to add a red Pioneer kerchief on the girl's neck—a symbol of the child's conscientious awareness and devotion to the Party. In another instance, Dmitry Antonovich portrayed a young Tatar bride, showing her long, black hair, not arranged in the more than thirty individual braids she had worn only the day before—braids symbolizing virginity—but hanging loose, free, proclaiming the fact that she had become a woman. Where previously she had worn a tunic over pantaloons, now at the lower point of the hips, almost touching the pubic bone was a scarf securely tied with a solid knot—a knot proclaiming her "being taken," and unavailable to any other man's courting. Then Dmitry Antonovich added to this painting an intricately decorated small metal vessel with a long neck that every Tatar woman always had near her. The vessel contained water used to purify and cleanse the body after relieving oneself—a ritual strictly observed by Crimean Tatars who were devoted Moslems. Party officials demanded that this object be removed, since it represented a religious relic.

Dmitry Antonovich began to withdraw, at first not realizing it himself. His paintings became dull, wooden. When he tried to catch the images of the new rulers, their lifeless faces stared at him angrily, as if to accuse him for lack of ardor. Finally he gave up, at first using "old age" as an excuse, then ill health. To sustain them, Praskovia Ivanovna periodically took some item of value—a ring, a silver cup, or a tapestry—and proceeded to the market place, quietly seeking to exchange it for food.

Slava and I were registered in the school closest to us, named after a fallen hero of the Soviet government, Comrade Kirov, who was ruthlessly slain in Leningrad in 1934.

Maya, the ashen-haired girl I had met on the day we arrived in the courtyard of No. 7 Karl Marx Street, was not only my schoolmate, but we were assigned to share the same school desk. I had learned by then from Praskovia Ivanovna that she was of Jewish descent, that her sickly mother was divorced from Maya's commissar father, who had remarried and lived in neighboring Caucasus, visiting his daughter often, and that the old lady was her maternal grandmother.

Slava, Maya, and I were all "Pioneers" by then. Previously we were called *Oktiabronok* (October child) in honor of the October revolution of 1917. As *Oktiabronok* we wore a five-pointed red star on the left side of our chest, a star replaced by a red cotton neckerchief when we graduated to Pioneers, and this often limp and wrinkled strip of cloth marked us as youthful scouts and explorers of the future.

After we became Pioneers, which was a mandatory duty, we spent hours after school in politically oriented meetings, where we were trained to become more involved, more alert to our surroundings, to people. Individuality was strongly frowned on, and the party call of "Out with individuality! Long live collectivism!" was on every Pioneer's lips.

In school, one very conscientious Pioneer was put before us as the ultimate example to follow. His name was Pavlik Morozov, a hero to all Soviet children. The life story of this boy was told even in the kindergartens, taking the place of outmoded fairy tales which were discouraged, even as dolls were, because they cluttered up the highly impressionable heads of the young. Slava and I were in our late teens when we first heard the tale of "Little Red Riding Hood," but the tale of Pavlik Morozov we knew by heart while still not able to write the alphabet.

The story was repeated several times a year in school, perhaps differing a bit in the telling as to exactly what it was—bread or potatoes—that Pavlik lost his life over. The point in the whole tale was not to be afraid to denounce one's parent, if that parent—in the child's opinion—was a "parasite." And Pavlik's father was definitely a parasite.

The events leading to Pavlik's heroism took place in the village of Gerasimovka during the devastating famine that followed upon the agrarian collectivization. Many highly motivated, successful farmers, derogatorily called *kulaks,* refused to part with their possessions, with their strips of earth, and join *kolkhozes.* Pavlik's father was one of the *kulaks.* Instead of turning over to the government all, in the form of food stuffs, he possessed, he began to hide potatoes (in some schools it was grain) so he could, on the sly, have enough to feed his pregnant wife and an eleven-year-old son, Pavlik. The *kulak* put those two ahead of all else; ahead of the welfare of the nation; ahead of the welfare of the

Party. Crime! Pavlik knew it instinctively. He was fed better than the rest of his neighbors because his selfish father, in the deep darkness of night, tip-toed to the secret place where the potatoes were hidden, and the next day Pavlik and his mother had a filling meal, while others, due to his father's tricks, were left to die of starvation. This could not be tolerated. And so, Pavlik, the good Pioneer, went to the Party representatives and courageously denounced his parasite father, pointing out to the officials the spot where the potatoes were hidden. (When done as a play in school, at the moment of denunciation we, the audience, were encouraged to utter a deafening "Hurrah!" and applaud.)

So the elder Morozov was shot as an enemy of the Soviet people. Pavlik, while a genuine hero to the Party officials, became, a traitor in the eyes of the villagers. One dark evening Pavlik was walking home from a Pioneer meeting, joyously singing a Soviet hymn:

> "Wide is my beloved country
> With its many forests, meadows, and seas . . .
> I know of no other single land
> Where one breathes with such ease . . ."

The boy was given no chance to start the next couplet, as revengeful peasants attacked poor Pavlik, clubbing him to death. Fists, axes, shovels—all fell upon the model Pioneer. A terrible death. . . . But! Not unlike religious martyrs of earlier times, Pavlik became a martyr too—a martyr of the Soviet Union. Schools, streets, *kolkhozes,* Pioneer clubs, libraries, theaters, whole villages were renamed in honor of Pavlik Morozov. And in Moscow a statue was erected in front of the Pavlik Morozov Pioneer Palace to the boy who had the courage to betray his own father.

As hard as I tried, I could not understand how Pavlik Morozov could denounce his father who, when all is said and done, only tried to save his pregnant wife and his young son from starvation. I visualized my own father, if he were ordered to hand over all that was growing in our Dulovo garden—to the last potato—to some faceless, nameless official, how he, too, would probably bury those life-saving foods and feed Mother, Slava, and me, so that we could live a bit longer and, perhaps, survive.

And yet, still an *Oktiabronok,* I almost emulated Pavlik's example, betraying my Mother to the authorities, unaware of my deed. It was during the winter of 1936–37, when our rulers professed to be vehemently anti-Hitler. My Russian language teacher, Sara Mikhailovna was instructing us—her forty young charges—on how beastly the German Führer was.

"Children!" she said. "The German people are suffering great deprivations under the rule of this mad dog, Hitler. They are literally starving, not even remembering the taste of sugar!" How terrible, I thought, not to know how sugar tasted. "Nazi Germany is as bad as old Czarist Russia was under the yoke of the bloodthirsty Czars, when only the Czars and their parasitic nobles could have sugar!" Sara Mikhailovna persisted.

I was strongly affected by this lecture from a teacher whom I trusted. She often smiled, helped me with my lessons, praised my efforts, and spent as much, if not more time with me than my mother did.

That evening, home at the samovar table, while sucking gently on a piece of sugar, I suddenly remembered the school lesson and blurted out, "Mamochka! I'll give you part of my sugar portion from now on."

Mother was touched. Sugar was not easy to come by, and it was expensive—five rubles per kilo. And that brownish-gray lump of sweet magic was awfully dear to a Russian.

"Why would you do such a thing, Ninochka?" Mother wanted to know. I faithfully repeated all that Sara Mikhailovna had said to the class, not omitting one word of the standard textbook jargon of accusing epithets, such as bloodsuckers, fascist mad dogs, parasitical pigs—words describing former Czars, American presidents, British prime ministers and kings, Spanish Generalissimo Franco, and of late, Adolf Hitler.

Mother heard me out, and then, with a slightly ironic smile, she shook her head and sort of absent-mindedly murmured while clearing the table, "Sugar? What nonsense! There was so much sugar I tried to limit myself, so I wouldn't lose my figure. Only a few kopeks a kilo it cost in the old days. Ah, those teachers."

It was a dilemma for me because until then I trusted both my parents and my teachers. I turned and twisted restlessly throughout the night, and by morning I reached the decision to confront Sara Mikhailovna with my newly obtained facts about sugar, and the obvious misunderstanding would be cleared up.

When the time came in the class for "questions and answers," I raised my hand and, being allowed to speak, I said bravely, "Sara Mikhailovna, last night I told my mother about the sugar."

"Sugar?" the teacher repeated uninterestedly, fussing with the stack of pupil's papers she was ready to inspect.

"Yes. Yesterday you told us about sugar in old Russia. Remember? My mother laughed."

"Why?" the teacher asked.

Recalling Mother's chuckle when she spoke of how she feared losing her figure, I, too, chuckled and continued confidently, "Mother said there was so much sugar she was afraid to eat it and get fat." The teacher was not laughing with me. Her face was quite grave. She gave the class reading to do, and left for a few minutes, instructing us to be absolutely silent while she was gone.

In those few minutes, my mother's fate was sealed. Just about the time Sara Mikhailovna returned to the class, an NKVDist assigned to the supervision of Dulovo's factory appeared at Mother's desk and quietly ordered, "*Na dopros*" (to questioning), two words that threw a Soviet citizen into a cold sweat of fear, because "*na dopros*" could easily be the first step on the death march to the labor camps. It also came as a total shock for, as a rule, the citizen felt no guilt of any wrongdoing, no reason to be dragged to questioning.

Mother did not return from work at 5 p.m., but her co-worker in passing our house on the way home, stopped and informed Father about the NKVDist and Mother's disappearance.

Hours went by in a tense, paralyzing wait. How afraid we all were: Slava and I, afraid of becoming motherless; Father afraid of losing his wife, afraid of following her route, afraid of his children becoming *besprizhorniks*. Such a demoralizing fear, embracing all. Father knew nothing about the sugar episode. It did not occur to him to question me or Slava, and it did not enter my mind that I had betrayed Mother.

She returned very late that evening. Slava and I were already in bed, but Father remained at the kitchen table with paperwork. We two heard Mother whisper for several minutes, ending up with the words, "Innocent babes . . . so trusting." And then, as if to still Father's angry, rising voice, again Mother's whisper, "Poor teachers. So much is demanded of them. Sara Mikhailovna is not to blame."

With this, Mother hurried to my bed. She took my face between her palms and kissed me three times, very ceremoniously, solemnly. There was something peculiar, unfamiliar in her face—a face that was dimly illuminated by a small candle on the kitchen table. Her eyes? Her nose? Lips? Yes! Yes! Her mouth was swollen. And that smell, that heavy, sweetish smell . . . of blood. I pushed her face back from mine to see it better, trying to part her lips a bit. Where just the previous morning had been a solid row of healthy, bright teeth, now a dark space was gaping at me.

"Mama," I whispered, "where are your two teeth? Two teeth missing! And your mouth is bleeding!"

"It's nothing, it's nothing, Ninochka," she started to say, but then, not trying to be brave any longer, she blurted out, "*Dopros* . . . about sugar. Tell your teachers nothing, little one. Nothing!"

From that day on I did not trust Sara Mikhailovna any longer. And if she could do what she did, then every teacher could do it. So no teachers were trusted anymore, either by me or Slava. We both became quiet and obedient, never questioning or expressing doubt. Instinctively, out of a natural feeling of self-preservation, we became reserved, neutral. We were not angry with Sara Mikhailovna. After all, her duty was not only to teach us to read and write. Her uppermost duty was to try ceaselessly to mold us into images of Pavlik Morozov.

CHAPTER FOURTEEN

Maya and I spent much time in each other's company during school hours, then hours in our courtyard. Yet, our hearts were not opening to each other quickly. After years of friendship in Dulovo with Lida, sharing so many happenings with her, I felt as if no other girl could become my true friend. By the same token, Maya did not rush to befriend me; she even seemed to avoid me at times. There were occasions when she appeared to be very sad, especially when Father took Slava and me to some outings, spending his free time with us on the beach, or just sitting on the porch steps with us, doing nothing.

Maya's father had deserted her sickly mother and married a healthy young girl who started a new family for him. It must not have been much of a marriage, people reasoned, if a man walked out on his wife as soon as she became sickly.

"Female troubles," they whispered knowingly. "Can't be on her feet, starts bleeding." And clicking their tongues, they proclaimed instructively, "There is a lot of truth in our proverb that 'a man likes his sister wealthy and his wife healthy.'"

I had not met Maya's father in person, but I saw his picture in her diary. A man of medium height, very muscular in the upper torso, in his late thirties, large, brown eyes, Stalin-type moustache. The photo showed him in his commissar's uniform—a uniform dreaded by many. Yet, Maya seemed not to dread this uniform at all.

"Father is a good man," she said once, when I commented on the commissar's uniform.

"Maya, could you ever do what Pavlik Morozov did?" I asked one day, walking home, after again being instructed in school about Pavlik's heroism. "Could you ever betray your father?"

"Never!" Like a bullet the answer shot out of Maya's mouth.

Taken aback at first by the girl's fierce reply, I looked at her determined face and, not being able to restrain a smile, said, "Neither could I."

Nothing more was said, but our deep "until death do us part" friendship sprang up at that moment.

Maya and I were taking piano lessons from a neighboring Jewish woman—Antonina Alexeyevna, a widow who was a retired concert pianist, of late beset with failing health. Kind, patient, she was adored by her pupils. Maya was already in her third year of study with Antonina Alexeyevna, who was preparing the girl for the upcoming grueling exams at the Feodosia conservatory. Me, on the other hand, Antonina Alexeyevna tolerated good-naturedly, for a while, then one day saying point-blank to my mother that I would not make it into the conservatory, no matter how hard I tried.

"Why?" Mother was crushed.

"Natalia Alexandrovna, dear, not all of us were born to be musicians," the good teacher said.

"But if Nina applies herself diligently?"

"Ninochka is tone deaf." Antonina Alexeyevna spread her arms wide, as if apologizing for my shortcomings.

"How can my daughter be tone deaf, when she runs through those Czerny exercises like a professional?"

Mother was right. I took to the Czerny studies with enthusiasm, repeating and repeating them until I knew many by heart, banging out those repetitious notes with a gusto, to Mother's great satisfaction and obvious pride. Yet the moment Antonina Alexeyevna spoke the words "tone deaf," I knew it was so. But Mother had to be convinced by my teacher.

"Ninochka, dear," Antonina Alexeyevna said patiently, "play the scale—and after each note, sing the note for me." The teacher turned to Mother, "It's not enough to be able to strike the notes properly. One must reproduce them accurately with one's throat, tongue, voice, and with one's ears . . . with one's memory. Hear, Natalia Alexandrovna? Listen. Ninochka sings false notes. Now, once more, girlie! Do-o-o, re-e-e, mi-i-i. No, no! Mi! Not fa sharp. Continue. La! La! Not si. Poor child," Antonina Alexeyevna sighed. "Natalia Alexandrovna, dear, Nina can't reproduce the notes accurately, and a musician *must* be able to do that."

Mother still refused to accept the fact. "But Nina memorizes the written notes very well."

"Your girl might memorize the notes on paper and read them well, but she would always remain a stranger to the instrument itself. And the instrument would always remain a stranger to her, Natalia Alexandrovna. There never would be a happy union—that union so necessary to create music. Ninochka will never be able to improvise—never! She would be lost when asked to improvise during the exams in the conservatory. So just forget about the conservatory, Natalia Alexandrovna," the honest teacher persisted. "If you wish, I'll occupy the girl with some intermediate instruction and teach her light Chopin pieces. Mozart and Beethoven have some selections I can give her. But serious study?"

Seeing how very upset this airing of my deficiencies made me feel, the wise teacher hastened to comfort me. "Darling, darling girl," she patted my limply folded hands, "to be tone deaf is not such a disaster. Many famous people couldn't sing or reproduce an accurate do, re, mi."

"Really? Like who?" I persisted, convinced that Antonina Alexeyevna could not come up with the name of a single "famous" person.

"Well," she said after a brief hesitation, "take for instance the Czaritza Ekaterina the Great. She was so-o-o tone deaf! She loved to listen to other people sing, but like you, Ninochka, she just could not reproduce the notes. Every time the Czaritza tried to carry a tune, she noticed people were smiling. And you know what she did? She organized weekly talent evenings. Only people with talent were admitted. She was asked what talent she possessed to guarantee her admittance to this select club. The Czaritza said, 'Singing!' And sing she did, but so off key, so outrageously funny and purposely ridiculous that the guests shook with laughter. So you see, Ninochka, nature's shortcomings can be turned into an asset."

While not being able to enjoy and exploit my tone deafness as the Czaritza learned to do, I nevertheless utterly, genuinely enjoyed my ballet lessons. As soon as we arrived in Feodosia, Mother hurried to enroll me in the ballet school. Her ultimate reason was to straighten out my poor body posture—the rising left shoulder, the slightly thrown-out left hip, the habit of bending my knees in order to cut off an inch or two from my height. After all, as Mother reasoned, I was approaching puberty, and needed help to become proud of my body.

I took to ballet like a duck to a pond. There I forgot my height, forgot that my stomach was empty, growling. Actually, the hunger pangs disappeared, the sluggish mood of my body evaporated; my knees, my shoulders, my back—all became strong, energetic. Another world embraced me, swallowed me for hours at a time. Surprisingly, not performance of the dance itself, but the hours spent at the exercise bar were the most enjoyable. Even after arriving home I continued, using a high-backed chair, to bend and stretch and throw my legs forward, sideways, back. My arms were in constant motion, trying to imitate the "swan's movements." I must have spent much time perfecting those movements because our ballet mistress, Elena Vasilevna, noticing progress in the agility of my wrists, elbows, and fingers, put me at the head of the class during the bar exercises.

"Now, class!" she clapped her hands for attention. "Watch Ninochka! Watch her arms! Don't hurry your arms! Don't slacken, either! Notice! There is no abruptness. Like a swan in the water—that is how your body must appear. Your arms are an important part of creating this illusion of a swan. Keep your eyes on Nina!"

I was euphoric.

CHAPTER FIFTEEN

*O*ur *host,* Dmitry Antonovich, although very ill, was still quite energetic and involved. Maya and I loved to spend our free time with him, while he entertained us with tales of foreign travels in years long past. Slava, too, often joined our company. We climbed the stairs leading from the veranda to the flat top of the building's roof and there, facing the rich panorama of the sea, the surrounding mountains, and the open steppes, we lost ourselves in the history lesson that Dmitry Antonovich poured over us.

"See how calm, how lazy the sea is now." He directed our eyes toward the endless expanse of emerald-turquoise water.

"But, visualize thousands of ships nearing the shores of our Feodosia in about 1475. The Ottoman Turks! Sabers, daggers! Violent chilling cries of the approaching invaders! They leap from their boats! Feodosia is prostrate, defenseless. The Turks slaughter every child, every mother, all the old, defenseless ones. All slaughtered because they were Christian. People were running in that direction to the Bald Mountain, to the steppes behind the mountain. But just then, the Tatars—Moslems like the Turks—appeared with bows and arrows. Poisoned arrows. They killed all the old. Thousands of young girls and boys were dragged into slavery. What sorrow! It is hard to imagine. Yet our Feodosia saw it all and listened to the human cries. Her soil was soaked with human blood."

We sat spellbound, relieved that we did not live in those times past.

While he talked, Dmitry Antonovich sketched scenes of the approaching Turkish fleet, of violent, deadly saber clashes, and of the desperate faces of the captives.

"And you know what the year 1345 meant to Feodosia, don't you? Plague! The black death—that frightening, frightful *chuma*. Yes, indeed! Feodosia was the spot from where it spread."

One day Dmitry Antonovich flabbergasted us with the news that vodka was the invention of Genoese settlers, who used it more for medicinal purposes than for pleasure drinking. When the Genoese fled from the Islamic conquest of Crimea in the 15th century, they carried with them this "medicine" which was then known as "aqua vitae" (water of life). The fiery liquid eventually reached Muscovy via Poland, after the Poles renamed the "water of life" "vodka" (little water).

Dmitry Antonovich was also filling our heads with another wonder— the wonder of learning a foreign language. And not just any foreign language, but English! Maya and I had begun to take German in school, while Slava had started it the year previous. Maya's grandmother spoke good high German, passing on the knowledge to Maya. My mother learned the language in Riga, but had had no opportunity to practice it of late.

Dmitry Antonovich, for some reason, was convinced that it was English we should study. "Children," he would say, raising his hand with his index finger pointed, as in prophecy, "learn English! It'll be the universal language. It's bound to be! German, you say? No. If your school will give you a choice, take English. German is for today, but English will serve you into the next century. What? Won't live that long? Of course you will! You'll only be as old as I am now." And patiently, yet with childlike enthusiasm, Dmitry Antonovich tried to draw us into the same enthusiasm of discovering the wonders of English.

"You won't believe how many similar words there are, in German and English," he insisted. "Now, take the German word 'haus.' In English? 'House!' German 'wetter' in English is 'weather.' 'Brot' is 'bread,' 'gut' is 'good.' 'Mann' is 'man.'"

Lines upon lines of words, similar in both languages appeared on our note paper. Maya and I marveled at the lucky circumstance that allowed us to acquire knowledge of two languages simultaneously. But then our enthusiasm for English suddenly and quite permanently evaporated. One day, Dmitry Antonovich started to instruct us about the specific form for addressing a person in English. And we exploded!

What? Everyone is addressed in English only as "you"? Where is "thou"? We demanded to know about that indispensable, warm, intimate form of address that a Russian could not get along without. Anglo-Saxons don't use it any longer? Out of fashion? Does Dmitry Antonovich mean that an infant is addressed in this . . . this "YOU"? And the President and kings are all addressed equally? And if we call a dog, don't we address an animal "thou"? Surely, an animal could be addressed more familiarly? No?

It was disturbing to learn that some people on this earth never used that wonderfully intimate "thou"—"Ti" in Russian. There was a profound difference for us in meaning between "thou" and "you." Relatives and members of one's family used the intimate "thou." Children were addressed by adults as "thou." Lovers, husbands, and wives used this form of address for each other. But then, a strict etiquette was observed, not allowing this familiar form to apply to anyone else, unless both parties agreed to such intimacy. Adults, after a long period of acquaintanceship, wishing to adopt the "thou" address, often drank a *bruderschaft* toast, a custom borrowed from Germany long ago, with arms entwined, holding a glass with some spirits, or even plain tea, and, with a kiss, sealed their "thou."

When we visited Feodosia five years earlier, I was allowed to address Dmitry Antonovich and Praskovia Ivanovna with "thou," not using their full names, but simply as Uncle and Aunt—regular forms of address permitted young children when speaking with non-relatives. Yet, five years later, it was out of the question for me to be so familiar with people outside my family. Unless they requested such intimacy, I would be considered a *nyekulturnaya*—uncultured, ill-mannered—to "thou" someone 60 years older than I was.

Not only was I expected to address them as "you," but I also had to call them by their full names—that is, by their personal first names given them at birth, and by a patronymic that every Russian inherits automatically from his father's first name. Since my father was Mark, I was Nina Markovna, while my brother Slava became Markovich— "-ich" being the proper ending for the male patronymic, "-na" for female. Family names also follow the male and female endings. Foreigners almost always address Russian wives by their husbands' names, turning the poor women into men—terribly annoying to a Russian.

Once two Russians had become friendly, using the intimate "thou," they expressed this friendliness by changing each other's first name into seemingly unending variations. My own name for instance, could be transformed almost endlessly: Ninochka, Ninushka, Ninok, Ninonka, Ninusia, Ninushok, Ninusenka, Ninchik, Ninunchik, and the angry Ninka, or the short, no-nonsense Nin.

When not sketching or filling us in with historical events, or instructing us in English, Dmitry Antonovich still succeeded in making us enjoy his company. We listened not only to what he said, but how he said it. The word "Russia" often slipped past his lips—a strictly forbidden utterance when applied to the present. This word, it was decreed at the time of the October revolution, could only be used when speaking in connection with pre-revolutionary times as, for instance, in Old Russia, Czarist Russia, Bourgeois Russia, and Imperial Russia, but not when describing the present. While to people outside Soviet borders— and particularly Russian émigrés—Russia still existed, being remembered and revered in teary nostalgia, for us—her citizens—there was only the Communist Party view that she died a shameful, disgraceful death. We were told that we needed not her storied past; nor her 1,000-year-old Christianity; neither did we need her ancient costumes, folksongs, and fairytales. Above all, we needed not her true and rightful name—Russia, that blood-stained name of a land that had been reborn as the Soviet Union. "Soviet" means "council," or even more precisely—"advice." I was born in the "Union of Advisers," not in Russia.

There were other outlawed words. "Soldier" was replaced with "Red Army man," "officer" with "commander," "police" became "militia," and Mr. or Mrs. changed into Citizen or Comrade. In school, it was extremely important for us children to realize the deep ideological differences that separated the beastly Czarist "soldier" of old from the new, benevolent "Red Army man," between the old bourgeois Mr. and Mrs. and the new, courageous Citizen or Comrade, between bloody Czarist "police" and the new, compassionate "militia man."

To speak the word *Woskresenie* (Sunday) brought severe punishment. *Woskresenie* means "Day of Resurrection," in dedication to Christ. While the Anglo-Saxons constructed their week by assigning every day to an ancient god or goddess, Russians did not do so. They avoided mythology and with clear-eyed realism identified the days thus:

English	*Russian*	*Meaning:*
Monday	Ponedelnik	—the beginning of the week
Tuesday	Vtornik	—second day
Wednesday	Sreda	—middle of the week
Thursday	Chetwerg	—fourth day
Friday	Piatnitza	—fifth day
Saturday	Subbotha	—from Hebrew "Sabbath"

All those names retained their place in the Soviet week. Then came the seventh day, the Anglo-Saxons naming it for the Sun and the Russians dedicating it to Christ's resurrection. Being anti-religious, the Soviet rulers outlawed this 1,000-year-old Russian word, replacing it with *wihodnoy,* meaning "day off" or, more exactly, "day of outing."

Neither my parents, nor Slava, nor I ever spoke those proscribed words, words that were nevertheless treasured, revered, and preserved, while wrapped in a cloak of silence.

CHAPTER SIXTEEN

*W*eeks *were* slipping by, turning into months. We felt quite crowded in our friends' apartment, aware that Dmitry Antonovich needed more rest and privacy than were possible while surrounded by us four. At night we heard his moans, stifled in the pillow so as not to disturb us. Dmitry Antonovich was definitely not getting better despite the powdered almonds and peach honey. Although quite often he still climbed with us on top of the roof, sketching and entertaining us with tales of the past, even more often he remained in his bed, tired and listless.

As if to be punished for my arrogance on the train to Feodosia, when I had so imperiously turned my nose away from the girl with the ugly *moskitka* sores, I developed *moskitka* in turn. Slava too, was bitten by that nasty insect, but recuperated in a few weeks with the help of quinine. So did I, it seemed. But then sores began to cover my legs, arms, and face, growing in size and exuding pus. One sore on the lower left leg grew to a wound one inch in diameter, reaching almost to the bone, refusing to heal. The *moskitka* cream was simply not available in Feodosia's pharmacies on a steady basis, and when we managed to acquire a small portion, it was applied to the most severe sores, but sparingly. My parents wrote to Dulovo, imploring Aunt Liza to try to find and send us a large jar of the cream, but received a reply that appeared uninterested in our pleas, and much preoccupied with her own problems. Aunt Liza was not able to make the trip to Moscow, she wrote, to hunt for cream, being very limited in her leisure time. She hoped we would understand. Uncle Shura, too, was very restricted, she informed us. He had been transferred from his old job—that of department supervisor in the Dulovo porcelain factory—and his new one severely reduced his free time.

I, meantime, received a short letter from my friend Lida. It arrived in a home-made envelope, as real envelopes were very seldom available. The home-made envelopes that cluttered the entire Soviet postal system were called *samocleika* (self-glued). The handwriting was obviously that of a young school child, yet—as with every letter we ever received—Lida's envelope was duly and neatly cut open, censored, and its contents approved, reglued, and sent on to us. The letter was short, pathetic:

> Dearest Ninochka!
>
> I send you my Pioneer greetings! Can't write as much. Don't go to school this year. Weak. Father is very good to me, saying I will see Mama soon. So, don't worry about me.
> With my Pioneer greetings,
>
> > Your loving friend,
> > Lida

And then, no more letters.

Because my parents were fully occupied with their work six days a week, Praskovia Ivanovna was the only person who had time available to hunt for lodging for us. Feodosia was not generous to us with offers of places to live. Many, who came to serve the assigned vacationers, decided to remain in Feodosia, even though they did not have the all-important certificate granting them official permission to do so. Still, a sizable number dared to take the chance and remain in this sunny, fertile corner of the Soviet Union. They often clandestinely acquired the needed lodgings by paying exorbitant sums to the greedy ones, or needy ones, who condescended to share their living space with the northerners. Some were on the move constantly, like vagrants or nomads, avoiding the militia by day and at night retreating into the mountains, seeking any cave-like opening in the privacy of the hills to give them at least a temporary shelter no matter how primitive. Eventually many succeeded in obtaining a permanent residence certificate from the officials through a *blat* (a payoff).

One Sunday morning, long before any of us stirred, Praskovia Ivanovna left home with a milk container, hoping to catch a Greek *sovkhoznik* who came only on this day. He brought milk to the market that was better than anybody else's, for he did not dilute it with water.

An hour later Praskovia Ivanovna burst into the main room where we had gathered for a morning glass of tea with Dmitry Antonovich, and waving the empty container like a flag of some sort shouted, "He is dead! Dead! Such luck! At the bazaar today!"

Dmitry Antonovich asked, concerned, "Who is dead, dear wife?"

"Yes, who?" we all wanted to know, taken aback by Praskovia Ivanovna's obvious exuberance.

"The old Tatar on the hill!" she replied, stretching out her arm toward one of the many hills surrounding Feodosia. "Oh, well, you wouldn't know him, I suppose. He used to sit in the bazaar, just to the right of the young Tatar boy with the smallest, sweetest watermelons."

"Yes! Yes!" Slava shouted. "We know the boy. Nina and I always buy his watermelons, on the way to the beach."

"And next to the boy sat an old Tatar selling sunflower seeds," I was happy to chime in.

Praskovia Ivanovna, glad that some of us knew of the person she was talking about, became even more animated. "Well, the old Tatar gave up his soul last week. Died! His widow is sitting in his place this morning. She needs money badly. She's willing to rent her cottage to you and move in with her son."

I froze. To think that I would be moving away from those two beings who had become like grandparents to me. How good it was to have an older person to turn to from time to time, who would not constantly correct, instruct, and criticize, as a parent was certain to do, but be patient, lenient, even doting. And to leave behind Maya, my new friend!

Praskovia Ivanovna, noticing my long face, began to braid my hair, comforting me. "Now, now, *ptenchik* [birdie]," she cooed, "we aren't being separated by the sea or by 1,500 kilometers. It's only 20 minutes walk."

She poured freshly brewed tea in our glasses, accompanying it with thinly, economically sliced lemon, and while we all sipped the aromatic beverage, our hostess began to discuss the pluses and minuses of the offered cottage. She spread open one hand, palm up, and listing minuses, began to bend one finger after another.

"Now, Mark, Natasha, listen. There is no stove, no *burshuyka*. That's a minus, definitely. But, see here," and she gestured vigorously toward a primus stove that had stood unobtrusively by the *burshuyka* ever since we arrived. Take it. It only needs benzene."

Praskovia Ivanovna bent another finger.

"No electricity. We are fortunate here. But on the hills a kerosene lamp will have to do, and we happen to have a couple in the storage shed."

Back to Dulovo, I thought, holding my breath for more negatives to come.

"No well nearby. Now, now, Ninochka, hold your horses! The well is at the bottom of the hill, twice as far as from us here. But," and Praskovia Ivanovna halted, smiling at me broadly, "it has a PUMP! Aren't you glad, *ptenchik?*"

I was.

Praskovia Ivanovna began to bend another finger, but straightened it out again, quickly. "No, no, my mistake. They *do* have an outhouse—in the yard. Some don't, you know. They just dig a hole in the ground. When it overflows they cover it with earth and dig another hole."

A couple more drawbacks were registered. The most important was that a bus stop was far from the hill, and Slava and I would have to change schools, or else add a half hour to our travel time. Praskovia Ivanovna stopped bending fingers.

"And what are the pluses?" Father asked, smiling, not expecting to hear any.

"Security, Mark. The woods are just behind. And caves. God forbid a new wave of arrests. You can hide in the caves, Mark! Natasha and the children could sneak you food and clothing. One could survive in those mountains until the wave subsides."

We needed no more persuasion.

Late that afternoon, with Praskovia Ivanovna in the lead, we marched toward the hill. As soon as I saw a wooden booth with a moon-faced woman sitting behind the glass window, collecting a kopek for each pail of pumped water, I knew we had reached our destination.

"There it is—the last roof on the right. See?" Praskovia Ivanovna pointed to the flat roof of a small building, its walls completely hidden by a row of overgrown lilac bushes.

"Come!" she urged, and lifting her long skirt, bending her knees slightly, but not her back, she propelled herself forward. We passed a dozen tiny, hut-like cottages with Tatar and Russian children scurrying around. When we reached the lilac hedgerow, a heavy wooden gate was flung open and an old, toothless Tatar woman greeted us with a respectful bow, inviting us with a gesture of her arm to enter the courtyard. The unpaved, neatly kept enclosure immediately disarmed me, mainly due to a big, vigorous apple tree spreading its branches and shading the entire courtyard with its lush foliage. Slava and I were reconciled on the spot. But our joy had no end when we spotted in the shade, under the apple tree, a huge, tail-wagging German shepherd.

"Name: Venerka," the Tatar woman announced, sending Slava and me into giggles, since Venerka meant Venus. We had expected some strange, hard to pronounce exotic name for a dog with Tatar masters.

When we saw the inside of the cottage, no cries of delight arose from any of us. Even Praskovia Ivanovna looked a bit crushed. The tiny lodging, although very clean, was dark, peeling, with very low ceilings and only one small, square window stuffed with rags where some glass was missing. The main room measured no more than 12 feet by 12 feet. A small area just big enough to accommodate a primus stove, a few shelves for pots and pans, some boxes on the floor, covered with tapestry and serving as a table, was called a kitchen. On the clay floor in the main room were two thin, old mattresses, covered with Tatar rugs and a mass of pillows, serving as beds at night and as low divans in the daytime. There was no other furniture in the room. Praskovia Ivanovna stood silently, as if not wishing to influence us in any decision making. Finally she said softly, "I'll continue to look if you can tolerate the veranda arrangement."

But Father knew that the temporary accommodations our friends were providing had to be replaced with more permanent quarters.

"Natasha, dear," he said, "let's not be discouraged. We'll whitewash the walls and clean the floors. Immediately the room will open up! And the window will be repaired. Then," he had to pause to think about what else could be done to make the cottage more acceptable before he shouted, "I'll make bunk beds for the children! Much space could be saved that way!"

"Yes! Yes!" Slava and I came alive. "And in warm weather we could sleep in hammocks, under the apple tree." Things began to look downright enticing.

Praskovia Ivanovna turned to Father. "Mark, that table on the veranda. Small, you say? It's not as small as you think. It opens up to seat twelve! Yes, a folding table! They don't build tables like that nowadays. When you're not using it, put it here by the window. It needs so little space. For meals, or children doing homework, or company coming— one! two! three! Unfold it! Afterward, again fold it, and dance in this cottage! So much space!"

Things were looking better and better. Mother finally was forced to admit that the cottage was acceptable. She said to no one in particular, "Well, one can't look a gift horse in the mouth."

The old Tatar who, until then appeared to understand no Russian, came suddenly alive, and with a heavy accent but in surprisingly good Russian began to sputter hurriedly, "No gift horse, madam. No gift horse, this house. Widow! Widow!" She banged her flat chest with her palm. "Need rubles. Need 100 rubles. Rent is 100 rubles a month."

Then the crafty old woman looked at Slava and me sprawled comfortably under the apple tree with Venerka's head on Slava's lap, while her hind legs and tail were in mine.

"Take dog!" she half-asked, half-ordered.

Not many people kept dogs, for one and only one reason—there was nothing to feed them. One had to sacrifice one's own portion to feed a household pet. The Tatar woman, sensing Father's concern, quickly said, "Tatars on this hill give little bit food here . . . little bit food there. Dog no hungry. Dog good guard." Then, more brazen, more bold, she declared, "No take dog, no take house."

We took both.

CHAPTER SEVENTEEN

*F*eodosia, *compared* to Dulovo, was a paradise in its abundance of vegetables and fruit. The bazaars were filled with high mounds of juicy, round, saffron-striped watermelons, golden honeydews. Peppers, eggplant, tomatoes, and cucumbers were available in bountiful supply, offered by the surrounding *sovkhozes*. As plentiful as the fruit and vegetables were, they nevertheless were very expensive, and appeared only rarely at our dinner table, and then as a treat and not as a main course in our diet. Only watermelons, through the whole season, were cheap enough to be enjoyed by us on a regular basis. Crimean apples, pears, cherries—these were easily obtainable. Grapes, on the other hand, although grown in profusion, were extremely expensive— up to four rubles a kilo—and were considered to be truly a treat. Delicious cheese, never tasted by us in Dulovo, but produced locally by those of Greek descent, entered our diet. We knew it as *brynza*, or feta cheese. Also we savored a dish the natives called vegetable caviar—this being the fabled *ratatouille*.

Feodosia had a mild climate, so we did not have to spend a major part of our budget on extra warm quilted coats and pants and felt snow boots. Clothing was a chronic worry, especially to the parents of growing children. While our parents could wear a coat for many years, Slava and I demanded a constant supply of ever larger shoes and clothes. I, especially, was a problem. A new dress bought only a few months earlier, would suddenly burst at the shoulder seams or under the arms or at the waist, because my body was growing relentlessly. Mother, out of sheer necessity, became a miracle worker in creating not only acceptable, but very attractive articles of clothing for me out of worn-out rags. She also excelled in fashioning skirts, vests, light-weight jackets—all out of sturdy burlap from discarded potato or flour sacks which she dyed brown, navy, or red. Mother's friends, seeing me in a new outfit, were highly complimentary.

"Natasha, dear," they quipped, paraphrasing an earthy old Russian saying, "you can truly turn manure into candy!"

But my schoolmates had no such reaction. Instead, they shouted on seeing me approach the school entrance in a new potato sack creation, with a matching beret—"Bourgeois offspring! Rotten capitalist!"

Not all my clothes were made of discarded old materials or burlap. A few years earlier, when we still lived in Dulovo, I received on my birthday, a dress made of adorable pink satin, strewn with forget-me-nots. My birthday came only a couple of days before the entire nation observed the celebration of May Day. On that day, a parade was obligatory and attendance was mandatory. Militiamen were out early and in force, banging on doors to make certain that all able-bodied adults and children were out on the streets carrying their assigned flags, placards, and pictures of our leaders. Schools organized their students, factories their workers, offices their employees, and *kolkhozes* and *sovkhozes* their peasants. Only a fever of 38 degrees Celsius could excuse one from parading.

One did not have to spend the whole day marching, unless one chose to do so. The most important thing was to appear by the tribune—the center of events—where living Party representatives stood under the huge images of dead idols. We cheered the announcement that "KARL MARX AND FRIEDRICH ENGELS ARE THE LIVING TEACHERS OF COMMUNISM!" and "OUR DEAREST COMRADE LENIN IS NOT DEAD, HE LIVES FOREVER IN OUR HEARTS!"

When one gave his due to shouting, waving, and singing, one could discreetly disappear. And as soon as they were out of sight of the tribune, people did disperse. After all, they could spend the rest of the day catching up on laundry, do some spring cleaning, or begin work on kitchen gardens.

Only we children liked to continue marching, running, and playing outdoors. To us, it was a festive, once-a-year occurrence marking the beginning of warm weather—the end of a long winter. By contrast, the October revolution parade that took place on November 7th was not an enjoyable affair. Cold, gray skies blanketed the spectacle with gloomy light, winds beginning to pierce through one's clothing, reaching to the very bone marrow, it seemed. One was not disposed to play or hop on one leg during the October revolution parade.

Before this particular May Day, preceding my ninth birthday, the Dulovo pavilion received a large supply of fabrics but still not enough to satisfy the needs of all Dulovans. It was decided, therefore, that Father and I would travel to Moscow and try to acquire some dress material. Our parents took turns once a month to go to Moscow for shopping, taking advantage of the law that allowed people living within a 90 kilometer radius of the capital to enter the city freely—that is, with only an internal passport and not the special certificate needed by anyone who lived outside the 90 kilometer radius. Fats, sugar, cereal, and tea were obtained in Moscow with comparative ease. The capital was supplied better than any other city in the country. It was called the "cradle" of the Communist world, and had to appear as a full cradle. The whole country was aware of this fact and people came to Moscow from as far away as the Ukraine, Crimea, and Caucasus. They came from the steppes of Asia and from distant Siberia—all hoping to replenish their supplies of food and clothing.

Before leaving home to hunt for dress material in Moscow, Mother presented us with a list, emphasizing the priority of the articles she needed most urgently. At the very top of the list were sewing needles, which were such a rarity that they were treated with the respect one would give to a precious jewel. My stoic Mother, withstanding life's many trials and tribulations without a whimper, broke out in tears when a sewing needle snapped in two in her hands, not being able to serve any longer, utterly exhausted from years of over use. Where to get another needle? Not in Dulovo's stores, for none carried them. Even Moscow stores seldom received supplies of sewing needles. Apparently the very top brains of the planning bureaucracy, while laying out the supply norms for the next five years, omitted sewing needles. The planners must have been all men, and they refused to correct the oversight. One five year plan succeeded another, but sewing needles remained chronically in short supply. Thimbles also, were not of top priority and became, more or less, collector's items.

Together with needles and material for my birthday dress, Mother, on the food list, requested eggs. Eggs, sold in fives and tens, were a great delicacy, used mostly to enrich our basic baking or cooking, and only in very good periods eaten by themselves.

Mother gave me a huge, sparkling clean linen kerchief, instructing me in a patient voice, "Ninochka, use this kerchief like a bundle. Carry the eggs with great care—like this." She stretched out her arm a bit away from her body. "Don't let anyone brush against the eggs. Even if some crack, don't throw them out. Just leave them in the bundle. But try, little one, try not to break any!"

I promised.

"No feathers nor down!" Mother shouted to us from the threshold, as a farewell. Following the custom, we ignored her last words, which were supposed to bring good luck. In the past, these words were used to wish hunters success so that they would return with birds of feather and down. The Moscow excursions for food and clothing were considered to be in the category of hunting, and Mother's words were quite appropriate.

While in Moscow, we did not seek out any special stores. Instead, our procedure resembled that of the scavenger fish on the bottom of an aquarium—we scooped up anything that came our way, since the purchase could later be exchanged with neighbors and friends for items we needed more than they did, and vice versa.

After filling our shopping bags with sugar, smoked herring, cooking oil, some hard candy, we finally happened upon a store where after a couple of hours waiting in line, Father and I each received 10 eggs. Twenty eggs! A fortune! While Father carried full shopping bags in both hands, I attended only to the safety of the 20 eggs, following Mother's instructions to the letter. But the dress material was still eluding us. We were getting in and out of trams, racing to lines of people wherever we spotted them, to find out if dress material was being distributed. Only three hours were left before we had to take the train back to Dulovo, for to be caught in Moscow overnight was inadvisable. No hotels existed to offer us accommodation—no inns, no guest houses. The railroad station waiting rooms allowed only long distance travelers to remain—that is, people whose destination was outside a 90 kilometer radius of the capital. We could be arrested and fined if we missed that last train. We hurried even more. Our tram brought us finally to a Moscow district called *Zatzep*, where Mother quite often came upon textile merchandise on her hunting trips. And sure enough, we immediately spotted a line of people, mostly women, standing, squatting, half-reclining on their small and large bundles, chatting in many dialects.

"What's being sold here, comrade woman?" Father asked the last person in line. A heavy-chested female, with a dark scarf covering her forehead to the eyebrows, said grimly, "Cloth. But don't waste your time. See?" She exhibited her left palm to us, marked with a number in red ink. "I am 540. There is no way the merchandise will last, unless new supplies arrive."

Father gave me a questioning look. "How about it, Ninochka? Are we to stand here or keep hunting?" Tired, hungry, I wanted to rest a bit. We both had our palms marked, settling down on the newspaper-covered sidewalk. We began the dreary wait.

An hour passed. Our plump neighbor with the 540 mark asked us to keep her place in line for a bit, while she ran to the nearby public toilet building. The comfort station was wide open inside, without any walls separating it into individual cubicles. One saw on entering, several dozen openings in a row, so close together that an exceptionally plump person could not avoid touching a neighbor's thigh with her own. One climbed on the wooden bench, for to sit on it was extremely unsanitary. A supervisor—an old retiree trying to supplement her meager pension—oversaw it all, orchestrating the progress of her many wards. Covered with a long oil-cloth apron, she marched from one hole to the next, observing diligently if all was in order. Was a woman too long on the hole? Why? If two neighbors, dawdled longer than necessary, the supervisor gave a strict command:

"Hurry! No idle chatter! Others are waiting!"

She also came as a saving angel when—already in position—the occupant discovered she had no paper tucked away in her pockets for this purpose. Because toilet paper, as such, was not available, the supervisor obligingly provided her ward with purposely wrinkled pieces of Izvestia or Pravda, from which images of Party members had been removed. In those communal super outhouses, the walls from top to bottom, were covered with vile graffiti. Although periodically scrubbed, painted, and repainted, graffiti—as if it were a living organism—sprang out of the walls, again and again. They were taken by all as a protest against authority. "Try to catch us doing it!" they seemed to be shouting.

After our neighbor in line returned, Father and I decided to visit the facilities. Later, while walking back to the queue, I spotted an ice cream vendor, and Father treated me to an "eskimo," a delicious ice cream on a stick, and always available in vanilla flavor only. Father, on the other hand, decided to treat himself to a couple shots of warming, soothing, *vodochka*. He ended up finishing a small bottle that he split with another fellow—a complete stranger—who consented to go *napopolam*—that is, half and half on the cost of the vodka.

So there, on a bench in a small park, opposite our store, we three sat—I, licking the eskimo, followed by another eskimo, and the two men toasting each other's health, then toasting the health of their spouses, then the health of their "birdies"—naming each child in the process.

When the bottle was emptied, Father suddenly slapped himself on the knee, jumped up from the bench, and said to me in a somewhat mysterious tone, "Ninochka! What an idea! I can't disclose it to you. You'll give it away. Now, don't ask any questions. Just stick close to me, all right? Yes, yes, of course, protect the eggs! And, whatever I do or say—agree with me! Don't start blurting out 'But, papa, it's not so!' Just remain mum. Promise?"

Grudgingly, I nodded, not at all amused. We headed back to the store, but instead of returning to our place at the end of the line, Father aimed straight for the store entrance. Reaching a group of tightly clinging women near the door, he assumed a happy, slightly daft expression and exclaimed, as if talking to himself, "Triplets! Triplets! My little darlings!"

One, then another female voice shouted harshly, "Hey, you, skeleton! You there, bag of bones! Where are you going? Might a three-wheeled cart run over you!"

Father stopped, as if in a daze, facing the angry women with a naive, absent-minded grin. Then, as though coming to his senses, he bowed to the group respectfully, and said, "I beg your pardon, comrade women. I am a bit under the influence. No, no! Not filthy drunk, just celebrating. My wife, the dove, presented me . . . with triplets!"

Father grinned from ear to ear, after thundering out the word triplets, then hiccuped. While the word triplets began to spread from mouth to mouth, Father began to apologize profusely. "I don't even know how I got in this line. What's being sold here? Women's attire, you say? Textiles? Oh, please forgive me. I am not interested in textiles. I must hurry to my darlings."

He made a move as if to go away, but the women, softened by the idea of triplets, surrounded him on all sides, hanging on to his jacket sleeves, questioning him about the babies.

"Now wait, wait, you old goat! Don't be in such a hurry! Tell us more, old horseradish." Smiling, friendly faces looked up at Father, showering him with affectionate epithets. "Tell us, what names did you give the new babies? Boys or girls? Or both? Tell us."

Father was warming up to his role. "All girls," he said, proudly. "All pink, fair, taking after my much-suffering wifie. I must hurry to her."

The women refused to let Father go. "Tell us, pickled cucumber, what names you gave to the little ones?"

It was fashionable to name girls after Stalin's daughter Svetlana, or after the Worker's Day in May, as my friend Maya was named, or after the October revolution, Octyabrina.

Father, no longer hiccupping, but solemn, with an almost stern expression, in a quiet, attention-demanding tone, uttered words that sealed our fate with those women.

"We named our little girls in the old tradition—Vera, Nadezhda, Lubov."

A hush fell. The women stood as though thunder-struck, mouths open in awe, some eyes moist. To Russians, those three names in old times were the most cherished, and lucky were the families where three sisters bore those names. Vera means "faith," Nadezhda means "hope," and Lubov means "love." Faith, Hope, and Love! In one family! At one stroke! The women started to moan, some reaching for handkerchiefs.

"Now, now, little pickle." They grabbed Father's arms and began to shove him inside the store. "Go in! Go in! Buy your little dove something pretty. You know . . . something lacy." They put their palms on their coat-flattened chests, showing Father what he should buy.

"But, comrade women," Father protested, "my wife needs nothing. Not yet."

"Dry up, you old turnip!" the women continued to grin and laugh. We know better if she needs it or not! Fine provider you are! Refuses to buy his wife a present!" And with new vigor, the women pushed Father inside the store, with me clinging tightly to his back. The sales girl, aware by then of the triplets' father, showed him lacy nighties and articles of underwear. Father expressed a desire for some dress material instead, selecting a rosy cloth printed with a mass of forget-me-nots, while I silently approved his choice.

"Needles. My wife needs needles badly," Father implored softly.

"Sure thing! For Vera, Nadezhda, Lubov, nothing is too much. Here . . . two needles per person—six for the little ones, two for you, and two for your tapeworm, here." The salesgirl pointed at me, loading us with 10 precious sewing needles. A find! She then very sternly gave Father a set of black lace underwear, instructing him in a no-nonsense tone, "Take those. Your wife will find use for them. Mark my word." She spotted my egg bundle and said in a near-whisper, "Some lovesick *sovkhoznik* would give 40 or 50 eggs for that underwear." Father refused no longer.

Loaded with our purchases, we were leaving the store, not feeling the ground we walked on from sheer joy at our unprecedented success. We had made only 15 or 20 steps when an angry voice reached our ears. It was the voice of the woman with the 540 mark, the one who was holding our place in line.

"That dry herring, there! That skinny fellow! How come he got in to shop? He was behind me!" After a few moments silence, as if listening for an explanation, the voice thundered again. "What? Are you going soft in your brains, females? Didn't you see the red mark on his palm? What triplets? He had no triplets two hours ago! Wh-a-a-t? Vera? Nadezhda? Lubov?"

Father spotted the approaching trolley in the distance, and, without turning his head, whispered a command to me.

"We'll be finished if we start running now. Walk normally, Ninochka. If we run, all will be lost. The militia will fine us for disorderly behavior. Don't get panicky, little one. I know, I know the women have started running. I hear their heels too. Watch me. That's our trolley. It's coming. What? Eggs? Throw them away! *Now* we must start running. Throw the eggs. Throw them away! Ninochka! I order you! Run! Run now! Jump! Jump, Nina! Throw the blasted eggs! I can't help you! My hands are full! Jump onto the trolley! Remember what the sales woman said! Mother can get 40 eggs for the underwear!"

Ready to cry from regret at sacrificing the precious eggs, yet needing both my arms to help me catch up with the speeding-away trolley, I threw the bundle over my head toward the enraged Number 540, and jumped in the car.

"That's a good girl! Now we're safe," Father grinned.

The trolley, moving faster, was carrying us away, away from the infuriated, fist-waving women, who only minutes earlier were so enchanted with Father's tale, determined to reward him for the triplets. After boarding our train, Father, cautioning me to keep an eye on our purchases, slumped in his seat, leaning his head against my shoulder. "Papa," I asked genuinely worried, "what would have happened if the women had caught up with us? Could they have torn us apart? They were so-o-o upset."

"Well," Father said fatalistically, "there is a good Russian proverb, Ninochka, that says, '*Dvukh smertey ne bivat—a odnoy ne minovat.*' Two deaths are impossible—but one is unavoidable!" And with that, he closed his eyes and snoozed blissfully all the way to Dulovo.

CHAPTER EIGHTEEN

Our first summer in Feodosia was coming to an end. It was September 1. I was scavenging the bazaar, trying to locate some potatoes for the lowest possible price. Potatoes, the steady diet of Moscovites, were a delicacy in Crimea, because they had to be mostly imported from the Ukraine. And we from time to time, longed unbearably for potatoes. Discouraged at not finding any that were affordable, I headed for home, when a loudspeaker creaked, squealed, and finally came to life.

"Attention! Attention!" The buttery voice of famed announcer, Yuri Levitan, called out, "Citizens of our great Soviet Union, pay utmost attention!"

People began to gather on the corners where loudspeakers were located, so as to better hear what the smooth voice was about to say.

And what the man was saying threw the bazaar into open-mouthed puzzlement.

What "Non-aggression Pact"? What "Friendship Pact"? What socialist country had our government joined in a pact? National Socialist Germany? Adolf Hitler?

Following the signing of the pact with the Nazis on August 23, 1939, the newspapers and movie theaters were filled with images of the benevolent Führer kissing adorable German children, waving to bosomy young women, saluting tall, good-looking German men. Such a handsome race of people! A great people! This fact was drummed into our heads from then onward, day and night, beginning with the morning news, continuing in school, in theaters, in newspapers, in books, more radio, more newspapers. A strong, honorable, moral people, the Germans, because Adolf Hitler and his Nazi Party helped, inspired them to be strong, honorable, moral people.

New school textbooks were hastily produced, replacing the unfavorable images of Hitler and Nazism. In my history book, under the title of "Today's Germany," appeared a picture of a neat brick house surrounded with flower beds. A smiling German family of four—called "typical"—was portrayed lounging under an apple tree, heavy-laden with fruit. Father in Wehrmacht uniform, on leave; Mother in a starched, snow-white apron, toothy, healthy smile; a boy Slava's age trying to reach an apple; a girl of eight or nine, ready to race after a puppy. Paradise.

So as to be able to communicate with our new friends and allies, we were expected to study German with the utmost zeal. A new teacher, Erika Karlovna, of pure German descent, replaced our previous teacher of German, who was Jewish. Erika Karlovna was very energetic, very enthusiastic about her job.

"Children!" she instructed. "You must pay much more attention to your German lessons! Learn to pronounce words correctly in *hoch deutsch,* high German, not some mongrel slang."

We were also taught to imitate the Nazi salute.

"The salute of Senators in ancient Rome! The salute of Caesars!" declared Erika Karlovna.

How romantic! And Hitler's troops goose-stepped. The SS men marched like highly trained athletes. Boom! Boom! Boom! Boom! Erect, proud, indestructible.

The pact with Nazi Germany brought us prestige, power. Our Red Army marched triumphantly into Galicia, proceeded into East Poland, spread its wings over Bessarabia, put its heavy boot into Finland, and—oops! To the Kremlin's utter surprise, the Red Army encountered terrific resistance. Finland's people rose like enraged lions, protecting their independence. Stalin, after a face-saving "victory," retreated, satisfied with small gains. Our army then moved on to rob Lithuania, Latvia, and Estonia of their national independence.

An enthusiastic young Soviet poet, Pavel Kogan, composed verses not different in spirit from *"Deutschland Uber Alles"*:

> "We shall yet reach the distant Ganges,
> Give our lives on the battlefield
> So that from Japan to Great Britain
> May shine my country's sword and shield."

The war was in full swing, engulfing the whole of Europe, but one could not feel it inside the borders of the Soviet Union. There was no war, neither the Red Army nor the Nazis were at war. The newsreels, the newspapers showed the whole population of eastern Poland, the whole population of the Baltic States welcoming our Red Army men. Flowers, more flowers, garlands, pretty girls, singing, dancing, kissing the "liberators." The newsreels showed almost identical scenes, only different national costumes on the girls who were singing, dancing, kissing, welcoming the gallant armies of Hitler's Wehrmacht. The two military forces, the most benevolent in our world's history, united their goals, and it was due to this union that they accomplished so much! And indeed, much was accomplished. In addition to more than 200,000 square kilometers of Poland, the Soviet Union now lorded over about 230,000 square kilometers of the Baltic States, Bessarabia, and Bucovina, with 40,000 square kilometers of Finland, besides.

Erika Karlovna, following Party instructions, lectured daily to us children about the benevolence that characterized our union with Nazism. The official voice of the Soviet government, *Izvestia,* and the official voice of the Communist Party, *Pravda,* every day drummed into the heads of Soviet citizens how this giant step—the union of Communism and Nazism—would change the world, and change it for the better. We were expected to adore our new friend, Adolf Hitler, and to trust him.

At the same time veneration of our own leader reached the highest pitch. Stalin's "genius" that led to this pact with Hitler was praised in newspapers, newsreels, and our school lessons. We repeated writer N. Avdyenko's earlier proclamation that "Our love and devotion, our strength, heart, courage—all is yours, Vozhd of the Great Land!"

Standing at attention beside our school desks, we chanted in joyous unison:

> "O Thou Mighty One, Chief of all the peoples, You
> Who callest man to life, Who awakest the earth to fruit-
> fullness, Who summonest the centuries to youth. . . .

Story tellers no longer know with whom to compare Thee.
Poets have not enough pearls with which to describe Thee.
O Sun, Who art reflected by millions of human hearts!"

The friendship pact with the Nazis created a horrendous shortage of food and sent prices sky-rocketing. A kilo of butter jumped from 16.50 rubles to 39.50. The bread supply was especially affected. Ships loaded with grain were departing from Odessa regularly for Germany. Trains, loaded to bursting with more precious grain hurried toward German borders. Feodosia's granaries began to empty. Crimea, which had served ancient Greece as a breadbasket, became exhausted under the heavy demands of our Nazi allies to be fed, and fed well.

Kerosene, which the majority of us relied on for lighting and cooking, was hard to come by, since Hitler needed all the fuel he could get from us for his army. Because our parents were not allowed to miss work, Slava and I were expected to hunt for food. There was a day when I found myself standing in four lines at once, all in stores next to one another. One line was for bread, a number scrawled on my chest in chalk. The second line was for lard, with a number in red ink printed on one palm, while on the other palm, blue ink recorded my number for the kerosene line. Fat, mouth-watering Kerch herring was distributed in yet another store, and a number in green ink was stamped on my forehead for lack of any other space. Successful with the bread purchase, and a quarter kilogram of lard, but missing out on herring and kerosene, I hurriedly dumped the purchases at home, and ran to school forgetting about my marked forehead.

Erika Karlovna's class was the first of the school day. She entered briskly, efficiently, encompassing us all with a surveying look. As a rule, we were neatly dressed, carefully combed and braided, due to the particularly doting attention our parents bestowed upon our appearance and attire. That morning my appearance was quite neglected. I did braid my hair—at four in the morning; by school time the braids had become sloppy, ribbons hanging loose, limp. My skirt was dusty and spotted from squatting on the sidewalk near the stores, waiting for them to open. My red Pioneer necktie hung askew, wrinkled, and the forgotten green number on the forehead!

"Nina!" Erika Karlovna exploded, her stern eyes settling on me. "How dare you come to class in such a state! I shall be forced to reproach your mother in your school diary."

"Please," I said, imploringly, not wishing for my mother to be punished for my sloppiness, "I left the house early today, Erika Karl-ovna. I stood in four lines . . . got messy."

"Four lines!" she interrupted. "What greed! Go! Go to the toilet room and scrub off those repulsive marks! Clean your palms as well! If I see once more such an undignified appearance, your citizenship course will suffer!"

Despite shortages, we were still comparatively well off, because Mother continued to receive one pound of bread at her place of employment, her original norm of one kilogram having been cut in half after the pact with the Nazis was signed. Father, too, managed to bring home some fish from time to time, mostly dried or salted *kamsa* (anchovies). Yet, dairy products were exceptionally difficult to come by. No stores carried milk. One could only find it at the bazaar, but to get it from this source required a routine that was, to say the least, extraordinary. Whenever Mother decided that she and I should look for milk the next day, she announced to the family, "Tomorrow, after milk!"

That meant we two went to bed soon after dusk fell. Father and Slava were expected to cooperate by staying very quiet, knowing of our need to sleep and rest up for the impending trip. At 4 a.m. we quietly rose, dressed, and headed for the dairy pavilion, an imposing, ultra-modern structure with cathedral ceilings, all of glass, and lined on either side with dozens of stalls. After several early morning expeditions of this sort, we began to realize that there was something wrong with our procedure, because we very seldom succeeded in obtaining any milk. By the time our turn came, the milk cans were empty.

By observing what others were doing, we learned that it was better not to go all the way to the dairy pavilion, but rather, to wait on the corner of the main highway and the road leading to the bazaar. It was there the *sovkhoznik* appeared first with his milk cart. As soon as we spotted his little horse-drawn wagon, we galloped toward him. Dozens of women arrived at the same time we did, or even earlier, and on seeing the cart, all started to run, as if on command. The very first woman to reach the milk cart grabbed its rear frame and clung to it as if her life depended on it. The second one to reach the cart clutched the first woman by the coat or back of the dress, the next woman doing the same, creating in this manner a long, unruly, swaying "tail."

While one hand was holding part of another woman's clothing, the other hand was firmly clutching a container for the milk, in the form of a bottle, pan, or bowl. Some *sovkhozniks*, just to be mischievous, gave their horse a playful touch of the whip, making the animal want to run briskly, and forcing the human tail to stumble while trying not to separate from one another. Remarkably, women would rather lose their grip on the milk container than to let go of their place in the tail; yet, without the container they could not carry any milk home.

One *sovkhoznik*, a blond, blue-eyed bully whose milk was the least diluted with water, was the most successful in creating the longest tail. But he also enjoyed playing the harshest tricks on us. He whipped the horses until the poor creatures broke into a gallop and, while pretending to aim at the backs of the horses, he often lashed out at the woman nearest to him, as if by mistake hitting her with the whip. But the woman, often young, with infant children waiting for milk, never gave up her grip on the cart. On days when rain created huge puddles in the unpaved road, he ran his horse through those puddles trying to hit the deepest one. The women blindly following the cart and not being able to see what was in front of them, found themselves suddenly sinking to their ankles in sticky mud.

The *sovkhoznik,* finally tiring of the circus, stopped several blocks from the dairy pavilion and allocated milk to his exhausted followers. His canisters were practically empty when he made his appearance in the dairy pavilion.

Mother and I, on returning from such milk expeditions, diligently scrubbed our coats, skirts, and footwear, removing the stubborn mud—planning already, the next "milk run."

CHAPTER NINETEEN

*S*ince *Feodosia* was far from the nerve center of the Soviet empire, it was not high on the bureaucrat's priority list of areas to be resupplied with food. A constant, gnawing hunger began to torment us all, particularly Slava and me. Besides Father's portion of fish and Mother's bread rations being cut, no more soup was carried home from the canteen at work. With the exception of watermelons, no fruit reached our table, having been picked earlier, and shipped to Hitler's Germany. Grapes vanished from our table altogether, and the hills covered with grape vines were closely guarded by armed *sovkhozniks* against looters. Fish was preserved and sent to Germany. Sheep that grazed the surrounding steppes and fields of Feodosia were slaughtered and shipped to Germany.

Mother decided that only in Moscow could we restock our supplies. She saved her early fall vacation time, and when I got out of school in December, we both set out for Moscow.

Near starvation conditions in Crimea were being duplicated in many other regions of the country, sending a desperate populace to Moscow. But there were so many food hunters that Moscow store shelves, too, became empty, a situation not long tolerated by the Kremlin. Abruptly, passes into Moscow were denied to virtually all "outsiders." Mother out-foxed the Party bureaucrats, however, insisting that she was going to visit relatives in Dulovo—Moscow being a necessary stopover.

We embraced Father and Slava in farewell and boarded the express train that was to bring us to our destination in 36 short hours. To get some basic foods—fats, sugar, grains—we covered a distance equivalent to a trip from New York to Atlanta, or from London to Rome, just one way.

We disembarked at Moscow's Kursk railroad station, at one o'clock in the morning. The weather was damp, cold, and windy—most uninviting. Fortunately, because we had come 1,500 kilometers, our tickets allowed us to remain in the waiting room on the wooden benches until daylight. The militiamen were patrolling the station constantly, checking every new arrival's papers, leading some away for questioning, if their documents were not in order.

Next to us on the narrow wooden bench sat a young woman with a four-year-old son on her lap. She came from a neighboring town, only 85 kilometers away, bringing her boy to an ear specialist. Wanting to be one of the first to get to the doctor, she took the very last train out of her home town, planning to spend several hours at the railroad station waiting room and then, with the coming of dawn, rush to the ear clinic. But because her ticket was a "short distance" one, she was not entitled to spend the night inside the station. The militiaman, after checking her ticket, immediately ordered her out of the waiting room. A few minutes later, we observed her entering the room through another door, trying to avoid being seen by the same militiaman. He spotted her, however, and began to push the poor woman toward the exit once more. The little boy broke out weeping, sending his mother into sobs of despair.

"Where can we go? Comrade militiaman, it's freezing outside. My child is shivering to his bones. Look at him! He's running a fever. Be kind. Allow us to sit here just a bit longer!"

She lowered her head, pressing it to her little boy's forehead, and both just sat there, as if one, rocking slightly. The militiaman, annoyed by all the begging, uttered a stream of vile epithets, and left. "Thank God," the young woman whispered and continued to rock her child until he fell asleep.

We, too, dozed. When dawn came, we swallowed some hot tea at the station cafeteria and joined the shoppers on the streets of Moscow. The city was coming out of its slumber, the trolleys filling up with toilers hurrying to their destinations. Some trolley cars were crowded to overflowing with people standing on the platform, on the steps, others resembling gymnasts clinging to window sills and to the roofs. Gloomy, unfriendly people appeared on the sidewalks; women seemed to outnumber men. While men, in most cases, marched with their hands in coat pockets, or with arms swinging free, women carried in one hand an empty shopping bag, while a young child clung to the other hand, on the way to kindergarten or school. Everyone walked determinedly, looking neither right nor left; few greetings were exchanged and those smileless. It seemed that everyone was in his or her own, impenetrable, separate world.

That morning promised to turn into a most productive one for us. We immediately bumped into a throng of people waiting for fabric to be distributed, mainly material for underclothing. After leaving Dulovo, not once had we been able to find goods in Crimea to refurbish our much-worn wardrobe.

But when it came time for the store to open its doors, the manager appeared and shouted to us, "Go away, citizens! No merchandise available today! Maybe tomorrow." And, in a strangely jovial mood, the balding man disappeared behind the door, locking it quickly. Everyone began to disperse, many grumbling at their bad luck. Mother and I sat on our cardboard suitcases—boxes that Father had constructed especially for us to use on this journey.

"Anything to be distributed here?" passersby asked us from time to time.

"No. We're just sitting here, resting. The store is empty," Mother answered listlessly, trying to decide in what direction to go hunting next.

Then the front door swung open and the same store manager shouted to the pedestrians, "Citizens! This store is full of merchandise! Welcome!"

We stared at the jolly, bald man open-mouthed, convinced that he was playing tricks on us. But he was not! The store shelves were bending under the heavy merchandise. Every shopper was entitled to five meters of material, giving us ten meters of tricot-type cotton for underwear. Mother was chattering excitedly about how she would sew a two-piece swimming suit for me, and decent swimwear for Father and Slava. Such items were normally unavailable in stores. Only foreigners and prominent vacationers were able to sport ready-made swimming suits. The rest of us wore plain underwear—briefs for men, homemade halters and panties for women. To see our underwear was to laugh, or break out in tears, considering the darning, re-darning, the patches. Often, I could not bring myself to undress and dip into the sea because I had no decent, undarned set of underwear that would not embarrass any girl nearing her teens.

We left the store carrying ten meters of precious tricot, when a thought struck Mother. Why not change our appearance slightly and try to enter the store a second time? She hid my waist-long braids inside the beret I wore, and rearranging her square neck scarf in peasant fashion—low over the forehead, almost to the eyebrows—she pushed me toward the store entrance.

"Let's try to avoid the manager's eyes, Ninochka, and go to the other salesgirl. My! People are beginning to pour in! Never did I count on such luck."

Ten meters of thick, beige cotton was allotted us this time. Terrific! Skirts, trousers, tunic tops—all could be created out of the stuff, just right for Crimea's fall and spring weather. We felt so lucky! Twenty meters of cotton fabric, divided by four—still, five meters per person! There were by now perhaps two hundred people jostling, pushing, shouting, and yet, very few standing in line outside the store. We joined the crowd once more, not really expecting the merchandise to last until we reached the counter, but we were rewarded a third time, with 10 meters of dark, unattractive cloth that seemed to have no place in Feodosia's climate.

"Mama, why are we taking this heavy, ugly stuff?" I wanted to know.

"Wait, Ninochka. We'll swap it with someone."

Leaving the store, we headed toward a group of women who were comparing their latest purchases.

One woman, obviously dissatisfied, displayed some cotton similar to that we received in the second line, and said to her neighbor, "Tell me, please, what good is this stuff to me, huh? That old horseradish of mine is a tractor mechanic in a *sovkhoz*—always greasy. Much good it'll do him. That's stuff for city folks' touch-me-not clothing. Such bad luck! And the sales girl said, 'Nothing else. Take it or leave it.'"

Mother, after listening to the grumbling woman, took the dark, ugly material out of the bundle, stretched it over her left arm, and approached the unhappy purchaser.

"Citizen," she said, soothingly, "don't despair. "Your husband is a mechanic in a *sovkhoz*, you say? Mine is a bookkeeper in one. I could use the light material. Let's swap."

The woman, utterly unhappy just moments earlier, shouted, "My savior! A heaven-sent dove you are! No more, no less!" And the stranger locked Mother in a prolonged, grateful bearhug.

Our next hunt was directed toward obtaining *galoshi* (rubbers). Rubbers were in such short supply that to locate a pair was considered a feat worth celebrating as if it were one's birthday—with toasts and congratulations. Rubbers were used all year round. One needed them desperately in the muddy fall, when unpaved roads sucked one's feet into the sticky soil. In winter months, rubbers were stretched over the bottoms of our felt snow boots (*valenky*), since *valenky* soles were made of the same felt as the rest of the boot and quickly soaked through if one stepped in a puddle. In spring, one simply could not step outside the house without rubbers. Even in summer, in order to protect the life of one's shoes, rubbers were often called upon to help. Yet, as in the case of sewing needles, rubbers were not of high priority to the central planners.

We left our purchases with a family of former Dulovan Rigavites who had established residence in Moscow after a seven year wait for a two-room apartment. The couple, in their 40s and childless, were very nice to us, but point-blank refused to accommodate us more than three nights, the 72 hour maximum allowed for an outsider to spend in Moscow. The couple's apartment was so tiny that Mother had to sleep on a thin pad spread under a long, narrow table against the wall. I, in turn, was led to a bathroom that counted as a second room, where a comforter covered the bottom of an old fashioned bath tub—the pride and joy of the couple, for very few could boast a private bathroom. The tub served me admirably as a bed, considering that the alternative was the hard benches at the railroad station.

The next morning we rose at 2 a.m., ready to march to the *galoshi* lines, but our hosts informed us that of late, extra vigilant militiamen were not allowing the public to gather anywhere until dawn. So, we waited for the ink-dark skies to turn charcoal gray, and headed once more to the *Zatzep* section of Moscow, where rubbers appeared more often than in other parts of town.

The entire forenoon was wasted on several unproductive lines. The afternoon was a repeat of the morning. Returning to our friends' place, we crawled into our resting corners and slept. The next morning we repeated the procedure, at one point joining a line of more than 700 people. The night had been cold, with a piercing damp wind. My body under overcoat and dress, was wrapped in layers of newspaper to protect it from the wind that seemed to reach to the very bone. My feet, too, were wrapped in newspaper, with old, worn-out *valenky* stretched over the wrappings. Out of one's nose and mouth, steam was pouring forth, and small icicles formed on men's moustaches and beards. I tried to breathe through my nostrils, but they were sticking together as if glued, and when I tried breathing through my mouth, my teeth became so sensitive I had to cover them with the scarf. People in line were jumping, moving constantly, throwing their arms out and then thumping them on their chests. They were rubbing their foreheads, noses, and cheeks. Some of the people, the ones at the head of the line, registered for their places at two in the morning, hiding under stairs and behind the gates and walls of the buildings when the militiamen approached.

The line grew to about 1,500 people shortly before 9:00 a.m., when a group of mounted militiamen galloped toward the store, shouting, "Hey! Hey! You! All of you in the front of the line! MARCH TO THE BACK! March! You lice! We'll teach you! F------ speculators! And you, in the back, march to the front!"

While the latest arrivals could not hide their joy at such a turn of events, the earliest were in despair. One obviously pregnant woman in her late 30s, holding on to her protruding abdomen, wailed shrilly, "Not fair! Not fair!" her cheeks covered with tears.

A militiaman grabbed the distraught woman by the sleeve and barked, "You much laid whore! Don't dare to accuse us of not being fair! *Na dopros.*" And with that, he hustled the woman to the nearest militia station. No one protested openly after that.

Our place in the line was undisturbed, finding us in the middle. The sales clerks inside the store worked efficiently, allotting each person a pair of black, shiny galoshes, then ushering them out quickly. We were moving nearer to the store entrance. The sun came out and began to warm us up, taking the chill out of our bones, but in the process melting the snow and ice. Under our feet appeared cold, slushy mud. Mother and I were in trouble. Our *valenky* soles were completely worn out—a mesh of small holes kept dry by rubbers. My rubbers were still in one piece, but Mother's were split at the heels from long years of wear. She had sewn the heels with thick thread before leaving Feodosia, hoping that the rubbers would serve her until they could be replaced.

"Ninochka," she instructed me before the store opened. "You stay behind me at all times and guard my heels. Protect me from pushing people or I'll lose my galoshes and my *valenky* will soak through."

For a while I was very conscientious in protecting Mother's rear, but then, during one exceptionally energetic push, I myself stepped on Mother's feet and her rubbers just gave way. They simply fell off, exposing the soles of her valenky to layers of icy mud. I almost wept, but Mother was more or less numb to her misfortune, preparing herself for the joy of receiving a pair of shiny, gorgeous galoshes, lined with a soft, reddish material, and smelling so deliciously of newness that one drooled in anticipation.

"*Galoshi*! Whose stinking *galoshi?*" a mocking militiaman called out, waving on a stick Mother's tattered rubbers. They were beyond redemption. No one laid claim to them, and the militiaman tore them into tiny pieces, flinging the pieces back at us.

Just when we were finally very close to entering the store, a clerk announced, "Finished! Out! No more galoshes!"

Relentlessly we tried again, but the galoshes eluded us. And then—a success! The very next day we came upon a store where we managed to stand in line twice and receive four pairs of darling galoshes. We tied two pairs together and carried them like some holy relics—two pairs in my arms, two in Mother's. On the way to our friends' apartment, a well-groomed man in a long, fur-trimmed overcoat, fur hat, wearing soft, black *valenky* encased in black rubbers, looked at our priceless possessions, then at our grinning faces, and more or less spat out words of anger and disgust:

"You hateful provincials. The likes of you rob our city blind! Four pair of galoshes. Not just one or two, but four! Pigs!"

Mother decided not to explain to the man with the glistening, python-like face that there were four in our family.

CHAPTER TWENTY

*B*efore returning to Feodosia, we paid a visit to our hometown of Dulovo. Mother was very uneasy about the continuing silence of her only remaining relative in Dulovo, her brother Shura. Aunt Lisa had written only once, informing us of her husband having changed jobs, and that this change made him very unhappy. Since then no more letters came.

My friend Lida had been silent since spring, when she implored me not to worry about her. Mother thoughtfully tried to prepare me for the possibility that Lida had died, blaming the cursed *chahotka*. Young and old alike, all succumbed. I understood, since I had witnessed with my own eyes Lida's sister Katya wither away. Yet, when we were approaching Lida's house on the way to Aunt Lisa's, I was filled with hope that I had only to knock on that familiar door, and Lida would be standing there, ready to embrace me.

A graying, older woman with one front tooth missing, opened the door and in a tired voice asked what it was we wanted. I had to correct my first impression of her being older. She was obviously very pregnant, with four or five children clustered around, some hanging onto her skirt. After hearing our inquiry, she said in a detached, emotionless voice, "Lida? Oh, that kid died in late spring. Lungs, you know. Better that way. No good spreading *chahotka* to others." She stopped for a moment, seeing me swallow approaching tears. "Your best buddy? Oh, that's life. The father? Just walked away one day. No one knows where. It's our house now. This one'll be my seventh." The woman patted her belly. "One more, and then I'll rest."

Mother wished the woman a safe confinement, and we slowly proceeded toward Aunt Lisa's, passing our former house, now dark, isolated, with no one looking out of the windows at us, its kitchen garden buried deep under drifts of snow. It was dusk, the fresh snow squeaking under our new galoshes, snow almost crystal blue, with its own peculiar aroma, so sharp, fresh, and clean, faintly reminiscent of newly laundered and ironed bed linens. And this snow was covering my friend Lida, I thought, blinking away stinging tears.

When we reached Aunt Lisa's place, she was just putting little Inna to bed. On seeing us, Aunt Lisa seemed to stiffen, no sound of welcome coming from her.

She then put her finger to her lips and whispered to us, "Stay in the corridor for a few minutes. I want Innochka to fall asleep. I don't want her to know you're here."

We did not understand why we received such an icy greeting from a relative with whom we had always been at ease, trusting and loving. Aunt Lisa after a while reappeared, and led us into the tiny kitchen, tightly closing the door to the room where Inna slept.

"Well, I suppose some hot tea would do you good," she said, looking at us as if waiting to hear a denial, but we truly were ready for a glass of tea, since we had been on the road for much of the day. While Aunt Lisa listlessly started to attend to preparation of the samovar, Mother offered to help.

Expertly, on her knees, still blowing at the sticks and charcoal, Mother casually, matter-of-factly asked her sister-in-law, "Lisochka, where is Shura? I would like to see my brother before leaving."

Aunt Lisa, kneeling next to Mother, dropped her arms limply, and whispered, "Didn't you get my letter? Yes, that letter! Couldn't you understand? Shura is *sitting*! Sitting! God! Natasha, I tried in as clear language as possible to let you know. I didn't want the censors to read about my problems."

Mother's arms, too, went limp at her sides. The two women kneeled on the floor, staring at each other.

"So Shura, my dear brother. . . . He, too, was swallowed," Mother mused, with her lips parting in a smile—a bitter, soul-wrenching smile of utter sadness.

Over tea, Aunt Lisa brought us up to date on the events. After our departure, several more Dulovans had been arrested; even crusty, old Pelagea vanished. The old woman, refusing to participate in the October revolution parade, was heard saying to the new partorg in an almost regretful tone, "One can lead a horse to the water, but one can't force the horse to drink it." After that, no one saw Pelagea again. Igor Ivanovich, the director, also vanished.

When Aunt Lisa was able to bring herself to tell us about her husband, we could not believe our ears, so completely unreal and nightmarish was the reason for Uncle Shura's arrest.

It happened on a Saturday, December 24, only a few months after we left Dulovo. Uncle Shura was returning home from work, taking a shortcut through the woods, observing with pleasure the huge, lush fir trees, surrounded by their offspring—the mischievous little *elochki*. Why not bring one to Inna, he thought. After all, in a few days the New Year will arrive—the fir tree will still be fresh and green then.

The old tradition of having Christmas trees had been outlawed since the Soviet takeover, specifically not being allowed in homes on the 6th and 7th of January, when Russian Orthodox Christmas was celebrated. But in time, the government yielded somewhat, and in 1936 began allowing its citizens to have a fir tree on the New Year, with its traditional companion, Grandfather Frost. Christmas carols were replaced with melodies dedicated to the tree itself—no saints, no biblical names or events entered the picture in this strictly secular celebration. The name Christ was taboo.

That evening, when Uncle Shura entered his home, dragging behind him a baby fir, Aunt Lisa a bit annoyed, said, "Shura! Why bring the *elka* so early? It'll start losing its needles by New Year's Eve."

But Uncle Shura would not hear of discarding the fir tree now that it had found its way into his apartment. Aunt Lisa retired early, while her husband proceeded to decorate the tree with old cotton for snow, paper rings and paper animals, all self-made, along with some hard candy and a few apples, in anticipation of the squeals of delight that Innochka was bound to utter the next morning. Blissfully pleased, Uncle Shura joined his already sleeping wife, and quickly he, too, fell asleep.

Then, violent knocks!

"Visitors," Uncle Shura murmured to his wife. The wall clock showed 2 a.m., the hour most favored by the NKVDists.

Uncle Shura knew his turn had come, but could not understand why. "Why?" That was the only word he addressed to his wife while walking toward the door to admit the NKVDists.

"Why?" he repeated the word to the intruders.

And they barked back, "Why do you have a Christmas tree in your home? How dare you break Soviet laws! No stinking religious relics in our society!"

While Uncle Shura was being marched away, little Inna woke up and shrieked in pure delight, still not knowing that her father was at that moment being taken away by force.

"Papa! Papa! Look! The New Year *elochka* has come from Father Frost! Papa! Why are you going away?"

During the dreadful *dopros,* Uncle Shura held to the point that the tree was not a Christmas tree, but a New Year tree. Then a question was put to him.

"In your city of birth, Riga, there were many Germans, Latvians, some Catholics, some Protestants. Isn't that right? Aha! When did they celebrate their Christmas? What? Two weeks before the Russian Orthodox? Aha! When was their Christmas Eve? What? Twenty-fourth of December was their Christmas Eve, you say? And last night, you brought the fir tree secretly, under the cloak of darkness, to celebrate Christmas clandestinely. Celebrate with stinking foreigners! Don't deny any longer! You're a spy! You MUST be a spy!"

Uncle Shura received a sentence of 15 years in the "corrective" camps of Siberia, where he soon died.

We stared at Aunt Lisa, wanting to cry, yet not being able to shed a tear. Crying brought a certain relief, cleansed wounds a bit, even helped to heal them. We were too numb to cry.

Aunt Lisa checked on the sleeping Inna and, returning to the table, said to Mother, "Natasha, I don't know who betrayed us. One of the neighbors must have seen Shura carry the tree. Who? Maybe now the same people watch us. They know you are Shura's sister . . . his blood relative. I don't want any trouble, you understand? No trouble for Innochka. Leave! I know, Natashinka, dear, I know it's late and it's cold out. But we must cut all family ties. What if someone reports your visit and your staying overnight in my place! Maybe it'll be all that's needed for the excuse to arrest me! And my poor Innochka, what will her fate be? *Besprizhornik!* I shiver just thinking of it. Oh, God forgive me! Natasha, you simply must leave! Right now! Go to the Likino station. It's only four kilometers away. I beg you, don't stay in the Dulovo station. Someone might spot you there and figure you came to visit me. Let's part, Natashinka. Don't weep, don't be hurt. I, too, loved you best of all my sisters-in-law. But we must live for our children. Stifle our conscience in order to protect our little ones from that bloodthirsty Moloch. So long he sucks our blood! And never enough, never enough! Oh! If only our children could be spared!"

Aunt Lisa's torrent of words, uttered in a frenzy of panic and anger, followed me all the way to Likino station. It was after midnight when we reached the unheated, heavily littered station waiting room and already, a black limousine of a type not seen in daylight, appeared on the streets of the slumbering town.

CHAPTER TWENTY-ONE

"*F*eodosia! *Last* stop!" the conductor announced.

We hurried to detrain. Mother instantly spotted Slava, then Father, and said, "Something's wrong."

I saw nothing wrong, except Father's face looked flushed as if he had been running.

"See your father's neck, Ninochka?" Mother persisted. "It's too outstretched, too tense. Something's bothering him."

We climbed down the steps of our car, loaded with bundles and bags and cardboard suitcases, more bundles hanging over both our shoulders, two packages on our chests, two on our backs, like growths of some sort. We wore our glossy new galoshes, but the clothing material, six kilograms of raw lump sugar, several glass jars of lard and sunflower oil, 30 kilograms of wheat flour, some pasta, some soap and matches, even two jars of *moskitka* cream for my slow-healing sores—all hung on our bodies in a mass of small and not so small bundles. Just looking at us bending under those bundles, straining to drag the overstuffed cardboard suitcases, Father and Slava knew that our Moscow trip had been a success.

Mother's premonition that something was wrong proved to be correct. After greeting us and taking over the bundles from our shoulders, Father, instead of leading us toward our cottage on the hill, turned toward Aivasovsky's gallery, in the direction of Praskovia Ivanovna's house.

"Dmitry Antonovich is near death," he said. "Let's hurry! I hope we'll find our friend still alive. He was conscious this morning . . . but failing fast."

In one of our bundles were ten lemons, purchased in Moscow especially for Dmitry Antonovich, to flavor his tea.

We did find Dmitry Antonovich alive, but barely. He lay still when we entered the room, his head slightly tilted toward Praskovia Ivanovna sitting in a chair beside him. His eyes—wide, wide open—moved like a clock pendulum, darting from right to left, left to right, as if counting away the very last seconds of life remaining to him. We sat ourselves next to Praskovia Ivanovna, surrounding the death bed. Dmitry Antonovich's eyes began to dart even faster when Praskovia Ivanovna spoke his name in a desperately anguished voice.

"Dima!" And his eyes, as if following her voice, found Praskovia Ivanovna's face and froze on her. Three grotesque spasms siezed the right side of the dying man's neck, as if choking him. His eyes, still wide open as though in wonderment, became very dark, their pupils spreading, reflecting light no longer.

Praskovia Ivanovna bent over her husband, sealing his already dead, yet still warm lips with hers. She did not stir for the longest time, as if waiting for his lips to move. Then, convinced that no warmth of hers could bring Dmitry Antonovich back to life, she crossed his corpse three times, kissing the cheeks, forehead, and hands. She opened the windows and quickly covered the mirrors with dark cloth, following the custom and beliefs of folklore that the soul of the dead must find a way to leave the confinement of the dwelling, either through a window or door. The mirrors, having stored in them the myriad reflections of the deceased, accumulated over the time of his existence on earth, interfered with the soul's departure, unless they were covered with dark cloth. Then, the soul would not be confused by the persistent images, and depart in peace.

While we stood forlornly by the bedside of the forever-stilled Dmitry Antonovich, Praskovia Ivanovna became very efficient. "Help me to bathe Dimochka," she said, turning to Mother and me. "And you two," she commanded Father and Slava, "load the Moscow purchases on the two wheeler and take them home. But bring back the folding table. Dimochka needs it now." She ran to the *burshuyka* stove and fetched a pan with warm water. "Here, Ninochka, you sponge this side and I'll sponge his legs."

How heavy, how unresponsive Dmitry Antonovich's arms, legs, head became. Only a few days before leaving for Moscow, Maya and I attended to his toilette. We bathed him, massaged the tired, sore body, while he insisted that we should clip his thick hair.

"Too thick, too bothersome. Girls, please!" he begged. "Cut all my hair off. Let my head feel light."

And we kept clipping in a childish, inexperienced manner. A tuft of hair came off here, another there, almost exposing his scalp, while the next patch was still full and vibrant. Praskovia Ivanovna was shocked to discover such butchering, but her dying husband insisted Maya and I clip off more of his hair. That day he was heavy too, yet responsive, cooperative, helping us to move him from one side to another, lifting his neck for us, lifting his arms when asked. Now nothing was lifting in its final heaviness. But even as I was sunk in a morbid sadness, Praskovia Ivanovna was chatting in a soft, lullabying manner while dressing the freshly cleansed corpse in silk moire pajamas, a burgundy cashmere leisure coat with matching suede slippers—all items to that moment carefully stored, and kept for this particular occasion in Praskovia Ivanovna's dowry blanket chest. They were Dmitry Antonovich's favorite garments, purchased three decades earlier and still bearing the labels of their origin, England.

"Now, my little berry, my darling husband. I'll fix you up. Like a bridegroom you'll look," Praskovia Ivanovna chanted soothingly. She stroked Dmitry Antonovich's hollow cheeks, put her own cheek to his, and said, "I shaved you this morning, my little mushroom. Good thing I did. Your face is smooth. Remember our honeymoon? I begged you to teach me how to shave you, remember?"

While I stole a sideward glance at Dmitry Antonovich's face, half expecting him to answer, Praskovia Ivanovna drastically changed her soothing tone and accusingly grumbled, "And now, Dima! Why have you done it to me? Deserting me! You hear me? Dima! You hear me?" She shook his slippered foot slightly. "I don't know how to spend a day without you. Orphaned, orphaned I am."

Mother and I threw ourselves at Praskovia Ivanovna, and the three of us sobbed, unrestrained.

When Father returned with Slava, Dmitry Antonovich was ready. Together, we placed him on the table, and he, in turn, accepted it in a regal manner, his long body stretching, dominating. Praskovia Ivanovna expressed her approval:

"Dimochka, you look quite comfortable. Are you comfortable?"

She moved a bit away from the table, giving a last critical look, fluffed up a small down pillow, placing it under the corpse's neck, and, finally satisfied, said, "Now, Dimochka, you look like you belong. I won't be ashamed for our friends to see you now." And she flung open the entrance door.

Mother returned to work the next day, while I took advantage of the school holiday, and slept and slept. When Maya ran in to visit me, I asked her about Praskovia Ivanovna.

"She's all right. Don't worry. Grandmother and I look in from time to time. Many are coming to pay respects. She's not alone," Maya said.

Late that evening, while we were busy arranging our beds for the night, we heard the gate flung open, and a voice hushing the vigilant, but not overly alarmed Venerka. Then a tumultuous call of my father's name—"Mark! Mark!"—rang through the courtyard.

Father, at first apprehensive, then visibly relieved at recognizing Praskovia Ivanovna's voice, shouted back through the window, "Wait! I'll unlock the door. What is it? What happened?" Indeed, we all wanted to know, looking at the distraught widow.

"It's so late, and you ran up the hill, with not one street light," Mother said, concerned.

Praskovia Ivanovna waved away all our concerns, addressing herself only to Father, "I need you, Mark. No! Dima needs you! Come, Mark, Dima needs a shave." She grabbed at Father's sleeve, and started to drag him toward the door.

"But . . . but," Father spluttered, staring at Praskovia Ivanovna in disbelief, "what are you saying? Dmitry Antonovich died! More than thirty hours ago!"

"Dimochka died, true. But his beard doesn't know it! I put my cheek to his, and it's scratching. People will come to pay respects tomorrow and Dima looks like a tramp. He needs a shave!"

Father's face looked pale, a bit gray, his head shaking in protest. "I can't shave the dead. I've never done anything like that. I simply can't do it, Praskovia Ivanovna. And besides, my razor is dull. It won't shave dead skin. . . ."

"Don't worry about the razor. I sharpened Dimochka's razor. Sharp as a saber it is—ready for you," the widow insisted.

"But, Praskovia Ivanovna, you shaved your husband for years. I humbly beg you, excuse me from this duty. Shave Dmitry Antonovich once more. I truly don't feel . . . too well." And Father sort of slumped into a chair, his forehead slightly perspiring in the cool, unheated room.

"I must tell you something, Mark," Praskovia Ivanovna came very close to Father, leaning toward his face. "Dimochka seems to be angry, displeased with me about something. He sort of groaned today, kind of snapped when I touched him."

"But that would be rigor mortis, nothing more," Slava announced, already tucked cozily in his bed.

Praskovia Ivanovna, no more in the mood to beg, dragged Father out of the cottage, while he took me by the sleeve and said, "Come daughter, I'll need a companion on the way back."

We found Dmitry Antonovich changed drastically. His natural majesty, the regal aura about him had disappeared. He had sort of shrunk into himself. Bending low over his face, I stared at him determinedly, forcefully, as if my stare could fill the dead body before me with the Dmitry Antonovich I used to know. And I saw Praskovia Ivanovna was right. Through the bloodless, lifeless skin, a gray stubble was protruding here and there—whiskers not visible when we last saw Dmitry Antonovich. How strange, I thought, that his beard was still growing. Strange and disturbing. Perhaps Dmitry Antonovich was not as yet completely dead?

With unsteady, sweaty hands, Father took the ivory-handled shaving brush, softened it in a bowl of warm water, trying to create some lather out of the brown laundry soap bar that we used for bathing. He began to apply soapsuds to the sunken cheeks, stroking them repeatedly with the softened brush, postponing the dreaded step of applying the razor to those unfeeling features. And when he finally did bring himself to start, the skin was immediately cut.

Praskovia Ivanovna jumped from her chair and, banging her fists on Father's bent back, exploded, "Don't you dare to hurt Dimochka! He suffered enough!"

Father wiped the perspiration from his forehead, and reached into his jacket pocket where he kept his cigarettes.

"Please, Praskovia Ivanovna allow me to smoke . . . to steady my hand."

"No smoking! Dimochka loathed that *mahorka* stink. Give me the razor, you coward!" And taking Father's place, Praskovia Ivanovna began to shave the corpse with self-assured, professional strokes, holding Dmitry Antonovich's jaw firmly in place, and chanting:

"Yes, yes, I know, I know. You grumble still. 'Praskovia this, Praskovia that.' Wait till I join you, my little mushroom . . . my little pickle . . . berry of mine."

Dmitry Antonovich was buried three days later. No clandestine priest could be located, and neither was there a brass band following the casket, because Dmitry Antonovich had always insisted that no tubas, no drums, no cymbals were to disturb his eternal sleep. "Only carry me by the seashore, for the last time," he requested.

The wake for the departed was judged highly successful. Everyone present ate, drank, later even sang and laughed. Praskovia Ivanovna was an excellent hostess—observing, doting. She tried to appear not only calm, but downright gay, the way Russian custom demanded one to be at a wake.

The next day, bent, aged, the widow walked into our courtyard. Venerka rushed to greet Praskovia Ivanovna, licking her hands. And the old lady, patting Venerka's handsome head, leaning lower, whispered hoarsely, as if sharing a secret, "So lonely, doggie. It's so terribly empty without my Dimochka."

CHAPTER TWENTY-TWO

The summer of 1940 we spent quietly, secure in our friendship with Hitler's Germany. Maya energetically pursued her musical studies, having been accepted in the conservatory. When her father learned of his daughter's achievements, he sent her an upright piano as a reward, and as encouragement for further efforts. And Maya did apply herself, spending hour upon hour at the piano, calling the whole courtyard outdoors to "better hear" the pieces she played. I, too, while visiting, and forgetting the chores that had to be done back home, would curl up on her doorstep, soaking in the sounds escaping from under Maya's fingers. How I longed to move back to this courtyard to be near Maya, near Praskovia Ivanovna. The widow often asked me to come and stay with her overnight, and on those occasions, she took out an old, musty-smelling canvas from a storage chest, some cotton and silk thread, special needles, and instructed me in the art of needlepoint. I, to my overwhelming surprise, began almost instantly to needlepoint so well that Praskovia Ivanovna once became very sentimental and said softly, "Ninochka, you are an artist! You must persist and excel! You could create masterpieces and win prizes!"

"But how? With what?" I asked, confused. The canvas, thread, and needles that Praskovia Ivanovna unearthed were all pre-revolutionary items. Such "frivolous" things were no longer produced. Needlepoint was considered to be an outmoded, bourgeois craft of parasites, useless to a Soviet woman. The needlework required time, much time, and only a housewife of those former days could waste so many hours on some useless piece of canvas that would become a pillowcase, or a hanging tapestry, or a book cover or some other unneeded, petty object. Handicraft was not encouraged or promoted and any craft work as a home industry was completely eliminated under Soviet rule.

While I loved to needlepoint, Slava liked to work with clay, to form animal figures, or cups and saucers. For hours on end he would sit and experiment with a piece of clay, changing it out of one shape into another, wrapped in wonder, yearning to discover, longing to create. But people were not encouraged to create on their own, out of their own ideas. Some, like Maya, with musical talent, were fortunate by comparison. Maya was given some freedom to lose herself at the piano with the everlasting genius of Beethoven, the gaiety that could be found in Chopin, or the moodiness of Tchaikovsky. She could improvise and escape.

And in a sense, I, too, was allowed to do so while dancing. Our ballet class was becoming quite a polished, disciplined group. It was made up of twenty boys and girls from the ages of 8 to 14. Many neighboring schools began to invite us to perform; then *kolkhoz* and *sovkhoz* stages were opened to us. Finally, the exclusive vacation sanatoriums, too, asked us to appear.

Returning home early one evening from ballet performance, I found my parents extremely perturbed. Father's face was buried in the morning paper, *Izvestia*, while Mother was scanning the later edition of *Pravda*. Both papers carried an article introducing a new law to the Soviet populace concerning job attendance. Over the signature of Mikhail Ivanovich Kalinin, Draconian measures were made public as to how "parasitical elements" in Soviet society would be dealt with from that day forward—July 26, 1940.

In the previous year a law had gone into effect that denied employment for up to six months to any citizen who was more than 20 minutes late for work. Upon losing employment, one could also lose one's living quarters. The latest decree was much more refined, emphasizing that every "toiling" Soviet citizen was to be punished in varying degrees for arriving late at his workplace. The new law proclaimed that the first time one showed up five minutes late, one would receive a stern warning. The second five minute tardiness was to be met with a severe reprimand, plus a warning. The third occurrence was to be punished by withholding of pay. A ten minute late arrival was to be punished as the five, but the wage deduction was larger.

And then, the axe fell. Anyone arriving at work more than 20 minutes late was to be punished the first time with a most severe reprimand, coupled with an extreme warning and the withholding of a quarter of one's pay for six consecutive months. A second-time offender was to be given a mandatory prison term from four months to a year!

My parents, always very conscientious about their jobs, became even more so when it was decreed a criminal offense to be late. They both enjoyed generally good health and never missed work due to any physical disabilities. Father lost not one day because of drunkenness, so prevalent among Soviet men. Yet, only in the previous few months Mother had begun to suffer from excruciating, nausea-inducing headaches, although she still was at her typewriter without fail. The doctors comforted her with persistent reassurances that the headaches were an ordinary occurrence among women of her age.

"Change of life. Bear with it. The headaches will disappear as suddenly as they appeared," the medical people declared unanimously. In reality, glaucoma was diligently at work.

After the new Kalinin law was introduced, my parents set their alarm clock one hour earlier so as not to be late under any circumstances. Mother's assignment began to involve much new material, primarily connected with those individuals who were late for work. She typed lists of offenders, the stated reasons for lateness, how many minutes they were late, how much pay to withhold, and, inevitably in some cases, which prison they were to be sent to.

In late fall the sanatoriums began to close. Winter set in, mild, unthreatening. January 1941 arrived with pleasant warm weather, accompanied at times by a sudden downpour of spring-like rain. On January 6, the director of the rail center at Sarigol announced abruptly to the employees during lunch hour in the cafeteria, "Today I come to warn you, comrades! To warn you about tomorrow! As our beloved Comrade Lenin said to our great proletarian writer, Maxim Gorky, 'Every religious idea, every idea of God, even flirting with the idea of God is unutterable vileness of the most dangerous kind, contagion of the most abominable kind.' "

His audience, mostly women, knew what the director meant since the next day was Russian Orthodox Christmas—January 7.

The director inspected the mute, blank faces of his audience, and concluded, "So, comrade women, anyone late for work tomorrow by more than 20 minutes—straight to jail! No first time warning! No pay withholding! Straight to jail!"

That evening was exceptionally mild, with a feeling of dampness in the air. Father had left the previous day for Simferopol—a trip he made twice each month to present a detailed report and balance sheet on the condition of the fishery *sovkhoz* to the regional headquarters. We all retired early, our cottage quiet and dark. Mother, perhaps, thought of her past Christmas Eves, of presents under the fir tree, but Slava and I had nothing to think about, since we had never in our lives experienced a traditional Christmas observance. No presents ever came our way on that day. And we all thought of Uncle Shura who had been arrested only two years earlier. No Christmas—new or old, Western or Eastern—existed for us.

In the middle of the night, rain began to fall, drumming on the roof, beating on the window, lullabying us into a deep sleep. When the alarm clock sounded the next morning, Mother jumped up and started to fix our breakfast.

She dressed hurriedly while Slava and I were still at the table. Our school day did not start for another hour. Because it was quite warm the previous evening, Mother decided to put on a light-weight skirt and blouse, a short jacket made of dyed cat fur, and thin-soled pumps. With a bowl of food for Venerka in one hand and her ever-present "in case" bag in the other, Mother departed. Only a few seconds later her desperate shouts reached our ears. Still in night clothes, barefoot, we ran to the window.

"Help! Help!" Mother screamed, lying flat on her back, the dog's food splattered over her fur jacket and skirt.

The ground outside resembled a smooth, endless skating rink. This rare condition was called *gololyoditza* (naked ice). While we slept, the frost had set in following the rain, and covered the ground with this mirror-like sheet of ice.

Slowly, Mother picked herself up, putting as much of the dog's food back in the bowl as possible. She walked toward the dog house as if on stilts—legs stiff, wide apart, knees unbent. Reaching it safely, she managed to put the bowl down in front of Venerka, but then abruptly lost her balance while straightening up, and landed with all her weight on top of the proud animal. Venerka growled in displeasure, not understanding at all her mistress's capricious behavior, and energetically shook herself free. Once more Mother climbed to her feet and step by step, at a pace resembling a turtle, she began to proceed down the hill. A young man passed her in his stocking feet, shoes tied together and thrown over his shoulder. Walking swiftly, arms outstretched like the wings of a bird, he was almost running downhill, gracefully as an ice skater. Mother tried, more or less, to imitate the young fellow but immediately fell directly on her face, shattering her eyeglasses. She again managed to get up, but fell on her side, and this time just lay there, defeated.

While hurrying to dress, I glanced at the clock and gasped. "Slava! Can't you think of something? Can't you make your big brain work harder? Think, Slava! Come up with something! Hurry!" I demanded.

Crushed, Slava's face reflected his helplessness. "If only we brought our sleds from Dulovo with us," he mused. "Mother could slide downhill in a hurry."

"Sleds! Sleds!" I screamed. "Slavochka! Darling brother! Philosopher! Thinker! Listen!" I was aflame with an idea. "In the shed there are some boards—Father's leftovers from building our beds. They could make a kind of sled. Let's hurry!"

By the time we reached Mother with a long, wide board, she had already begun to throw off the air of defeat, and was trying to crawl on all fours down the slope.

"Mama! Here! A board! Like a sled!"

Understanding in a trice, Mother sat on the board, pushing herself with both hands, oarlike, down the hill. But she could not restrain an involuntary cry of pain with each movement, for she had in the very first fall landed directly on the base of her spine, injuring her coccyx. Mother had to change her position and after briefly experimenting, decided that lying on her belly, head facing the bottom of the hill was the most productive way to slide down.

"Goodbye, my cherubs, my saviors!" she shouted in a bright, unconcerned voice, reaching the bottom of the hill in a manner every child could envy.

But inwardly, Mother was very concerned. It was already eight o'clock when she reached the highway leading to her office, still two kilometers away. She missed the train for Sarigol by a few minutes. Slowly, cautiously, she went forward, walking, never stopping. If only not to exceed the 20 minute limit! If only to reach the office before those crucial 20 minutes had passed! She pushed herself unceasingly, in a super-human effort to walk as briskly as the ice allowed, trying desperately not to fall, and if falling, then to get up again and walk, and walk.

And then! A noise from behind, the sound of a motor vehicle. A truck! Heavens! Help was coming! She stood in the middle of the highway, waiting for the truck driver to spot her. When she knew he could see her, Mother put up her right hand, all five fingers open, then the left hand went up, thumb raised. The trucker got the message—six! Six rubles was the price for a half liter bottle of vodka. He stopped.

When Mother entered her office 27 minutes late, the heads of all her co-workers remained lowered; yet she knew that an unspoken sympathy was expressed by those purposely averted faces. She went before the management with a puffed-up and bruised face, broken eyeglasses in her hand, her fur jacket wet and dirty from many falls and the spilled dog food, skirt partially ripped at one seam. In her defense Mother could utter only one word, *gololyoditza.*

The management, serving as court, judge, and jury, after lengthy deliberations, came to a decision, announced by a grave, stern director:

> "Due to the unforeseen, undeniably disastrous weather condition of *gololyoditza,* Natalia Alexandrovna is granted pardon from the designated jail sentence for her 27 minute late arrival on the 7th of January, 1941. Her only penalty is the withholding of her entire salary for two consecutive months."

That evening in our cottage we celebrated. Father, returning from Simferopol, produced a bottle of sparkling Caucasian wine, treating even Slava and me to a small glass.

We had reason to celebrate. Mother survived the outlawed Christmas Day. It was the very first Christmas present Slava and I had ever received. And the very best.

CHAPTER TWENTY-THREE

*S*pring *was* marching by, a bit too fast for Slava and me. We were nearing our final school examinations for 1941—exams I dreaded to face. And when they were over, I—shamefaced—presented my parents with a report card showing that I had passed, but barely. While previously I had been called an "all-around excellent" student, earning straight A's in all subjects, this time many of my subjects received "barely satisfactory" marks. Yet my parents did not punish me in any way, Mother expressing worry over the fact that cod liver oil was harder and harder to get.

"Children need it. Nina is getting listless, phlegmatic. She grows too fast," she fretted.

Yet, I never was listless or phlegmatic while in ballet class. There I glowed, rejuvenated and invigorated by the strenuous bar exercises. Intuitively I knew that I could never reach a big ballet school, because all of them followed Moscow's example, not accepting girls over five feet five inches in height. After all, put the girl on her toes and she will appear to be a giant next to her male partner.

My legs, too, were not finely chiseled creations with delicate ankles and small, high-instep feet. Like Father's, they were strong, straight— not the legs created for classical ballet. I knew it, yet my mother did not. She saw me excel in the regional dances—Ukrainian *gopak*, Caucasian *lesginka*, in the Spanish *flamenco*—and she was pleased. But my dear ballet teacher, Elena Vasilevna was very unhappy watching me steadily adding inches to my height. That year I was already five feet seven inches tall, and growing. Gradually, not wishing to upset me, she was withdrawing me from female roles. She dressed me in boys' costumes, covering my braids with wigs or fur hats, sticking moustaches of all sizes and colors on my upper lip, adorning my torso not in floating dresses and the very short classical ballerina tutus, but in trousers, tunics, and caftans.

Ironically, while my body was being camouflaged by male clothing, my long familiar silhouette began to change—as if to give Elena Vasilevna even more trouble. While before, waist and hips measured the same, and chest followed the flat line of the abdomen, now, imperceptibly but inexorably, my waist began to shrink, become smaller, sending, in my opinion, this migratory flesh below the waist to the hips—rounding, filling them out—threatening to rob me of even male dancing roles. And my chest, that comfortable, familiar chest, began to be invaded by some outsider, demanding to be recognized, accepted. Not that I was unaware of those changes in the female body, observing for years women of all shapes and ages during the communal steambaths in the *banya*. Yet those changes of my own body did not please me. They annoyed me.

Strange, how the populace felt about ballet! While many adored the art of expressing oneself through dance, others loathed it. When *Izvestia* or *Pravda* carried the portraits of grinning prima ballerinas, like Galina Ulanova, or Olga Lepeshinskaya, or Natalia Dudianskaya, posing with masses of roses, and receiving 100,000 ruble prize purses, some people openly expressed their displeasure.

Osip Osipovich, a crusty old retired civil engineer, whose apartment was next to Maya's, reading about the ballerinas, grumbled aloud, "Great Fathers! How is it that those dames receive such rewards? For what? No one is going to persuade me that to lift one's leg high in the air is such a big achievement! Not big enough for the hundred thousand! Tax free, too. Oh, those jumping crickets. They know how to get paid. Whores! All of them!"

Deep resentment, aimed at the prima ballerinas for being on the receiving end of such extravagant, excessive awards was very prevalent. Even my father grumbled, while Mother was enchanted. She still fantasized and remained hopeful about my future in dance.

At the beginning of June, in that fateful year of 1941, we had a group of male visitors—officials from the Crimean capital of Simferopol. They informed us that on Sunday, the 22nd of June, a Crimean ballet olympiad would commence, lasting perhaps a week. All Crimean ballet schools were given a chance to compete for the privilege of being selected to appear in the Simferopol Olympiad. The pupils were in a state of great excitement, and even more so the teachers, while our parents were beside themselves with anxiety.

"Ninochka," my mother implored, "try to do your very best during the Feodosia competition. Yes, yes, I know how tall you are. But even as a boy, try to excel. What? Your chest? So, we'll tie it flat. What? Can't forget that you're not a boy? Well . . . try!"

I had already decided to excel—for my own inner satisfaction. Moscow was out of my reach, I knew, just by looking at some of my slightly built, agile classmates who were truly meant by Nature itself to be dancers. Perhaps one of them would make it to Moscow, but my aim was to reach Simferopol.

Elena Vasilevna began to polish us feverishly, inflaming us with her enthusiasm, her determination. Hour after hour we bent, stretched, jumped, repeating and repeating the steps of each dance until we needed not to think of the next step any longer. This super effort paid off. The judges selected seven dances our troupe performed. Only two were classical, the rest were folk dances, and I appeared in three of them. In one dance called *Polianka* (the meadow) I was onstage as a totem pole! Standing straight, in a tight tricot, I did nothing for a time, holding on to a mass of colored ribbons, while my colleagues were performing a vigorous folk dance. At the finale, each dancer—after a picnic in the meadow—came to me, the totem pole, and receiving a long, colored ribbon, began to dance around me, holding one end of the ribbon, and I the other. About 12 dancers ran around me, expressing joy at the coming of spring. I, in order for the ribbons not to twist, moved my feet imperceptibly, so as to turn with the flow of the dancers. No great artistry was required of me, to say the least. Only my height to represent the totem pole was appreciated.

The second dance was Elena Vasilevna's own creation, which she included in the repetoire more or less for fun. Yet, the deadly serious, stony-faced judges liked it so much, they included it in the winning category. The dance was called *Mesiatz* (the moon), which was danced to a Russian folk melody, "Bright Shines the Moon." In this dance I appeared solo, playing two parts. During the first section, I came out on the stage with slow, graceful movements, garbed in a floor length, ancient Russian gown and head dress. Reaching the middle of the stage, I performed an uncomplicated folk dance, always facing the public. And then, in a *pava* (peahen-like movement), to the opposite side, I disappeared from view, but only for a second or so, immediately reappearing with my back to the audience. My dress was of a different coloration in the back, and instead of the head gear, my head and neck were covered with a mask of a grinning moon. Because skirts covered my feet, dragging a bit on the ground, and long sleeves hid my hands and fingers, the audience was led to believe that a different person executed the part of the moon. It was only at the end, to a quickening, whirlwind tempo, that I abruptly turned to the public once more facing them, and the judges broke out in delighted laughter, shouting, "*Molodyetz! Molodyetz!*" which strictly translated was male gender "Good boy!" or "Courageous, brave youth!" But nonetheless, the compliment was accepted gratefully by females, too.

Again, no great skill was demanded of me. No road to fame would open with this dance. Elena Vasilevna was quite surprised that "Moondance" was selected for the Simferopol Olympiad; it was to liven things up, the men told her.

The third number selected by the judges was a regional dance from the Caucasus called *Lesginka*, reportedly highly favored by Stalin. In it I portrayed a warrior prince courting a Lesginian princess. The princess was attired in a floor-length flowing gown and magnificent headpiece with floating veil, while I wore knee-high, black, glove-leather boots over wide trousers, and a long, dark tunic. The tunic had special breast pockets on both sides in which dozens of dummy bullets were displayed. The weight of the bullets was welcomed since it helped to camouflage my chest. My braids were tucked out of sight under a typically Georgian black lamb hat.

The judges unanimously approved my performance, although they stated frankly to Elena Vasilevna that a "natural" boy would have been preferable. One judge, shaking his head sadly, said, "No one had succeeded in dancing a better *Lesginka* than that girl," pointing grudgingly at me.

The next several days were spent in a frantic swirl of excitement and exhilaration. While Elena Vasilevna continued to polish and perfect our routines, our parents kept polishing, kept perfecting our wardrobe. These costumes were not provided by the state, nor were they available in stores. Most were Elena Vasilevna's possessions from "former" days.

For hours, Father was bent over the leather boots worn in *Lesginka*, trying to mend their fragile, paper-thin, glove-leather soles. How many different dancing feet those boots had served over the years, if only for a few minutes at each performance! The soles were worn out to the point where my toes protruded vulgarly. And those leather boots were utterly unobtainable, irreplaceable. Father succeeded finally in securing the thinnest, weakest spots.

"They'll serve you this time, Ninochka. But they'll fall apart instantly at the end of the Olympiad," he warned. At the end of the Olympiad, I dared to hope, the state might reward me with a pair of new boots.

Saturday, the 21st of June, my parents and Slava escorted me to the Lenin Prospect station to catch a 9 p.m. train to Simferopol. Father's leather suitcase was loaded with my refurbished, refreshed dance wardrobe. We all sat on the bench not far from the one we occupied in our very first hours in Feodosia. And the same prune-faced old Gypsy was scavenging Lenin's Boulevard for new prospects.

Mother pointed to the Gypsy and laughed openly, as if challenging the fortuneteller. Seeing the Gypsy approach nearer, Mother called out, "Gypsy! Nothing, but nothing you forecast three years ago has come true! Nothing! Thank Heaven!"

Passing by without stopping, the brazen Gypsy mumbled, "Tears are coming. A sea of tears, an ocean of tears, for all of us." But her words, once unfulfilled, carried no weight this time.

The air was exceptionally soft, caressing. The evening sky appeared to be a bottomless, huge purple dome over our heads, while the stars were piercing the sky like peekaboos, and sea breezes pleasantly cooled our excited, anxious faces. The town was already filling with arriving *kurortniky* (vacationers). The gay chatter of their different accents, different dialects came from all directions. A wonderfully promising summer had begun.

CHAPTER TWENTY-FOUR

Our dance group was assigned a first class coach, with soft, cushioned bunks spread out for us, with blankets and small pillows to provide more comfort. As soon as we settled down, Elena Vasilevna instructed us quite sternly.

"Children! Now, listen to me with great attention! We must all get a lot of healthy, restful sleep. A lot! We must! Otherwise, we won't perform well. Understand?" She observed our earnest, glowing eyes answering her in the positive. "We'll arrive in Simferopol before midnight. The Olympiad will start at 10 in the morning. We'll be fetched by the Olympiad authorities some time after dawn. The Olympiad will be held in the Pioneer Palace where we will wait our turn. I wasn't given a schedule, so I don't know when our turn will come. But, we must be ready. So, *ptenchiky* [little birdies], sleep tight now. Tomorrow we'll excel. Tomorrow! Now we sleep. Good night!"

And with an all-understanding, "Goodnight, Elena Vasilevna," we were ready to meet the approaching sandman. My parents' last words to me—"Neither feathers nor down!"—rang in my ears for a while, and then warm, soft comfort embraced me. I slept.

All of Crimea, all of the Ukraine slept as securely. The whole Soviet Union was sunk in slumber. And while we slept, "Operation Barbarossa," Hitler's invasion of the Soviet Union had begun.

In a building near the Pioneer Palace at the Olympiad in Simferopol, we were stretched out on comfortable beds, waiting our turn to perform. The bell had rung only a few moments earlier calling us to the cafeteria for the noon meal. Just then, Elena Vasilevna, lifting her head toward the corner where the loudspeaker was located, gave us a sign to remain in our places, saying, "Shhh. Our Comrade Foreign Minister is about to speak."

And then the shaking, stammering voice of a frightened man assailed our ears. What was Comrade Molotov saying? Our country attacked? And even as during the Napoleonic war—the Patriotic War—we, too, will rise to a man, and defeat the aggressors? "The government expresses its unshakeable conviction that our armed forces will inflict a crushing blow upon the aggressor."

Elena Vasilevna, frightfully pale, her eyes widening in disbelief, uttered only one word: *"Wo-o-yna-a-a!"* (War) stretching out the "o" sound and the "a," as if moaning in pain.

The Olympiad was cancelled, and we were ordered to pack immediately. When we reached Feodosia, Slava was waiting at the station, appearing very much concerned.

"What do our parents say about the Germans attacking?" I asked my brother.

"Mother is awfully worried for Father."

"Why?"

"Father going to war . . . maybe being killed," Slava said.

"But, Slavka! Think! How could they take Father? He is old! Fortyeight years old! He'll be 49 this fall!"

But Slava was not dismissing the possibility of Father being drafted. "Besides," he said, "I'll be 16 next year. If the war drags out they'll take me, too."

The meaning of the word "war" was beginning to sink slowly into my carefree, unconcerned brain, still preoccupied only with the personal letdown connected with the cancelled dance competition.

On Monday, the 23rd, one day after the attack upon our Soviet borders, the population of Feodosia found most of the fences plastered with posters announcing the confiscation of all radio transmitters. A few days later, posters demanded all binoculars, daggers, swords and sabers, hunting rifles, typewriters, telescopes, and bicycles and motorcycles.

A bit later, new posters were glued to the fences—all horses in private possession must be brought to the authorities for confiscation. And then one day a militiaman came, instructing Father to bring

Venerka to a specific square at *dom Krestianina,* square of the farmer. The Soviets used dogs in the mine fields, and also began to train them to blow up German tanks. During training, meat was thrown under the tanks, so that the animals would learn to accept the link between the vehicle and the food. Before action, the dogs were kept hungry for several days, then fitted with explosives strapped to their bodies. A detonator was attached, standing like an antenna, its head fitted with a graze fuse. When released, the starving animals ran under the oncoming German tanks looking for food, activating the graze fuse, blowing themselves to bits, together with the tank.

Our darling Venerka was doomed. If we had a radio, or a typewriter, or a pair of binoculars, or even a bicycle, we could have hidden it somewhere, somehow. But how could one hide a lively, energetic dog? Our neighbors would betray us at Venerka's first bark.

On parting with our pet we all wept. Mother, who was not sentimental about animals, was moist-eyed, while our father sobbed unashamedly as he was putting a chain on Venerka's neck. And she, as if knowing the reason for our anguish, stretched out her neck, helping to be chained. Licking Father's hand, she stood still, waiting. Slava and I embraced her head with those all-knowing eyes, stroking her back and her strong, proud neck.

"Let us at least feed her to her heart's content," Mother said, serving Venerka for the very last time a bowl overflowing with our own rations. While she gulped down the food, Mother disappeared into the cottage once more and soon returned with a good-sized bag of dried *suhary.*

"Take it, husband. Who knows when she'll be fed again."

While Slava and I whispered loving phrases to the devoted, affectionate creature, Father, abruptly, to escape the unbearable scene, shouted, "Venerka, come!" and briskly led our doomed pet away.

Hours passed. No Father. Dark came. Still no Father. Slava and I were beside ourselves, and when the hour struck 10, we offered to go into the streets and start looking for him.

"No need," Mother said. "Your father is probably trying to forget himself—to *sabytsa.*"

But it was not like Father to *sabytsa* in a bar or on a park bench sucking on a vodka bottle. When he wanted to *sabytsa,* he bought a bottle and forgot himself at home, at the kitchen table, surrounded by family, supervised by Mother's watchful eye. Besides, in Feodosia there were no *sheltoks*—those egg-yolk yellow bar stores—as in Dulovo.

Midnight came and went. Then, there were hurried steps, the squeak of the gate. Father entered our cottage, his clothes soaked from perspiration. He was dead sober.

Seeing our tense, questioning faces, he said in a tired, but strangely upbeat voice: "Our Venerka is safe."

He described to us how he had started to take Venerka to the designated square, but then decided to lead her into the steppes, behind the mountains, away from the coast, away from the authorities.

"About 30 kilometers I covered, there and back," Father said, and seeing his small vodka glass being filled by Mother, accompanied by a plate of hearty stew, he laughed, "Tastes awfully good! Helps to wash away the dust from my throat." A bit later, taking my hand and Slava's in both of his, Father comforted us. "I left Venerka in a little woods with a stream nearby. The *suhary* will last for a while and there are many small animals. In the wild Venerka has a chance, but she must learn to fend for herself."

He turned once more to his plate, but then, as if not able to swallow another bite, Father dropped the spoon and, covering his face with his palms, sat there, motionless.

Slava and I, as if waiting for a signal from Father, began to sob, calling out: "Venerochka, darling Venerochka! Where are you? Don't die. Catch a rabbit, or a bird . . . or something. Just don't die!"

Finally, Mother, her eyes dry, put a stop to our wailing. "Venerka was saved from the mines. A good deed was done. Don't ask too much of life, children. Be satisfied with little. To bed with you now."

She straightened out our beds, patted our heads, and kissed us good night. Only then, while kissing her in return, did I notice that her cheeks were damp and salty.

Things were going badly for the Kremlin. The Germans overwhelmed the Soviet forces by thrusting into Russia so unexpectedly, advancing up to seventy kilometers a day. After only the first few months of war, two million Red Army men were in German custody. Many were encircled and were unable to escape captivity. Others raised their hands voluntarily, seeking to surrender. The Kremlin instituted grave measures with regard to the behavior of Red Army men, giving the commissars and NKVDists absolute power to shoot on the spot any soldier who was caught without personal arms. Even if the soldier was found wounded and had parted with his weapons involuntarily, he was often sent to the rear for further interrogation. Despite such strict disciplinary rules, Soviet soldiers were still surrendering in droves, encouraged in part by the flood of leaflets the Germans were dropping, in which they promised to restore individual and political freedom to the populace. Many of those who wore the Red Army uniform were of peasant stock. Only a few years earlier Stalin had persecuted this segment of the population as a "class enemy," exterminating them by artificially created famine and harsh exile. Now those men were only too willing to raise their hands and surrender to the Germans. The memory of that devastating famine which engulfed the entire country in the years 1928–32 was still frightfully real. Although the famine affected primarily the "black belt" of Russia, claiming the lives of three million children in the Ukraine alone, it spread to all corners of the country, reaching Dulovo as well.

Slava and I during that time often lullabied ourselves into sleep with repetitious begging for "just one *suhar* . . . just a crumb of a *suhar!*" Neither candy nor apple, nor even a chicken leg inflamed our imagination. Just to suck on a *suhar*. . . .

Stores sprang up in all major cities of the Soviet Union, stores called *Torgsyn* ("torg" meaning trade, and "syn" an abbreviation for syndicate). In those trade syndicates gold, silver, and other precious metals, precious stones and jewelry, gold watches, gold and silver icons, oil paintings with famous signatures were negotiable. All were exchanged for food coupons. The nearest *Torgsyn* to Dulovo was established in nearby Orehovo-Zuevo, where Dulovans dragged their intricately carved, much-cherished walnut chairs, ivory inlaid desks and headboards, their sables and minks and silk oriental carpets, their samovars. Small items such as coins, jewelry, and icons were brought to a *Torgsyn* in Moscow where one hoped to receive higher quality bread or sausage in exchange.

My parents parted with good oil paintings Father inherited, along with his collection of old Russian coins. They turned in their gold pocketwatches, all jewelry, Mother's Persian Gulf pearls. Every icon— some in Father's family from pre-Nikon times—one by one were eaten away. Our parents also had the gold crowns removed from their teeth, and still Slava and I grew weaker, more listless. Not one egg, not a glass of milk passed our mouths in the year 1932. Lice covered Slava's and my scalp, not touching our parents though. Our heads were shaved but lice infested our clothing, sucking on our blood as if it was tastier than our parents'. Foot-long, dark burgundy worms began to crawl out of our bodies, usually at night, while in bed. At first Slava and I screamed in fear, calling Mother, who took the worms by their heads and pulled them out of the way. Later, not being afraid of those parasites any longer, we ourselves pulled them out.

When Mother brought us to our physician—Moisey Grigorevich—he listened to her attentively, stroked our heads and helplessly spread his arms.

"Poor children. Their bodies are crying out for fats, for protein. Those worms. . . . Strange, I see them attack starving people, just as lice, and disappear when one's gut is lined with at least some fat." And to Mother's half apology, half explanation that she kept our bodies very clean, the doctor waved his hand: "No, no, dear Natalia Alexandrovna. Don't feel shame. It's not your fault. Try to go to Orehovo-Zuevo's *apotheks*. Or better, try Moscow's. They might provide you with some cod liver oil. I can't get it in Dulovo. Dose your little ones with that stuff. Perhaps . . . perhaps they will get better soon."

But things were not getting better. And one day at the end of 1932, nothing was left to turn in to the *Torgsyn* for food. Our samovar was rejected—not enough silver content. So my parents took off their much-cherished gold wedding rings. Mother walked home with seven loaves of good Moscow bread in her bundle, while Father—since his ring was bigger, heavier—carried nine loaves. Marching toward home from the railroad station, Mother silently wept, from time to time looking at her right hand, fourth finger, where Russians wear their wedding rings. The finger was empty, robbed of the "till death do us part" ring. And while she wept, not uttering a sound, Father comforted her, near tears himself.

"*Nichevo. . . . Nichevo,*" he kept repeating softly. "It's nothing, Natashinka, nothing."

But to Mother it was not nothing—it mattered terribly.

CHAPTER TWENTY-FIVE

Feodosia began to prepare for the worst. All sanatoriums emptied almost overnight, extra trains rushing the privileged patrons back to their homes and duties. Local Party members began to evacuate their families to safer areas. All able-bodied Feodosians were organized into digging squads that spent two hours daily after the regular day's work, excavating anti-tank trenches, building barricades, and generally securing Feodosia against possible enemy onslaught.

While Father was digging the trenches to provide his fishery *sovkhoz* with a defense against enemy tanks, Mother, in Sarigol, right on the shore of the Black Sea, was part of a work brigade piling sand into a pyramid-type structure, securing the railway buildings from attack by sea. Every female employee was required to carry one hundred stretchers of sand, sharing the load with a co-worker. Mother returned home even later than Father, totally spent. The supervising NKVDists stood guard over the exhausted women building the pyramids of sand, making certain that the stretchers were fully loaded. "No sabotaging the Fatherland's security!" they yelled.

To build barricades out of heavy damp sand after just finishing a regular eight-hour shift was very hard on a woman's physique. Nursing mothers, to their great alarm, began to lose breast milk and artificial formulas were not available. A great many girls and women suffered a variety of disorders after weeks of such labor; some complained of dropped wombs, others of continuous menstruation, while still others experienced the cessation of menstruation altogether. No one was excused from evening labor for any of those reasons.

The NKVD men and commissars were no longer restraining themselves in their behavior toward the populace, becoming extremely hostile. The distinction between the "they"—the masses—and the "we"—the Party faithful—became clearer than at any time since the revolution. Any pretense of equality was dropped.

"We'll show you!" the NKVDists screamed. "We'll teach you!" And they shook their revolvers in the air forcing the utterly exhausted people to scramble a little faster, struggle a little harder.

"They're afraid," Mother's young stretcher-carrying companion whispered one evening. "They know their ship is sinking." So critical was the situation that all Party members were issued guns in case the need arose to have to defend themselves against the populace.

When schools reopened in August, the German language was dropped and the book showing the apple tree with the attractive German family vanished. Instead, we were shown a series of gruesome photographs that we were assured had been snapped by an objective observer in Berlin. Long-faced, sad people stood inside a meat store, while others waited their turn on the sidewalk. All the shelves were empty. Those waiting looked distraught, children weeping from hunger.

And then, a crow! A fat, black crow was hopping near the crowd. One desperate woman threw herself on the crow, clutched it tightly to her chest, and began to run—evidently toward her home—to prepare a meal for her starving family. But the others, also starving, ran after her, grabbing the bird, tearing it apart. Afraid that the meat would be snatched out of their grasp, the people ate it raw! Under those pictures was the explanatory comment: "THE FASCIST RULERS BRING UPON GERMANY INHUMAN DEPRIVATIONS."

Other photos shown to us at school, depicted masses of sad, downtrodden people, who, we were told, were being punished by Hitler for no other reason than for being born Jews. Turned out of their own homes, they were crowded into rows of barracks, kept apart from the rest of the population in detention camps.

When those illustrations were introduced to us, Maya kicked my foot under the desk calling my attention to a single word she had spelled out on her notebook: "Lie!?" Then the incriminating word was quickly, thoroughly erased. Our young minds were in turmoil. What to believe? If one were to believe in the mistreatment of Jews under Hitler, then one must also believe in the crow being eaten raw by starving Germans! The Soviet officialdom, just three months earlier, was pounding into our heads that Comrade Hitler and his Germany represented a land of paradise, a land of true socialism. And then such changes! Maya and I chose not to believe the illustrations—neither the sickening, graphic crow story, nor the persecution of Jews.

August 18 was the day that truly marked the beginning of the war for our family. A draft notice was delivered while Father was away on his mid-month trip to Simferopol. Mother, on arriving home late that evening, tore open the notice with trembling hands. It ordered the recipient "immediately to report to the nearest mobilization station." It emphasized that the severest punishment would be administered to those who disobeyed.

Father was past his 48th birthday. His internal Soviet passport noted that he had a heart defect. We were sure Father would be excused from military duty. But he was not.

The next day when Father returned home, Mother took a small broom made out of soft tree branches, a bar of soap, a couple of tin bathing basins and said, "Come, husband, I'll help you bathe and scrub your back. Go to them clean."

She took a sheet and secured it to the laundry line, making a tent-like cubicle in the part of the yard where Venerka's dog house had stood. Our parents were alone for a long time, it seemed. At one point, when I wanted to bring some more hot water into the enclosure, Slava held me back, hissing, "You stupid girl! Leave them alone. They need privacy. They're parting, don't you realize? And who knows for how long?"

There was quiet after the splashing, scrubbing, rinsing. Then we saw Father's freshly mended, freshly ironed clothing disappearing from the laundry line.

His soft voice caressing Mother, reached our window. "My poor Natashinka, my faithful spouse. To leave you like this with the children. . . ." His voice broke off, as if choked by tears.

Soon Mother's voice, mellowed by their intimacy, began to speak words never heard by me until then—the words of a prayer? "Our Father, Who art in heaven, hallowed be Thy Name. . . ." Father's baritone voice joined Mother in unison: ". . . and forgive us our trespasses, as we forgive those who trespass against us. . . ."

"Slava," I said for some reason weeping, "they're praying!"

And my brother as if in answer, almost in a whisper, joined our parents, ". . . and lead us not into temptation, but deliver us from all evil. . . ."

So! My parents quietly, privately prayed, and my brother knew a prayer. And I was totally excluded from their confidence. Was it, perhaps, because I still was not trusted following the sugar episode leading to Mother's brutal questioning in Dulovo's NKVD basement, after I so thoughtlessly betrayed her to my teacher?

Yet was I not also praying only a couple of years earlier, at a gathering with hundreds of my peers? We were the Pioneer worshippers under the supervision of the Komsomol priesthood at a festive-holy occasion in a cathedral—the Pioneer Palace. We stood in front of icons—portraits of the gods and saints of our new anti-god religion— Marx, Engels, Lenin, Stalin—and in front of the cross-like symbol of the Communist Party—the hammer and sickle.

Was I not intoning the ultra-modern prayer chant of the new religion?

> "I, a Young Pioneer of the Soviet Union,
> in the presence of my peers, solemnly
> promise to love my Soviet Union passion-
> ately, to live, learn, and struggle, as
> the great Lenin bade us, as the Communist
> Party teaches us."

And instead of kissing the icon, I sealed my oath with the crisp, military-type salute of a Red Pioneer—a zealot of the anti-god religion of the future. And was I not following in this ceremony, by this action, with this commitment the dictates of our Founding Father, Comrade Lenin when he said, "OUR STRUGGLE WILL NOT SUCCEED UNTIL THE MYTH OF GOD HAS BEEN EXTIRPATED FROM THE SPIRIT OF MAN!"

When he could delay his departure no longer, Father crushed Slava and me in his farewell embrace and rushed out of our cottage. I watched him being accompanied down the hill by Mother with a bag of dried bread in her hand, as was done previously with Venerka. War was greedy, robbing me of beings I loved most. Would the war soon lead Slava down that hill?

I wanted to run after my departing father, but instead I ran toward the grape vineyards at the back of our cottage, and crawling through a hole in the fence I hid my head in the grape leaves and the arid, sun-baked soil that was so kind to the grapes, and I prayed. Prayed childishly, ignorantly, trustingly.

"*Boshinka*," I said aloud giving the forbidden God an affectionate diminutive of "little God," not the strict, formal *Bog*. No! *Boshinka* was nearer, easier to reach.

"Darling *Boshinka*," I chanted, soaking the soil under my cheek with tears. "My papa is gone. Taken to war to fight Germans. Papa is no warrior, *Boshinka*—a good bookkeeper, but not a warrior. I beg of You, if You spot a bullet flying toward my father, make him duck. Please! And forgive me for bothering You, *Boshinka*. Many people try to reach You. They beg You for this and for that, but I promise I won't bother You with petty beggings—only with big, important ones. Thank You, *Boshinka*, thank You for listening to me. And so, in the Name of You, *Boshinka*-Father, in the Name of Your Son, in the Name of the Ghost, the Holy Ghost, Amen."

Feeling as if a very heavy weight had been lifted from my chest, I began to rise, wiping my tear-stained, muddy face with the red Pioneer scarf, having nothing else to use.

That Pioneer kerchief and its pledge—to what, to whom? A strange, rebellious thought possessed my whole being. Can I serve two masters? Can anyone serve two masters? Gently I took off the soft, red scarf, my constant companion for so long, and folded it neatly. Then I scratched out a small but deep hole with my bare hands and placed the Pioneer scarf on the bottom of the hole, as if in a grave. And as though it were a real grave, I put back the soil once more and laid a small stone on top, a tiny monument.

There, I thought, in great relief—now *Boshinka*-God will truly watch over my father.

CHAPTER TWENTY-SIX

*F**ather was* taken to a training camp at Dalnie Kamishi, a village about 15 kilometers from us, but we were not allowed to visit with him. While young men were kept no longer than two to three weeks in this camp, and then shipped promptly to the front, Father, perhaps because he was nearing his 50s, remained in Dalnie Kamishi for almost five weeks.

Then, at the end of September, early in the morning, a still beardless fellow in Red Army uniform knocked at the gate, calling out Mother's name.

"Hurry! Your husband wants to see you! Maybe tomorrow we'll all be shipped out. Who am I? His buddy doing him a favor. I'm in town on a chore for our commander. Your old man begged me to let you know."

Without any delay, we all three put on our sturdiest shoes, tieing them for security with an extra string. We took all our available *suhary,* a jar of lard, and brown sugar pieces, and hurried toward the camp. Word spread that many Feodosians were in the Dalnie Kamishi training camp, sending hundreds of women of all ages on the road to the village. Many women had infants in their arms; some women led a flock of four or five children to see their father before he would be shipped to the front. Also in that steady stream of anxious relatives were many fragile, bent, toothless men and women, making their steps with visibly painful effort, slowly but determinedly.

The training camp was encircled by a high wire fence, and within this heavily guarded enclosure were hundreds of freshly turned-out warriors, sprawled on their army coats or standing by the fence waiting for their relatives to locate them. Father spotted us immediately, and ran to the guard.

"My wife and children have come to visit me," he said pointing to us.

"Prove it!" the guard demanded.

Mother, who never left home without her identification card, produced it quickly and we were allowed to enter the enclosure.

Father was unrecognizable! His entire scalp was naked, his moustache was gone, and he looked somehow very young. His crisp, long tunic top was freshly laundered, ironed; the galife-type trousers made Father look as if he were ready to mount a horse and gallop away. The small Red Army man's summer hat sat daringly on one side of his shaved head, and it was perhaps the position of this little hat—its sort of devil-may-care, cocky attitude—that made Father look younger. He grabbed us in a sweeping embrace and led us toward a spot of grassy ground where his long, heavy winter overcoat was spread—a coat that served the Red Army man also as a blanket or a tent. And on that army coat the four of us sat, picnicking.

A couple of hours after our arrival, when the whole field was crowded with the new, untried soldiers and their visiting families, a loudspeaker was abruptly turned on. The speaker was not the smooth, familiar voice of Moscow radio—the fabled Yuri Levitan—but rather one of the local political commissars, with an uncouth, harsh delivery.

"Comrades! Today, the 27th of September, a new law is going into effect in our Soviet homeland!" The whole field was alert. What law? No newspapers had carried it yet. Was it so severe, so frightening, that it had been kept a secret from the general public?

"Over the signature of Marshal Voroshilov, this wartime law proclaims that all persons in the military uniform of the Red Army and Red Navy who make any attempt to surrender to the Fascist enemy will be executed on the spot!"

The speaker halted for a moment. Father tensed, his grip on Slava's and my shoulder tightening. Those words were not altogether new to us. Back on June 29, a similar law went into effect. But what followed was new.

"Comrades! The new law states that every member of the family of the traitor to our Soviet Union will also be subject to punishment. Wife and children of the turncoat will be jailed or sent into exile. The parents, if the traitor is unmarried, will suffer the same fate—that of imprisonment!"

A hush fell. No human voice was heard for several moments. Then, the deafening sounds of the Soviet National Anthem engulfed the field, and we all rose, many heads bowed so as to hide approaching tears and to conceal the deep hatred rising to the surface, into the open.

The Voroshilov law was the cruelest the Soviet citizen had yet encountered. From one end of the land to the other, every family whose father, son, husband, or brother was in the armed forces, was held hostage. There was no excuse for becoming a prisoner of war, no matter that the Red Army man might be severely wounded or even unconscious. One was ordered to die—to commit suicide—rather than surrender, or be called a traitor, bringing down retribution upon the entire family.

Our town was in upheaval, the populace shifting to and fro, moving, evacuating, others arriving in the uniforms of commissars and the NKVD. Only one day after Father's departure for the army on August 19, a proclamation was issued by the government that there existed within the Soviet population a faction antagonistic toward the well-being and security of the Soviet Union. Therefore this disruptive element had to be resettled, by force if need be, in the "depths" of the country, clearing the cities of its "parasitical" presence.

The directive applied to all citizens of German descent who in their internal passports claimed to be German. The NKVDists went from door to door dragging utterly unprepared, surprised people out of their dwellings, marching them toward the Sarigol station where cattle cars were waiting for the deportees. We stood on the sidewalk, watching the unfortunate creatures passing our gate. Erika Karlovna went by, with a huge suitcase and a featherbed, looking neither left nor right. Only last spring she was glowing with enthusiasm during lessons about the land of her ancestors—Germany. She was then following the Party's orders to teach us about the benevolence of the Führer and his National Socialist Germany. Now, following the same Party's orders, she was being marched into exile as an "enemy of the People."

Terrible human tragedies arose out of one specific technicality during this forced relocation of Soviet Germans. Under Soviet law, a child of a mixed marriage was allowed to choose his nationality at the age of sixteen when he received his internal passport. Consequently, on that 20th of August many families were forcibly split up and separated.

In our neighborhood lived a family by the name of Muller. Mr. Muller, a carpenter, was German according to his passport, while his wife of mixed parentage chose to register on her passport as Russian.

Their older daughter was registered as German, while the younger one who just the previous year turned sixteen, registered as Russian. We watched Mr. Muller with his elder daughter being led away by the armed men, while Mrs. Muller with the younger girl ran after, pleading to be taken along so as not to be separated.

"We are as much German as they are. We are all Germans, the whole family!" Mrs. Muller pleaded. "Take us! Take us! We don't want to be separated!"

The guard barked, "Where is your proof? Show me your passport with the word German and I'll shove you out of here in a hurry, you damned Hitlerites!"

But she could not produce a passport with the word German on it. Thus, husband and wife were torn from each other and two sisters dragged in different directions—the family unit destroyed. The radio that evening proclaimed that Feodosia was "cleansed of the parasitical Hitlerites."

CHAPTER TWENTY-SEVEN

*F**eodosia was* being deserted at an accelerated speed by Party members and their dependents. Jews too began to depart—mainly the Party members and not the rest, who were called by the people "our Jews." While 3,000 Communist Jews left, about 1,000 of our Jews remained in Feodosia, my friend Maya among them.

On October 29, 1941, Mother was called to the office of the director of railway operations in Sarigol, where she and all her co-workers were handed back their Soviet internal passports and told that they were dismissed. The railways in our region ceased functioning.

Shortly after Mother returned home, Maya and Praskovia Ivanovna ran into our cottage. Puffing from hurrying up the hill, Praskovia Ivanovna called out to us, "Pack! Pack! An apartment is empty in our courtyard! Yes, Natasha!" she exclaimed trying to convince Mother. "Pack now—let Slava bring my two-wheeler." The Krimchaki just left their apartment. . . ."

Krimchaki and Caraimi were two separate peoples living in Crimea, who at one time were all Hebrews, but split over religious differences. The Caraimi, claiming to speak a tongue closest to the ancient Khazars, recognized no Talmud, only the teachings of the Bible and the Laws of Moses, and worshipped not in Hebrew but in their own language. They also recognized no rabbis. The Krimchaki, recognizing rabbis, likewise did not profess their faith in Hebrew but in Turkic dialect.

It turned out the only Krimchaki family living in Praskovia Ivanovna's courtyard had at the very last moment decided to accept the Party's offer to evacuate. This family of seven occupied a "double" apartment—that is, instead of a single stall, two were united into one dwelling.

While we were still dazed at the sudden prospect of moving back to Karl Marx Street, Maya shouted, "I stationed my grandmother on the porch steps to guard the apartment for you! How long do you think she'll sit there?"

In three frenzied trips, loading and unloading the two-wheeler, Slava and I, with Maya's help, moved all of our belongings into the new apartment, not believing our luck at such spaciousness—even a wall between the rooms! A real wall to give us all a bit of privacy. A black, wonderfully efficient *burshuyka* was left behind too. A sink with a porcelain pot hanging over it, constituted a "bathing corner." Slava and I had our cots arrayed in this part of the apartment, while Mother arranged her bed-divan in the main room where a nice large window brought much light and sunshine into the room. The Krimchaki family had left behind a rectangular oak table that seated all seven of them, and an Oriental carpet, covering much of the wooden floor.

"What do we do about those things?" Mother asked, afraid she might be blamed for some unlawful deed.

"Nothing you can do now," Praskovia Ivanovna declared reassuringly. "If they come back, then we'll worry about it. Besides, before they left, I offered them some rubles. The man laughed and said to put the rubles on the nail in the outhouse!"

The next morning, with the sun just beginning to rise, a strong, persistent knock on the window woke me out of deep sleep, induced by hours of scrubbing and cleaning on the previous evening, bringing our new home into tip-top condition.

Maya was staring at me through the freshly washed window glass, shouting, "Our troops are retreating! People are plundering! Let's go!"

"Go where?" I asked, standing on the threshold by the open door. While I was asking this silly question, I saw men and women running out of our courtyard with all sorts of containers, and some ran just to follow the others without anything in their hands. I awakened Mother and Slava and, dressing quickly, we shouted to Praskovia Ivanovna through her veranda window, "We're off! To the mill! Follow us! We're taking the two-wheeler!"

The mill was about one kilometer from our place. Already hundreds of people were in front of us, all headed in the same direction, all hoping to secure the most important item in our diet—bread. Some early birds even then were on their way back with 70 kilo sacks of flour. Some, the very strong ones, carried the flour on their bent backs, or else the sacks were piled on two-wheeled carts that were groaning under the weight of 300 or 400 kilograms of flour. Others were dragging their booty along the ground, a few steps at a time.

Inside the huge, dome-like granary, people behaved wildly, some screaming to one another across the entire building.

"Anka!" A bearded, middle-aged fellow was booming at the very moment we entered the mill. "Anka! What've you got there! White? No-o-o! Get rye! What? Just white flour? Drop it! Keep looking for the dark flour!" Then, giving up shouting instructions to his wife, he produced a long, dagger-type knife and slit a sack of flour closest to him. "Crap! More blasted white!" He jumped to a different pile and did the same thing—splitting the bulging bags with his knife, looking for dark flour since his wheelbarrow was already loaded with sacks of white.

Many others were doing the same thing, so that hundreds of sacks were slashed, their contents spilled, before the desired color was located. In a very short time the floor of the mill was covered with flour half a meter deep and people looked like giant, awkward herons, slowly walking with one leg sinking in the flour, while the other was being lifted high in order to make the next step.

We had no containers of any kind in which to carry the spilled flour. We had to crawl on our knees, digging under the ever-thickening layer of precious flour in order to come across a full sack. Our fingernails were broken, bleeding in the process, leaving red splotches on the surface of the flour, but there was no stopping us. To be able to have a supply of bread for several months in the future was the height of security. Survival itself seemed to be sewn into those sacks of flour.

An hour passed. Outside, on the two-wheeler guarded by Praskovia, lay three sacks of flour, what color we as yet did not know. While Slava dragged this treasure back to our courtyard with Praskovia Ivanovna steadying the load, we continued to dig. By the time Slava returned, two more sacks were ready to be loaded.

"Enough! Five sacks. One for Praskovia Ivanovna, two for Maya's family, two for us," Mother declared while hurriedly leading us out of the mill, pointing to a man all bedecked in black leather. The figure stood still for a while—high above us—like a statue erected on the beams of the ceiling, looking down on the plundering public. Then he moved his arm, and a shot rang out.

"An NKVDist! That bastard! He'd shoot us for less than a kopek! Let's run!" And many people quickly dispersed, but even more remained, bent and sinking in the deep layer of spilled flour, still trying to fill their containers.

The NKVDist produced a hose and pointing it at the people below, screamed, "You treacherous vermin! Instead of fighting the Hitlerites, you plunder! Mother f-----s! I'll show you what to do with this stinking flour! Neither the Germans nor you will get it! Turncoats!" And the NKVDist began to spray the flour with kerosene.

The people broke out in a wailing, sobbing chorus, imploring the man not to destroy the flour, not to doom the civilian population to starvation. But at this point, more NKVDists arrived to help their comrade and shots began to ring out from all directions, with all those still inside fleeing in panic to the exits. The mill very quickly billowed in flames. Many people sat on the ground nearby and wept, rocking back and forth in anguished frustration.

With the flour divided and stored by the wall behind our hanging clothes, and refreshed by a glass of tea, Maya and I, together with Mother, stepped outside our courtyard. Seeing a group of running women, we asked simply, "Where?"

"To the canned goods warehouse! The shelves are still full!" The puffing women did not slacken their pace while answering us, and we, wasting no time, energetically tailed them.

When we arrived at the storehouse, the shelves were being emptied with frightening speed, but not in a productive way. All the items were preserved in glass jars, since tin cans still did not exist on a wide scale in the Soviet Union. People who arrived before us, coming upon jars that did not meet with their approval, flung the containers on the floor, so that by the time we entered the warehouse, a pudding-like substance covered the floor and reached to our ankles. The broken glass made it dangerous to take a step.

There were jars containing sweet cherries, stewed tomatoes, green peas, pickled eggplant. Others held macaroni in tomato sauce, some offered pickled pigs' knuckles. Our footwear was bathed in a mixture of those rarely obtainable foods. We stood there, ready to cry from frustration, watching helplessly as a group of youngsters, all self-restraint cast aside, climbed like acrobats along fully loaded shelves shouting to one another: "Vanka! Look for macaroni! Look for meat! Eggplant? Oh, that's garbage!" And with that, the hooligans, wrinkling their noses at items not to their taste, threw jar after jar to the floor, seldom looking as to where the rejected loot would fall. The containers were quite heavy, each weighing close to one kilogram. In order not to be hit on the head, we had to dodge quickly and in the right direction.

One fellow spotted Maya's pretty braided head and shouted, "Hey, *kukla* [doll]! You there, with that thick snake of hair! Want some meat jars? Any jars? Okay!" Turning to his buddies, he instructed, "Hey, fellows, let's throw a few jars to that girl there—the ashen one—and that long-legged heron next to her," meaning me.

Maya brought home ten jars of ratatouille, while I was thrown ten jars of pigs' knuckles. Mother, separated from us and stumbling upon a dark, out-of-the-way corner not yet discovered by the scavengers, dragged home 25 jars of macaroni in meat sauce.

The town was being robbed of its life-sustaining food resources. Every person knowing that food would not be distributed to the civilian population remaining behind, plundered. Like some animals in the wild do before a change of season, so, too, Feodosians tried to supply their nests with needed nourishment against the scarcity they knew was coming. Everyone passing our gate that day was loaded in the fashion of coolies, bending over double under booty. Some carried sacks of onions, others bags of processed sugar or—so precious in Crimea—potatoes. People continued to stagger by, bowed under the weight of boxes of *mahorka*, sauerkraut, perfume, or feta cheese—all depending upon what storage they happened to uncover—knowing that every item found would have bartering value later on.

We stood by the gate feeling as if we had put in a good day's work. A very rewarding day, we thought, acquiring flour and canned food, not feeling envious toward those still filling the street loaded with goods. Then we saw two women nearing our gate carrying a rolled-up Persian rug of huge proportions. "The Hotel Astoria is being stripped!" the women announced, answering our inquiry about the rug. That beautiful place, formerly open only to a very few chosen people, was now open to us. We hurried over.

When we arrived, we saw people running through the hotel's revolving doors dragging pillows, mattresses, chairs, tables, sofas, mirrors, potted palm trees, bundles of towels, and bed linens. We entered the vestibule facing a mirrored wall. One group of youngsters was smashing the mirror with rocks, while another gang tried to reach a massive crystal chandelier. As we stood there, feeling genuinely sad at seeing such rich beauty being senselessly destroyed, one young vandal shouted to Mother, "Hey! *Baba!* Want this piece of mirror? No stinking bolshevik *baba* will need this mirror any more! Hey! *Zaplia*

[Crane]! Don't you want a mirror? Better than looking into the samovar! Ha! Ha! Ha!"

We ignored the rascal, especially since addressing a woman as *baba* was quite disrespectful. We continued inching nearer to the marble stairs, planning to go to the second floor, when a shot was fired, sending the vandals out of the building. We expected a commissar or NKVDist, but instead, a stocky, bearded man appeared at the top of the staircase. He was dressed in soiled, unkempt civilian clothing, holding in one hand a long leather whip, in the other a revolver. He was very drunk.

"Bandits!" he shouted, his tongue thick, slurring. "Goddamned Russians! Wait till the Germans come! Our own people will soon be here! We'll show you, Slavic swine!" He spoke in heavily accented Russian, as if he had spent his whole life in one of the Crimean villages occupied wholly by people of German descent. He continued to yell, frothing at the mouth. "I survived! Survived! In the caves! In the mountains! Soon it'll be your turn to try to survive! Goddamned Russians!"

An elderly, intelligent-looking woman near us said quietly, "Perhaps our proverb will be proven right."

Her companion asked, "What proverb?"

"The one that says a native tyrant is better than a foreign tyrant."

Her companion disagreed. "One can forgive the foreign tyrant just as a stepmother can be forgiven for mistreating a child not her own. But the true mother?"

CHAPTER TWENTY-EIGHT

*T*he *day* after we provided ourselves with flour and canned food, Feodosia appeared to be calm, deserted by local authorities and Soviet troops. There were no airplanes over our heads, dropping bombs, no artillery shells reaching our town. At rare intervals some muffled, unthreatening noise of faraway artillery fire would reach us, but did not arouse any fear for we had heard various rumors that the Soviets had decided to surrender Feodosia without a fight. The flour mill was still burning, and people were trying desperately to extinguish the flames with all available water and sand. Maya and I, while helping to carry sand from the beach, overheard women talking about *banya* (the steam baths). Despite the chaos, Feodosia's *banya* was still functioning, and we hurried to take advantage of the situation.

The bath-*banya* was very important to our well-being, visited faithfully by us once a week, and more often on special occasions. One did not march to the *banya* empty-handed, but carried a neat bundle containing a towel, a change of clean underwear, sponge, a short, fat broom made out of fresh leafy branches—preferably birch—and a bar of brown soap that was used for everything, from washing one's hair to scrubbing the laundry. Hair shampoo did not exist and a delicately scented fancy bar of toilet soap was such an extravagance that we could only wistfully long for it.

The building housing Feodosia's *banya* was a tall structure with small windows, different from Dulovo's in that it was built of stone. Inside the building all was of stone also—floors, benches, ceilings— echoing the influence of earlier Turkish rule, while Dulovo's *banya* was all of wood, the Finnish influence prevailing there. At the *banya* entrance, an older woman sat at the cashier's booth collecting money for a *banya* ticket. With this ticket in hand we entered a room called *oshidalnaya* (the waiting room), not very large, with benches back to back in rows, and all the walls taken up with very narrow, almost to the ceiling, individual storage lockers. Upon being assigned a locker, we undressed, stored our belongings, tied the locker key to the handle of the tin wash basin, and pulled open a very heavy door leading into the *kupalnaya* (bathing room). This vast room had nothing in it but stone benches lining the walls and a stand in the middle with several sets of hot and cold faucets.

On entering the *kupalnaya,* the clamor of women's voices combined with the noise of dripping, splashing water—echoing and re-echoing off the bare stone walls—was at the first moment disturbing, resembling the roar of a huge seashell when put to one's ear, only much stronger. One had to remain at the entrance a while to get used to the thick, blinding steam, and then cautiously proceed into the center of the room, looking for vacant bench space. Once located, the bench was then vigorously cleaned with a harsh brush located underneath it, and several pails of hot water were splashed over the freshly scrubbed space before occupying it. The bathers would undo their braids and start beating each other's back with soft, aromatic, leafy brooms—"opening the pores." From the top of the head to the soles of the feet one's body was scrubbed, slapped, literally whipped with the leaf broom, while one's hair received its dose of laundering. The young ones squealed with delight at the end of the procedure, splashing cool rinse water on each other. Now, if there was enough room on the benches, a bather could stretch out for a while to "catch one's breath."

There was a third room in every *banya* called *parovaya* (the steam room). In size it was about one-fourth of the main *kupalnaya*, consisting of many steps leading toward the ceiling. The bigger and higher the building, the more steps there would be in the *parovaya*. In Dulovo, one *banya* that could accommodate several hundred bathers had a *parovaya* with 32 steps. With each step the steam became thicker, until the upper steps were utterly camouflaged behind a dense curtain of steam, daring only those with exceptional stamina to enter its realm. I utilized the *parovaya* quite often, but after climbing to the seventh or eighth step, where the steam was already blinding, and gasping like a fish out of water, I ran back to the *kupalnaya* where it seemed cool by comparison.

To many women the *banya* was not only a place to cleanse themselves, but also a place where they could gossip to their heart's content. Information of all kinds was gathered and exchanged there. While the neighborhood waterwell was another convenient place to gossip, the *banya* represented more security. One could not see clearly beyond a few steps and the constant noise of running water made it difficult to be overheard. During the mass terror of 1937–38, the first word exchanged between Mother and our nearest neighbor in Dulovo's *banya* was "Who?" One word only. The name of a friend or neighbor would be the answer to Mother's "Who?" Then a newcomer would ask Mother "Who?", receiving in reply the name of the latest victim. In this manner the whole *banya,* and very shortly the whole town, knew which family was newly orphaned by the NKVDists.

The *banya* supplied information on other subjects as well: who married whom; who had to get married; and who became a Party member—meaning his wife should not be trusted in the *banya* conversations.

One knew right away which wife had been beaten by her husband because of the painfully obvious bruises marking the woman's body. The victim was pitied and comforted while her husband was duly castigated. The thrashing occurred as a rule, on the 1st and 15th of the month—pay days. I had a father who after a few drinks became quite merry, cracking sharp jokes and singing, or he simply retired and slept it off, but many men became angry and violent, taking out their frustrations on their mates. Afterward, the wife ran to the *banya,* where soothed by a couple of hours of steaming and broom "massaging," she exclaimed with an all-forgiving sigh, "Ah . . . the poor horseradish needs to forget himself, to *sabytsa.*" And with that, the pacified wife would leave the *banya* in the best of moods. Her bathing mates, murmuring compassionate goodbyes as she departed, would then say to one another shaking their heads in surrender to the wisdom of the old proverb: "*Lubov ne kartoshka—ne vibrosich v okoshko.*" (Love is not a potato—that could be thrown out of the window.)

While women often fought and argued with each other in their overcrowded living quarters, they did not do so in the *banya,* where the steam and heat were too relaxing for the strenuous activity of physical fighting. Only once did I witness two dark-haired young women of Italian descent pulling each other by their waist-long braids all across the *parovaya* and *kupalnaya,* through the *oshidalnaya,* and suddenly found themselves in the open courtyard, being observed by the bathers in the men's part of the *banya*. They quickly ran back into the *kupalnaya* where a few pails of ice cold water flung over their heads by the superintendent, separated and calmed the women down.

While physical squabbling was a rare occurrence in the *banya*, a more constructive activity was quite prevalent—that of matchmaking. During one *banya* visit, Mother and I seated ourselves on a bench next to a girl in her late teens, accompanied by her mother. A little later, another woman—apparently an acquaintance of theirs—joined them. She looked the young girl over from head to toe in an openly admiring way. "Zina!" The newcomer turned to the girl's mother. "Where on earth have you been hiding yourself of late?"

"What do you mean—hiding? What nonsense are you saying? I saw you only last week at the well," the girl's mother shot back, irritated.

"I somehow haven't noticed your little Galinka. She's grown up! My, my! How everything has grown!" The woman measured the embarrassed girl's chest with her eyes, then her slender waist, her rounded hips.

"Everything grown, you say? Why not? Galinka'll be 18 this month. And besides, what's it to you?" the girl's mother snapped.

"What's it to me, Zinochka? Foolish question! My Petya is ready to take a bride. That's what it is to me! Zinochka, little dove, how about arranging a picnic for the young folks, eh?"

The newcomer had lowered her voice to a very intimate soft murmur, even as the girl's mother held her ground.

"My Galinka is too good for your son. She won't want him."

"Think about a picnic, Zinochka." Her friend, too, was not retreating. "If they won't take to each other, we won't force them." And the determined woman took her new, freshly cut leafy broom, landing it repeatedly on the reluctant mother's wet back. With harder strokes she began to whip the woman's arms and lower torso, "opening the pores." Then both retired into the *parovaya* (steam room) climbing slowly, giving each step a few minutes, until they reached the ceiling. By the time they returned, the picnic date for their children was arranged and the last words of one mother to another were "A good pair they will make—our *ptenchiky* [baby birdies]!"

Many interesting stories came to light in the *banya* that I would not have heard in other surroundings, often concerning the newborn. Horror stories abounded about the unsanitary conditions of maternity clinics, where there were instances of infants being attacked by rats.

While those accounts frightened me for a long time after hearing women talk of them, one story of a newborn baby was different.

Back in Dulovo, during one of our weekly *banya* sessions, while I was sitting on a hot, wet bench, beating my legs with a birch broom, a young, full breasted, obviously nursing mother came in, seating herself not far from us.

Mother shouted to the young woman in a particularly friendly voice. "Luba! How are you, dear? How is your little *pusir?*" *Pusir* could mean a bladder or a bubble. In this case it was a bubble—an affectionate nickname given by Russians to especially chubby infants.

Other women shouted their greetings, wanting to know how Luba was doing. "And your husband—might he burst to pieces!" one bather bawled out, rolling with laughter, not offending the new mother at all, only making her laugh, too.

"My *pusir* is fine," the young woman answered to satisfy the curious group. "He's a strong screamer, that little boy of mine—real strong!"

Women's breasts and bellies shook in merriment, while they hastened to agree with the new mother. "That screaming saved him in the first place!"

All Dulovo knew Luba's story. She gave birth to her first child in the same one-story, outdated maternity clinic that I was born in. It had no other function except to accommodate women in childbirth. Luba's baby, a male, was pronounced dead at birth. Luba, heartbroken, took a last look at her stillborn before her husband, accompanied by a friend, came for the little corpse, to prepare it for burial. The husband was not allowed to see his wife, so as not to infect her with any germs. And she herself would remain on her back for ten days, not permitted to get out of bed at all. Soviet doctors were much concerned over the possibility of the uterus dropping, if the new mother was on her feet too early.

It was bitter cold outdoors—the middle of winter. The baby was naked, wrapped in a discarded piece of a hospital sheet. Luba's husband and his friend walked slowly, each reaching from time to time into his coat pocket for a small bottle of vodka—to *sabytsa*. They discussed the funeral arrangements until abruptly, the new father, overwhelmed by sorrow at his first-born's fate, started to sob. From the darkening sky the tender snowflakes were falling steadily, while a lonely star here and there blinked at him, and the bluish-white blanket of snow crunched under his felt boots, and that little boy, his flesh and blood—dead.

Suddenly, both men were startled by a peculiar noise.

"Frog?" the unhappy father asked his friend.

"Frog? In this frost? Most unusual," the friend commented, and plans for the funeral arrangements resumed with expressions of worry over the price of a casket for an infant.

"My angel. My white angel. For you—a white casket. Nothing's too good for you, little darling boy."

More and more overcome by grief, the young man put the bundle, now thickly covered with snow, close to his chest and in a sorrowful wail, with a few drunken hiccups, began to sing a lullaby to the little corpse. His friend joined in. People on hearing two drunkards bellowing out a cradle song at the top of their voices, peeked through the windows to see who these half-wits could be—these *duraks*.

"Ah! It's not *duraks*. It's Luba's husband. He is carrying his stillborn home." And they shook their heads compassionately.

The men had to walk through a park before reaching their destination. Both sat down on an icy bench for a while, resting. The father soon reached a state of mind unconsolable any longer even by vodka. He embraced the little corpse and began to cover it with kisses, flooding it with his hot, freely rolling tears. While he was so engrossed, the corpse uttered a lusty cry and stirred. Arms, legs, head—all came to life at once! The father, in shock, dropped his son in the deep, soft snow and ran as if from a ghost. His friend, sobering up instantly, lifted the baby out of the snow and wrapping it in his overcoat, chased after the father.

"Hey! *Durak!* Stop running! Your baby is not dead! You hear me? The baby is crying, breathing! You! Half-witted drunk! Come back!" He finally caught up with the father and persuaded him to take his little son into his arms once more. Both men, by now shocked into sobriety, returned to the clinic where the nurse, seeing the previously dead baby alive, began, very unprofessionally, to scream in wide-eyed disbelief. When the doctor appeared, both he and the nurse started to argue with the father that the baby was dead at birth, and that was all there was to it.

The young couple tried to charge the doctor with negligence, but nothing came of it since the doctor was a Party member. Dulovo's local newspaper in commenting on the case, stated that "no harm was done in the end. The baby did not even catch pneumonia during his first snow bath. Strong baby!"

CHAPTER TWENTY-NINE

*F**eodosia was* completely deserted of Soviet foot soldiers. Only trucks full of retreating NKVDists and commissars were seen speeding by. One such truck stopped by our gate. The commissar at the wheel jumped out and ran toward Maya's door. Knocking impatiently, he shouted to Maya's grandmother through the window, "Leave with us! Your granddaughter's father gave us a message to help you get away!"

The old lady came out and, standing on the threshold, said in a dismissing tone, "Go! Go! All of you! May God help you." She extended both arms in front of her body as if forbidding the commissar to come near her.

He, nevertheless, did move closer, and slowly, solemnly, as if spelling his words said, "May your God help *you,* old woman."

"Go! Go!" she still persisted.

As soon as the truck with the commissars sped away, leaving Maya's family behind, people poured out of their homes, strangely animated. "Let's scrub the cobblestones in our courtyard!" someone proposed, and immediately locating a stiff broom, began to do so. Another started to disinfect and "beautify" the outhouse, inside and out. Someone else started to straighten out the gate, while still another began, without being asked by anyone, to walk from window to window washing and polishing the glass with a lot of outdated Soviet newspapers. Others—those who did not visit the *banya* as we had done—began to heat water and wash themselves in their small apartments, completing the ritual by scrubbing the floors, entrance doors, and porch steps of their dwellings. Freshly laundered curtains appeared on windows. From many apartments the aroma of baking bread began to tease one's sense of smell.

Mother brought out flour and yeast, saying to me, "Ninochka, start making bread dough. Knead it hard for me. I have such a headache, and rainbows in my eyes ... especially my right eye." Mother was very often attacked by these mysterious headaches, but still was not worried, remembering the Soviet doctors' explanation—menopause.

While I vigorously kneaded the dough, Mother watched me for a while, then said, as if a bit embarrassed: "*Dochka ... dochenka....*" She seemed to be at a loss for words, addressing me with the tenderest diminutives for the word "daughter." "Nina, *dochenka* ... you are pretty, very tall. You look eighteen." I continued to knead. "Germans ... they're soldiers away from their womenfolk. Who knows how they'll behave toward us? Try to be very, very discreet ... unnoticeable."

"Mama!" I interrupted. "How can I be unnoticeable? My head is above everyone else's! When I try to hide behind others I stand out like a telegraph pole!"

Mother still persisted. "It's all right to be tall, *dochenka*, but. ...." She looked at my chest that wanted to proclaim my adolescence, and became more direct. "Let's tie your chest flat." Interrupted by my moan she quickly abandoned the idea. "All right! All right! No tying your breasts, but, please, wear my brown blouse. It's cut very full. Here! This one! It'll hide you. And your skirts are terribly short, revealing. This skirt of mine ... take it and wear it until we know how the Germans will behave."

I kneaded with double zest, pleased not to have to flatten my chest as I had to do so often in ballet, trying to pass for a boy.

After the dough was ready, and put on a tray to rise, Mother said, worried, "Not enough bread for us and for the Germans."

"For the Germans?" Our gorgeous, fresh-baked bread would be shared with Germans?

"*Dochenka,* it is an old Slavonic custom to greet guests with a loaf of bread and salt."

"Mama!" I made a step backward, away from the dough, away from my mother. "The Germans are not our 'guests,' they're invaders! Fighting men! They might already have killed Father!" I abruptly burst out in tears. My dear father, where was he? Some German soldier, right now, while we're baking bread, might be putting a bullet in Father's chest. And I! I must knead the dough to give that German freshly baked bread—bread that symbolizes the mother earth, and salt—life itself. Then some German will stuff his mouth with our bread, while earlier perhaps, he was killing my father.

I was furious with Mother. "On the one hand, you order me to tie my chest! On the other, you order me to make bread for . . . for our 'guests!' " I protested fiercely, shoving away the unfinished batch of dough.

Mother sat on her cot, hands folded in her lap. "*Dochenka,*" she began, very quietly, a bit sadly. "So proud you are, so naive and direct. Ninochka, child, in order to survive life's upheavals, you have to learn to . . . to bend with the prevailing wind."

"To bend with the prevailing wind?" I repeated skeptically.

"Yes! Like the cattails in the swamp in Dulovo. Remember? When we dug to make *torf*, the breezes would come and bend the cattails. Don't you remember? You always liked to look at the tall, agile cattails. Well, *dochenka*, if those cattails didn't bend, didn't sway with the wind, they would've been snapped off—broken by the power of the wind. Perished. And so it is with life. We must bend too. No, no, *dochenka*, not to beg. What? No! Not to fall on our knees. What? Oh, Ninochka, not to turn into crawling worms. You express yourself so graphically! Only bend a little . . . survive." Mother, covering her face with both palms, sighed, "If only your father was with us. So frightening to be alone—no one to lean on." She remained withdrawn, silent for much of the day, while I, recalling the long, slender cattails gracefully bending under the prevailing breezes, with renewed energy kneaded the bread dough.

I'll bend some, I decided. But not much.

The next day—Monday, November 3—was clear, warm, with spring-like weather still lingering. By early afternoon our courtyard resembled a bee's nest, swarming with excited tenants. Our street and the street parallel to us were both crowded with rows of people standing shoulder to shoulder, as far as the eye could see. Several hundred faces greeted mine, when I found room enough to squeeze between the neighbors. Mostly they were animated faces—some laughing, some jesting; others appeared as if thunderstruck, eyes wide open in wonderment. Several very old people stood in silence, but with their lips moving—in prayer, I surmised.

Were all these people wishing to bend with the wind so as to survive? And if that was all it took to survive—to dress nicely, to have children hold a few chrysanthemums in the hope of lightening the yoke, softening the oppression—why then, had the same people never before, never in my life's time, behaved in this fashion? Why, for instance, during the May and October revolution parades, did it take two armed militiamen to "visit" every dwelling and chase people out to show their loyalty and devotion?

While we all jostled for position on the sidewalk, a former cavalryman, Osip Osipovich, was stretched out on his belly right in the middle of the deserted highway, his ear glued to the roadbed.

"Osip!" people called out from time to time, bending over his prostrate form. "How far? What do you think? How far away are the Germans?"

Until midafternoon Osip kept reporting no hint of movement. Then, at about three o'clock, he jumped up shouting, "Prepare yourselves, friends! They're near! I can hear the wheels . . . only about five kilometers from us and moving fast now!"

People started to shout, "Germans! The Germans are coming!" Some were weeping, jumping, laughing, all at once. "Our liberators are coming! Thank God!" Some fell on their knees right there on the sidewalks, on the road, and for the first time in a quarter of a century began to pray openly, unafraid.

Maya and I stood still and stiff, shaken by this unfamiliar emotional scene that led almost everyone to kneel. Even old Praskovia Ivanovna gracefully lowered herself to the ground, praying. What to do, I wondered? Fall on my knees? Give thanks?

Just then Slava's hand grabbed me by the sleeve. He was not standing with the rest of us, but had been sitting all by himself on our little porch, sulking. When he noticed my knees ready to bend, he leaped up and tried to prevent me from kneeling. "Don't be stupid!" he hissed in my ear, dragging me toward our steps. "Sis, remember Dmitry Antonovich when the three of us were alone—how he talked about the October revolution? How he had hoped for a change in Russia? No Czars . . . democracy. He told us, 'It was a *false* dawn. The revolution brought a false dawn.' Remember? The revolution didn't liberate anyone."

"So?"

"So, the Germans aren't our liberators, either. They're bringing nothing but another false dawn. And you, like a fool, ready to kneel, to thank God."

I looked at the eager faces of my neighbors, all in an exuberant, hopeful mood, and shot back at my dear brother, "You're just a born pessimist! That's all you are! Look at Praskovia Ivanovna. I bet Dmitry Antonovich would be kneeling, too, if he were alive!"

Then I heard Maya and Mother shouting, "Nina! Hurry! The Germans are near! They're coming! We can see them!"

I ran toward Maya, while many around us began to shout, "Hurrah! Hurrah! Germans are coming! Germans are coming!" Many started to run toward the approaching army, Osip Osipovich in the lead. Maya grabbed me suddenly by the sleeve of Mother's ugly brown blouse, and whispered close to my ear, so that others would not hear.

"What if the rumors are true? You know?"

I thought at first she meant the rumors about German cruelty toward Jews, but she interrupted, impatiently.

"I mean . . . breasts! Young girls' breasts!"

I stared at her, motionless. The reports that Germans were cutting off the breasts of virgin girls, salting them, and eating them, was widespread and persistent, yet discounted by our elders. But then how could one be sure? Perhaps this time our elders were utterly wrong. Maya and I ran back to our apartments, and a few seconds later reappeared with bulky old shawls covering our upper torsos. The older girls seemed to have no fear. Our neighbor in the next apartment, 19-year-old Nadia, was very brave. She was of Greek descent, with the lush figure of a grown woman, and she stood there unafraid in a tight, green sweater. She had a pretty, oval face with green eyes and curly, black hair. But it was not her pretty face that interested us. It was her heavy, pear-like breasts, very obviously unrestrained by any undergarments, protruding through a thin sweater as if wishing to burst out of their confinement.

"Let's stick close to Nadia," I whispered to my friend, convinced that even if the rumors proved to be true, no one would notice us two next to that beautiful, full-breasted girl.

A noise, thought to be a shot, was heard coming from the next block, followed by a spectacular flare directly over our heads. Immediately a very large detachment of motorcycles zoomed into our neighborhood, piloted by men in unfamiliar uniforms with strange-looking headgear. They all seemed to be concentrating on the road ahead of them, not paying us civilians much attention. "Scouts," Osip Osipovich informed us. Every few blocks the scouts would fire another flare, letting their comrades following behind know that it was safe to proceed.

After the motorcycles, columns of tanks began to crawl into our view, with young men atop them—some sitting, some standing, many taking off their heavy headgear to be more comfortable. A mass of grenadiers marched behind the tanks and people started to throw flowers toward them, some mothers shoving their youngsters forward to approach the huge tanks and push wilting chrysanthemums into the hands of the Germans. People shouted in broken German the only word they had memorized.

"*Willkommen! Willkommen!*" Welcome!

The tank troops responded graciously by shouting back in broken Russian, "Russky our friends! Bolsheviks kaput!"

I waved for Slava to join me, but he remained sitting at the porch step. How I pitied my brother. His pessimism was uncalled for. There was no chance those good-looking, good-humored Goths were bringing us a false dawn. If only Slava could be made to see it.

How the soldiers carried themselves! As if they were born in uniform! What discipline! And how clean they looked! Crisp and neat, as though they had just stopped at the seashore and taken a quick bath in order to face us at their best.

The Feodosians carried their small trays with bread and salt to the marching soldiers, some older folk bowing in the old Slavonic fashion, bending from the waist, voicing their greeting by saying, "Welcome to Mother Russia, in the Lord's name."

Praskovia Ivanovna stuck a tray in my hands with a fresh loaf of bread and a container of salt, instructing me to offer it to a group of approaching soldiers. While I debated within myself what to do, wanting genuinely to believe in our liberation, yet still hearing Slava's gloomy words of a false dawn, a young, straw-haired officer drew near our group, moving confidently toward the tray I held.

To make certain I understood him, the officer spoke in clear slow German. "Fraulein, may I?" He reached for the bread loaf, pinched off a piece, sprinkled a bit of salt over it, and ate it with a solemn expression.

"Thank you," he said, his face still serious. He bowed, first to the older people, then to the rest of us. The other soldiers in his group followed their officer's example, accepting our bread and salt. Older people wept openly, overwhelmed by the apparently genuine friendliness and good will of the occupying army.

Maya and I were given permission to walk to other neighborhoods, leaving the pretty Nadia flirting with the blond officer. We covered street after street, block after block, and what our Karl Marx Street had done, so it seemed, had every street in Feodosia, with every gate crowded by the inhabitants greeting the Germans with childlike trust.

When at the onset of dusk, we returned to our own courtyard, Maya's grandmother took her by her young, slender shoulders and said with the same naive trust which permeated our whole town that day, "Nice fellows, those Germans, Mayichka. No need to worry any longer."

CHAPTER THIRTY

*T*he Germans were settling down in Feodosia, occupying the villa-sanatoriums along the beach, providing their wounded with pleasant quarters to help them recuperate from battle wounds and fatigue. German medical personnel established a field hospital in the freshly scrubbed and disinfected old synagogue, which, under Soviet rule, had been functioning as a nightclub. The Germans also took over civilian housing that was spacious and attractive. Inevitably, an officer very politely "asked" Praskovia Ivanovna to move into the veranda, while he occupied the main room.

An older lame man, reportedly of German descent, was presented to the populace of Feodosia as the mayor, and he very diligently proceeded to bring law and order into the occupied town. At once he began to hand out daily rations of flour which, even though it smelled of kerosene, was desperately needed by thousands who had not been successful in providing for themselves as we had done. He started to disinfect and purify water wells purposely polluted by the retreating NKVDists. He was also able to extinguish the stubborn fires set by the Reds, which blazed up sporadically in the mills, stores, factories, and government buildings. People fluent in German were recruited into clerical jobs at German headquarters, or as interpreters, receiving pay not so much in money as in food.

The Moslem mosques were cleansed, purified, and reopened to the faithful, as were the Christian churches. Practically overnight, the bazaar plaza was turned into a truly capitalistic enterprise. Because rubles were of no value, people began to cart to the marketplace things they reckoned they could barter. Men and women also began to advertise their particular talents. Seamstresses appeared in droves, carpenters walked from door to door, and shoemakers were welcomed with shouts of delight and relief at every dwelling. These occupations had all previously been forbidden to function, except under state supervision. And Jews—"our" Jews—too, advertised their readiness to give instructions in the German language and in music. Some Jews registered with the German authorities as experienced watchmakers and cobblers. Tailors came forward offering to mend and repair the Wehrmacht uniforms.

The new mayor—or, more exactly, the first mayor since under Soviet rule no such position as city mayor existed—opened the schools almost immediately, and many Jewish teachers registered to resume their careers in music and in German. Almost magically vulgar graffiti disappeared and vile words dropped out of people's everyday vocabulary. The word *Tovarich* was forgotten overnight. Instead, the respectful *Gospodin* and *Gospozha* (Mr. and Mrs.) made their debut after 25 years of enforced absence.

General Guderian, of the German High Command, on entering Russia wrote:

> "The people look on us as liberators.
> It is to be hoped they will not be
> disappointed."

Three weeks of German occupation passed uneventfully, peacefully. November 20 arrived—a cool, crisp day. Slava was listless, his face flushed, his head aching. He pushed himself away from the oak table and dropped on the cot in the next room. Mother had just covered him with a comforter and went to the stove to fix some broth to give him, when our gate flew open and a neighbor from the next courtyard shouted at the top of her voice, "Females! Hey! Females! Where are you hiding yourselves?" The courtyard was immediately filled with women eager for news.

"What is it?" several voices at once demanded to know.

"Our men! Hundreds of them! At the Sennaya Plaza by the bazaar! All prisoners of war! I'm off. Who knows? My falcon might be there!" With that, the messenger sped away. Mother and I started to follow her.

The booming voice of Praskovia Ivanovna stopped us before we reached the gate. "Natasha! Think! Where are you galloping empty-handed? If Mark is among the prisoners, he must be starving. Take some *suhary,* some lard. I've got some good tobacco in my apartment. The officer pays me for fixing his room."

As we loaded ourselves with a bag of *suhary,* a loaf of fresh bread, lard, and some hard candy, Praskovia Ivanovna returned with a bundle of warm clothes and a package of tobacco stuffed in a woolen sock. She reached into her coat pocket and gently pressed into Mother's hand a golden Russian Orthodox cross. "Put it on Mark, if you find him. To protect him."

The day was quite cool, but sunny. The earth was still dusted with a light frost, but no snow had fallen, leaving the roads dry and easy to walk on. We were not the only ones hurrying to Sennaya. Just as back in September, when the road to the training camp in Dalnie Kamishi was filled with anxious people, so now, the same people were hurrying to the bazaar plaza in hope of finding their loved ones alive, even if a prisoner of war. When Sennaya came into view, Mother and I instinctively increased our pace, as if afraid that those preceding us would take all the prisoners away, leaving us no Father.

Mother started to mutter to herself in a kind of self-hypnotism. "Be there, Mark; be there, Mark; be there."

I, too, silently repeated the same word over and over, "Papa, Papa," as though my call, unheard by anyone, would be heard by him.

A seven-year-old girl holding on to the hand of her practically running mother kept asking: "Papa'll be there, won't he? Won't he? He'll be there, mama?"

The plaza was like an ant hill, swarming with men. Several German soldiers surrounded the field, guarding it, but not very strictly. Mother approached one of the guards and asked if her husband, Mark Illarionovich was among the prisoners.

"Woman, you don't think we know every prisoner's name, do you?" the guard snapped. "Go and start looking for your man. There are many Feodosians out there. If you find him we might release him into your custody. But remember this, Frau, you'll be responsible for him with your life!"

We squeezed into the midst of the prisoners. The wounded, stoically restraining moans of pain, avoided eye contact with us, like suffering, mortally hurt animals do. Blue, swollen from malnutrition, some of the men were in a pathetic state. The ones who were not from Feodosia were withdrawn, uninterested, not expecting to receive any help. All were unshaven, unwashed, some naked to the waist, others without trousers, sitting by small bonfires, inspecting the seams of their tattered uniforms, or each other's scalp.

"Look there," Mother nodded wistfully toward a half-dressed prisoner, leaping up and running to a young woman, embracing her in an unending hug, both weeping with joy.

The guard, on approaching them said to the woman, "Take him! Take him! One less mouth to feed. But don't hide him in case we call him back," and he put his gun near the woman's temple, only half in jest.

We continued walking slowly around the field, looking intently at every man resembling Father in height and age, asking again and again if anyone knew or heard of Mark Illarionovich. At one point we stopped to ask a young fellow, about 19 years old, if he knew of Father.

"No-o, auntie." The boy shook his head sadly, adding with faint hope, "But, if you don't find him, auntie, give the bread to me. Please."

Mother looked at the boy, not much older than Slava, his blue eyes tired, watery, his skin gray, tight, his slight frame sunk into the much too big army overcoat. "When did you eat last, son?" she asked.

"Not one bite in the last two days. I am starving, auntie. Older men don't want to eat as much as I do. I am really awfully hungry." The boy did not take his eyes from the loaf of fresh bread we carried.

"Where are you from, lad?" Mother asked.

"From Ukraine. . . . No one will come and look for me in this town."

Mother, eyes lowered as if to hide her true feelings, ordered me to break the loaf in two and, spreading some lard on it, she handed it to the boy. He sank his short, white teeth deep into the loaf and began to devour it, staring at us wildly, as if afraid we might decide to take the bread back. The other prisoners, seeing that Mother was feeding one of them, surrounded us, pleading, "A crust, lady. . . . Just one crust of bread . . . one *suhar*." Mother gave me a wave, pointing to the bag of suhary.

I opened the bag and began to pass one *suhar* to each prisoner. "There," I advised, "suck on it slowly. Don't gulp it down too fast!" There were only a half dozen *suhary* left when I sternly announced that my father would be as hungry as they were, and only if I did not find him on that field would I divide the remainder of the food.

"All right, girlie," the prisoners good-naturedly agreed, following us in a large group, waiting to see if *suhary* and bread with lard would be theirs.

We seemed to have looked at every face, asked everyone if they knew Mark Illarionovich. By then, there were more civilians on the field than prisoners, all searching, moving from man to man, questioning, walking away disappointed. Dusk was threatening to descend suddenly, as it often does in Crimea, and with the approaching darkness the Germans would chase us away.

"Come, Ninochka!" Mother persisted. "Once more we must circle the field. Let's get deeper—into the very center."

"I was there earlier. No one looks like Father," I said, utterly discouraged.

We went again into the very center of the field, separating slightly from each other, I, walking more briskly than Mother did, trying to inspect as many prisoners' faces as possible. I approached every tall, slim man, erect in posture, resembling Father. All were strangers. By a small, dying bonfire, two men were hovering near the embers, trying to get some warmth. One was sitting, bent, stretching his hands toward the smoldering logs. The other, tall, broad-shouldered, was standing facing the dying flames, his back to me. That back! So familiar! Father? Excited, I pushed through a group of searching women, hurrying to reach the tall prisoner. I knew! I knew that this man was my father! Reaching him, I stood for a few seconds filled with such joy, before lightly touching his shoulder. I was ready to say, "Papa," when the prisoner turned and the word "Papa" froze on my lips. A much younger man, no more than 35, with blue eyes—not my father's eyes—looked at me questioningly. Terribly disappointed, but also embarrassed, I stuttered, "Forgive me . . . I thought. . . . My father is tall, like you. Mark Illarionovich . . . from here . . . from Feodosia." I kept sputtering, starting only then to realize how utterly empty I felt inside, after the bitter letdown of mistaking a stranger for my father.

While I stood there, stammering, the sitting prisoner, who appeared to be dozing when I approached his companion, stirred suddenly and tried to get up. He was wounded in the left hand, the fingers dark, thick like sausages, sticking out from under the charcoal-gray bandage. The man pulled himself up from the ground and made several steps toward me, looking at me intently through the cracked lenses of his eyeglasses. Number 410 was painted on his chest.

He appeared to be about 60, maybe older, his face covered with gray, unkempt whiskers. The man's posture revealed his total exhaustion, as if his waist had no more strength to hold him erect. He stood there, in the wrinkled, mud-covered tunic, his feet wrapped in smelly, damp leggings, an empty, bent canteen dangling from the tunic belt. He took the wounded left hand in his right, as though to help the pain in some way. I felt so sorry for this old man, perhaps also from the

Ukraine, the Urals, or the Caucasus. And he kept coming nearer to me as if he was ready to beg for bread, like the youngster did earlier.

The wounded man was in front of me, bending a bit lower toward my face, taking off his eyeglasses. His huge, dark eyes opened wide. Joy, pain, and tears were in those eyes. Those peculiar color eyes—the color of overripe sweet cherries! Could anyone else on this earth have Father's eyes?

"Mother!" I screamed wildly. "Come!" And still shaking my head in disbelief I stood there—stiff—until a soft, familiar voice, a voice that had changed not at all, reached my ears, my senses.

"Ninochka, *dochenka,* it's me." And he stretched out his arms to embrace me.

"Papa! Papa! My papa!" I sobbed on his chest.

Mother hurried to us, pushing through the crowd. "Mark, darling! My husband!" She stroked his tired face, his hair, holding his left hand in hers, as though trying to share the pain. "The Gypsy—remember the Gypsy, Mark? The Gypsy was wrong! Wrong! Oh, how I was afraid of her forecast, to lose you. Now, all is well. My Mark, my husband, you're back."

And there we stood, surrounded by hundreds of strangers, embracing and weeping, envied by all.

CHAPTER THIRTY-ONE

*M**y father's*** fighting experience was brief and violent. After parting with us on September 27, he was marched to the Perekop Isthmus where the Soviets tried to stop the German army from entering Crimea. A fierce battle ensued, lasting 10 days, accompanied by non-stop October rains. After very bitter fighting, the Germans were victorious, taking 100,000 prisoners, and on October 28, they broke into the Crimean peninsula. Father's unit began to retreat in utter disarray, but not for a moment could Father allow himself to forget about the Voroshilov law, which punished family members for the unpatriotic behavior of their kin in uniform. It was of the utmost importance not to be separated from one's rifle. Even if it was empty, without bullets, the instrument itself had to be in the physical possession of the Red Army man. Otherwise, he was shot on the spot by the commissars or NKVDists as a deserter, or as one who was ready to surrender to the Germans.

One day early in November, the men in Father's unit—all in their twenties, and who called Father *Papasha,* a half-affectionate, half-respectful word for an older man—fomented a revolt within their unit. Evidently, on a previously arranged signal, instead of firing at the advancing Germans, the Red Army men turned on their commissars and emptied their rifles into the men who were "guarding" them in the rear. The young soldiers had not taken Father into their confidence. He could only stand helplessly, observing the fury of the revengeful soldiers. A bullet hit his left hand grazing it deeply—whether it came from the rifle of a commissar or a soldier he could not tell.

That day many men in Father's unit sought out the Germans and surrendered. But Father and six others, not knowing if their dependents were still in Soviet hands, and afraid to expose their families to certain punishment, decided to run from the advancing Germans. For an entire day the small armed band traveled through the fields and through the deserted villages, avoiding both Germans and Soviets. At dusk they came upon a field with several haystacks arranged in a tidy group. A late autumn rain began to fall, chilling the tired, sleep-hungry men to the bone. The soldiers dropped their rifles in one pile and began to crawl into the nearby haystacks.

Father stood off to one side, pondering. Should he drop his rifle? The thought of being able to sleep through the night inside a warm, aromatic haystack was tempting, especially because his wounded left hand was throbbing angrily, sapping his body's strength. Yet something—some inner voice—restrained him from crawling into a warm, inviting haystack.

"Hey! *Papasha!*" a Ukrainian fellow shouted. "Aren't you sticking with us? You need sleep, old man."

Father shook his head, "No, too risky. I'll crawl into a cave somewhere. But not here. It's too close to the highway."

The Ukrainian persisted. "You'll drop dead on your feet before you find a cave. You're gray in the face, *Papasha*. Sleep with us."

Father turned toward the road. "I'll walk a bit longer, maybe meet you fellows tomorrow." And taking leave of his comrades, he headed for the highway. After only a few minutes of walking, rain started to pound on Father's heavy army overcoat, and just for a moment he was ready to turn back, toward the haystacks. Then he spotted a group of thin, undernourished Crimean fir trees directly ahead, and he decided to proceed, hoping to dig a foxhole near one of the trees and rest. His ears suddenly caught the faint sound of a motor vehicle, and soon a covered truck came into view, racing toward Father at high speed. It stopped abruptly and a young NKVDist jumped down from the passenger side. Several more NKVDists peered through the canvas opening at the back of the truck.

"Deserter! Traitor!" the leader shouted, brandishing his gun in the air.

"No, comrade," Father responded calmly, "I am not a deserter. I became separated from my unit, but never separated from my rifle. I am walking on the highway, in the open, not hiding."

The angry NKVDist lowered his gun, disarmed by Father's straightforward words. Then he looked in the direction of the haystacks.

"What's in that field, there? Maybe you were in the hay—hiding, eh?" He laughed coldly. "Mother f------! In every field—the same thing! All the f-----g haystacks full of traitors! That human offal! Like rats, they hide from us in those haystacks."

The NKVDist motioned his crew to follow him. "Let's see if the haystacks are empty!"

Dear God, thought Father, if only his young comrades would hear all that commotion. But, it was too far. If only they would crawl out and reach for their rifles, take a chance.

But his former fighting comrades had no chance. A dozen of the young NKVDists jumped off the truck and each grabbing a bayonet, ran toward the doomed men.

Father stood frozen, his face and body wet not from the drizzling rain, but from the cold sweat of fear. He felt as though he were shouting at the top of his voice, only no one could hear. Lord, why? Why such a beastly slaughter? So much slaughter!

Screams—inhuman in their agony—shook the heavens. The NKVDists, two or three to each stack, probed deeply, fiercely into the haystacks with their bayonets in a coordinated move. Finding their quarry, they tossed the mortally wounded man back and forth like a rag doll on the point of their weapons, before dropping him, lifeless, to the ground, still continuing to stab the motionless body over and over.

On returning to the truck, the NKVDist leader asked Father mockingly, "Where are you from, Soviet patriot?"

Again, as though following some inner warning, Father hesitated in saying "Feodosia," and heard his lips pronounce "Dulovo—a Muscovite. . . ."

"A Muscovite? Hah! Away with you, son of a whore! We'll cut your balls off if you desert! We'll string you up on your own guts!"

The truck surged forward, carrying the execution squad away. Father stood for a while, watching the truck grow smaller, finally disappearing in the distance. Then he resumed his slow, deliberate walk, trying to force his weary, leaden legs to move—one, then the other—plodding forward with heavy stumbling steps. He had to keep moving, he felt, otherwise death would overtake him, would swallow him.

Time passed, marked now by the darkening autumn sky. The rain stopped. Father was hoping desperately to spot an earthen ditch where he could crawl in and catch a few hours sleep. Then his nostrils caught the smell of smoke, and soon a huge flame sprang up, lighting the horizon like a beacon of sorts, calling Father nearer. Fire, and not a wild fire, he figured. A building must be burning. There was a strange, sweet-smelling tinge to the smoke.

Another half hour of laborious walking brought Father to the scene of the fire, to a small village where a two-story barracks was engulfed in fiercely crackling flames as if kerosene had been poured on the building. Women were running wildly, aimlessly, holding their heads in their palms; some were carrying pails of water, splashing it on the leaping, mocking flames. One young woman hurried past Father, repeating as if in a trance, "Our own . . . our men . . . our own men. . . ."

Father approached an old man leaning on a cane, his eyes hidden under a worn cap.

"Citizen," Father asked, "what's it about? That fire, those distraught women, and their water pails? In no way can they help stop that fire."

The old man looked at Father's Red Army uniform, at the exhausted face, the blood-covered hand, and said in a toneless voice, "Be glad you're not in that building, son. Seventy of our men are in there, all severely wounded. This morning, 400 lightly wounded were evacuated. The real bad ones were left behind." The man's dry, clouded eyes stared at the burning building.

"But, this fire?" Father asked, still trying to chase a horrible thought from his mind, wishing to hear some explanation, any explanation that would not be so appalling, so horrifying as his suspicions were.

"A squad of NKVDists before evacuating an hour or so earlier— sprayed the field hospital with kerosene, and set it on fire."

"But why?"

The man's voice was a monotone, answering Father: "Stalin's orders. Nothing be left behind. Not one Red Army man be taken alive by the Germans. Not even the wounded. That's what the NKVDists were saying. Stalin's orders. Women were kissing the NKVDists' boots, their hands, begging them not to do it."

Father was certain that it must have been the same group of NKVD-ists he had watched with horror earlier, as they slaughtered his fellow Red Army men in the haystacks. To kill healthy young deserters was one thing. To roast alive the helpless, the wounded. . . .

With his very last bodily strength, he dragged his feet toward a half-destroyed, unoccupied shack and, discarding his rifle, crawled under some loose floor boards and was swiftly engulfed by sleep that was closer to unconsciousness.

It was there he was found at dawn by the Germans. They shook him, pouring some cognac into his mouth to bring him out of the stupor, helping to get him to his feet.

"Come, *Opa,* come!" They urged their new prisoner to follow them, addressing him by the diminutive for "Grandpa." At a field hospital a German doctor cleaned and dressed Father's wound, putting his arm into a sling.

"There," the field doctor exclaimed in passable Russian, while securing a number to Father's chest, "now you are prisoner number 410. Try to always remember your number. It's your name from now on. Where is your home? Feodosia? Wife waiting, two children. Hmm. . . . Afraid they'll be punished because you became our prisoner of war? No need to worry. Feodosia is in our hands. We'll try to ship you back there to your family."

CHAPTER THIRTY-TWO

*O*n *being* released into our custody, Father became the center of our attention—bathing, shaving, filling him with all the nourishment we could, to hurry his recuperation. Our neighbor Tanya, a surgical nurse, came daily to dress Father's wound, bringing medications from the German field hospital where she was employed.

Tanya did not like the looks of Father's wounded hand. "Dirty," she said, when she first saw it.

"Of course it's dirty!" Father retorted. "No one's changed the dressing since the field doctor."

"Dirty in the way the bullet hit it, Mark Illarionovich," Tanya quickly explained. "The wound didn't bleed much, didn't cleanse itself. It will take longer to heal. But then, the Germans don't heal well either," she continued. "Only the very young seem to heal all right."

The Germans began to suffer severe deprivations. While Hitler planned to complete "Operation Barbarossa" before the start of winter, fate decided differently. December was nearing, with no German victory in sight. The summer, with its suffocating heat and unbearable dust, with its clouds of mosquitoes, was over. Autumn, with its bone-chilling rains and oceans of mud, claimed hundreds of thousands of horses and stalled endless columns of tanks, trucks, and gun carriages. The German march on Moscow was stopped in its tracks. Now came a winter that promised to be the coldest on record; and the German soldiers had no winter uniforms. General Guderian wrote to his wife: "At night I lie sleepless and torture my brain as to what I can do to help my poor men, who are unprotected in this crazy weather. It is terrible, unimaginable." Even in our southern town, German soldiers were suffering in their light short jackets, with no overcoats, no mittens, no warm socks. Looking at them hurrying past our gate, skipping, stamping icy feet, blowing on their bare, blue hands to warm them, we could not help but wonder how their brethren were faring in the north, where they had to face the hurricane-force freezing winds on the unending steppes, winds so devastating that soldiers could not even perform their everyday bodily functions. When the Germans were only about 100 miles from Moscow, all their food supplies were cut off, due to disastrous road conditions, forcing the starving soldiers to eat their horses. The frozen, uncooked meat brought on serious stomach disorders with violent vomiting. The Germans suffered horrible agonies, yet still they endured. The Red Army commanders acknowledged this fact, and prompted their own men to fight "like Germans fight!"

By December, 800,000 Germans became casualties of Hitler's blitzkrieg, including General Guderian, who was fired. Thirty other generals met the same fate. Goebbels described these men with the words, "They are incapable of withstanding severe strain and major tests of character."

And while many Wehrmacht high officers were dismissed, the prestige and power of the SS troops led by Himmler, grew. And the tentacles of Himmler's special power were reaching all the way to Feodosia, to Karl Marx Street, to our courtyard.

The last day of November arrived. Maya had vigorously resumed her musical studies, trotting out daily to Antonina Alexseyevna with her heavy, thick cardboard *papka* (a portfolio especially used for music), a heavy, awkward annoyance to carry. I accompanied Maya several times carrying her huge *papka*. Mother, too, came at times, not only to listen to Maya play, but to swap some merchandise with the piano teacher. While Antonina Alexseyevna had secured no flour for herself, she, on the other hand, had stumbled on a storage cache of honey in her neighborhood, and a liter of this precious commodity found its way into our possession, while flour was delivered to the teacher in exchange. During that particular swap, following Maya's lesson, Antonina Alexseyevna treated us to a samovar. Mother had brought some fresh yeast dough *lepeshky* (flat yeast rolls, resembling English muffins), her specialty. Piercing the tops of still warm, tender *lepeshky* with a fork and drenching them with honey, we ate them slowly, and drank hot, aromatic tea. Life seemed to smile on us. All Feodosia was at peace; we were not starving; the Germans were not looting or raping. People, exhausted emotionally and physically from all the recent upheavals were glad to just let go, to relax.

Antonina Alexseyevna was exceptionally talkative on that day, animated, young in appearance, with her dimpled cheeks even at her ripe age giving her a girlish look. Her voice, too, was so very clear and bright, not dull or coarse as some women's voices turn with age. After we all had several glasses of tea—until perspiration appeared on our foreheads—Antonina Alexseyevna lifted her very swollen feet up on a small stool and reached toward a round side table where a framed photograph of her late husband was standing.

"Such a good man my Jascha was," she said, taking the picture in her hands, "and such a good musician. You know, we met in Germany about 40 years ago. We were both performing in Berlin."

Maya and I were enchanted with the fact that our Feodosia music teacher had traveled so far. Open-mouthed, we listened, absorbing every gesture, every word, as if trying to be with Antonina Alexeyevna mentally, wherever recollection led her.

"We were in Paris, too. Later we went to Milan, to Vienna—we were already married by then. But Berlin! Such cultured people! Such appreciation of music! Perhaps, if my health allows, I'll visit Berlin again some day, where Jascha and I met."

We regretfully left Antonina Alexeyevna's apartment that evening, wishing to hear more, but curfew time was fast approaching. On the way home my mother turned to Maya and said with a certain wistfulness, "Mayichka, what a blessing to have your natural talent! Why, you may one day reach the Berlin Conservatory!"

Maya vigorously nodded her braided head. "Definitely! Definitely, Natalia Alexandrovna! I'll practice my fingers off from now on! Wait and see!"

That evening our courtyard was filled with the sounds of the ever-haunting "Moonlight Sonata." How Maya played! How she wanted to succeed, to follow the road of Antonina Alexseyevna, the road to Berlin! German soldiers passing our courtyard, slowed their steps and stood, leaning against the fence, engrossed in the sounds Maya created.

The very next morning, December 1, we found a pink poster glued on our gate, announcing that all Feodosia's Jews were given 72 hours to appear at Sennaya Plaza for the purpose of "resettlement," taking only their "most precious personal possessions."

Some Jews—the more perceptive ones—ran into the mountains, while others panicked, rushing to seek out Russian Orthodox priests in order to be baptized, immediately displaying brand-new Orthodox crosses. Those were in a tiny minority, though. The rest, including Antonina Alexseyevna and Maya's family, although perturbed at the thought of moving, seemed not afraid.

Reading the poster, some of the non-Jews were skeptical. Father, sitting on our doorstep, trying to take advantage of the pale winter sun, was gloomy. "Our Jews are doomed," he said. Mother sitting next to him, was rolling a homemade cigarette. After gluing it, she placed it in Father's mouth and lighted it. "Doomed, you say?" She shook her head in mild disagreement. "You're a *kohldoon,* just a *kohldoon.*"

It was true that very often Father was called a *kohldoon* (a wizard) in jest by friends and relatives, for what seemed to be his unique ability to predict events. He was not a *kohldoon,* of course, but rather an exceptionally intuitive and farsighted man. On that December 1st, studying the pink poster at the gate, Father remarked, "The sickle came upon a stone."

The whole courtyard was by then scrutinizing the poster. "What's behind your riddle, Mark? Why quote this particular proverb? Explain!" Praskovia Ivanovna demanded, while the others gathered around Father. He sadly, but matter of factly said, "Jews for thousands of years have believed they are the chosen people. They believe it fervently. It's part of their religion. And this belief has sustained them for so long."

"Stop rambling, Mark," old Osip Osipovich interrupted. "Get to the point."

"The point is," Father threw the cigarette butt to the ground, crushing it, "the point is Hitler comes along and decides his people are the chosen race—not the Jews. He is the sickle, Jews are the stone. The stone has to be removed. You understand? Natasha, dear, don't you understand? Our Jews are doomed."

Mother saw my questioning, rounded eyes, and perhaps only to ease my anxiety said, "Well, my *kohldoon* husband, the sickle might just easily break to pieces in trying to remove the stone."

"Sure!" someone in the crowd piped up. "The sickle might break, but our Jews might not live to see that day."

A heated debate broke out, as if people were at some meeting, arguing a point. Someone shouted, "If Hitler is exterminating Jews, why would the Soviet government leave them behind?" Someone else said, "The Soviets evacuated all Party-member Jews—all! The rest don't interest them. They gave them a half-hearted warning, and our Jews elected to ignore that warning." "True," another neighbor chimed in, "our Jews chose, mind you, *chose* to remain in Feodosia! And why? Because they were lied to so often—like us. They couldn't believe that this was not just another Kremlin lie."

How awful, I thought, listening to my neighbors. Could it be that this time, just once, the Kremlin was not lying in urging the Jews to evacuate, warning of atrocities committed against them by Hitler? But how could it be? It was only as recent as the previous spring that Hitler was a benevolent and kind man. Then, there was no mention of his mistreatment of Jews. And if the Kremlin leaders did know, would it not be their uppermost duty to load all Jews—not just immediate families of Communists, but all Jews—on ships, on trains, even cattle trains, like those on which the Soviet Germans were loaded, and transport them, by force if necessary, to safety? Would that big-shot Jew, Stalin's right-hand man, Lazar Kaganovich, betray his own people, just because those people were not Party members?

The cynical words of old Osip Osipovich reached my ears. "Those Jews who didn't leave Feodosia are traitors to Stalin. He doesn't give a damn what happens to them!"

Mother, once again decided to let her voice be heard. "Why are you all dooming our Jews? The poster says, 'to gather for purpose of resettlement.' Why read all kinds of evil things into this?"

Just then, our pretty neighbor Nadia, walking quickly toward the gate, shouted as she approached, in her girlish unconcerned voice, "Guess what the rumors are in the whole town? Jews are going to Palestine! Yep! Palestine. I asked some officers. They didn't know. But one SS officer laughed and said, 'Ja! Ja! Palestine!'"

"That's more like it!" Mother's voice rose as if to say expressly to Father, "I told you so!"

And this rumor spread like wildfire, jumping from our gate to the next, from one street to another, until all of Feodosia, in its utter ignorance chanted, "Our Jews are going to Palestine! Our Jews are being resettled in Palestine!"

Seventy-two hours passed. I sat in Maya's apartment, overwhelmed by the sadness of separation. The apartment was already emptied of her piano, the bags of flour, the big wall clock, the set of beautiful old porcelain dishes. The floors were naked, stripped of Caucasian rugs. The dark-uniformed SS had shown up hours after the poster appeared, led by a Jewish *starosta* (an elder), the former director of Feodosia's theater of performing arts. He volunteered to take on the duty of *starosta* so that he would not be evacuated with the others. One of his duties was to comfort the anxiety-filled Jews by stressing the honor of the Nazis, and to express and instill trust in their word. He led the SS men from house to house, identifying those occupied by Jews, in order that their belongings might be impounded.

Strangely, Maya and her family were not distraught by this confiscation. After all, the posters had announced point blank, that only "most precious personal possessions" were to be taken along. And those "most precious personal possessions" were interpreted by all as being jewelry and gold.

Terribly oppressed by the plundered apartment, by Maya sitting quietly, prepared for her journey, I mumbled, swallowing approaching tears, "Mayichka, you'll write to me, won't you? I won't know where you'll be, but you'll know my address."

"Sure," Maya wholeheartedly agreed. "Here, Nina, take this book on Khazars. I can't carry it." She handed me a book titled *Studies in Ancient Khazar History*. Its author, Soviet historian-archeologist M. S. Artamonov, claimed that most Russian Jews descended from the Khazars—a Turkic tribe from central Asia. The Khazars wielded great power and influence at one time over the still weak, disorganized Slavic tribes inhabiting what was to become known as the land of "Rus," receiving a heavy tribute from them.

In the 8th century, the Khazars accepted the Hebrew faith, according to Artamonov's study. It was another two hundred years before their power began to decline, as the power of Russia began to grow. Other central Asian peoples started to harass the Khazars, forcing them to disperse, with some settling in the Ukraine, others in Poland, in Lithuania, and in Crimea which at one time was called "Little Khazaria."

Many Russian Jews, especially the religious ones, were offended by the Soviet historian's claims. Yet, Maya's father thought Artamonov's findings plausible, and sent his daughter this book, inscribing on the flyleaf, "Daughter, read and learn." I opened its cover and under her father's inscription, I read hers to me:

"TO NINA, 10 PERCENT TATAR—
FROM MAYA, 90 PERCENT KHAZAR"

Maya was all in white, a small pink bundle on her lap, containing a change of clothes. "Take provisions for only 2 days," the poster proclaimed. Her mother, too, had a similar bundle, as did the grandmother. They would travel truly *na lechkye* (light weight). But in their ears were gold earrings I had never seen before. In Maya's ears were small rubies; in her mother's were diamond clips set in platinum. Grandmother had large pearls half hidden by gray hair. All wore golden watches, and on Maya's creamy white wool dress, on a thick gold chain, was a locket with her father's picture inside the cover. While I implored Maya not to be lazy and write to me promptly, Mother knocked and entered with a pile of *lepeshky* so hot that one could not touch or eat them just yet.

"For the journey!" she announced. "*Lepeshky* will keep for days and won't take up much room."

"But Natalia Alexandrovna," Maya's grandmother protested weakly, seduced by the aroma of the fresh yeast rolls, "the Germans promised to feed us. The *starosta* said as much. They don't want to take up space with . . . with. . . . Ah, well, Natalia Alexandrovna. We'll make room for your *lepeshky*—in our stomachs!" And we all burst out with approving laughter.

Actually, looking at Maya, dressed in her best outfit, white rabbit fur coat covering her trim, strong body, her legs in high white leather boots, a white, fluffy beret lying prettily on one side of her head—I felt envious, even perhaps a bit resentful.

"You're ready to travel, going out into the world. You'll see so much!" I said sulking, staring at Maya's glowing earrings, at her glowing eyes, her smiling mouth.

"Oh, yes, like an adventure!" she said. And then suddenly, as if something or someone struck her from within, she stopped smiling and holding on to my cold palm, said, "What if . . . what if. . . ."

"What?" I blurted, all at once feeling no longer envious.

"What if the Germans decide . . . decide to kill us. What if the rumors are true?"

Everyone in the room grew still, and for a few moments remained so. Then my mother putting the *lepeshky* plate down on the small iron stove, said in a comforting and utterly convincing voice, "But, Mayichka, think, child. Why would anyone want to harm *you*?" She embraced Maya, stroking her freshly washed, thick, ashen braids and continued, completely unselfconscious of her words that at other times could have offended one's ethnic pride. "You're not even real Jews. No religion in your lives. So, one plus for you. And then another plus, you're not even Jews by blood! That book you gave Nina. . . . It says so. No, no, little one. No need to be afraid."

Amazingly, like a drowning person would grab for a straw, so Maya and her family grabbed at the straw Mother was offering them, convincing themselves that the straw was a life boat. At once the family—

three generations of Jewish women—perked up as if by magic and started to chat, started to plan.

"Nina, remember Dmitry Antonovich telling us about Pliny? Pliny the Elder, or was it Pliny the Younger? The botanist?" Maya excitedly tried to recollect our former history lessons. "Remember when Pliny returned home from a long botanical trip and a friend asked him if Pliny didn't miss his home? And the botanist said, 'To a happy person, the whole world is his home,' or something like that. Remember, Nina?"

I was just ready to say that Palestine wouldn't be a bad place to make one's home in, when two SS men burst into the small apartment without knocking. Their barking voices were not mean, but very impersonal. "Jews! Out! Time to march!"

Our longtime neighbors clutched their small bundles in their hands, and we all exchanged kisses, Mother saying repeatedly and tearfully, "Godspeed. . . . Godspeed, friends. God bless you all. God bless you all," absentmindedly making a Christian cross over the three departing Jewish women, the way Russian Orthodox custom dictates when bidding farewell.

"God bless you too," Maya's grandmother said, kissing and embracing Mother and me. She came up to Father who stood rigid and pale with Slava by the gate, and said quietly, "Good-bye. No. It looks like farewell, Mark Illarionovich. Let's hope that the sickle won't . . . won't hurt the stone."

God! I wanted to fall through the ground, embarrassed at the realization that Maya's grandmother had heard us the three days earlier discussing their possible fate. Maya kissed my beet-red face once more and, not turning again, left the courtyard.

"Write!" I shouted, and ran out of the courtyard, to the street. She already was turning the corner, holding on to her mother with one hand and carrying the bundle in the other.

Snowflake: that was my very last impression of Maya. All in white, fragile, vulnerable, melting . . . melting . . . like a snowflake.

Others followed Maya and soon the entire highway was filled with marching Jews. Not hurrying, but marching steadily, with the SS guards positioned discreetly on either side of the marchers, not shouting, not swearing or harassing anyone. Not many carried feather beds or large bulky bundles. All were dressed in their best as if for some very festive occasion—some women in mink or in black Persian lamb coats with matching hats and muffs.

My adored mathematics teacher went by. What a "crush" I had on him last year. I would blush to the roots of my hair when he entered the classroom, and could not figure out how to stop this blushing. And the good, compassionate doctor. How he had tried to help me get the unobtainable *moskitka* cream. He carried no bundle, only his black medicine case. And there was our baker, marching a bit preoccupied. He always used to throw an extra *baranka* in my bag, knowing with what relish I would devour it on the way home.

And there was our dear Antonina Alexseyevna, her ankles swollen terribly. Yet, she walked upright, briskly, in order not to lag behind. The small suitcase she carried must be full of music, I thought. I started to push toward Antonina Alexseyevna, to kiss her farewell, but the guard stopped me with his rifle across my belly. "No bodily contact with the Jews! Go!" Why no bodily contact, I wondered.

Antonina Alexseyevna shouted, "Goodbye, dear girl! Goodbye! Stay well! Natalia Alexandrovna! *Dosvidanya! Dosvidanya!*"

Dosvidanya means literally "until seeing each other again." It is not the final farewell, which is *Proshaite* ("Forgive, and be forgiven"). No, I thought, this parting was not forever, only until the next meeting. Perhaps until war's end. Then travel will be allowed across all the borders.

We watched as all "our Jews" marched by. We followed them with our eyes as they receded in the distance, until almost abruptly they faded from sight, the highway empty, deserted. And all was quiet.

I sat sulking on the porch steps, staring at Maya's lifeless apartment, its door and window boarded with crisscross wooden planks. Darkness was approaching. Then the sound of steady, uninterrupted machine gun fire muffled by distance, burst into our courtyard. "Partisans again," Mother worried.

"No, Natasha. That gunfire is too steady," Father observed, and whispered to Mother, thinking I would not hear. "Our Jews. Let's hope . . . let's hope they're not dying now."

But they were.

At Sennaya Plaza, the same plaza where we found Father and where the Jews were ordered to appear, trucks were waiting to transfer them to the port, supposedly. Instead, all 917 persons were delivered to an area on the outskirts of town, past the Bedrisov iron foundry, which was surrounded by rows of deep anti-tank trenches. The Jews were ordered to drop their bundles, to take off their clothing, to surrender all their jewelry. Then the very young children were carried to vans marked with the Red Cross insignia. There, SS medical personnel were waiting. Youngsters met their death quickly, painlessly, with ether masks over their faces, not disturbing the parents with their cries. The rest of the Jews were lined up facing the trenches and then . . . the steady, uninterrupted machine gun fire . . . reaching our courtyard, reaching the porch steps I sat on, no more muffled by distance, but bursting into my life, into my memory with a thunderous, deafening force never to be silenced.

CHAPTER THIRTY-THREE

December 7th came. It was for many in America a tragic day—a day of newly created widows and orphans. Across the Atlantic, in London, however, Sir Winston Churchill admitted to feeling "the greatest joy," because giant America was now bound to enter the European War.

For me, it was a dreary, dull day. Those events, which happened so far from Feodosia, somewhere in the Hawaiian Islands at an unheard of place called Pearl Harbor, were of utmost importance to my ultimate fate, but not on that day.

My tormented mind still sought to deny the stark, grim reality of Maya's fate. But when my brain grew tired of denying the truth, for hours on end I visualized what Maya's last moments could have been like. The unease, when the trucks instead of heading for the port, turned into the wooded, deserted area by the iron foundry. The moments after she took off her white *shubka* (fur coat) and her earrings, together with the watch and the locket with her father's picture. Had she opened the talisman for the last time and kissed her father's image in her last, eternal farewell. . . .

Days, weeks crawled by, and the end of December was near. Nadia was organizing a Christmas party, inviting the whole courtyard to her place later that evening. Her pleasant soprano drifted through the thin walls of her apartment, as she was giving voice to the song most popular among the German soldiers—"Lili Marlene." All of Feodosia was caught up in a kind of fever for the pleasant and easy melody. Women sang it in the *banya,* at the bazaars, on the streets, in their apartments. Wherever two or more females got together, that song sooner or later burst forth.

> *"Vor der Kaserne, vor dem grossen Tor,*
> *Stand eine Laterne, und steht sie noch davor."*

> "In front of the barracks, by the big gate-door,
> Stood a lamp post, and it still stands there.
> Let us meet there once more,
> Let us stand by the post once more,
> As before, Lili Marlene, as before, Lili Marlene."

A neighbor of Nadia's, hearing the girl sing, joined in helping her to serenade.

> "Out of the silent past,
> Out of the land of my dreams
> Your loving lips call to me
> As before—Lili Marlene, as before—Lili Marlene."

It was not our Christmas. We celebrated it two weeks later, because our church calendar had not changed since the time of Peter the Great, while the Western nations had changed theirs to the calendar named after Pope Gregory. Still, we were looking forward to marking this holy day with the Germans in a quiet way, if only by listening to their Christmas carols. Just the day before, Father and Slava had brought a small fir tree from the bazaar. And while we tried to create some homemade decorations, finding a few tufts of old cotton to simulate snow, Mother, clearing the breakfast table, said to us, "Now, children, finish decorating the tree. Then, clean the floor for me. Scrub it! I'll run to the *banya* with Praskovia Ivanovna." She threw a towel, change of underwear, soap, and a small broom into her basin, and turning at the threshold, said, "A couple of hours and I'll be back. Then you two run to the *banya.*" She pointed to Father and Slava. I felt lonely and sad at Mother's words. I no longer looked forward to the *banya*—no one to beat my back, no one to share a giggle, no one to have a contest with over who will climb the highest on the steamroom steps. No Maya.

* * *

After Mother left, the three of us sat around the Christmas tree in the room permeated with the aroma of fresh *lepeshky* and the fir. Outside, an unpleasant piercing wind began to blow, coming suddenly from the sea, dumping heavy, wet flakes of snow from the leaden skies on our window sills.

An hour passed. Then a booming voice over a loudspeaker burst into our apartment.

"Lend an ear! Lend an ear! All Red Army prisoners of war in the custody of their families! Leave your homes immediately! Fall in behind this vehicle! You will march to Sarigol railway station for transfer to another area! Obey these orders, prisoners!" And again, "Lend an ear! Lend an ear!"

Almost at once, a paunchy, heavily armed German soldier stepped into the courtyard. "Any prisoners of war in here?" Not one resident volunteered a word or gesture.

"Papa," Slava and I pleaded, "let's hide you! Once the train leaves Sarigol, the Germans'll forget about you! There are so many prisoners. We'll hide you, Papa."

"Where, little ones? Where could you hide me?" Father smiled sadly, while already putting on the warm felt boots we had found for him.

"*Detki,*" he addressed us in the softest terms, the way one would speak to toddlers, "one can't escape one's own fate." He started to put on a warm sweater under his army tunic. "It might be for only a short time."

The fat German, looking into every apartment, reached ours. "Where is Mother?" I cried. "Leaving us like that!"

The German stepped into our apartment and said sternly, but not loudly, "Hurry, Russky, hurry. You're older. We'll put you on the truck. You won't have to walk to Sarigol." The soldier even tried to help Father put on his heavy Russian army coat, holding the left sleeve wide open for Father's bandaged, still unhealed hand.

"Why are you taking our father?" I jumped at the fellow like a protecting mother cat, and started to drum on his expansive chest with my fists. "His hand isn't healed yet. What good is he to you? Leave him home! Leave him to us!"

The German, while leading Father into the courtyard seemed to be unhappy at having to drag an older, wounded man away from his family. "Don't you dare to hurt my father!" I demanded, my fists now pounding the German's back. The soldier did nothing to stop my fists from landing on his huge bulk. At one point he just mumbled, "You scare me stiff."

At the gate, Father quickly pressed Slava to his chest. And tearing himself away from Slava's clinging grasp, he crushed me in the same desperate embrace, then, with the help of the stout German, climbed into the truck.

"Tell Mother not to worry! It might be only for a short time!" he shouted as the truck, spending not one extra moment by our gate, raced off. "I'll be back! Wait for me!"

Slava and I started to run after the truck, but the moment it turned the corner and reached the highway leading to Sarigol, it sped away, leaving us behind. Devastated, we returned to our empty apartment. In the kitchen, on the table, were Father's half-finished glass of tea, his cigarette holder, his tobacco, and his reading glasses! He forgot his reading glasses! He even left his tobacco! Stuffing all these items in my coat pockets, I started to run to the *banya* to find Mother. She, however, had already heard from newly arrived bathers about the sudden recall of war prisoners.

Her hair still wet, covered with a shawl, she ran toward me in tears. "*Dochenka!* Ninochka! We lost him! We lost him!"

I was quite unprepared to see Mother in such a defeated state, and snapped back angrily, "Why bury poor Father? He believes it'll only be for a short while. The war is almost finished."

Mother shook her head in disagreement and said: "This morning your father woke up and said, 'Natasha, such a lovely dream I just saw. You and I in church, getting married. You in a snow white dress, ropes of pearls.' So I asked some women in the *banya* what such a dream could mean. And Ninochka, all of them said it means separation— *eternal* separation." And not holding herself back any longer, in front of dozens of strangers, Mother began to moan. She sat on the washbasin she carried to the *banya,* rocking herself back and forth.

I looked at this act of hopeless anguish for a while, and suddenly screamed in a childishly helpless, angry voice, "Don't bury my father yet! He said to wait for him! And you—over a dream, a stupid dream—you are burying him!" I stamped my foot in protest and turned to run toward Sarigol.

Mother raised herself quickly, following me. "*Dochka!* Nina! Wait!" She caught up with me. "Something snapped inside me. Something gave out. I don't know why. Some feeling of foreboding. Come! Let's try our luck at the Commandant's office first. We'll beg him to spare your father."

We ran to the German headquarters, but the Commandant was in conference. For an hour we paced the corridor, keeping an eye on his office door. He came out flushed, barking to his adjutant, "Put out the new posters for the populace, 'For every German life—30 hostages!' Let's stop this banditry at the very roots!" The Commandant's order was in retaliation for the murder of one of his soldiers, presumably by the partisans.

Mother, intimidated by this angry outburst, gathered courage nonetheless, and approached the military ruler of Feodosia.

"Herr Commandant," she just managed to say, when the man cut her off.

"*Donnerwetter*, woman! Don't bother me today! No petitions! No begging!"

Mother desperately persisted. "Herr Commandant, my husband is a war prisoner. He is wounded in the left hand, and it's not healing." She extended her left hand toward the Commandant's face, showing where Father's hand was not healing. "They just took him away."

"Orders, woman, orders!" The Commandant continued to march briskly to his car.

"But his hand! I beg you. Have compassion! Leave him to me till his hand heals." Mother ran ahead, and leaning her back against the car door, said in a sort of mad fashion, eyes wide, unblinking, "Herr Commandant, I know—how I know I can't explain—but if my husband is taken away from me today I'll lose him forever. Forever! Save him for me. Free him! His number is 410. Please! Recall number 410!"

The German swore vigorously. "What am I? God? I am already in trouble with headquarters! I . . . I. . . . Woman!" He lowered his face toward Mother's, "I, on my own recognizance allowed the prisoners to be released to their families! Now I am getting hell all the way from Berlin! Don't pester me any longer. I can't help you."

The Commandant, although sounding angry and mean at the outset, ended up in an almost sad, defeated tone that allowed no more room for negotiating. Mother was all at once very old, very tired.

"Let's go to Sarigol, Mama," I proposed, and took Mother by the arm.

On the highway, we tried to catch a ride but none of the passing Tatars in their rickety carts would stop for us. The three kilometers took almost an hour because Mother was not able to walk any faster. She stopped from time to time, clutching her forehead and moaning, "Headache. Such a headache. And rainbows. My right eye can't see."

I was regretting every angry word that passed my lips earlier. What a shock it must have been for Mother to leave our home without a kiss or embrace, to steam and bathe with friends in the relaxing *banya,* and then to be told by a newcomer about prisoners being taken away.

The station was packed with prisoners and relatives. We started to move quickly among them, looking for number 410. Parents, wives, children surrounded their loved ones, comforting one another. One young, pretty woman—still in braids—with a month-old infant near her breast, was weeping soundlessly, while her husband was trying to reassure her.

"Dovie, don't suffer so. Your milk will disappear. No good for you to cry like that. The war is almost over. Rumors are we'll be sent to Germany. Now, that's not so bad, away from the front, away from the minefields." He embraced the braided head, wiping the tear-stained cheeks with his palm. Such a young, healthy palm. But my father's palm? I tore my eyes away from the young couple and resumed my frantic search. "Had anyone seen number 410," and "did anyone know Mark Illarionovich, my father?" God! Only four weeks earlier, we were doing the same thing on the Sennaya Plaza—looking for him, asking everyone about Mark Illarionovich. And found him! Found him! Now he was being taken away from us, again taken away. How will he survive without us? Who will feed him? The Germans could not feed all the prisoners. So many prisoners! And still more were surrendering every day! We were saving every scrap, even shriveled, musty vegetables dark with age, along with every vegetable peel and scraping, every moldy *suhar,* and tried to turn all this into a hot brew, rushing it to Sennaya Plaza to feed the prisoners. Only Feodosians had been allowed to go home to their families. The rest remained at the plaza, housed in flimsy tents, sleeping on the ground. And starving. People daily carried water pails full of the hot liquid to the prisoners, to try to give each one at least a ladle full, to warm him. To keep the brew hot we wrapped the pails in pillows, in down comforters, in winter coats. But nothing was enough. The men were dying. The mass graves, open pits near the cemetery, were daily receiving truckloads of fresh corpses. Those corpses would be sprinkled with lime, and the next day another layer of corpses would cover the ones below.

Father. . . . If only he were younger! If only his hand were healed! Someone said the prisoners were being sent to Perekop Isthmus to dig trenches. How will Father hold a shovel or any other tool in that sick, raw palm of his? It'll be infected in no time. And then . . . gangrene? Death? And open pits, like those near the cemetery in Feodosia?

"Try that train there. It was loaded earlier and they're ready to leave." One young prisoner was directing my desperate mother toward a train about half a kilometer away, a train we thought was meant for those on the platform with us. Instead, it was ready to depart. While we were waiting for the Commandant, this train was being loaded, I thought bitterly and ran toward it, shouting to Mother, "Try! Try to hurry, Mama!"

Reaching the very last cattle car, I called Father's name. No answer. Then to the next car, shouting his name, his number. No voice answering, only men's heads shaking in the negative. I decided to run to the very first car, bypassing the others, and began to shout at the top of my voice, "My father! Mark Illarionovich! Number 410! Is he there among you?"

Then at the second car, at the third, the fourth. No Father. The cars shook a bit, the engineer acknowledging a signal from the conductor.

"Please! Please! Is my father in your car? No?" As if impatient at standing still, the train was eager to start moving. Mother caught up with me. "Mark," she tried to call out loudly, but her voice was weak, shallow.

Then the train gave out a loud noise and shook convulsively. The German guards started to wrench away the relatives, the children who were trying to steal a last embrace, the last kiss, clinging to the doors of the cars.

I again ran toward the locomotive. "Papa! Papa!" I called. "Your tobacco! Your reading glasses!"

The wheels rolled faster. The same cars, familiar faces, were passing me now. I was no longer running forward. The moving train made me feel as if I was running backwards: the fifth car, the sixth.

Then an arm tried to wave, an anxious face appeared. Father's face! A hoarse, choking cry escaping the door of the seventh car, "N-i-n-o-ch-k-a-a-a! N-a-t-a-sh-a-a-a! Fare-ew-e-l-l!"

"*Papochka!* Papa!" I threw the tobacco and the eyeglasses at the door of cattle car number seven, but missed. The tobacco fell under the wheels turning to dust, and the eyeglasses too, were crushed.

"Wait! Wait! Father! Don't go away! Don't!" I commanded, pleaded, begged the train to stop. It would not, could not stop.

CHAPTER THIRTY-FOUR

*C*ruel, cold weather, unprecedented in Crimean memory, settled over the peninsula. Frost visited us daily, and so did the snow. While in other years snowflakes seldom survived their descent, this winter they lay stubbornly intact, covering the ground. Frigid sea winds were lashing at us, knifing through the thin walls of the dwellings, dropping indoor temperatures almost to the same level as outdoors. The oldest residents could not recall a time when the sea froze, but this winter thin layers of ice appeared where the sea waters lapped the shore. People ran to look at this wondrous sight, not believing their neighbors' eyewitness accounts.

On one of those wind-whipped mornings, three days after Father had been torn from us, Praskovia Ivanovna entered our apartment and, without being invited to do so, started to prepare a samovar. We knew that the old lady was perturbed by our crushing sadness and wanted to bring us out of our apathetic stupor.

When the samovar boiled, Praskovia Ivanovna seated us at the table. She spread jam, which she had received from her German tenant, on some warmed up *lepeshky,* and began to stick small pieces of it into our mouths. A few minutes of this and we simply had to smile, even laugh aloud at the devoted woman's determination to see us fed; and she sighed in relief that her method worked. Relaxed somewhat after breakfast, we sat looking out of the window, watching the snow steadily falling on the cobblestone courtyard.

Suddenly, the gate was flung wide and a group of Germans entered, led by Nadia's lieutenant. Some carried boxes and bags spilling over with foodstuffs; one had a *bayan;* another was loaded down with photographic equipment. At Nadia's porch, the Germans put down their parcels and started to throw snowballs at each other. Mischievously roaring as if they were high school students, they shouted curses at one another. But how mild their curses were! *"Donnerwetter!"* one fellow boomed at his partner, when a snowball found his eyeglasses—*donnerwetter* meaning "thunderous weather." Another supposedly vicious epithet heard from the soldiers was "Sacrament!"—meaning just that. The Germans continued their mock battle in the snow as Nadia started preparations for her party. I was invited, too, because her lieutenant after finding out about my father's departure, had told her that he would like to see me dance or just sit in the company of other young people. When Nadia said that I was not even fourteen yet, he seemed to be taken aback, but still repeated again his wish to see me at the party. Early that afternoon, nurse Tanya appeared at our apartment as she often had done on her lunch break. She gratefully accepted a glass of steaming tea, and said, looking at Praskovia Ivanovna and Mother with wide, wondering eyes, "Something is funny. I can't put my finger on it. All kinds of rumors in the hospital. . . . The Soviets presumably are planning a descent on Feodosia."

We stared at her open-mouthed. "What do you mean, 'descent'?" Mother finally managed to ask. "What kind of descent? Air? Land? Sea?" Questions flew from all of us.

"Rumors are spreading, perhaps purposely by partisans, that Soviet ships were spotted at Coctibel Bay!" Tanya pointed toward the highest mountain peaks beyond which, about 20 kilometers away, was the bay called Coctibel.

Praskovia Ivanovna said, not unduly concerned, "Coctibel Bay is far from us. The Germans will spot the ships." We calmed down immediately.

But Tanya was still very distraught. "There are rumors," she kept on, "rumors that the Soviets are doing it on purpose—the Coctibel business—to distract the Germans . . . to make them think Coctibel will be attacked, but instead, they'll attack Feodosia!"

"What about the Germans? You work with them. The doctors, what are they doing?" Mother asked.

"Oh, they're not worried. They're saying that everything is under control. They think a captured partisan spread those rumors on purpose."

While we continued with our lunch tea, Nadia knocked, surprising us all, for she very seldom came into our apartment. We informed her of Tanya's warning.

"What utter rubbish!" Nadia hooted, dismissing it with an impatient wave. She turned abruptly to me. "So, are you coming tonight?"

"Don't know. Maybe," I answered moodily.

"Say! Let's go to the *banya!*" she proposed. "Olga and Vera next door are going." The girls she mentioned were in their late teens, perhaps early twenties, and "going steady" with German soldiers.

"Go, go, Ninochka. It'll be good for you," Praskovia Ivanovna insisted, throwing all that was necessary into an empty tin washbasin and pushing me toward the door.

The *banya* that day was filled to overflowing with young girls and women, beautifying themselves in anticipation of approaching New Year's Eve parties. Some already sported engagement rings from their German lovers who promised to marry them as soon as they were able. Some girls carried with them—even to *banya*—family photos of their German fiancés, showing them off proudly to other bathers in the *oshidalnaya* (dressing room).

The girls being chosen by fate itself to be favorites of the victorious Germans—the prettiest, the cleverest, the most talented ones—all were beating their skin with the leafy brooms, opening their pores to breathe, shampooing their long, luxurious hair. All were getting ready to meet the coming new year—a year promising so much—promising to change their lives.

Evening came. Nadia's apartment was filled with *bayan* music, laughter, dancing. She threw the door open to the whole courtyard. When her place became overcrowded with dancers, people spilled outside, continuing to dance, not noticing the biting cold. "Lili Marlene" was bellowed enthusiastically over and over. Women, a bit later, began to sing other songs—of their beloved birch tree and of the rebellious, Czar-hating Cossack, Stenka Razin. They even belted out the popular Red Army song "Katusha"—about a young woman and her farewell to her loved one, who was being taken away from her, taken away to guard the Soviet borders. The Germans, too, liked this easy on the ear melody, adding their baritones and tenors to the female chorus, politics forgotten.

It was pleasant to lie on my cot and listen to the singing. Mother, earlier in the evening, decided that the party was too raucous. "Not for you. You're too young." She pointed to my bed. And there I lay, as always a bit envious hearing others sing.

Slava, listening to Nadia's unrestrained shouts, commented, "I never expected Nadia to be so . . . so pro-German. She's a Komsomol, you know, and I remember in school the day she was accepted into the Komsomol. There was a big hullabaloo! She really acted devoted to the Party."

By 11 p.m. the courtyard and Nadia's apartment began to empty, soldiers walking away arm in arm with their dates, while Nadia's lieutenant remained in her apartment. It became very quiet, with only the wind persisting to sing its melancholy tune. Everyone in our apartment was quickly embraced by blissful sleep. And not only in our apartment. By two in the morning, even the German guards who were supposed to patrol the beaches were disarmed by the need to sleep. Feodosia's shores were wide open as if in invitation.

The Soviet battleships *Red Caucasus* and *Red Crimea,* accompanied by smaller ships and more than a dozen torpedo boats, carrying the 23,000 man invasion force from the Red Army and Navy, guarded by countless NKVDists and commissars, were crawling stealthily toward our shores, unheard and unseen through impenetrable darkness and fierce winds.

All at once, thunderous explosive shells began to land on Feodosia at random, chasing us out of, and under, our beds. The *Red Caucasus* alone, in the first fifteen minutes, emptied one hundred and fifty shells into the heart of town. The ships blasted at us in such an unceasing barrage, that after a while, one could not distinguish the individual shots. It was a deafening, continuous roar. Although there was no moonlight, with heavy clouds blanketing the sky, the winter night nevertheless at times was so brightly lighted that one saw whole blocks of the city as if by daylight. The whole sky was decorated with golden "Christmas Trees"—the target-spotting flares sent from America.

At 2:40 a.m. the *Red Caucasus* succeeded in locating the main German ammunition center, blasting it to high heaven. The blast was so severe that our dwelling, more than five kilometers away, was in danger of collapsing on itself. Sections of the ceiling fell, all the shelves with dishes and books fell, the window was partly shattered, and our underground shelter in the courtyard ceased to exist.

Then one of the battleships zeroed in on the gasoline storage tanks and a large part of town was set ablaze. Feodosia was alight from end to end, its asphalt roads aflame, its telegraph poles crackling like matchsticks. It was so bright that one had to squint to protect one's eyes from the fierce light. The town was roaring with flames, roaring with explosives, roaring with human cries. On one street, a line of German tanks was spotted crawling into action, and in a matter of minutes, the column was incinerated.

After the initial devastating surprise, the Germans were able to organize their defenses, retreating to Bald Mountain. The Soviets, spotting the telltale flash of German artillery, started to bombard the mountain, every fireball flying over our heads before reaching Bald Mountain. Some fell short, not reaching their designated target, pulverizing many dwellings, together with their inhabitants, and sending the rest of us trembling under mattresses, under porches—forcing us from time to time to stop breathing, as if this could save us from being found by the mindless, wayward missiles and blown to bits.

The Germans, caught by surprise, were a pathetic sight. The victorious men, who only seven weeks earlier had marched so smartly into our town, were running in panic. Many, barefoot or in their night clothes and slippers, were dashing for their lives in the direction of Stary Krim, a town more than 20 kilometers from us, where the Germans eventually made a stand. At first, feeling cornered, many raised their hands in surrender. No acceptance of surrender took place during the heat of battle; all Germans who were signaling surrender were mowed down.

Slowly, the Germans rallied their scattered forces and began to fight to the death. Their artillery began to respond forcefully to Soviet fire and succeeded in giving some protective cover to their retreating forces, setting afire some Soviet ships in the process, including *Red Caucasus,* but they did not put it out of action.

At dawn, firing from the sea stopped and Soviet ships began sneaking away, avoiding possible German reprisal from the air. On the ground, though, every building, every apartment and room, every flight of stairs, every attic and basement, every inch of Feodosia was taken in savage combat. At mid-morning, the Germans were still holding out, protecting their retreating comrades who zoomed past our gate in trucks, on motorcycles, or on bicycles. Others galloped by, straining to control the frightened horses. Several horses fell, caught in the crossfire, and the wounded ones filled our ears with soul-searing whinnys, moaning in predeath spasms as if hundreds of human beings decided to moan in unison.

Some retreating Germans, on reaching our gate, hid behind it with a grenade or machine gun in their hands, waiting for the advancing enemy, then dying themselves in the ensuing exchange of fire. Our fence on both sides was lined with fallen soldiers and the gate was becoming blocked by the mound of dead Germans who, one after the other, tried to hide behind their already fallen comrades, only to fall themselves a few minutes later. Bullets were flying in all directions: past our broken window, over our roof, ricocheting from the cobblestones in our courtyard, pinning us to the floor.

At eleven in the morning Karl Marx Street appeared to be "cleansed" of Germans, and the dull, more angry than joyous "Hurrah! Hurrah!" of the victorious Soviets flooded our neighborhood. Just then a lone German soldier squeezed through our gate and like his comrades before him, slumped down behind a mound of corpses. A few moments later a group of Red soldiers—intense, determined—began to climb over the pile of bodies with "Hurrah!" on their lips when one of the "corpses"—the very last German—hurled a grenade in their midst. But an alert Soviet soldier, coolly catching it, threw it right back at the German, while hitting the ground for self-protection. The German's body was literally torn apart, his head almost severed, flung back, touching his shoulder blades, his lower abdomen ripped open while his right hand was cut off at the wrist as if by the sharpest surgical instrument. From the force of the explosion, this hand flew high in the air toward the telegraph wires and, caught in the tangled lines, did not fall back to earth. Like some ghastly glove airing on a laundry line, the hand just hung there. For days, for weeks, it remained hanging, dripping blood at first, then dropping rotting flesh, then just hanging like a thick, ivory spider web.

"Hurrah! Hurrah!" Cries of victory filled our courtyard—a courtyard resembling a cemetery with all its graves dug up and the corpses spilled out helter-skelter. Wild-eyed, faces pale, the young Soviet sailors burst into every apartment, rifles ready to shoot, bayonets ready to stab. Once inside the apartment, they used the bayonets to pierce needlessly through the ceilings and walls, firing their rifles into the floors, furniture, mattresses.

"Any fascist pigs in here?" A party of four rushed in through our unlocked door, not really expecting an answer. They blasted the thin walls with bullets, put several holes in our leather suitcase, shouting, "Any German pigs hiding in here?" Spotting the bags of flour, they slashed the sacks to ribbons with their bayonets, spilling the precious flour all over the apartment floor. They saw a bag with soiled linens, awaiting wash day, and deciding that a German could perhaps hide in there, quickly reduced it to ragged strips. As if disappointed to go away empty-handed, one fellow grabbed our Christmas tree, tossing it outside, his boots stamping furiously on the green branches. "We interrupted your f-----g fascist celebration! Ha!"

The Reds inspected every dwelling in our courtyard and even peeked in the holes of the outhouse and probed with bayonets to make sure that no German was hiding inside. This first wave was comprised of strictly professional warriors whose only concern was to flush out every German in hiding, to clean Feodosia completely of enemy forces. This initial military sweep rolled over, not engulfing us, only paralyzing us with its violent efficiency. The second wave, we knew, could be devastating in its fury.

There descended a short period of calm between the waves of soldiers, as in a hurricane, while the eye is overhead. And in that eye we hastened to finish our survival preparations that we had started earlier, during the battle.

Praskovia Ivanovna, after the thunderous explosion at 2:40 that morning, when her German officer tenant ran away in great panic, dressed quickly and with a small bundle of clothing and framed photographs of Dmitry Antonovich in her arms, she stood at our doorstep. "Natashinka, take me in, dear. I can't face it alone," the old lady shivered.

"But of course, Praskovia Ivanovna, stay with us," Mother warmly responded, covering Praskovia Ivanovna with a down comforter, protecting her from possible shrapnel pieces. Hiding under the bed, I heard Praskovia Ivanovna intoning strange, yet melodious words. They were words out of times long past, but they fitted our circumstances as if written for us—for three defenseless females and a boy, hiding under tables and mattresses from the deadly explosives that men were hurling at us, all around us—hiding from this frenzy of human madness.

"The Lord is my Shepherd," Praskovia Ivanovna was saying aloud, pillow covering her head. I liked the words instantly. To have the Lord for a shepherd appealed to me. "Yea, though I walk through the valley of the shadow of death, I will fear no evil." That, too, was comforting. "Surely, goodness and mercy shall follow me all the days of my life." I started to repeat the prayer, shouting the words at the top of my voice when shells exploded close by, as if to silence and chase away violent death knocking at our door, demanding to be admitted.

Although at that time we were not sure if we would survive the fighting, we were sure that if we did survive, we would then have to face the wrath of the returning Soviet army. After the heaviest bombardment subsided, we knew that the victors would soon be in our neighborhood, and we began—as our only defense in this fateful encounter—to get ready for the "masquerade."

CHAPTER THIRTY-FIVE

*E*ven *Praskovia Ivanovna* had to take pains to look as repulsive and as old as possible. Both upper and lower dentures were removed, her hair arranged in an unkempt fashion, falling over her wrinkled forehead and a faded kerchief full of holes was tied under her chin. She needed to do very little to turn into a real old woman, but it was foolish to take chances, for even 80-year-old grandmothers were known to be sexually assaulted during the retaking of towns.

"Natasha," Praskovia Ivanovna said at one point lisping, her tooth-less mouth fallen in, chin suddenly sticking prominently forward, "I know I could pass for Baba Yaga, the witch! You must pass for one as well." Mother's upper bridge with two steel teeth—replacements for her own that she lost at the *dopros* in Dulovo—came out, exposing a gap on the opposite side, teeth she had lost naturally. The upper lip became wrinkled, fallen in, causing her to lisp also. She next took the big scissors and began to chop indiscriminately at her thick, wavy hair, reaching to the scalp in many spots. Then she made a stiff paste out of mustard and flour, sticking chunks of it on the bald spots. "Disease, contagious. I used to do it during the civil war. I was young then, but it worked," Mother announced matter-of-fact. She put on a dreary old dress, darned and mended in many spots—no waist, no breasts, no hip outline showing—a sack.

Slava was safe, but Mother and Praskovia Ivanovna were openly apprehensive about my safety. They tried to tie my chest, to put flour on my face, to dress me in Mother's long, ugly skirt. Still there I was, almost 14 years old by the calendar and about 17 at the first glance.

Face pretty, oval, large hazel eyes, long brown hair, taller than the average Russian man. What to do? Mother at one point sat on the cot, her face in both palms, crying, "They'll rape her. They'll destroy my little one. They won't spare her."

While in English the four letter word "rape" is quite inexpressive, often meaning "to snatch and take away by force," as in the classic painting "Rape of Europa," in Russian the word rape means "to ravish, to violate, to outrage" and not only strictly to penetrate a female's body. *Isnasilovanie* in Russian is a dark, frightening word stemming from the root word *sila* (power, strength, might, force), all coming from an avenging male toward a much weaker female body. Consequently not only one part of her body is violated in *isnasilovanie,* but all, all of her—her mind, heart, her very soul.

We had a book in our household library which Mother at first kept hidden, but then allowed me to study thoroughly. It dealt with the female body, its reproductive organs, pregnancy—all illustrated in no nonsense, nakedly scientific drawings, including the very first penetration through the skin of virginity. It must hurt, I figured, to break that layer of nature-provided protection. Yet it was done when girls marry or fall in love. Yes, to fall in love, to know the man intimately, to have his tenderness, to long for it to happen. But to be violated by a stranger, a brute whom one never saw before, stinking of vodka and raw onions, his vile words pelting one's ears, one's human pride—and never to see this stranger again! Only always to remember! What torture, what an ordeal rape must be! I was so afraid and turning to Mother I pleaded, starting to weep, "Mama, don't let me be raped. Do something, Mama."

She seated me on the bed next to her, embracing me in a protective hug, as if to hide me from the world. Rocking with me gently she said, "*Dochenka,* remember poor Lidochka, your friend in Dulovo, and her sister, Katya? They died of *chahotka.* Remember how Katya looked? Pale, with bluish lips, red spots on her cheeks . . . feverish. Those drunken soldiers are more scared of *chahotka* than bullets. We have no attic, no cellar here. Nowhere to run. Yes, *chahotka* must be tried!"

Our masquerade was complete. In one room two toothless old women huddled on a bed with a fifteen-year-old boy recovering from malaria, while in the second room isolated from the rest of the family, lay a *chahotka*-wasted girl, a hanging sheet protecting others in the home from the infectious germs. I lay stretched out, clad only in my nightgown, since it was feared that were I to lie under the blanket dressed and with my chest tied, the masquerade would be revealed. A thick winter blanket covered me to the chin and in my hands I held a bloodstained handkerchief, with countless bright spots of blood spattered on the top sheet near my face—blood Slava donated by cautiously cutting his leg with Father's razor. Deep, dark shadows encircled my *chahotka* eyes. Uneven red spots on the cheeks were applied with the help of juice from a grated beet, diluted with water. No rouge or lipstick could be used to create such spots, because the soldiers could wipe away cosmetics. And those spots held the key to the whole charade, since it was those feverish spots and the blood on the sheet and handkerchief that the Soviets were almost superstitiously afraid of.

It was near noon when, already intoxicated, Red Army men appeared in our courtyard, splitting into several groups, and dashing into the apartments. At once piercing, animal-like screams of women rose in an anguished chorus. The children began to bawl, "Uncles! Don't hurt mama! My mama!" And the vicious, peculiarly dull voices shouting back, "You whore's maggots! Shut your f-----g mouths or your skulls'll be split in two!" In apartments where only old people resided, dishes were heard breaking, surviving window glass shattered with rifle butts, sacks of flour and other foodstuffs dragged out of the apartments. People pleaded with the soldiers, "Leave us some food! We'll starve."

"So! Starve, f-----g bastards! Greeting the fascist dogs with bread and salt! Starve!"

As soon as the group of three charged into our place, the very first fellow—red hair, red eyelashes, pale eyes—yelled at Praskovia Ivanovna, "Washed fascist laundry, didn't you? Old whore!"

Praskovia Ivanovna shook her head in denial, but the man screamed at the old lady, "Sure! Bitch! Hitler's cock-----rs! All of you!" In a rage, he covered us all with a barrage of verbal abuse that paralyzed us into complete apathy. Pausing, he pointed to my corner, but before he could snatch away the sheet, Mother, regaining her alertness, said mournfully, "Poor child, dying of *cha-ho-ot-ka*. Not long now. The doctors say this spring. We keep her separated. Don't want to catch her germs. Those *chahotka* germs are infectious. . . . Deadly."

The words were pounding on my brain like teardrops, making it so believable. If only those words would pound on his brain, I silently prayed. Abruptly, he reached out and threw aside the sheet isolating my bed, then just stood there. God! Why is he just standing! Don't just stand there. Move! Turn your back on me. Move away. Shepherd! Shepherd, help!

Eyes half-closed—hiding all my fear, panic, and anger behind the lowered eyelids—I directed my gaze past the suspicious, calculating intruder. Remembering how Lida's sister appeared on her near-death bed, I opened my lips and hardly moving them, said, "Mama . . . thirsty. . . ." His hand had moved to the buttons on his fly. But then! Shepherd! Abruptly the intruder spat on my top sheet and turning, ran out the door. His two buddies, not even checking my corner, followed the redhead out.

Mother threw herself on her knees by my bed and wept in prayerful gratitude. Praskovia Ivanovna kept crossing me in blessing, while Slava repeated over and over, "Bastards! Bastards!" I, too, prayed—a bit ashamed that even as I prayed for my own deliverance, someone else was being raped.

And that someone was Nadia. The girl's screams from next door reached us as if she was in our apartment, and not separated by a wall. The same redhead and his comrades, after leaving our apartment had burst into her place.

"I am a Komsomol! Listen! I carried messages to the partisans. I am one of you! Ahhhh!"

A man's voice rumbled back, "German mattress! You spread your legs for German swine! Now we'll spread them ourselves! Stuck your tits out like flags. Let the fascists suck them. Now! We'll show you how properly to suck them."

Nadia's screams pierced the air—and then—abrupt silence, as if Nadia no longer felt any pain, and only ever more violent verbal terror from male voices kept roaring through the walls of her apartment.

After emptying their wrath on the defenseless women, the soldiers headed for the gate and there a gory scene was taking place over the German corpses. One by one those corpses were inspected for wedding rings and other golden jewelry. Soviets peered into the mouths of dead Germans looking for gold crowns and fillings. When sighted, they tried to pry out the metal with their knives, but quickly losing patience, they chopped out part of the gum itself together with the entire tooth; or they banged the gaping jaw with a rifle butt hoping for the gold to fall out. When a ring refused to come off, they sliced off the whole finger.

After relieving the dead Germans of rings, watches, fillings, and wallets, the Soviets began to strip them of their woolen scarves, socks, sweaters—many articles just received from home, for Christmas.

This terror held us in its grip throughout the whole day, while the most violent wave was passing. Then the Soviets started to appear singly, or in pairs, and no longer in large, ravaging packs. We saw several soldiers individually entering Nadia's apartment, but quickly retreating, as if what they saw repelled them.

The only young married woman to avoid rape in our courtyard was Tanya. Handsome, in her early thirties, surely a prime target, she nonetheless saved herself by sheer courage and presence of mind. When soldiers charged into her apartment, she greeted them at the front door, dressed in a nurse's uniform, holding a bag of medical equipment. "Comrades! Thank goodness you arrived!" she shouted, shaking the soldiers' hands in vigorous greeting. "Look! Come! Look at this order." She shoved before their uninterested eyes an official-looking piece of paper. "Read! Read! The head of the NKVD, Comrade Kalcovsky—how do I pronounce his name correctly? Do you know him? No? His field wife is wounded. He is expecting me. Can you give me a ride? You came on foot? Well, can you get a commissar to bring me to Comrade Kalcovsky?" Tanya persisted, shoving the men slowly out of her apartment, pretending to be leaving with them.

NKVD boss! Field wife! Order to appear! Who needs it! The men ran toward other apartments where the occupants—soon to be victims—were not as intelligent and coolheaded as Tanya was. She repeated this procedure for the next three days with complete success, her main concern being that the same faces not appear a second time. And none did, for who wanted to bother with the nurse to the NKVD boss and his whore field wife? And may the devil take his last name!

Even as the sex orgy was subsiding, an orgy of executions began. At night, the doom-like silence was often interrupted by the echoing steps of the victims surrounded by heavy-booted NKVDists on the way to *dopros* (questioning). Many never walked the same street back. The Soviets, surprisingly, disciplined Party members more severely than non-Party members, meting out harsh punishment to them for the "betrayal of Party principles." The Jewish *starosta* who led the SS men to the Jewish families, threw his entrance door wide open when he heard the NKVDists coming.

"Comrades! What a blessing! You returned!" he cried out tearfully with his wife at his side.

"You were *starosta? Na dopros!*" the secret police ordered. And a few hours later they informed the wife that she was a widow. "Why? Why?" she sobbed.

"He tried to save his miserable skin at the expense of others! Well, now his turn has come."

The town *burgomistr,* too, was dragged toward the NKVD cellars but because he was lame and could not walk as briskly as his guards wanted him to, he was shot right on the street and left there to rot. Many translators, who worked in German headquarters, were executed, as well as people of German descent. Scores of Tatars were shot or sent to the front as minesweepers. About 200 young women who dated German soldiers were arrested and put in the town prison, their bodies found later—rotting.

Someone betrayed our old Osip Osipovich, who only seven weeks earlier lay on the highway with his ear glued to the roadbed, listening for the first sounds of German troops. Hundreds of neighbors on that November day had hung on his every word, anxious to know how far away the German army was. Now, one of those people had informed on the old man. He was summarily shot and flung on top of the Germans lying by our gate, his ear touching one of the corpses beneath his own, as if still listening.

"If only to live through this night," Mother prayed, as New Year's Eve approached.

The New Year traditionally was celebrated by Russians as gaily as possible. The final midnight of each year as it passed, supposedly took all unhappiness, all misfortune with it, while the approaching first hour of the New Year, it was hoped, would bring better, happier times.

Mother always at that time had undertaken an energetic program of cleaning, dusting, washing, mending, so that the whole abode would meet the new, coming year in a better form than previously. Every saucer, every spoon, every towel, every sheet was cleaned; shoes were polished, shirts and dresses were ironed, floors were scrubbed—all should be sparkling clean at the stroke of midnight. *Banya* was high on the list and even one's pet did not escape grooming.

As far as the festive table was concerned, even if one had to starve for a week in order to save rations for the New Year's Eve feast, then that is what was done. The New Year had to be met with full stomachs, with drink, with music and singing. Soon after the clock struck midnight, anyone who was curious as to what the New Year would bring started to burn a tightly crumpled ball of newspaper on an upside down plate. Whatever shadow the burned paper threw on the wall would give a hint as to the fate in the coming year of the person holding the plate.

We blew out the candles early on New Year's Eve, not wishing to attract any attention from the celebrating Red Army men. Earlier, a large group of soldiers occupied Praskovia Ivanovna's vacant apartment, and throughout the night shrieks, cries, laughter, and drunken female voices were mingled with the slurred, curse-filled grunts and exclamations of their male companions. The sound of breaking dishes and glass echoed through the courtyard, keeping us awake. Shouts of "Bull's-eye! Bull's-eye!" were heard from inside, but no shots accompanied those cries and we wondered what they could mean.

"Dimochka, all alone. What are they doing to our home?" Praskovia Ivanovna lamented as if she had left her husband there to fend for himself.

The following day when a comparative quiet settled on our courtyard, with the Soviets gone, we stood speechless at the threshold of the once lovely 'rich' apartment of Praskovia Ivanovna. The silk rugs still hung on the wall but were ripped in narrow strips like hula skirts. Bayonets had destroyed the big floor rug, pierced through every few inches. The pictures, paintings, photographs, books—all were torn to shreds. The precious, centuries-old icons that had survived so much upheaval in previous centuries, found their end under the merciless boots of the "anti-gods." All ivory, all sterling silver had disappeared. The magnificent old Czechoslovakian chandelier was pulled down and its crystal pendants pounded by heavy boots into a mass of small-size pellets, still glowing with diamond-like light. The handsome high ceilings, decorated with carvings of juicy grapes and other fruit, had new decorations, especially around the spot where the chandelier had hung. There, a brown, dried substance clung to the ceiling, stuck on one side with pieces of newspaper. The drunks were throwing their own feces at the ceiling with the help of newspaper, turning the chandelier's supporting rosette into a bull's-eye for their target practice. The smell of vomit and urine seemed to permeate every divan pillow, every piece of upholstered furniture, dampening the old silk wallpaper.

Praskovia Ivanovna slowly walked to the bed where her Dimochka met his death two years earlier. The bed linens were covered with semen and blood.

"Forgive me, Dima, but I must leave now. Dimochka, I must leave this place. I'll take you with me wherever I go, but this is no longer our home." Praskovia Ivanovna was weeping softly as she turned toward the blanket chest standing at the foot of the bed and tried to lift the heavy lid.

"I need a comforter stored here, Slava," she called to my pale, stricken brother. "Lift that chest cover for me, please. It's awfully heavy."

Slava had opened the wood and iron top only slightly, when a vile stench overpowered us all. "God in heaven!" Mother gasped, as if not quite believing what by this time, we could see. The old, treasured blanket chest that Praskovia Ivanovna brought with her into her marriage as part of a dowry, had been turned into a communal chamber pot. The old lady almost ran out of the place she had called her home for more than half a century.

"God have mercy on their souls . . . have mercy on their souls," she whispered.

Why? My brain wanted to explode. Why have mercy on their souls?

CHAPTER THIRTY-SIX

*F*eodosia appeared to be a city of the dead and dying. The streets literally belonged to the corpses. Fallen German and Soviet soldiers were lying next to one another, often embracing as if best of friends ready to drink *bruderschaft* to the familiar "thou." Here and there as if to break the monotony, a civilian corpse peeked through. Nature, taking pity on us still living, tried to preserve the corpses under a blanket of snow, accompanied by sub-zero temperatures.

Tanya came over the morning after the New Year, wearing her uniform and carrying the bag with medicaments, still having the official-looking certificate in her uniform pocket. We had a glass of tea together, then Tanya got up and pointing to Nadia's apartment, said, "Have to see the poor girl. Maybe she needs help. Should've gone earlier, but I was frightened to leave my place."

We, too, were wondering about the stillness in Nadia's place and were fearful of going there. From time to time we could see a shadow moving, meaning Nadia was on her feet, but not once did she appear at the window or light a candle in the evening. Tanya left Nadia's apartment about an hour later and, catching our inquisitive glances from the window, she put a finger to her lips. We understood. Nadia must have begged the good nurse not to tell the neighbors how she had found her.

The next morning Tanya again went to the girl, stopping by our porch and hurriedly whispered a few words to Mother that nevertheless reached my alert ears, " . . . tried to bite both nipples off. . . . Breasts infected now . . . gang raped . . . needs stitching. . . ."

Mother moaned as if in pain. "Beastly. Beastly," she repeated.

"Beastly?" Tanya exploded, forgetting to whisper. "Not one beast in the wild would do such a thing to his own species, to his female!" And she hurried off to nurse the ravaged girl.

I began to spend some time every day on our porch steps, inhaling the crisp, fresh air, but always remaining on the alert, ready to jump up and run to my *chahotka* bed. Slava stood guard by the gate. Seeing approaching soldiers, he gave me a hand signal, showing with his fingers how many men were nearing our courtyard. On this day it was only one. Regretfully, I left my outdoor constitutional and was heading for my bed, when Slava rushed toward me and whispered, "A commissar. All alone. Something familiar about him." He pushed me inside, while remaining on the porch observing the newcomer.

Entering our courtyard was a middle-aged man, with a thick moustache and stern face. He stepped carefully over the snow-covered mound of corpses, turning toward the very first apartment to the left of the gate—Maya's. It was a vacant, deserted place, its window blown out, door ajar, no furniture inside. The commissar stood in front of the door for a while, then he took off his hat, as if at a burial, paying respects. A familiar man, now that his hair was uncovered. Ashen hair, like Maya's braids! That's where Slava and I had seen him—his photograph in Maya's school diary!

I ran in, calling to Praskovia Ivanovna at the kitchen table. "Someone's at Maya's apartment! Help! Praskovia Ivanovna, help! You know him! You met him. I just saw his photo." I puffed, gasped, choking the last words with the fresh ones, stuttering.

"Know whom?" Praskovia Ivanovna asked.

"Maya's father!" I shouted, hurrying the old lady to follow me, dragging her outside by the sleeve. Eyes narrowed, she looked intently at the forbidding figure in the hated uniform while he, with apparent uninterest, watched us approach.

"Comrade Commissar," she began, looking at the man with calm, direct eyes, "I met you during one of your visits."

"Yes. Praskovia Ivanovna, isn't it?" The commissar was cool, but not hostile. "So we meet again," he said, turning a bit away from us and staring at his daughter's empty apartment.

Maya's reassuring words rang in my memory, "My father is a good man." Overcoming my deep-seated fear for the commissar's uniform, I stepped a bit closer to him and blurted out, as if in challenge, "Maya

was my best friend! We went to *banya* just before the Germans came."
And remembering that day, I burst out in uncontrollable sobs. Until
then I had been mourning Maya dry-eyed, numb. "I have a book on the
Khazars. Maya's present . . . your present." I managed to squeeze out
between the attacks of weeping, motioning the man to follow me to
our apartment. And obediently, head lowered, he followed.

Mother stiffened at seeing the man in commissar uniform entering
our apartment. "Afraid you've come to arrest her," I half apologetically
explained, introducing him to Mother. She looked at the pale, unemo-
tional face of Maya's father and said, more to herself than to him, "Poor
suffering man." Perhaps not expecting to be approached by anyone in
the courtyard and not prepared for any sympathy or warmth from
others toward him in his sorrow, the commissar reached for the back of
the nearest chair and slumped into it. With his elbows on the table for
support, he hid his face in both palms and just sat there, as if hiding his
grief from the prying eyes of strangers.

Mother turned to the cupboard where some Crimean wine was
stored in an old teapot, and pouring a waterglass full, she offered it to
the commissar. "Please, drink. It'll help you some. I'll fix some tea,
meanwhile."

He took a sip, his dark eyes settling on my flustered face. "What's
your name? Nina? Ah, I remember Maya talking about you. Pavlik
Morozov . . . something connected with Pavlik Morozov's lessons."

Yes. I, too, remembered. It was the true beginning of our
friendship—three years earlier when we both proclaimed our love for
our fathers above love for the Party, and elected not to follow the
example of Pavlik Morozov—the perfect Pioneer.

"Bring me Maya's book." He took another sip of wine. Reading
Maya's inscription, he started to shake from silent laughter; or was it
weeping? Dry. Harsh. Bitter. "Much good it did her to be ninety
percent Khazar," he said.

The man's laughter crushed, oppressed me. I wanted to shake off this
heavy, unbearable feeling and brazenly asked Mother for a glass of
wine. Sternly put in my place and still aching to become free of my
numbing desolation, on impulse, I reached out to the commissar's
almost full glass of wine and quickly drank it all. While Mother proceeded to scold, and to apologize for my behavior, my thoughts became light, my tongue loose. By some intuition dictated from within
me, I had to open my soul to this bereft father, and tell him all about my
relationship with Maya: about our music lessons, our *banya* sessions,
our talk of world travel, our discussions about the Khazars, even about

our greeting the Germans and the four weeks that followed, before the cursed poster . . . before the machine gun fire.

"The girl is intoxicated." Mother tried to cut off this flood of words. Yet, I felt he needed to hear those words as I needed to tell them. And I continued for a bit longer, until the words began to slur, refusing to leave my suddenly tired, heavy tongue. I excused myself, feeling all at once very cold and crawled into my sheet-protected corner.

"Why the sheet?" the commissar's words reached me already from a far, far distance, and Mother's explanation followed about the fear of rape, the masquerade of *chahotka*. Then, I slept.

Maya's father did not leave right away, having tea with the family, while I snored quietly in my corner, for the first time since the "descent" not afraid of being raped.

It was from him we learned that at the same time the Soviets launched their 23,000 man assault from the sea in Feodosia, they also invaded Kerch, driving the Germans out of there as well. Maya's father was with the Kerch invasion. Anxious to know of his daughter's fate, he reached Feodosia much too late to help her.

Mother, utterly exhausted from constant fear of everyone and everything that happened in the past turbulent week, lowered her guard and truthfully admitted to Maya's father how she more or less was waiting to be fetched by the NKVDists one day soon, and punished for being the wife of a prisoner of war.

Before leaving, he said coolly, "Don't worry on that account. I'll look into it. But, thank your lucky star your husband wasn't with you on that 29th. We had no mercy."

Feodosia was starving. Since the return of the Soviets, no food had been distributed to the populace, not even the kerosene sprinkled flour. Women implored the Red soldiers to let them wash their laundry in exchange for some food. The laundry was washed, but the laundresses were paid not with food as the Germans had paid, but with worthless Soviet rubles that bought nothing in the bazaar.

Actually, the bazaar plaza was quickly abandoned as a barter place. At first people tried to barter, to swap, but all had bad experiences with the soldiers who, after asking to inspect the merchandise and having it in their hands, ran, or pushed rubles into the seller's hand, setting their own price. Feeling crudely betrayed, the populace soon stayed away from the bazaar altogether.

Russian Orthodox Christmas arrived—January 7. One could not

even think of bringing a Christmas tree into one's home, nor dare to visit the church that had been immediately opened by the Germans. Yet in the courtyard, away from prying eyes of officials and strangers, neighbors exchanged a barely audible "Congratulations" in place of the forbidden "Merry Christmas!"

During the previous night someone had moved the frozen corpses from the inside of our courtyard, stacking them on the sidewalk facing the highway. I stopped wearing my night clothes 24 hours a day and for the first time in more than a week, appeared in my winter clothes and boots.

At noon on that day, Tanya ran into our apartment with the news that the Soviets were opening the Jewish mass grave. I reached for my beret and mittens.

"No! No! Ninochka! Listen to me! Don't go!" Mother insisted, worried.

And I insisted that I must.

Old Praskovia Ivanovna got up from her cot, put a warm shawl over her head, made me put on an old shawl too, instead of the pretty beret, and led me to Maya's grave. Many older people came out of their homes, walking toward the iron foundry, toward the anti-tank trenches. The long, deep ravine gaped at us from afar. Much of the thin layer of soil covering the bodies had already been removed, spotting the snow with dark, dirty patches. Tatars in prison uniforms were doing the actual opening of the grave, while several Jewish survivors bent low over the yawning mass grave. We were stopped about ten yards from the pit, not allowed to come closer to look right into it, as the surviving Jews were doing. NKVDists were all over the place, even supervising filming of the scene, cameras being manned by two of their agents.

The Jews at the site were weeping, some silently, crushed, while others were almost hysterical with grief, calling the names of their loved ones. A pretty woman in her late twenties, with wavy, reddish hair falling over her forehead, eyes, nose, was crying out the same name over and over.

"Lilia! Lilia! My little girlie! Lilia! My child! Where are you?"

The woman ran from one end of the grave to the other, bending low, crawling on her knees, eyes searching wildly. The NKVD cameramen, favoring her out of all others, zeroed in with their cameras on the grief-stricken woman while she continued to lament.

"Oh, why didn't I die with you? Lilia! I deserted you, ran away! I didn't think they would harm a child! Oh!" The Jewess beat her chest with her fists, inconsolable with grief.

One of the men filming the scene shouted to her after a while, "Easy! Easy, woman! Don't put on so much. Can't get your Lilia back anyhow."

The woman, utterly lost in her sorrow, unaware of surroundings or film makers, continued to lament. The cameraman again shouted once more, this time not hiding his annoyance, "Don't open your mouth so wide! It looks like hell! Hey! Lilia's mother!" Not getting through to the oblivious woman, the film crew deserted her, turning their camera eye on us. The young woman's anguished screams and tears affected us so that we could not move, or speak, or cry.

"Weep!" the cameraman yelled in our direction. "Weep, you bastards! Don't stand there like paralysis struck you! Tears! I must have tears!" he commanded, exasperated with our lack of compliance. "You! Jew haters! Came here to gape? Cry!" he ordered once more. "Can't you squeeze out a tear? Hitler lovers! Wanted to have the Jews killed, didn't you?" He shook his fist in our direction.

"Come, Ninochka." Praskovia Ivanovna took my elbow. "Let's walk back home by the sea. We haven't had a glimpse of the sea in a long time." And she led me away.

But our walk to the sea afforded no comfort. Feodosia's streets were littered with bodies, not allowing us to walk easily, but forcing us constantly to lift our legs over a corpse, or mound of corpses. The Red Army dead were being picked up and truckloads of their bodies were dumped near the cemetery, destined for mass graves. No one was removing the German corpses. Ruined, burned buildings gaped at us, dark, accusing. The magnificent villas on Lenin Prospect were without window glass, scorched, some walls damaged by shellfire. But most villas survived intact, because they were not targets during the attack, and the artillery shells flew over them, causing minimal damage.

In front of one villa, a crowd of civilians was gathered, heads tilted back, watching something. On coming near we saw naked bodies flying out of the French doors of the villa's second floor, over the heads of the onlookers, landing with a thump on the sand below.

The Soviets were cleaning out the villas, where many wounded Germans had been hospitalized, to make room for their own wounded. At our approach, we could hear the soldiers, after each hurtling corpse, counting, ". . . 69! Parasites! 70! Hitler's arse lickers! 71! Fascist dogs!" And another body flew out.

A mountain of 72 corpses rose on Lenin Prospect, spilling over to the shore, where already the cold waves of the ever-cleansing sea began to play with the human remains, gently.

"Comrades!" the leader of the work crew shouted. "Let's march to the next villa!" And so, villa after villa gave out a pile of corpses. Stamboli Villa—the most magnificent of all—former residence of a Jewish tobacco mogul, where I danced once with my ballet troupe, came into view. I hurried up the graveled walk. So familiar, that walk, leading me into the past. Was it only last summer? I entered the huge hall that had served as a dining room with a raised platform where we had danced for the vacationers. The stage was still there, but the hall had no tables, no chairs. Instead, row after row of hospital beds stood. And by every bed, or in it, or under it, lay the corpse of a German soldier. Some were partially dressed, as if trying to escape. One young fellow, looking no more than twenty, lay near the door, his leg in a cast, short top jacket pulled over one arm, with no time for the other arm to go through the sleeve before bayonets pierced his body. And out of the jacket pocket had spilled Christmas cards, greetings from family, from far away Germany. I bent low over one card, reading a line, "Stay warm, darling Kurt!" From Mother? Sister? Fiancée? Stay warm. If his family could see his rotting body now. Smell him.

"Such a stench. Praskovia Ivanovna, why does the human body stink so?" I asked.

And the old lady, trying to comfort me, said, "The human body may stink, Ninochka, but the human spirit remains pure, clean."

Old Praskovia Ivanovna must be joking. This Kurt's spirit is pure? And the dead commissar we passed in the graveled yard, his spirit is pure? And the hundreds of corpses we stepped over this day, wearing both Russian and German uniforms—all rotting, moldy, being devoured by fat, juicy maggots—all had a pure spirit? If everyone's spirit was clean, why did it lead them into such inconceivable slaughter?

I overheard Praskovia Ivanovna quietly praying, the same verses she had recited to comfort me a few nights earlier during the battle for Feodosia.

"The Lord is my Shepherd. I shall not want. . . ."

Shepherd! I silently called in numb despair. Where are you? Do you see me now, walking through the valley of the shadow of death? I am stumbling through the valley of death itself. I am so utterly tired of this valley of death. I want so much to lie down in green pastures, to inhale the aroma of young grass, or of hay. No more smelly, rotting corpses with their mouths agape, eyes glassy, and the greedy maggots, competing with one another, devouring the corpses. Shepherd, lead me beside the still water. No! No! Not the water of my Black Sea. It is awash with maggots. Shepherd! Shepherd!

That evening Mother implored Tanya to give me something—anything—to calm me. Nothing could help, Tanya said. Only time. And time was crawling by with such cold, heartless indifference. During the day, my esophagus protested with violent spasms, allowing no food to nourish my body. In the dark of night, I saw corpses—German corpses, Jewish corpses, and Red Army corpses—in a mound of such size as to reach all the way to the sky, the whole mound glowing with special light. Arms, legs, heads, necks, all mixed, intermingled, as though they were toys in a child's toybox, thrown there carelessly, hastily—all glowing. At daybreak the glow faded from the corpses, only to be replaced by maggots. And Praskovia Ivanovna still insisted that the human spirit was pure and had no stench.

Days passed.

On January 15, the sound of artillery fire reached us, sounding not too far distant, west of us. A fierce battle for Feodosia was going on several kilometers away—a battle the Soviets appeared to be losing. The highways soon became choked with heavy war machinery. Artillery gun carriages were dragged in a long procession behind trucks filled with Red soldiers, followed closely by a straggling mass of humanity on foot. Some of those retreating on foot were in uniform, others were civilians.

Jewish survivors, joined by the Krimchaki, were leaving Feodosia. Many Caraimi, who were not previously afraid of Hitler's policies, were not sure any longer that their turn would not come to be "relocated," and they, too, chose to leave their hometown. The surviving and forgiven Party members tagged along, including Nadia, whose loyalty was established after intensive interrogation by the NKVD. It turned out she *did* deliver messages to the partisans. She used the German lieutenant to gain information and she had purposely arranged the party on December 28, knowing all the time from the partisans of the forthcoming invasion. Nadia could not count on surviving the approaching Germans for a second time.

While the highway was echoing with the endless rattle and clatter of retreating Red Army men and machinery, fires began once more to illuminate the sky. No food stores, no grain mills were allowed to fall into German hands, nor into the hands of the populace. No electric facility, or telephone, telegraph, or radio equipment remained intact. Most of the water wells were purposely poisoned or polluted, our well serving as a wet tomb for several dead Germans. Those taken prisoner during the "descent" presumably were executed, with only high-ranking officers spared.

Not daring to stay at the gate in the open and gape at the retreating men, I sat with Slava on Maya's porch, feeling very gloomy and lost. What to expect next? More fighting? More slaughter? More corpses? One of the trucks chose to stop its motor right at our gate, putting Slava and me on instant alert. Should we run? No time. The gate was flung open.

"So, that's where you are. . . ." Maya's father's voice at once put us at ease. He came closer and said, obviously hurrying to return to the waiting truck, "Nina, tell your mother that the papers in the case of number 410 are all destroyed, understand?" I nodded. "And don't, don't suffer. You're too young to suffer so deeply." He took both my braids in one of his hands, tugging at them slightly. Then he tucked them under my chin and, lifting my face to meet his gaze, he looked at me intently. Trying to see his Maya or trying not to see her in me? And then, the banging of the gate, the racing of a motor, and he vanished.

On January 17, Feodosia was on her own once more, without the supervision of anyone in authority. The Soviets had deserted the town, while the Germans had not yet re-entered. Observing the calm settling over our neighborhood, Mother asked Slava and me to try to find some clean snow for drinking purposes. We each took two pails and began to scout our immediate neighborhood for fresh patches of snow, avoiding the spots where corpses were still lying. One full pail of solidly packed snow, when melted, yielded only a few glasses of water, so that we had to spend several hours, running home repeatedly, delivering the snow and running out again.

It was late afternoon, nearing sundown. Mother was quite satisfied with our snow gathering, and Slava was too. But I once again took the two empty pails and proceeded toward a spot I had noticed earlier that was still pristine white. The clear patch was off to one side of our water well on top of the hill, quite noticeable but probably ignored by our neighbors, since no one wanted to get near the foul-smelling well opening, where corpses of German soldiers were floating.

While crawling about on the hill searching for clean-looking snow, I was at the same time observing all that was going on around me, alert and prepared to run home if I spotted the German troops re-entering Karl Marx Street. The highways were empty. I continued to scoop snow into the pails, when my eye caught a movement that put me on guard. I turned my head to the right, from where the Germans were expected to enter, but instead of Germans I saw two Soviet foot soldiers. They were broad shouldered, husky, short-legged, dressed in unkempt uniforms. Perhaps drunk? It was too late to run. I could not cross the highway and reach my gate without being spotted or intercepted by those two Soviets. And if they intercepted me, would they harm me? Abuse me? All those past weeks of trying to survive without being ravaged would be in vain. I decided there was nothing for me to do but stay put, trying to hide behind the water well, trying to blend with the low brick structure.

I could see the soldiers' faces clearly as they approached our gate. They were not Slavs, I realized, but olive-skinned Turkic natives of the Caucasus. Over the left shoulder each carried a rifle, while holding on to something big, dark, and round with both hands. Why were they walking at such a leisurely pace, so relaxed, I wondered? After all, if they wanted to escape the approaching Germans, they should be hurrying away, running. When they came nearer, I realized that the round, dark objects in the soldiers' hands were five kilo loaves of rye bread, and they held on to it as if it were some extraordinary prize they had just received. I could hear their excited guttural voices, often interrupted by laughter, but could not understand a word of their native tongue. They reached our gate, passing it, walking steadily toward the beginning of our street, toward the triangle where the Kerch and Simferopol highways blended into one road. Because all the houses on our street had very high wooden fences, this triangle could not be seen by the soldiers until they came right upon it. And of course, nothing could be seen by them of what was happening on the other highway, which was blocked by a row of houses. But I, from the well hill, could observe everything that was taking place on Karl Marx Street, on the triangle strip, and on the second highway that was partially visible to me through the open space of the triangle.

Just a few steps from this open strip of land, the soldiers suddenly stopped and as though reaching a mutual decision, they took their rifles off their shoulders and, with care, stood them against the wooden fence. Slapping each other on the back, laughing, they began to walk away from the rifles. Deserting! I scarcely had time to register this when I saw on the second highway a truck heading toward the triangle. My first thought was, God Almighty! The Germans are returning! I must run home! But then I realized that the truck had a red star on its side. A Soviet truck! And it was full of retreating NKVDists! I could see all this, but the two soldiers could not, because the high fence on their right was still obstructing their view. But they could see me on their left. I must give them a signal, a warning, I decided. Overcoming my ingrained fear of being seen by the Soviet soldiers, I shouted, "Stop! Stop!" and ducked immediately behind the water well structure. The two soldiers turned their heads toward the well, while continuing to walk, and reached the open triangle, exposing themselves to the Soviet truck. Instantaneously, a stream of bullets flew toward the two men.

"Traitors! Cowards! Take that! And that in your filthy guts!" the sharpshooter screamed, remaining seated all the while. The truck did not even slow down, perhaps because the driver simply had not seen the weaponless soldiers.

The shooting took only a few seconds, but I, crouching behind the water well, watched it unfold like a slow motion film—from the moment the soldiers walked into my view, discarding their rifles, slapping each other's back, laughing in self-congratulation. Then . . . a shower of bullets. And there they both lay, on the slushy snow of the triangle, moaning, rolling from one side to another, as if to ease the pain, still embracing their bread loaves.

I ran toward the men, followed by other women, who were gathering snow nearby. We surrounded the wounded, bending over them. One soldier whispered something through his bleeding mouth. No one understood him at first. "Col . . . col . . ." he muttered, shivering.

"He feels cold," someone decided.

With his last bodily strength, the wounded man lifted his arm a bit, pointing to his breast pocket. "Bab . . . bab . . . wuma. . . ."

The same interpreting voice announced, "He is saying 'baby, baby, woman.' His wife."

The short, middle-aged woman in a tattered head scarf, her eyes brimming with tears, bent over the stricken man and located a small, soiled folder with a photograph of an infant girl with black, thick bangs framing her round, grinning face, sitting comfortably on her mother's lap.

"Bakk . . . bakk . . ." the Caucasian urged. The weeping woman looked at the back of the picture where the names of the soldier's wife and child were written and their address. She arranged her water pail upside down at the side of the man and, sitting on it, stroked his forehead. Then she spoke slowly, precisely, hoping to be understood.

"I will let them know. I will write." And she showed with a gesture that she would write.

The dying man tried to stretch his lips in a grateful smile. "Tha-nng-y-u-u," he breathed, and as if relieved of an overwhelming burden, he lowered his eyelids slowly and straightening his bent legs a bit, lay still. We stared at him, waiting. Will he move? Moan? The heavy bread loaf suddenly began to roll away from the man. "Dead," someone said. We all turned to the man's companion. He was younger, with no sign of a beard on his smooth, handsome face. Tears were running down his cheeks while he was hoarsely repeating something over and over.

"Calling his mother," someone decided. "Poor creatures. They dropped their rifles five seconds too soon." And another voice lamented, "Ah! They thought they were safe from the NKVDists. Like flies they both died. Just like flies. Those bullets hit them just like a flyswatter hits flies."

Then we were all aware that the second Caucasian, too, was still—no more tears escaping his eyes, no more murmur of unintelligible words crossing his lips. And then his bread loaf rolled away, freed.

"There he goes, poor creature. Gave up his soul," the kindly woman said, and took a wallet out of the fellow's tunic. "I'll try to let his family know. Terrible . . . to wait . . . not to know."

All stood for a few moments, motionless, then some began crossing themselves and the dead men.

Soon a woman's brisk voice proposed, "Well, neighbors, nothing more we can do for them. Let's divide the bread loaves and beat it. Not safe to stay here."

I picked up the almost empty pails and began to walk toward my gate, feeling crushed at watching the two young men die, while only moments earlier the same men were full of life and laughter. I felt as if I had betrayed them by not shouting a warning more persistently. Instead of ducking behind the well, could I not have shouted "Stop!" again and again, until they understood? Until they stopped walking toward the triangle of earth on our Karl Marx Street that became their execution ground?

"Hey, kid!" A cry from the woman who was dividing the bread reached me. "Don't go away empty handed." Then, seeing me almost run toward the gate, she grumbled, offended, "Look at that long-legged prima donna! She turns her nose up at good black bread. Give her a slice of 'Napoleon' and she wouldn't be so quick to run off."

CHAPTER THIRTY-SEVEN

When the Germans were re-entering Feodosia, no bread and salt, no flowers, no children and lovely young women were there to greet the troops. The streets were mostly deserted, with only a few older women standing by the corpse-littered sidewalks, their *babushka* scarves tucked under their chins, mouths grim and sad.

The Germans, too, were grim, their cold faces set in an attitude of standoffish determination, but after observing the effects of three weeks of Soviet rule on the civilian population, they softened. At entering Feodosia's prison, they were greeted by hundreds of corpses, many belonging to young, lovely women they had become friendly with earlier. Some were devastated to stumble on the remains of girls they had genuinely loved, particularly those soldiers who had applied for permission to become legally engaged. They found many Tatars who had worked for them only three weeks earlier, the interpreters, the wives of prisoners of war—all slaughtered as traitors.

German military commanders, before any direct orders could come from the main headquarters, began to help Feodosians get back on their feet. Within hours of their return, the Germans mobilized medical personnel among the civilians, putting them to work at the field hospital where all the wounded were gathered. Tanya, immediately at work, witnessed a severely wounded Russian soldier receiving priority treatment before a less severely wounded German soldier was attended to. The physician in that case must have followed the Hippocratic Oath to the letter.

When the Germans walked into the villas, they found many

wounded Red Army men left behind—the same men who so savagely fought the Germans on December 29, the time of the invasion. Probably the Soviet high command had no heart to liquidate those men, knowing that not one of them was a coward or deserter, and they left their wounded to the mercy of the Germans. Mercy, truly, was what those wounded received. Perhaps, not unlike young, wounded Kurt with Christmas cards in his jacket, those Soviet casualties greeted the Germans with terror-stricken eyes, perspiring in expectation of the forthcoming massacre. No massacre came. Instead, the German army doctor, with the assistance of Russian nurses, began to clean and dress the Red Army men's wounds. The less experienced nurses and aides began to faint and vomit at the sight of maggot-infested lesions, but the German doctor sternly commanded them to continue, until every Soviet soldier who had been left behind had been attended to. Some of the wounded wept in gratitude. Many of those who recovered fully, enlisted as *hilfswillige* (volunteer auxiliaries).

While generals and high officers of the German field army in occupied Russia gave opportunities to literally hundreds of thousands of Soviet citizens to participate in the *hilfswillige* force of the Wehrmacht, Hitler himself was kept uninformed of it. German Lieutenant Colonel Reinhard Gehlen, who was chief of the intelligence branch known as Foreign Armies East, only weeks after reoccupying Feodosia told Major Heere, his co-worker:

> "The Russians were ready to receive us as allies, except, of course for the Communist Party organizations. Unfortunately, all the orders from the Army High Command forbid us to exploit this attitude. God alone knows what will happen if Hitler or people around him find out what is going on, if they learn that there are Russians wearing German uniforms. But we have to carry on this struggle. Our aim should be not to colonize Russia, but to liberate the Russian state from the Soviet system."

Three months went by under the re-established German occupation. The town was healing, recuperating, and looking forward to April 5, Sunday—a day that held special significance for the Russian Orthodox, for it was *Paskha* (Easter). The Orthodox have a midnight service on the eve of *Paskha*, walking around the church three times with lighted candles, and at exactly midnight reach the church entrance with doors wide open, where the priest greets them with the phrase, *Christos*

Woscrese!" ("Christ is risen!"), and the people answer, "Woistinu Woscrese!" ("Verily, risen!")

The midnight service was not allowed by the Germans due to the violent sniper attacks coming from the partisans hiding in the mountains, who were looking specifically for worshippers with lighted candles. So, being forced to forego the traditional midnight service, we visited the church in the early morning hours, greeting one another with the ancient words acknowledging Christ's resurrection, and asking the priest to bless the Easter bread.

Our courtyard was cleaned, scrubbed, and decorated for the communal feast. A long, narrow table stood in the middle, with the traditional cake (kulich) rising high, accompanied by a sweet cottage cheese spread called paskha, surrounded by platters of hard boiled eggs colored with beet juice and onion skins, and there was even some ham. People ate, drank, and embraced each other in the traditional Paskha three-way kiss—a kiss that was meant to wipe away past wrongdoings, past hurts and abuses, and to forgive. No person, after exchanging the three-way Paskha kiss, should remain a foe to another person. If any impaired relationships could be restored, they were on that special day of Paskha.

The long forbidden words—words punishable at times by death under Stalin's rule—were ringing loud and clear, "Christ is risen!" and even louder and clearer the answer rang back, "Verily, risen!" Those words could be heard in every Christian dwelling, echoing through every courtyard, spilling over to all the neighboring courtyards, to neighboring streets. "Natalia Alexandrovna! Praskovia Ivanovna! Ninochka! Slava! Christ is risen!" Tanya, for whom it was the first freely celebrated Easter since her early childhood, shouted the greeting to us and our "Verily, risen!" was followed by a three-way kiss.

Not only the Russian Orthodox took part in the celebration, for the Western Easter as well fell on April 5 that year. So the Germans also joined us, and it was they who provided such traditional things as eggs and ham for the table. They seemed to take a special interest in our custom of the three-way kiss. I pleaded pathetically with Mother to be excused from this exchange of the traditional kiss. "They're not Russian, Mama," I whispered, cheeks aflame, facing a seemingly endless line of waiting, earnest-looking soldiers. "They're not Orthodox. I don't have to kiss them."

Mother said softly, while loading my hands with red colored eggs, "Ninochka, the greeting of love and peace is universal and that's what the Easter greeting is—a greeting of forgiveness, and of peace. Now, give each of our Paskha guests an Easter egg."

Our guests. Strange. Back in November, while kneading dough, I argued with Mother over the word "guests." Yet, that is how those young fellows acted on the Easter of 1942—no ill will in their eyes, no hatred. Easter spirit seemed to prevail.

A deep sorrow immediately followed the joyous mood of Easter. Praskovia Ivanovna, while helping to clear the *Paskha* table, complained at one point about feeling a bit headachy, nauseated—and retired. Since it had been a long, active day for all of us, we retired early too. Praskovia Ivanovna called out to me before I blew out the candle.

"Ninochka, I can't understand it, but I'm so-oo hungry! Slice me a thick piece of *kulich*. Don't be stingy now."

Impatiently she took the *kulich* from me, eating it with great appetite. Her right hand seemed to shake a bit while holding the *kulich*. The unusual feeling of uncontrollable hunger and the shaking of Praskovia Ivanovna's hand disturbed me a bit, but I did not dwell on it, attributing it to the extraordinarily active day.

"Nighty night, Ninochka. Sleep tight." Praskovia Ivanovna called out, while I was climbing under the blanket. I turned once more to wave to her, but her head was already thrown back, resting on the puffed pillow, as if she had instantly fallen asleep.

At dawn, when we all began to stir and awaken, Praskovia Ivanovna did not. She remained in the very same position as when I left her, not responding to our calls. Her eyes remained shut and her right arm and leg were lifeless to our touch. But her chest rose and fell in even, slow waves. We ran for Tanya who, after observing Praskovia Ivanovna for a while said sadly, "A stroke. Perhaps a series of strokes. Who knows, maybe even now new strokes are occurring."

Mother was aghast. "But, Tanya, she *can* recover? She *will* recover, won't she?"

Tanya signalled us to follow her into the next room, speaking in a half whisper. "I do know people who got better. . . . The stroke disabled them some. But . . . but Praskovia Ivanovna might very well die."

Not prepared for that final "die," we started to cry, insisting that it could not happen to our Praskovia Ivanovna. Tanya told us that even if Praskovia Ivanovna was in a deep coma, as she appeared to be, it was advisable not to behave as if we were already burying her.

"Who knows?" the nurse cautioned. "Perhaps Praskovia Ivanovna can hear everything, understand everything, but can't respond." Tanya's advice was to stand watch for the next 48 hours, because in her experience those 48 hours were decisive to the fate of the stricken person.

When we returned to the room, Praskovia Ivanovna was making a strange, snoring noise, and her tongue seemed to rise a bit, then fall. "She tries to say something," Tanya observed. "Praskovia Ivanovna! Can you hear me? It's Tanya. If you can hear me, try to squeeze my fingers with your left hand. Try!" And only seconds later, Tanya shouted, "She hears us! She is aware, lucid!"

Mother wanted to be sure, and her finger too, was squeezed quite determinedly. To me, it was at once joyous and frightening, that the human body could be so disabled physically and remain so alert mentally. And not to be able to communicate this alertness with voice or eyes or even with change in the rhythm of breathing.

We took turns sitting by our friend's bed—to watch and wait. Another 24 hours passed with Praskovia Ivanovna remaining completely motionless when, suddenly, violent spasms twisted the left side of her mouth.

"God," Mother whispered, "she must be having another stroke. It must hurt so."

And yet no sound escaped, no change occurred in the rhythm of her breathing, as if Praskovia Ivanovna was undisturbed. After this stroke, her body began to contract in repeating spasms, every 16 seconds her arms and legs jerking involuntarily.

Another 24 hours passed. Praskovia Ivanovna seemed to become deeply comatose. No more spasms, no more tongue movement, yet surprisingly, while in the first two days after the stroke, her face turned pasty, now a slightly rose color settled over her whole face, and even her ears, until then as pale as if made of wax, took on some color. We were bewildered, even encouraged by such apparent improvement, but Tanya shook her head, dashing our hopes.

"Her blood pressure must be rising. If it rises too high and then drops low, it's the end."

Mother began to sob, placing her head on Praskovia Ivanovna's chest, lamenting in that peculiarly female way—natural, unrestrained—when one forgets about the surroundings, giving one's self over to the expression of pure grief.

"Praskovia Ivanovna, darling Praskovia Ivanovna . . . our dear, dear Praskovia Ivanovna," Mother chanted. "We took no leave of one another, so suddenly you were stricken . . . without saying farewell to one another, without a chance to beg forgiveness. To part with us in such a sudden way, and just after *Paskha* . . . after such a joyous *Paskha*. And now, not a word from you. You are silent. Not even a last *proshaiyte*—farewell. If only we knew that you hear us now! Feel our love for you, our sorrow to part with you. Praskovia Ivanovna! Praskovia Ivanovna!"

Slava and I, crushed by Mother's lamentations, dropped on our knees together at Praskovia Ivanovna's bedside and started to repeat the words, "We love you, love you, Praskovia Ivanovna. Like our own blood grandmother you are to us, Praskovia Ivanovna. We love you."

For a time we were deeply absorbed in lamenting and weeping. Calming myself a bit, I lifted my head from the bed sheet, turning my eyes toward Praskovia Ivanovna's face.

"Look," I tried gently to lift Mother's head from the dying woman's chest. "Mama, Praskovia Ivanovna is . . . crying. Crying!"

Praskovia Ivanovna's face was unchanged, not one muscle moving, while her breathing too, was rhythmic, her eyes tightly shut. And there they were. From under those tightly shut eyelids, heavy, clear tears appeared, one tear following another. Two, three, four teardrops. Grudgingly, as if forced by superhuman effort, the tears were slowly rolling down Praskovia Ivanovna's cheeks, and remained hanging there, as if they had no more energy to roll.

Those tears, living tears, were Praskovia Ivanovna's parting words, a final farewell—that "Forgive and be forgiven"—that Mother so desperately needed to hear. What torturous effort squeezed out those tears!

Death claimed Praskovia Ivanovna a few hours later. Her grave was dug by all the able-bodied tenants in our court; no gravediggers were to be found in Feodosia. A casket out of unpainted, uneven boards was crudely put together, and we carried Praskovia Ivanovna to the cemetery, to her Dimochka. We stood there at the open grave, watching Praskovia Ivanovna being lowered to the bottom, and could not take shovels in our hands. Instead, as if to throw the earth on her casket with shovels was somehow sacrilegious, we all started to sift the earth a handful at a time, gently, as if not to hurt Praskovia Ivanovna, not to disturb her rest. And for some reason, each fistful of earth brought fresh tears to my eyes. And the more the casket was being covered with this earth, the more tears came. If only no one would throw any more earth into the grave. As long as the coffin was visible, Praskovia Ivanovna was still with us, among us.

Then, as if on command, many mourners took shovels in their hands, hurrying to cover, to hide Praskovia Ivanovna, and very quickly, a gentle earth mound rose. As if satisfied with their labors, the mourners said, "Well, now Praskovia Ivanovna is finally with her Dimochka. May they both rest in peace. . . . May Feodosia's soil serve them as a soft, warm, down comforter."

At the wake, I behaved childishly, not eating or drinking, only weeping. Weeping for my dear Praskovia Ivanovna, missing her terribly.

CHAPTER THIRTY-EIGHT

Spring covered the steppes, hills, and new graves with young grass and field flowers. The sea was losing its wintry chill, soon to invite us to take a refreshing dip in its eternally self-cleansing depths.

May 1, arrived. When early in the morning I headed for the water-well, my eyes were greeted by a large, fresh poster glued to our fence. The poster was calling all able-bodied Feodosians from the age of 15 to 50 to register for work in Germany. The announcement promised that the volunteer workers were to receive the same salary, the same food rations, the same accommodations as German citizens. Further, they would be free to return home after the war's end, if they so chose, or they could remain in Europe.

The posters were greeted with a burst of contagious enthusiasm. The Germans hoped to meet a quota of 1,000 persons for this first ship-ment. Three thousand registered.

Since I, only 48 hours earlier, had just reached my 14th birthday, this offer did not apply to our family. Besides, Mother still lived with hope that Father one day would walk through our gate at Karl Marx 7, across that cobblestone courtyard of ours, climb the two steps of the little porch, throw the door wide open and be there—once again husband, father, head of our family—our protector.

What was very disturbing to us of late was the activity of the parti-sans in the hills surrounding Feodosia. The past November, before the Soviets retreated for the first time, they opened all the jails, allowing the criminals held there to go free. The looters, rapists, murderers—mostly young and able-bodied men, many of *besprizhornik* background—on being freed, decided not to face the discipline of the Germans. Instead, they ran into hiding, making the caves their home and biding their time.

The populace at first called them simply bandits, and not partisans. From time to time they raided the unprotected parts of town near the caves. After plundering mainly for food and taking advantage of defenseless women, they retreated. The Germans, catching one or two periodically, hanged them on the lamp posts, leaving the dangling, rotting bodies for weeks at a time, to discourage others.

With the retreat of the Soviets for the second time, in January, many commissars and Communists who were too late to join the retreating units went into the mountains, organizing the previously undisciplined, wild band of men into a fighting unit. Attacks upon the town became more frequent, more menacing. The partisans' main objective was to antagonize the Germans against the populace, and at the same time to cow the people into passive submission to their ever-increasing harassment.

In this they succeeded with Mother, denying her the opportunity to earn daily food rations for us three. Because many interpreters were killed during the "descent" revenge, on their return, the Werhmacht tried to recruit civilians who spoke German, paying fantastically well with food rations. Mother seriously considered becoming an interpreter, but changed her mind when Tanya described the mangled body of a middle-aged Russian woman brought into the military hospital. On the woman's forehead was carved out the word "Traitor." She was marked a traitor because she worked as an interpreter, and was ordered to take part in the interrogation of captured partisans. One day, while returning home from a late work session, she was ambushed and so viciously cut up that no efforts could save her life.

My mother had been suffering from violent headaches for two or three years now. Soviet doctors, after a cursory eye examination insisted that she had to have patience.

"Menopause," they kept saying. "You must let nature take its course. Don't whine. Many women go through this hormone disbalance, but in time it will fall into a normal pattern. You must wait." Mother waited. And the headaches worsened. More and more often she began to see rainbows—bright, blinding rainbows. Only a few days after the posters appeared, Tanya was having tea with us when Mother started to get up, moaning. "Tanya, dear, can you get me something for these headaches? Those rainbows . . . I feel I am going blind."

Tanya put her glass down with a determined gesture. She seemed for a moment uncustomarily timid, as if afraid to say what was on her mind. But then, with her natural courage she blurted out, "I, personally, have a suspicion. Now don't get panicky, Natalia Alexandrovna. But I *do* believe that you are, in fact, losing your sight." Tanya put her hand over Mother's, and, holding it tightly as if not allowing Mother to escape, she continued: "Your symptoms might be symptoms of glaucoma, chronic glaucoma. It blinds eventually."

Mother did not move, did not protest. She even seemed to be relieved to hear words that for the first time presented a reasonable, if frightening, explanation for her terrible headaches.

"Tanichka, glaucoma always blinds?" she asked.

"Not if you could get an eye operation and special eye drops."

"Drops? Can you supply me with these drops?"

Tanya pulled up her chair and put her arm around Mother's slumping, dejected shoulders. "Natalia Alexandrovna, you need surgery if it is glaucoma, and there is no way you could get such surgery in Feodosia, at least not until the war ends. And when will that be?"

Mother lowered her head and began to cry. "What to do? What to do?"

Tanya briskly wiped Mother's cheeks. "No crying! That's what you can do for a start, Natalia Alexandrovna. No tears. They are bad for the glaucoma condition. So, try not to be emotional, since all those things affect your eyes." And then, seeing Mother, almost like a child, trying to follow her instructions, Tanya poured out what she had really been thinking about.

"Natalia Alexandrovna, now try to hear me out. Why don't you three register to go to Germany. That's where your eyes could be helped. What? Will they take you with glaucoma? Of course they won't. But don't disclose your symptoms during the physical. After all, they only check eyesight, not the eye itself. What if they won't operate on you in Germany? Well, you still have a very big plus on your side—your relations in Riga! Try to locate them immediately. But you must act. Otherwise you might just wake up one day totally blind!"

Totally blind! Slava and I were beside ourselves, picturing Mother blind. "Mother," Slava declared, as if deciding the entire matter for us all, "you must select out of two piles of soot the cleaner one."

Is there such a thing, I wondered. The proverb says there is.

"At least choose the smaller pile, Natalia Alexandrovna," Tanya persisted.

"And my Mark? He might return any day now."

"Return to a blind woman!" Tanya snapped. "In war? To have the burden of providing for a blind wife! Come now, Natalia Alexandrovna, let's stop the sentimentalities. If you allow yourself to go blind, you'll be a burden to your poor husband *and your children!* How about your children? How are they going to manage to provide for themselves *and* for you?"

Tanya got up as if to leave, but Mother instead of being hurt or offended, begged Tanya to stay a bit longer, to talk things over, to figure out how to proceed with the registration. Seeing that her purposely calculated outburst had done the trick, Tanya again took Mother's hand in hers and over a fresh glass of tea, continued to comfort:

"Natalia Alexandrovna, I know how you feel about Mark Illarionovich. My husband, too, is at war. Where? Wounded? Dead? Prisoner? I know nothing, nothing. So, I know it's hard for you to leave. You're still waiting. I am still waiting, if only for a word. So"— and lifting her young, energetic head high, Tanya, as if giving a command, decided—"why don't I wait, just one of us wait. If Mark Illarionovich returns, I'll be here. You'll send your address, and in no time we'll all get in touch. And you might help your man more if you repair your eyes. God! If only my Kolya would surface! Alive or otherwise. Just to know . . . to know!"

As if ashamed in front of this younger woman whose family life was so brutally disrupted by the war, Mother stood up determinedly, and announced that if it was not too late, we would register the next day for work in Germany. Only then a thought occurred to me, that I was not eligible for the registration.

"What about me?" I shouted indignantly. "I'm not 15! Only 14! Am I to be left behind?"

Tanya looked at me as if deciding for herself how old I was.

"Ninochka, you have lost your birth certificate. Yes, dear, you have lost it! And actually, even if you say 16, no one will doubt you. But no need to age yourself more than necessary. Fifteen will do."

The next day we three marched toward a sprawling building complex not far from the bazaar plaza, where hundreds of people stood in line with Soviet documents in their hands, waiting to exchange them for newly issued German documents. One of the first questions asked was if one knew German. We all three claimed to know it, and were ushered toward the front of the line for the physical examination. This we passed quite easily. Our hearts and lungs were found to be in good condition. As Tanya had predicted, eyes were examined only to determine if one had generally normal vision and, much to our relief, Mother passed. The Germans did take exceptional care to examine the teeth of the volunteers. Russians, on the whole, have very good, strong teeth, so much so that the Germans were paying us compliments. And yet many people walked out of the dentist's examining room with bleeding mouths, their teeth pulled out without any warning or any anesthetic. Slava came out spitting blood, minus one healthy molar that was found to have pinhead-size cavity. Mother was outraged at such needless loss of a good, sound tooth. She stood by me when a young German in uniform—the dentist's assistant—was peering into my mouth.

"How old is the girl? Fifteen?" He smiled. "Good teeth. Not one cavity!" A stamp of approval was put on my certificate.

"Why have you pulled my boy's molar?" Mother complained. "Why not to repair his tooth? Such a small cavity."

"Madam," the man sternly announced, "we are at war. We have no time to waste on fixing your molars!"

Slava received a certificate of general approval as to his physical state and was dismissed, but Mother and I were directed toward one more examination room—that of the gynecologist. We were ushered into a sunlit, square room, all its wall space taken with women clinging to one another, staring intensely toward the middle of the room. There, directly in the center, stood the examining table, altar-like, with a white-garbed army doctor performing the ritual of examination, while a Russian nurse assisted him. A young woman's bare lower torso spread on the table, knees high, greeted us as we entered. A few moments later the doctor boomed in German, "Passed!" The nurse, translating, called out, "Next!"

I stood behind Mother, wanting to die, while watching another woman climbing on the table. How repulsive those bare-bottomed females looked on the ugly table, their underpants previously removed, helping themselves to get situated comfortably. In the *banya* the same women were attractive, but there the naked body was cleansed, cared for, as if belonging on the wet benches, to be scrubbed and rinsed, broom-beaten, and rinsed again. But here in this stark, barracks-type room, bright with the spring sunlight, a moustached, foreign-speaking male in a military uniform, standing over the spread female form! And what was he doing? His right hand disappeared almost to the wrist inside the woman's cavity, and the left hand pressed hard on the naked abdomen. Both hands feeling, hunting, for a growth—for even a pea-size growth. A baby? Detecting something suspicious, the doctor—to the obvious regret of the woman on the table, often mixed with utter surprise, tears, and moaning—shouted, "Not passed!" and the nurse, after translating, again commanded, "Next!"

The doctor, not changing the glove, continued with the examinations. I was staring at the bodies of the women facing me, especially their legs and feet. Some had stockings tied with rubber bands or thick cord, to keep them in place. The shapeless cotton stockings or socks were often full of holes, darned over and over, and split open once again, while shoes and boots were exposed in all their undisguised shabbiness and disrepair, many not replaced in years. Although legs and feet could not be hidden, the faces of many younger women were covered with the hems of their flung back skirts. Yes, I thought, that's what I must do—cover my face while I lie on that cursed table. No one must see my face. It's most important to cover one's face. At one point, desperately yearning for privacy, I felt I could not go through with the examination. I literally felt faint. Mother led me to the farthest corner, where I lowered myself onto the cool floor.

"Mama," I implored, "when your turn comes, ask the nurse to take me last . . . when no one will be there to stare at me. I beg you, Mama, or I'll run away!"

Sitting on the floor made me feel better. I hid my face in both palms and just sat there. Not seeing the female applicants paraded and inspected in front of me, my stomach relaxed, and I sighed, somewhat relieved.

Mother's turn came. My palms became glued to my face. I heard Mother say to the doctor, "But it's impossible for me to be pregnant. No husband, and I am over menopause."

"No exceptions, Frau. Hurry now. Knees up! Relax!" And then, matter of factly, "Passed."

Mother's voice again reached me, begging the doctor to spare me the embarrassment of this degrading procedure. But the doctor repeated, that his duty was to inspect every female who registered for work in Germany.

"If your girl is a virgin, there's nothing to worry about. One, two, finished!"

"But of course she is a virgin! She's only 14 . . . I mean 15."

"Well," the doctor persisted, "be happy that the Bolsheviks spared her. I saw girls younger than your daughter, much younger, not spared."

I heard nothing for a few moments, and when I was just ready to lower my hands and see what was going on, a tap on my forehead brought me to my feet. The doctor stood facing me, his look tense, searching, judging. Then his face broke into a half-smile and he led me by the hand to the hateful table. Limply, I followed his quiet directions, climbing up, taking off my underwear, and lifting my skirt. I was prepared to stretch out as I had observed others do, and quickly cover my face. But instead, the doctor's hand in one moment's time, unnoticed, unobserved by my eyes, had reached something that forced me to cry out.

"Passed," he whispered, only for me to hear. Or was he shouting at the top of his voice? "Passed!"

"Passed!" His voice was still ringing through my brain while I ran toward the sea, leaving Mother behind, leaving the ugly examining room behind. What a relief! I passed! I would not be separated from Mother, from Slava. I would not be left alone in Feodosia. The borders of the Soviet Union—so tightly sealed for a quarter of a century—were opening up for me. They were letting me out—to see Europe, to see the world! I passed!

CHAPTER THIRTY-NINE

M *ay 25,* the day of our departure, was sunny, breezy, and warm. As dawn lightened the sky, we sprang out of our beds and started to attend to the last items to be packed and taken with us to Germany. We were told beforehand in no uncertain terms, that only what we could carry ourselves should be taken, because there would be "no porters" waiting to carry our belongings for us. "Don't fuss over your junk," German soldiers had good-humoredly shouted to us just the previous day.

"In Germany, ah! In our beautiful Germany! You can get everything! Nice furniture, nice clothing. . . ." They had a wistful, faraway look. "Oh! If only we could go with you! Back to our *Deutschland,* to our *heimat!*"

We sincerely hoped that those Germans would soon return to their *heimat* (homeland). And it seemed that they soon would. Only ten days earlier, Kerch, had been retaken by German troops. One hundred and seventy thousand Soviet soldiers were taken prisoner. Sevastopol was soon to follow with another 100,000 joining the ranks of the more than 4,000,000 Soviet soldiers who had thus far become prisoners of war. By July 1942, all of Crimea would be in German hands.

At seven in the morning on May 25, we were by the door of our apartment, ready to leave it.

"Let us pause now, as custom demands," Mother said, seating herself on a bundle, while Slava and I followed her example. For about a minute we sat in total silence, not moving, mentally leaving behind all unwelcome happenings that occurred in our lives, while wishing for a clear, undisturbed road ahead of us. We crossed ourselves three times and stepped over the threshold.

The courtyard of Karl Marx No. 7 was empty. No one waited to shout to us, "Godspeed!" No Praskovia Ivanovna, no Dmitry Antonovich, no Osip Osipovich, no Maya, no Father.

As we had entered Feodosia with bundles on our backs four years earlier, so now we were leaving Feodosia with bundles on our backs, only smaller ones, and no Father to help us. My duty was to carry blankets and bed linen, while Mother carried our comforter and three pillows, Tanya having warned her not to lift anything heavy. Slava manfully lugged the leather suitcase containing all our clothing that we thought would be decent enough for stylish Germany, leaving most of our rags behind. Because the rampaging Soviet soldiers had punctured the suitcase through and through with bayonets, Mother had sewn a very sturdy canvas jacket to cover its holes and allow it to serve us a bit longer. Our samovar we left with Tanya, or to Tanya actually, for all she had done for us and still proposed to do. We left Father's civilian clothes with her, in case he returned to Feodosia before we did.

Tanya was the only person accompanying us to the Sarigol train station, helping Mother carry the bundle, and repeatedly reminding her to attend very quickly to the condition of her eyes.

"Now, Natalia Alexandrovia, today is the 25th. You'll probably be at your destination in two or three days. Sit down at the very first available moment and send me your new address. And I beg of you, don't torture yourself over Mark Illarionovich. Right now you can't help him in any way and you'll only drive yourself toward blindness. You can't afford it." The kind nurse shook her finger good-humoredly at Mother. "Remember, in the hospital I hear a lot of rumors. If anything surfaces about your poor Mark Illarionovich, I'll hear about it!"

Marching the two kilometers toward the waiting cattle train, we had no overwhelming sadness at the impending separation from our homeland, since we were not leaving for long. What opportunities were opening for our self-improvement, for rising above the misery of wartime existence, when one's life was constantly in danger of being ended by one side in the conflict or the other.

Tanya envied us openly. "If only my Kolya were back. I would sign up so fast! Spend a year in Europe, earn enough money to start my own nursing home for war invalids."

"That's why I am going to Germany," Slava proclaimed, puffing under the weight of Father's suitcase. "To save money to start my own business."

Mother and I were genuinely taken aback by Slava's remark—it was the first time we heard of his plans for the future.

"Your own business? What have you in mind, Slavochka?" Mother prodded.

"To open my own shop and make those enameled silver cups, saucers, and trays. Remember we saw them in the Moscow museum? People in old Russia used to make all those fantastic things. I'll learn how to start doing it again."

I felt generous toward my ambitious brother and not having any specific plans for spending my soon to be acquired capital, I proposed to donate my savings toward his enterprise.

Full of hope and lightheartedness we hastened toward Sarigol. The open, spacious field was already partially occupied by hundreds of people bent under heavy bundles, looking for a place to drop their belongings. We selected a spot nearer to the railroad tracks and waited for ten o'clock, when our train was scheduled to depart. Although exactly 1,000 people were to leave Feodosia with us, many more had gathered to see off friends and relatives. Near us, a family of five sat waiting, but only the woman and her two children were going, while her husband, over 50, and their youngest child, under 15, were not eligible to go with them. Yet no real deep sorrow or tears were to be seen at their parting. The husband, very business-like, was instructing his spouse to send him immediately any money the three of them would earn so that he could put a down payment on a shoe repair shop he wanted to open. His wife and two boys were nodding in solemn agreement.

"And Masha," the husband was very practical, "don't squander the money on pretty dresses or silk hose! Once I turn into a millionaire, I'll cover you from head to toe in silk!" And all grinned approvingly, perhaps visualizing such times in the near future.

In front of us, on large bundles, sat two young women, one holding a little girl in her lap. The women resembled each other in appearance, both with chestnut hair, both tall, with full bosom and slender waist. The one holding the child turned to the other and said, "Don't worry, sis. Just leave with a light heart. And I beg of you, don't worry at all over Sonichka. She'll be safe with me. I'll take good care of that favorite niece of mine, won't I?"

The girl, tickled slightly under her armpits, jumped in delight. She climbed into the lap of her departing mother, grinning. "Auntie and I will have a good time and wait for you. And send me some chocolate, Mama! Promise?"

The mother promised on her honor that the chocolate would arrive in a jiffy. As many other families had done, those sisters decided, when the posters appeared offering jobs in Germany, that the younger one with the child, already widowed in the war, would leave, while the older sister who still waited daily for some news about her soldier husband, would remain behind to take care of the younger sister's child.

Families were splitting up, yet no heartbreaking sorrow overshadowed the parting, because the separation was voluntary.

At 10 a.m. The German guards came to life.

"Russky! Russky! March to the train cars! Hurry now! Ja! Ja! Frau, go there. You, Frau, come in this car. Fraulein, follow this group. Ja! Ja! Very good! Very punctual!"

Thirty-three cattle cars, the floors covered with fresh hay, made up our train, each one accommodating about 30 people. Slava and I climbed aboard and ran very quickly toward a corner where the three of us could be situated more cozily than in the middle of the car. It was away from the door, regretfully, but also away from the *parasha* (the pail destined to be our outhouse throughout the journey).

The locomotive was already chuffing, wheels creaking impatiently, ready to move, the way the wheels were creaking while getting ready to take Father away five months earlier. The same railroad station. The same rails.

"Mama!" I heard my voice screaming. She was kissing Tanya goodbye. "Mama! I am afraid! Afraid to leave Feodosia!"

Mother patted my braids. "I know you're sad, Ninochka, but don't be afraid. No, we won't lose track of Father, not if he comes to Feodosia. You want to stay here? But, *dochenka*, how will we survive here? Interpreter? So, I'll be an interpreter and it'll feed us. But the partisans might carve my eyes out. And speaking of eyes, only in Germany can my sight be repaired. Ninochka, I, too, am afraid, afraid to become blind."

Ashamed of my sudden outburst, I threw my arms around Mother's neck and—as if I were the adult and she the frightened child—I patted her head awkwardly, and murmured, "Sorry, sorry, Mama. No question about it, we *must* leave Feodosia. Only promise, not for long, Mama. Promise?"

"Not for long, child, not for long."

Part Two

Outside Soviet Borders

Perhaps there will be only one flock
And one shepherd with an iron staff
And a flock of human sheep
All shorn alike and bleating alike! . . .

The future smells of Russian leather,
Blood, godlessness and many whippings.
I should advise our grandchildren
To be born with very thick skins on their backs.

HEINRICH HEINE—German poet
writing in the year 1842.

CHAPTER FORTY

A girl, unaccompanied by any member of her family, was looking out of the small, square cattle car window at retreating Feodosia, until the town completely vanished from view. Then she lowered herself onto the hay, next to me, and was motionless. I turned to the girl and, tortured by the sadness of separation from Feodosia, point-blank asked her, "We *will* return, won't we?"

"Naturally," she said, matter-of-fact, and smiled.

I was hypnotized by that smiling face. I had seen her somewhere, but where? In the *banya*? In the bazaar? Where did I see her? She was quite tall, with a slender, almost boyish figure. Her short, dark hair fell in bangs over a very prominent forehead, and while it camouflaged the unproportionately high brow, nothing could hide the girl's nose, which was very long, somewhat sharp, and covered with freckles. It was this long-nosed profile that was familiar to me. Not many people have such profiles—not at all pretty, yet so striking that to see it once was always to remember it. And when the girl smiled, as she did after saying "Naturally," her whole face was transformed. It no longer was just unusual, but turned into an unusually attractive face, dark eyes sparkling, thin-lipped mouth revealing pearly teeth, and the long nose played no role in detracting from the sudden, unexpected beauty. My questioning mind, for a while could not comprehend what my eyes saw, so that I continued to stare at the girl, waiting for another smile to convince me.

Then a mental picture arose in my memory—August 20, 1941, only a day after Father's departure for the Red Army, the forced relocation of Soviet Germans out of Feodosia, the breaking up of families, and Mr. Muller, the carpenter, marching by with his older daughter while his wife and younger daughter pleaded with the NKVDists to be taken also. I was convinced that the girl was the younger daughter of the Mullers.

The girl, trying to escape my intense look, turned to her small suitcase and took out a tattered, obviously much-handled book.

"My name is Nina," I said wishing desperately to be sure if the girl was a Muller, "and your last name is Muller, isn't it?"

The girl nodded, adding softly, "Lana."

"Lana," I repeated, liking the sound of her name. "I saw you that day, on the 20th, saw all of you." Lana looked down at the book cover. "And your mother, she allows you to go to Germany alone?"

Not raising her eyelids, Lana replied quietly, "Mother didn't survive the descent. I hid."

I asked no more, becoming still at the memory of that dreadful time. Trying to sound very adult, I stretched out my hand to Lana, offering my friendship. "You are an orphan, Lanochka—no mother, no father. I have no father. Let's stick together and be friends."

The girl took my hand eagerly. We again fell silent for a while, listening to the train's wheels churning. Lana then lifted the book she held in her lap and said, pushing it toward me, "*Uncle Tom's Cabin*. You read German? Have you read it? No? Well, here. Take it. I've read it several times. A German soldier gave it to me."

I accepted the book and slowly, a bit laboriously at first, began to read the account of slavery in 19th century America. Only the onset of twilight forced me to put the book down.

By then Feodosia was far, far away.

Our train crawled at a snail's pace, giving way to military trains and to the Red Cross trains that were hurrying wounded Germans to hospitals in Europe. For many of us it was not a very comfortable trip, especially for those who fell ill with gastro-intestinal disorders brought about by bad water. Our *parasha* pail was constantly occupied, exuding a suffocating stench. The June sun beating down on the car's roof intensified the foul smell. More than thirty young, able-bodied men, soon after leaving Feodosia, not wishing to put up with such discomforts, decided to run away as soon as we crossed the Soviet border, forcing the Germans, who were quite lax until then, to guard us more closely, bolting the car doors. The stench intensified even more.

A few days later, at the Polish town of Przemysl, we were ordered out of the train cars, and marched with our belongings to the baths for disinfection. At the huge town square, about 5,000 men, women, and children were assembled, sitting on their bundles or suitcases. There were several hundred Red Army prisoners of war with thin, gray-skinned faces, dull eyes. They were being shipped to the Reich to be employed in factories and by farmers. Their only possessions were their ragged uniforms.

Aside from the Russian prisoners and our group, the rest of the people assembled in the huge square were Polish Jews. Whole families sat or stood by their suitcases and bundles, waiting to be disinfected. They were the richest in appearance, with rows of matching leather suitcases, flanked by large bundles of belongings, even carrying musical instruments and sewing machines. Their mode of dress, in our view, was very chic, with women sporting gold earrings and bracelets and massive neck chains. The Jews did not appear to be unduly disturbed by this "resettlement." The youngsters were scurrying around, shouting greetings, looking for neighbors and friends. Several enterprising men were bartering as in a bazaar, carrying apples or boiled eggs or bagels in small baskets and in their hands. Women were calmly feeding their infants.

"*Ost! Ost!*" A portly, dull-faced SS man appeared at our side. Who was he calling this denigrating *Ost,* we wondered.

"You there, *Ostarbeiter!*" he shouted once more, pointing directly at us, calling us "Eastern workers." "March after me! Drag your junk with you. It'll be disinfected. No need for your Russian lice to spread into the Reich!"

How differently he acted from Feodosia's soldiers. Russian lice! As if lice can choose a nationality. With our traditional weekly *banya* sessions, lice had difficulty surviving. Still stewing over the SS man's words, I was propelled by the surrounding mass toward the building that housed the baths. *Banya!* How good it will feel to scrub my skin, to beat it with a soft broom, making it "breathe," to splash pails of water, refreshing myself after so many days in the stifling train. While Slava was marched away to the men's section, two hundred of us females were led into a huge, cold room lined with benches. There we stripped and our clothing was rushed into the disinfecting chamber. The same fat, unfriendly SS guard accompanied us right into the room where we undressed, watching us strip, from time to time hitting his left heel with a leather whip. Then pointing to an adjoining room—also very cold, without any steam or water faucets or benches as in our *banya*—he barked, passing to everyone the smallest crumb of soap, "Go bathe!"

We stood in the big room, confused, forlorn, not knowing how to proceed, when all at once cold water began to sprinkle out of shower heads in the ceiling. "*Banya?*" a nearby bather grumbled. And another echoed, "That's bathing? If Germans bathe that way, they must stink," and she bravely marched up to the guard who remained standing at the entrance, watching us and tapping his boot with increasing relish.

The young woman asked to be given a sponge or broom and hotter water. The guard stared at the woman's exceptionally luxurious pubic hair and abruptly stopped the rhythmic drumbeat on his boot. Then, almost unnoticeable to our eyes, he produced his whip and landed it on the woman's behind. While she ran back screaming, he roared with laughter, watching her rear end sporting a dark pink mark left by the whip. Later, all two hundred of us, naked and cold, sat for an hour waiting for our belongings to be returned, while a gloomy, dark mood settled over us. Things did not look, did not feel right. Our reception in Przemysl somehow did not correspond to the rosy promises in Feodosia's posters. And that ugly *Ost!* Not even calling us by our ethnic name, Russians.

Several more days en route passed in slow, crawling fashion, often detouring, due to destroyed rail lines, or being shunted aside by military trains; creeping across the rest of Poland, following a meandering route through Yugoslavia, Austria, and Czechoslovakia, making countless unscheduled stops, then again renewing our slow progress forward.

On the fifteenth day of travel, our train came to a halt in a beautiful mountainous spot. The guards began to run from car to car, unbolting the doors and shouting, "Detrain! Detrain! You've arrived!"

While the first fifteen cars began to move toward a different destination, our fifteen cars remained standing. I rushed to the opened door and read on the station wall the name of the town, MARKTREDWITZ—a Bavarian town near the border of Czechoslovakia. Stretching our limbs and dragging the bundles out of the train cars, we stood on German soil for the first time, delighted with what we saw.

Such a pretty Bavarian town, sparkling in its cleanliness, as if its cobbledstoned streets and alleys were scrubbed with brooms and soap-

suds. Not one speck of litter anywhere! And the abundance of blooming plants! In gardens, in hanging baskets, in window sills—blooms,
blooms, blooms—well fed, well attended flower blooms spilled forth
in such profusion. And the fruit trees! Where have I seen this town? It
was strangely familiar, as if in the past I had already visited Marktredwitz.

Yes! I knew where I had seen this town! Back in 1939, right after the
Friendship Pact was signed between our two countries, Soviet school
books carried a picture of a "typical German family." The picture could
have been taken in this very first Bavarian town that we reached!
Perhaps it was taken by that neat brick house facing the station, with its
fenced-off, tidy little garden, beaming at us with multi-colored blooms.
The house itself seemed to be teasing us, its sparkling clean windows
framed by starched snow-white curtains, and there—sitting on the
threshold—were the neatest children I had ever encountered. It was
Sunday, and the children were dressed for church.

Our belongings in hand, or on our backs, we were lined four abreast
and ordered to follow the guards. "Where?" someone asked. "To the
marketplace."

Why to the marketplace? I wondered, a bit perturbed, but my uneasiness quickly passed. On such a pleasant, sunny day, one could not
remain troubled for long, being disarmed by the friendliness of nature.
To think that not one home in Marktredwitz, not one building was
destroyed or damaged by a bomb or artillery shell! After Feodosia, after
the war-ravaged countries we had passed through, Germany seemed to
be a land out of some beautiful fairytale.

The local residents were hurrying to church. Several old people
shouted to us, "*Grüss Gott!*" (God's greetings!), but the rest paid no
attention to our large gathering, as if they already were used to such
scenes. We, on the other hand, devoured the natives with avid curiosity. Could it be that the females of Marktredwitz were of the same
race as the tall, handsome soldiers we encountered in Feodosia? We
expected their women to possess the same characteristics, but the ones
we observed hastening to Sunday services were stocky, a bit bow-
legged, with heavy bosoms. They arranged their thin, greasy-looking
hair in unappetizing, sausage-like buns, while evidence of baldness was
apparent on the top of some women's heads. And so many natives had
an enormous, turkey-like goiter, hanging grotesquely over their col-
lars. Mother knowingly remarked, "Not enough iodine in their water."

While many of the younger women wore flowery patterned dresses, the older ones were bedecked in short, fancy Bavarian jackets with long, dark skirts covered with freshly laundered "Sunday" aprons. And all, without exception, walked in low-heeled, thick-soled shoes that made their feet look large and unfeminine. Not one woman we passed wore gold jewelry. But some, as if to replace their jewelry, wore a narrow band of black crepe around their left arm—a symbol of mourning.

CHAPTER FORTY-ONE

"*Marketplace!* Unload! Get ready for disinfection!"
The guards kept repeating these orders, directing us toward a huge square. A wave of people began to spread over the block-wide area that was still called a marketplace, but of late served only to greet the newly arrived human cargo from the East, while the market for foodstuffs was moved to another part of town. The trains arrived daily in Marktredwitz, delivering fresh additions to the labor force. Hundreds of thousands of Poles, who fell under German occupation much earlier than we did, were already on the soil of the Reich. Arriving in even greater numbers than Poles were Ukrainians and Russians. Then, millions of captured Red Army men followed. In order to cleanse all those people before dispersing them, several large barracks were erected on the former market square of Marktredwitz. This time the procedure was much more thorough than in Przemysl. After the disinfection, all leather articles, including suitcases, were ruined, together with many articles of clothing, which turned stiff as boards or became permanently wrinkled. The inspection of our bodies was much stricter this time also. Some people lost their hair due to lice infestation, and women wept when, mercilessly, their braids were chopped off. I could feel Mother's anxiety when I was called into the examining room, where a young German nurse minutely inspected my scalp and my skin. Popping out of this room with my braids intact, I heard Mother's relieved voice.

"Thank heaven! My Ninochka still has her braids! Sacrilegious to rob a virgin of her hair. It's her pride and joy."

As did many Russians, Mother held to the old-fashioned custom of a virgin proclaiming her purity with braided hair. I, on the other hand, longed to shed my long hair, annoyed at the care it demanded to keep clean; annoyed at the tight, pulling sensation braiding induced. To me braids brought no pride and joy. But what could I do?

While Mother and I felt no ill effects from the two-week journey, Slava was suffering terribly from the impure water. He often sprang up from the suitcase he was sitting on, and rushed to the lavatory, returning exhausted and dehydrated from his ordeal. Not being able to stand watching Slava growing weaker, his lips cracking, I ran to the nearest guard, demanding to know how much longer we were to sit under the baking sun, waiting for what? For whom?

"You will just wait, young lady! Don't throw tantrums! Soon your owner will come," said the guard, waving me away.

"What owner? I don't belong to any owner! Please, explain!" I tried to catch the guard's glance, tried to interpret what he meant. The word "owner" sounded ominous, foreboding.

The guard suddenly snapped into a stiff pose, his eyes observing a string of approaching Mercedes limousines, followed by several trucks. "There!" He pointed toward the cars. "There are your owners. Run to your family, Mädchen, and stick together. Take my advice."

I hurried back, repeating the guard's words to Lana in a half-whisper, not wishing to upset Mother. "The Germans tricked us. They lied to us in Feodosia. Remember how they wrote on the posters that we'll be 'equal' to German citizens? Rubbish! See those men? The guard called them our 'owners.' Owners, mind you! Not just employers," I sputtered.

Lana was not unduly disturbed. "He probably tried to make fun of you," she decided. And looking around me, I preferred to believe her, since no one appeared to be frightened or agitated.

The limousines stopped one by one, discharging portly, middle-aged men in Bavarian *lederhosen*. Some of the men were factory owners and mine owners, while others were farmers, and all needed workers to till their fields, to dig in their mines, to attend to countless tasks in the factories, since most of Germany's able-bodied men were called away to war.

A sprightly little fellow in police uniform, with a stack of official-looking papers in his grip, greeted the men, and began to lead them from one group of people to another. Reaching a sturdy, robust-looking Ukrainian family that was situated near us, the policeman said in a businesslike tone, "Now, gentlemen, here I have a strong, healthy family of pure peasant stock. Tireless workers," and he signaled with his finger for the head of the family to come nearer.

The marketplace became hushed, all watching what the Germans would do next. A jolly, ruddy-faced farmer reached out both hands to the Ukrainian man's upper arm. "Strong. Good, good. Mark him for my farm. Wife? She'll pass. . . ." The policeman put cross-like marks by the names of the ones who were selected. The Germans were looking over every man, every woman, every teenager offered them. They repeatedly felt men's arm muscles, pinched women's buttocks, even breasts. They opened people's mouths to check the condition of their teeth the way horse traders do. One such employer, satisfied with the appearance of a full breasted young woman, went away in thorough disgust when she smiled, exposing a row of upper teeth covered with steel caps, which were quite fashionable in the Soviet Union.

The marketplace was no longer hushed or placid when the Germans began to break up families by selecting some members and rejecting others. In some instances, husbands and wives were separated, or parents from their children. Realizing the awful truth, people became frantic with grief. I sat on my bundle between Slava and Lana, feeling as if I not only knew the Marktredwitz railroad station and neat, flower-decorated houses, but that I also knew about the town's marketplace. How, where did I learn about this?

All at once, piercing cries shattered the air. A pretty, slender girl, perhaps twenty, ran after a Bavarian, pleading in halting German. "Sir! Sir! Be merciful! Don't separate me from my spouse! Take both of us! I beg you!" And then, as if exhausted by pleading, by the sorrow of approaching separation, she added in despair, "We just got married four months ago."

A guard grabbed the young woman by both arms and held her until a truck carrying her husband and a group of young men, sped away. The employer, before returning to his limousine—perhaps disturbed by the woman's plea—wrote on a piece of paper his name and the address of his place of business.

"There," he said, pressing the paper into the woman's hand. "Your husband will work in my mine. He won't be far from you. I can't use women."

I sat on my bundle, bent almost in two, holding onto my belly. Wide-eyed, I stared at Lana, all at once remembering where I saw the marketplace before.

"*Uncle Tom's Cabin!* Lana! Remember? In *Uncle Tom's Cabin!* The marketplace! Slaves! Dark-skinned slaves. We're light-skinned, that's the only difference!"

The sprightly policeman was leading a tall, well-built Bavarian toward us, a very handsome man with full mouth, his hazel eyes large and sparkling. He was perhaps forty, or a bit older. The policeman pointed at us three.

"Here, dear sir, I have a family just right for your porcelain factory. They are from a Muscovy porcelain town. The mother spent her whole life working in the Dulovo factory." Mother was ready to correct this statement, but the policeman kept pressing. "No syphilis in the family history. All speak passable German." The factory owner glanced at Mother, at Slava, at me. "The mother is in good health. The girl is only fifteen. Strong, well-built. The boy? Well, sir, if you wish to take only the woman and the girl?"

The factory owner's glance once more scanned Slava's exhausted, dehydrated face, Mother's prematurely wrinkled, anxiety-filled features, and measuring me with bold, impersonal eyes from head to toe, he announced, "The girl, I'll take her. And this one," he pointed at Lana.

The policeman was just in the process of putting a cross mark beside Lana's and my name when Mother, as if coming out of a temporary stupor, slid from the bundle she was squatting on, and landed at the factory owner's feet.

"Sir! In the name of justice, don't separate us! I implore you!" she moaned, surprising the factory owner, perhaps, by her fluent German. "Don't ruin our lives, sir! Don't tear our family apart! We're all three good workers. My son is a bit under the weather. We had poor water during the journey. I beg you! I beg you!"

I watched my mother on her knees at the feet of that long-legged man in boy's pants, and wanted to die.

"How ugly life is, Lana," I stated matter-of-fact, surprised at the dull, lifeless tone of my own voice. "I just want to get it over with. To die . . . die this second." And while wishing for death, I also wished desperately for tears to come and ease my unhappiness. I could not squeeze out a single tear.

Lana had remained as though stunned until then, but hearing me speak of death, she all at once sprang up from her suitcase, threw her head back a bit, and made a step toward the businessman.

"I am ashamed . . . utterly ashamed to be of German blood, sir! Ashamed of my German name." She stared at the industrialist, her eyes ablaze with anger.

"You are German? *Volksdeutsche?*" The man looked surprised, but pleased. "What is your name?" He followed the finger of the policeman, pointing on the list to Lana's name. "Aha! Lana Muller. And why are you all by yourself? Where is your family?" The factory owner was friendly, interested, involved.

"My family?" Lana paused, lowering her eyelids, perhaps reliving her separation from father, from sister. "The Soviets have done, back in Feodosia, less than a year ago, what you are doing now. They destroyed my family, tore us from one another." While both German men remained silent, even after Lana stopped talking, she pointed at my weeping mother, at my ill brother, at me, and very quietly said, "They are my family, Herr Fabrikant." And as if challenging the rich man to be humane, and not to dispute her claim, she stretched her whole body, adding inches to her height, and in her proud, fierce defiance she was as beautiful as when she smiled. The factory owner looked at her with amused, embracing eyes, his voice soothing, kind.

"Calm yourself, Fraulein Muller. I shall sacrifice my better judgment and accept all four of you. Good?" He bent slightly toward Lana's uplifted face, and looking deeply into the young girl's eyes, answered for her, "Good!"

CHAPTER FORTY-TWO

*T**he truck* sped us toward a picturesque neighboring town, surrounded by mountains and forests that gave way to a valley,
where among fields of wildflowers stood adorable one and two-story
brick and stone buildings, housing people whose whole economic life
was dominated by the porcelain factory, as it was in my native Dulovo.
But how different the towns were! How different the factories were!
While Dulovo's factory was a dingy, old-fashioned structure with walls
crumbling for need of repair and with soot-covered small windows,
surrounded by pathetic barracks where workers lived on the level
of serfs, this Bavarian factory glowed, its grounds immaculate, and
its employees energetic and involved. And the houses of those workers! How rich they were compared to Dulovo's barracks. Surrounded
by white fences, each house was a miniature estate where children
played on swings among the neat flower beds, supervised by doting
grandparents and pet dachshunds. No dust, no grime was allowed to
accumulate and settle on buildings or inhabitants. The door knobs
were constantly polished, windows washed, floors waxed, gardens
weeded.

The truck, with forty of us selected by the handsome factory
owner—mostly single, good-looking females—approached the factory
gate about half an hour after leaving Marktredwitz. The guard pointed
to an imposing, one-story building directly across from the factory,
with a high, peaked roof and large, rectangular windows adorned with
flower pots.

"Your place," he announced, and we grinned. To be housed in such a building was the very next best thing to being allotted one of the private houses we had just passed. Things were looking up. The memory of Marktredwitz's market square was quickly receding.

We were preparing to get off by the front entrance of the handsome building, but the truck was not stopping just yet. It was turning the corner, and as I looked at the series of steps leading to a broad front entrance, I saw a sign in bold letters over the impressive double doors—CLUB.

What a letdown! The building was a club for the factory employees, and not meant to house us. The truck stopped at the side of the building and the guard directed us to get out. Then, pointing to a narrow, uninviting door, he snapped, "Hurry! Hurry! Don't stare open-mouthed. I have to drive back to Marktredwitz to fetch more people." And he pushed us into a dark corridor toward narrow stairs leading downward.

"A basement! A goddamned basement!" an angry voice hissed. Stumbling down the unfamiliar, poorly lighted steps, we crowded into a large room. Thick metal pipes rose out of the basement floor and through the ceiling, supplying the club above with heat and water. Between the pipes were arranged rows of double-decked bunk beds, and a long wooden table pushed against one wall. Spartan. Almost immediately a slight, middle-aged man in a peculiar suit resembling a uniform of sorts, appeared in the basement. In a crisp, efficient, but not unfriendly voice he addressed us.

"Welcome, everyone! Welcome. I am your supervisor. My name is Ordnung." When people giggled at hearing this name, which means "Order" in German, the man continued, unperturbed, his lean face breaking into a half-smile. "That's right. It is my real name and I am good at keeping order." Half-jest, half-warning. "Now, people, let's get acquainted." And Herr Ordnung seated himself at the large table, spreading a file of papers, ready to appoint each one of us to a specific job at the factory. When we demanded to know why we were housed in a basement, while the posters in Feodosia promised living arrangements equal with the natives, the supervisor shook his head and waved a hand in front of his face.

"Folks, learn to take the posters, the promises, with a grain of salt. After all, it's wartime. Perhaps later things will change." He took out of one large envelope a bundle of small cloth badges, where on light background in dark blue ink were printed three letters—OST.

"There. Put it on the left side of your chest. Wear it always. What?

You think it's degrading? Nonsense! All foreign workers wear badges. Poles wear a letter 'P.' You'll wear 'OST.' "

The warm summer months were passing, wilting the abundant flower blossoms, but turning the tree foliage into an exuberant earth-hued bouquet. All through the late summer, Germans invaded the surrounding woods on weekends, armed with small baskets, picking strawberries, blackberries, and juicy, fat blueberries. After the first few weeks under strict supervision, we, too, were allowed to leave the factory premises and wander into the forest to pick berries.

Life was not as rosy as we had fantasized it would be while still in Feodosia, but it was not pitch black, either. Working hours were long and tedious. Mother was assigned to a comparatively easy job—to sort chipped dishes from the perfect ones. Slava's job was to pack the undamaged dishes in crates and cart them to an adjoining storage room where they were kept awaiting shipment. I, on the other hand, together with Lana, was given an easier and more interesting task—to paint a very simple pattern of flowers on the cups and saucers. We two were employed in a department where only Germans worked—all women.

When the first pay day arrived, twenty marks were given to each person. This was one-tenth of what German workers received. On expressing our indignation at such minimal pay, the factory owner explained patiently—was he not feeding us? For this, part of our pay was taken out. Was he not quartering us? In a basement? Never mind where. He was providing us with adequate shelter. And then, who did we think would pay for our transportation from Feodosia to his factory? German taxpayers?

The Germans were quite decent toward us in that small Bavarian town. They did not abuse us, either physically or psychologically. Only once, while we were being marched to work, a fifteen-year-old Hitler *Jugend* hissed at our group, "*Verfluchte untermenschen!*" ("Damned subhumans!") Our supervisor must have given the boy quite a tongue lashing later, because the young fellow apologized to us the next day.

Some Germans were truly kind to us, bringing to the basement baskets of apples, cherries, and baked potatoes. Some carried to work extra flasks with milk or good ersatz coffee, and shared it with us, often accompanied by a cheese or sausage sandwich, or a generous slice of their delicious thin cake, called *kuchen*. When cool weather arrived, the supervisor, observing the lack of warm clothing in our possession, all of which we had left in Feodosia due to our optimistic belief that we could buy all we needed in Germany, rallied the town folk to donate some clothing. Bicycle after bicycle rolled up to our basement, their riders dumping on the bunks piles of coats, jackets, skirts, socks, boots—all well worn, some mended, yet still better than anything we had left behind in the Soviet Union.

During the monthly "mail day" when we were allowed to send postcards to friends and relatives, the supervisor diligently inspected the mail for proper postage and correct addresses, making sure it was sent out promptly. He also periodically supplied us with necessary medications such as iodine, aspirin, or bandages. Strict and demanding when it came to work attendance, he nevertheless was very decent and kind. And in Mother's case, Herr Ordnung proved his compassion when, one early November morning, on entering our basement to check if everyone had left for work, he found Mother by the table, moaning, her forehead tied with Slava's dark sock.

"What is the matter, Frau?" the supervisor demanded.

Mother decided to be open with the man, no matter what the consequences would be. And the consequences could be disastrous, because people who could not labor were sent back to the Soviet Union. Already two young women whose bellies had begun to balloon, their pregnancies undetected during Feodosia's medical examination, had been promptly shipped back to Feodosia.

Mother was frightened, but could not avoid any longer letting the supervisor know of her condition. While the man stared at her sock-wrapped forehead, Mother blurted out, "I must confess to you, Herr Ordnung, that back home a friend, a nurse, thought that my headaches could be caused by . . . by glaucoma." She forced herself to utter the · frightful word. "I never had an eye examination for glaucoma. So, I still am not sure if these headaches are caused by glaucoma. But, if it's so, then I won't be of use to the factory owner much longer. If I am sent back to war-torn Feodosia, no operation can be done there. I'll go blind as sure as the sun will set tonight. Help me, Herr Ordnung!" Mother challenged the supervisor.

He sat opposite her, studying her face intensely. "No question about it," he finally said briskly. "If you go blind—out you go. But Frau, your children will remain in Germany. We won't let healthy, young people go back. We need them. So not only will you be blind, but you'll be separated from the children."

The sound of a moan and a sob escaped Mother's throat. "Help me,

Herr Ordnung! Can't you help me? Bring me to an eye specialist," she pleaded.

"I can't bring you to an eye specialist. Doctors aren't allowed to treat you people—the ones from Soviet Russia."

Mother was near hysteria. She banged the table with her hand in exasperation. No one to turn to for help—no husband, no strong, grown son who could fight for her interests. Not even allowed to go to a medical doctor for help. "If only I had never left my Riga, never went to that cursed Dulovo. If only I remained in my native Riga and never became a 'Soviet subject,' " she cried. Herr Ordnung suddenly slapped his knee and jumped up.

"Frau! Frau! That's it! We found a way out! Riga! We'll say to the eye doctor that you're from Riga! He is not forbidden to treat people from the Baltic States. I'll bring you to Hof—a town about 20 kilometers from us. I know a good eye specialist. Next week we'll go to Hof. Let's see what the eye doctor will say."

"Glaucoma," the eye doctor announced. And the prognosis was gloomy. The right eye was probably beyond saving, but the sight in the left eye could be preserved if an operation were performed within two to six months. Could he perform the surgery? No, he could not, because Mother was a foreigner, unless a special permit was obtained. The doctor gave Mother eye drops, but warned her that they would only postpone the blindness, not prevent it, because her eyes were damaged beyond permanent help from medication.

Herr Ordnung would not give up. He sent a letter to the High Command in Riga, imploring on Mother's behalf to find out if any relatives of hers, whom she had not seen since 1915, still remained, who could sponsor her trip to Riga—her birthplace—to undergo a glaucoma operation? He wrote also to the monastery where Mother was brought up, requesting the abbess to look into Mother's case. After all, she was once their ward.

Lo and behold! The nuns did locate Mother's single remaining relative—her maternal aunt, after whom she had been named and who was now a widow in her late sixties. She was willing to sponsor our trip to Riga, paying for our transportation and for the critically needed surgery. Yet, due to typical German thoroughness, nothing could be hurried. All had to be in perfect order—stamped, signed, and approved. We were forced to wait. But would glaucoma wait?

CHAPTER FORTY-THREE

While Mother was full of anxiety, desperately wishing to reach Riga and hurry under the eye surgeon's scalpel, anxiety was also filling many Germans. More and more often the word "Stalingrad" was heard. At first the word was uttered with a certain optimism, supported by the letters of Wehrmacht soldiers, telling their families how close to final victory they were getting in Stalingrad. Newsreels in the early Fall showed grinning, cheerful Germans marching on the roads near Stalingrad, taking thousands upon thousands of Red Army men prisoners. Later, the newsreels became sort of stuck—the same roads, the same faces of German soldiers, still grinning, the same columns of captured Red Army men—as if events had frozen. Herr Ordnung, who managed to obtain permission to escort us to a movie theater once in a while, became openly concerned while watching the same newsreels for weeks at a time. He knew that things were being hidden from the German population when no war newsreels in connection with Stalingrad appeared at all, but were replaced by a morale boosting sequence showing the successful rehabilitation of Wehrmacht casualties—all young men, who had lost an arm or leg, or both legs—learning to ski down the Bavarian slopes, after being fitted with artificial limbs in a sanatorium created especially for this purpose.

And all the time more and more black crepe appeared on the left arms of grieving relatives. By November 1942, the word "Stalingrad" was no longer pronounced optimistically or casually or hopefully. It became a curse. "Devil take that place!" Herr Ordnung once muttered, while leading us back to the basement, after a two hour outing in a movie house. And it looked that way to the ones trapped in it—"The Devil's Place."

Many changes began to take place on the Soviet-held territory of Russia by then. Frightened by German successes, Stalin went so far as allowing for the first time in twenty-five years the word "Russia" to creep back into the people's vocabulary. He opened the churches—not just the "anti-god museums" that the most venerated cathedrals were turned into—but little, crumbling, wooden churches in out-of-the-way villages. They were scrubbed, cobwebs removed, windows cleaned and repaired, icons, altars returned. The church bells began to ring throughout the length and breadth of the country. They were ringing not only in villages, towns, and cities, but they burst into every home, including the faraway *kolkhozes,* through the ever-present radio loud-speakers.

The ancient name for Sunday reappeared, the cherished *Woskre-senie*—The Day of Resurrection. And people wondered whether per-haps it truly was a time of resurrection of the whole land, the resurrection of their much-suffering Russia?

Stalin began to call upon people to fight not so much for Commu-nism, but for the "Holy Motherland," and for the "Holy Cherished Fatherland." Heroes out of the "holy, cherished" past reappeared, calling people to sacrifice in this "Patriotic War." Prince Alexander Nevsky called to them out of the 13th century, a special order for bravery being created in his name. So was General Suvorov calling the Russian people to duty all the way back from the days of Catherine the Great, joined by General Kutusov—the famous commander in the war with Napoleon. Those long dead heroes were raising their voices as if they were still among the living, exhorting the people to rouse them-selves out of their leaden apathy so prevalent in the year just past, and to start fighting. Even Czars—all of whom were until then considered to be "bloodsuckers"—began to boom out of the long past with a call to arms, led by that giant of a man—Peter the Great. Czars became acceptable, respectable, admired.

Stalin allowed shoulder epaulets to be worn once more on military tunics. The significance of this step might escape a non-Soviet person. After all, what was so important about shoulder epaulets? But to the Soviet Red Army man it meant a lot.

Epaulets marked the same designation of rank as those that had been ripped off during the Civil War, when anyone wearing them was shot, since the wearer was a White—a mortal enemy to the Red who wore no epaulets, emphasizing his "redness." A quarter of a century went by in which every child—from the cradle, more or less—was taught to loathe, despise, and downright hate the warrior with shoulder epaulets. Those filthy epaulets represented Czarist Russia, the "Bloody Russia," which had no place in the hearts of Soviet citizens.

And there they were—the exuberant, rich, heavy epaulets of Czarist days, jumping up onto the shoulders of not just Red commanders, but "officers"! This long forbidden word, too, returned, together with the word "soldier."

No longer was the soldier expected to give his life only for the "Union of Advisers," the Communist Party, or Josef Stalin personally. While at the start of the war Stalin ordered his people to fight and die for "the Party of Lenin-Stalin," now he dropped this order like a hot potato. And the Soviet people, encouraged by the promise of a better, brighter future, began to fight.

On February 1, 1943, Radio Moscow ecstatically broadcast news of the Soviet victory at Stalingrad. We in the Bavarian porcelain town, together with the rest of the Reich's population, heard the news only two days later, when Hitler declared three days of national mourning for the 6th Army that had perished at Stalingrad, leaving behind, according to the Soviets, 300,000 men—killed, wounded, or captured. Crepe strips appeared like some gruesome black blossoms on the sleeves of Germans, and kept appearing for a long time thereafter, since only 5,000 German soldiers out of the 92,000 captured at Stalingrad were destined to return to their native land.

CHAPTER FORTY-FOUR

Germany's *period* of official mourning for the 6th Army had just come to an end when Herr Ordnung, not waiting for evening—his usual time for visiting our basement with the day's mail—rushed into the department where Mother worked, shouting, "Frau! Frau! It's here! Arrived! You're free to go to Riga!"

What joy! To be able to get away from those dreadful basement living quarters, to meet our relative, to have Mother's vision repaired! I only dreaded to say a final farewell to my friend Lana. She was no longer living with us, having been moved out of the basement soon after our arrival. We were sitting one evening at the big table, eating the supper delivered to us daily from the cafeteria, when the factory owner entered, looking for someone.

Spotting Lana, he said quietly to her, "If you're finished with the evening meal, please take your belongings and follow me."

"Why?" Lana looked up at him and blushed. How her eyes sparkled. Did she know how her face lit up at his nearness? She must have known it, and lowered her eyelids, hiding the spark.

Helping the flustered girl to her feet, he said soothingly, "You are *Volksdeutsche,* of German blood. You must have different accommodations. I have seen to it. You will have a room of your own."

I watched Lana follow him as if in a trance. She was situated in a private room located at the factory's rear wing, where previously some exceptionally fine china was stored. The carts were moved somewhere else, giving Lana an airy, cozy room on the second floor with a large window opening on a magnificent view of the hills and forest, away from the town's traffic. Utter privacy.

Not many of us could visit Lana, and then not often, for she was given to understand that she should not associate with the *Ost*. But I continued to come in contact with her daily at our workplace. During the lunch break we often sat on some crates in a quiet corner, and gossiped to our heart's content. Lana received much better rations than we did, and she never failed to bring an extra sausage or cheese sandwich for me. She also was allowed to make use of the town's library, and book after book was devoured by us with a never truly satisfied hunger.

One day she brought a thick book bound in a black leather cover. "Nina," she said solemnly, her voice full of reverence. "Friedrich Goethe! His *Faust*. You must read it. Such love! Such torture!"

I opened the cover and moaned. "I can't read it! The print is in Gothic! So twisted and curled!"

But Lana insisted. "Take your time. I'll help you. What love!" she again exclaimed.

Then one morning as we two were sitting almost elbow to elbow on high, revolving stools, bent in concentration over the dishes, with thin brushes in our hands, the factory owner appeared on an inspection tour, accompanied by several supervisors.

He neared Lana's stool, and bending low over the cup she was working on, said to the supervisor of our department, "This girl has a real talent! It's a waste to keep her at this work. Find a place for her in there." He pointed to the adjoining department where only a few women were working, each enjoying her own room-like cubicle.

From that day onward, Lana began to withdraw from me. While in the past, after working hours, I often sat on the basement steps, waiting for Lana's signal, letting me know that all was clear and I could come for a visit, now no window opened, and no white kerchief waved "all clear."

Just before the three-day national mourning was announced, when we were almost certain that soon the papers, allowing us to move to Riga would arrive, I cornered Lana in the factory corridor at the end of our shift. I had not met with her for the last two months, and wanted to say goodbye. She was wearing a new, fullcut, squirrelskin coat—a Christmas present. When we saw Lana wearing that coat for the first time, one of the women in the basement hissed, "Don Juan's present. Doesn't come free, that coat, does it?" Don Juan was our nickname for the factory owner, who did not let any attractive young woman escape his attention. Two girls—Feodosians—were his willing victims already, living in private rooms as Lana did, and receiving extra food rations, although still sporting the *Ost* sign on their clothes. Those two were used to not taking things close to heart, but only exploiting the situation to their benefit. But Lana?

In that corridor meeting, while Lana tried to pass, I reached toward her soft, pretty coat and said, "Wait, Lana. Please don't run away. I want to let you know that any day now we'll be leaving for Riga. Lanochka, is it true? I mean, those filthy rumors . . . that . . . that our factory owner. . . . Is he . . . you and he . . . sleeping together?" Even as I said it, I wished I could fall through the floor. To accuse my dear Lana of such indecency! After all, could not a married man, a family man as our factory owner was, could he not look upon a teenage girl as a father would? And besides, the man was seen of late with a new conquest—a Russian woman with generous hips, full breasts, a coppery glow to her thick, long hair, almond-shaped emerald eyes, a lusty smile. And my poor Lana, just a teenager.

I felt ashamed for even uttering such ugly words, and quickly I came near my friend, throwing my arms around the stiff, unresponsive girl. And then I, too, became stiff, backing away. Lana's body was no longer familiar, boyishly flat. Instead a very hard, protruding belly touched my own belly. Could it be? Could Lana be hiding behind this wide fur coat, and behind the wide, loose frock she wore to work, because she was pregnant? What a disaster! To be unwed and bear a child was still, to a Russian, a terrible stigma. Only a "whore" bore a bastard child. No matter if she was a virgin and "forgot" herself only once—she became automatically a "whore" and that was it. Even if she succeeded later to marry someone, in his first drunken bout, the indignant Russian husband would call his wife a "whore." Could my Lana—shy, proud Lana—become a "whore"? Remain forever a "whore"? I reached toward her coat, wanting not only to feel the protruding belly, but to see it, too, so as to be totally convinced. She did not protest, only brownish, peculiar spots appeared on her cheeks. Slowly, reluctantly, I drew back the front of her fur coat. Yes. The girl's waist had disappeared, her breasts had become quite prominent, and that watermelon-shaped abdomen! A whore.

"Lana, Lanochka, what will you do? He's married. What will you do?" I whispered, rearranging the girl's coat. Married? I did not dare to mention the copper-haired woman and the two others before her—a harem!

Lana, perhaps relieved that I finally knew the truth, said in a crushed, quiet voice, a voice that tried to hide the girl's inner turmoil, "I don't know what to do, Nina. At first, I was not afraid. Even when I knew I was pregnant. He loved me. Loved me! All was bearable. Now he doesn't even come to say hello, to ask how I feel. You can't imagine how I suffer."

I wanted to comfort Lana, to say that I knew how she was suffering, knew it just from reading Goethe's *Faust,* reading about the young virgin, Gretchen. But then I remembered the almost awe-stricken Lana when she spoke of Goethe's tragic love story, saying, "Such love! Such torture!" And I held my tongue. She looked at me, suddenly her eyes flashing, angry.

"I know what you're thinking. A whore. I am a whore in your eyes, aren't I?" And, sobbing, she hurried away, not listening to my protestations.

The day of departure arrived. With big bundles on our backs, and holding smaller bundles in our hands, we were leaving the basement. While we were climbing the stairs, Herr Ordnung opened the basement door, and instinctively I turned toward Lana's room. Her window was wide open, white curtains blowing in the frigid February breeze, silhouettes of people scurrying back and forth.

"What happened?" Slava asked, pointing to Lana's window. Herr Ordnung's face was sad. "Oh, that poor girl. Cut her wrists." And, anticipating our next question, he continued, "She's alive, but barely. Had a miscarriage, though." And a bit later, as if reasoning with himself, added, "Perhaps it would be better for the girl if she succeeded. Such a young thing, trusting."

Crushed by the news of Lana's predicament, I wanted to drop my bundles and rush to the stricken girl. But I could not. The train to Riga was waiting.

CHAPTER FORTY-FIVE

*T*he train came to a halt. "Riga!" the conductor announced.

"Riga!" Mother's voice was choked with inner excitement. "My darling home town! After twenty-eight years I return to my Riga." She hurried to leave the coach, impatient to see her birthplace.

The railroad station was huge, ultra-modern, surmounted by a cathedral-type glass roof, with cafés and restaurants, flower shops and souvenir shops, making Moscow's stations seem drab by comparison. And the exuberance of the arriving passengers, and those meeting them! Presents, flowers, kisses, embraces—all calling out their greetings in several utterly unrelated tongues. The German language was most prominent with hordes of military men arriving and departing, wearing not only German uniforms but the uniforms of all the different foreign contingents that had joined in Hitler's crusade to free Russia from the "Bolshevik cancer." But no matter what national insignia they displayed, all communicated with one another in commonly understood German. The Latvian language—not a bit similar to either German or Russian—was tumbling excitedly out of the mouths of vigorous, sturdy-bodied, blond, and blue-eyed natives. The Russian language was not heard very often, coming from the downtrodden, subdued minority.

While quite friendly and submissive toward the occupying Germans, the Latvian natives were demonstratively hostile toward their Slavic brethren, and we immediately experienced this hostility personally. Because we could not inform Aunt Natasha of the exact time of our arrival, we tried to telephone her from the station, but no one answered. Mother led us to the trolley, which she knew would bring us to "Moskovsky Forstadt," where her aunt lived. We started to push ourselves into the trolley car, when the Latvian conductor, hearing us converse in our native tongue, and perhaps recognizing a difference in our pronunciation from the Riga Russians, whistled to the driver to start the trolley moving. Seeing Slava still clinging to the door of the trolley, the conductor kicked him in the shins, saying to the boy in Latvian, "Soviet swine!" And then, to make sure we understood, he repeated the curse in German.

Very angry at first over the conductor's behavior, Mother forced herself to calm down, and directed us to another trolley just arriving. "Let's climb on that one, children. But no conversation between us, understood?"

And so, once again we ran to the car, and without any dialogue being exchanged, we boarded it safely. Slava and I, almost hidden under our bundles, devoured the city out of the trolley windows. From time to time, Mother brushed away approaching tears at recognizing a building, one street or another, all bound up with memories of years past.

And how beautiful Riga was! Mother had said earlier to us that Riga was called the "Paris of the Baltic." Wide, clean boulevards, parks, fountains. And the magnificent stone buildings! Some still glowed with beauty and vigor after more than half a millennium in existence. Some buildings were built by the very first German merchants in the 1200s. And to enchant the town even more, the River Dvina ran parallel to the trolley rails, seeking outlet into the Baltic Sea.

The original inhabitants of Latvia were called Letts, and the country was named after them—Lettland. The region was so productive that— in half jest—it was called "Fatland" by the Germans. In addition to the Lettish tribe, there also lived in the vicinity of Riga a people called Livonians. They were still pagan when Germany was already thoroughly Christianized. With the blessing of the Popes in Rome, German missionaries proceeded to infiltrate and dominate the Livonians. More or less by force, the missionaries succeeded in baptizing the natives. But then the subjugated Livonians turned on the Germans and defeated them in a bloody massacre, at once plunging into the River Dvina to thoroughly wash off the "stain" of baptism. Whereupon, their pagan gods once more embraced their devoted flock. But not for long. Pope Innocent III mounted a crusade against the Livonians and Bishop Albert, encouraged by Rome's blessings, entered the Dvina with his fleet, subjugating the Livonians to German rule in 1201. To celebrate this Christian success, the Bishop erected a town on the spot where the very first baptized pagans slaughtered the missionaries. He called the town—Riga.

Two religious-military orders, the Livonian Knights and the Titonian Knights, completed the conquest of the Baltic lands for Germany. Riga was ruled by the Order of Livonian Knights until 1561, prospering phenomenally under the hand of the baron-merchants. Then, powerful Catholic Poland grabbed rich Latvia, losing it later to another great power—Sweden. The Swedes in turn, lost Latvia to Russia's Peter I. Under Czarist rule, the "Baltic Barons" still retained their powerful influence, German remaining Latvia's official language until the year 1885, when it was replaced by Russian. Only after the conclusion of World War I, when Latvia received its cherished independence, was Latvian recognized as the country's official, primary language. And with what vigor and relish the trolley car conductor exercised his privilege on that February day in 1943, by calling us "Soviet swine."

A massive, locked iron gate was separating us from a handsome, two-story brick house that was surrounded by several large trees, their naked, sprawling branches seeming to embrace the building over the high, peaked roof. While we tried to locate the bell, a window opened on the second floor and an older, gray-haired woman poked her head out.

Mother was ready to call out her aunt's name, when the woman shouted to us in broken Russian, "You . . . Soviet relatives? Your aunt gone to doctor. Sick. I open gate." And soon a short, thick-set woman was facing us, her eyes round with curiosity. "Come! Come!" She helped to drag our bundles. Seeing Mother's concerned, worried look, the woman said, "Your aunt, very ill. Long time ill, with heart. Ah! There is taxi! She returns."

Once more we dropped our bundles and hurried toward the approaching taxi. A very tall, or more exactly, a very long woman climbed slowly out of the car, her hand touching the left side of her chest, as if to still any undue excitement. Her hair was dark, parted in the middle, showing only a few streaks of gray, while silky, dark eyebrows prominently dominated the high forehead. Hazel eyes were surmounted with surprisingly long, thick lashes. And those lashes seemed to make her eyes appear young, inquisitive.

"Natashinka! My dearest, long lost niece," a bit hoarse, but still resonant voice greeted Mother, who rushed to embrace the sick woman, weeping.

"At long last!" Mother cried out. "Auntie, at long last!"

Slava and I did not weep, but were a bit sad at not being able to feel an overwhelming joy. Aunt Natasha was never part of our lives. We never even heard of her during our life under Soviet rule, perhaps because our parents did not wish for us to know about relatives living outside Soviet borders, since this fact alone often brought imprisonment to Soviet citizens.

As if understanding such feelings, our great aunt did not insist on immediate expressions of affection. She patted our cheeks, kissed lightly those cheeks, and said while wiping her tears, "Come, come. Let us get comfortable inside." She led us into a very spacious apartment. It was elegantly appointed with furniture imported from England and silk curtains and drapes from France. The pastel Oriental rugs were laid over marble and parquet—all harmonizing in a calming, unostentatious way. While Aunt Natasha occupied the four rooms downstairs, she rented out the upstairs, where originally all the bedrooms were located. This brought in necessary income for the widowed woman, all of whose savings had been lost during the Soviet invasion of 1940.

That evening, for the first time in my entire life, I was given a separate bedroom. I was so intimidated by the utter quiet of such unaccustomed privacy that I needed to hear someone's voice, someone's breathing. I opened my door slightly, leading to the adjoining, much bigger room where Mother and Aunt Natasha had retired for the night, and for a long time I felt as if lullabied by the murmur of their voices. But then, I soon wished that my door had remained closed and I never heard that which reached my ears.

Mother, at one point, was more or less apologizing for our descending on Aunt Natasha when she herself was not well. Her aunt waved away Mother's apologies.

"The important thing is to get you to the eye surgeon," she said. "Right away! Don't worry about my heart, Natasha. It gives me trouble for the past ten years, and still I am able to lead a pretty normal life. But glaucoma might blind you. It won't give you much more time." And Aunt Natasha informed her that there was an appointment made with the eye surgeon, Dr. Jansonis.

"Jansonis?" Mother's voice was uneasy, apprehensive. "It's a Latvian name. Couldn't a Russian or German doctor take me as a patient? I don't trust a Latvian."

"Natashinka," her aunt said, gently, "Dr. Jansonis is the best among eye specialists. Don't fear."

When Mother described the Latvian conductor's treatment of us on the trolley, Aunt Natasha said, her voice full of anguish: "If you only knew what was going on in Riga under the Soviet occupation! Thousands deported. Doctor Jansonis escaped deportation only because he was visiting one of his patients. When he returned, no wife, no children. Vanished. And if you could have seen the prisons. Slaughter houses! Corpses dismembered . . . children tortured to death! People took pictures of the corpses. So many torture instruments were found! People's nails were pulled, their shins were broken, skin from their hands was pulled off. Some men died while their testicles were crushed. The Soviets raped pregnant women, then hanged them by their ribs. Nightmare! Absolute nightmare!"

CHAPTER FORTY-SIX

A middle-aged man with reddish-blond hair was staring intently at Mother, his thin moustache twitching from impatience, as he sought to find out if the eye surgery was successful.

"Open your eyes, madame," the doctor commanded gently, wiggling his finger in front of Mother's left eye. "Aha! Good! Good!" He clapped his hands as if in applause when he saw Mother's left eye faithfully following his finger. He did not even want to know if Mother's right eye would do the same. He knew it would not.

While the doctor was exuberant with the results of his superb effort to save Mother's vision, she herself seemed crushed by disappointment.

"But, doctor," she said so quietly that the doctor had to bend toward her in order to hear. "My right eye. . . . I see nothing with it. Nothing!"

Doctor Jansonis knew what tone to adopt. "Madame," he said sternly, "two more months and your left eye would've gone 'pffft' under my scalpel. I wouldn't have been able to save that eye, either. So, dear lady, thank your lucky stars for getting here in time."

Mother very quickly regained her natural common sense, and only asked meekly if the salvaged left eye would serve her well and long.

"It'll probably serve you your life span. Only you must religiously— religiously, mind you!—use the drops I will prescribe for you."

Forgetting the angry, vindictive trolley conductor, forgetting the unfriendly looks other Latvians gave us during our streetcar ride to Aunt Natasha's house, Mother—in heartfelt appreciation and admiration of this man's efforts—raised his hand to her lips and, before he could withdraw it, she kissed it.

With rainbows and headaches gone, armed with new eyedrops and eyeglasses to help her see better, Mother did not lament too long over the loss of one eye, but began helping Aunt Natasha provide food for the table by taking up knitting. She proved to be a genius at salvaging the yarn from worn-out articles and creating brand-new ones. She was especially partial to knitting baby items—booties, hats, mittens. Soon the whole neighborhood had heard of "the Soviet Natasha" who could turn "manure into candy," as she had done in Dulovo, fashioning attractive clothing for me out of potato sacking. Unbeknown to us at the time, Mother began to put a small part of her earnings aside, saving. Saving for what?

And then one day, returning from an excursion downtown, Mother—her face glowing, somehow young, as if reliving a moment out of the past—sat down to tea with us, holding her right hand in a peculiarly stiff manner. And we saw it—a wedding ring! A ring that she took off, together with Father, almost ten years earlier, exchanging it for loaves of bread—it was back! Not the same one, certainly, not as thick, but a gold wedding ring banding her to Father still.

"Natashinka, dearest, don't you think you should wear it on the left hand. After all, Mark is gone," Aunt said, not unkindly.

"No!" Mother shook her head. "For the first seven years the ring stays on the right hand. And in that time I might yet find my Mark-usha."

One day in early June, an envelope arrived addressed to Mother. It contained a soiled, crumpled, brownish postcard. While the card was very tattered, the envelope was neat and clean, with a recent postmark, indicating it came from Germany, from the porcelain town we had left behind months earlier. In Herr Ordnung's handwriting, a few words were crowded on one corner of the card, "Thought it might be important to you."

Mother, looking at the card, became very agitated, her hand flying toward her forehead, the way she used to do when glaucoma-induced headaches attacked her.

"Slavochka, son, read it," she said, sitting down.

"Who is it from? Lana?" I suddenly was filled with hope that my former friend was sending me a few words.

But it was not from Lana. It had come all the way from Feodosia.

How many letters and cards we had sent to Tanya in the past year! No answer. When the porcelain factory owner was sending back two pregnant girls, we gave one girl, Irina, a letter, begging her to pass it on to Tanya, together with our new address, convinced that our letters were for some reason not getting through to Tanya.

And there it was, the long awaited reply from our dear friend, who promised us faithfully to keep an eye and ear open for Father's whereabouts.

While Slava was staring at the card, remaining silent, I took it from him and at first in an energetic, but soon a subdued voice, read aloud:

> "Friends, forgive the long wait. Was ill with infection after premature delivery. Was at Karl Marx St. No. 7. Your Tanya died soon after you left. Mountain people. . . . Much unrest. Sorry about everything. Irina."

Our Tanya . . . dead. And the "mountain people," the partisans, must have trapped her as they did the woman interpreter whose tongue they cut out. They killed Tanya because she worked in the hospital, attending to the wounded.

So while in Riga we lead peaceful lives, war still raged in Feodosia, claiming poor Tanya. No one left of those we knew and loved. No one to keep watching for Father's return, to tell him of our whereabouts. And yet, wouldn't we ourselves soon be returning to Feodosia? To a free Feodosia? Our hopes were nurtured by Riga's Russian language newspapers, which were printing more and more about a former Soviet general—Andrey Andreevich Vlasov, calling him a liberator. The general was taken prisoner by the Germans in July 1942, and since then had been trying to organize an army of anti-Communist Russians from among the prisoners of war to fight Stalin's rule. We felt Vlasov's Army was destined to free our land—to liberate Russia.

July was ending its hot, sunny reign, oppressive to humans, but Riga's gardens and parks were grateful for this heat, exuding, as if in thanks, sweet fragrances perfuming the whole city. The blossoms of summer flowers were so exuberant that pedestrians in the parks stooped over the sweet-smelling blooms and, grinning, complimented them for putting on such a show.

That late July Sunday we all attended a service in Riga's Russian Orthodox Cathedral, standing for more than two hours, pressed from all sides by worshipers. Aunt Natasha felt faint toward the end, and we hurried outside to the benches in a nearby park. There, by the cooling water fountains we sat a bit longer, soaking in the beauty of the profuse, luxuriant blooms. A nearby ravine, which centuries ago had served as the city's defense against invaders, was now filled with water and turned into a joyous, life-filled canal, traversed by several bridges.

Slava and I leaned over the bridge railing, trying to spot some brightly colored carp that were hiding beneath the purple and white water lilies. Aunt Natasha came to us and said with an apologetic smile, her face ashen, "Let's hurry home, children. Awfully hot outdoors today. Perhaps it'll be cooler in the house."

When we reached home, Aunt Natasha went toward her favorite leather armchair in the study, refusing to lie down in bed. Mother lifted her legs onto a footstool and said comfortingly, "Sit and rest, dear. I'll fix you some cool, sweet lemonade."

She sent Slava to a nearby store for ice, and minutes later with a tall glass of lemonade, Mother hurried to Aunt Natasha's chair.

"Here, auntie." Aunt Natasha's eyes were closed and the eyelids did not lift in response to Mother's voice. Neither was her chest lifting. She must have died instantly, not even having time to utter a cry, a moan. Only her long, white silk scarf was clutched tightly in her right hand—the hand that was lying over her heart, perhaps only seconds earlier trying to still the sudden, the final pain.

Four days later, we were returning from Aunt Natasha's funeral, sad, forlorn, longing to enter the cool, pleasant dwelling—and try to lift ourselves out of the depression and helplessness that overwhelmed us. Nearing the house, we were surprised to see a Latvian policeman standing with his bicycle by our gate. The Latvian woman-tenant stood alongside, engaged in animated conversation with him. Seeing us, the woman scurried upstairs, as if to avoid facing us, and the policeman, thrusting a slip of paper at us, said in excellent German, "The German Commandature demands your immediate expulsion!"

"Expel us? From my aunt's home?" Mother asked, not believing a word the Latvian was saying.

"Not from this house only," the man persisted. "You are expelled from Riga."

"Why?" Slava stepped forward, trying to act adult-like, helping Mother to cope with the official.

"Because you no longer have any sponsor. Out you go! You're *Ost.* Go back to the *Ost* camps."

Was the policeman smiling when he turned away from us, facing the upstairs window? And the tenant, peeking from behind the curtains, was she smiling too? The arrangements, involving several people, must have been made as soon as Aunt Natasha's death became known to the neighbors. Did the greedy tenant, wishing to take over the lower floor of the house, inform her friend, the policeman, and he informed . . . whom? He must have informed the German authorities and secured the certificate ordering our expulsion from Riga. Not a half hour after we returned from the funeral, a truck stopped in front of our gate, and another officer marched briskly toward us. The man, wearing the uniform of the Latvian SS, barked, "Let's go! Load your junk. What? Help you? How about that!" The fellow assaulted Mother with an obscene gesture of the arm.

Slava, his voice breaking with resentment, said, "If you're so full of hatred for the NKVDists, take your anger out on them, not on my mother."

The Latvian merely spat in reply and pushed us aboard the truck, where we squatted on our bundles and sped away in the direction of the main road. While the driver stopped for the approaching traffic, we three embraced with our eyes and minds the house where we had so happily lived for several months with dear Aunt Natasha. The policeman, not a bit intimidated by our stares, was loading the bicycle basket with Aunt Natasha's priceless crystal, throwing over it one of her Oriental runners. Then he pedaled away, perhaps to return once again—to plunder. The tenant was already in the downstairs apartment robbing the windows of their magnificent French silk curtains that reached from the ceiling to the floor. Through the naked, lonely windows we could see her climbing the stairs, her arms full of loot. She, too, would probably hurry down again, and yet again, to Aunt Natasha's orphaned home, and plunder.

CHAPTER FORTY-SEVEN

The train was taking us farther and farther from Riga. We presumed it was taking us into the Reich, as the gendarme at Riga's station told us, when we tried to learn our destination. The car was uncrowded, allowing us each to occupy a wooden bench as a cot. Across the aisle sat a middle-aged couple with a girl of Slava's age. They spoke Russian, not in our Muscovy accent or in Ukrainian, but in that peculiar "Piter" way, as only natives of Leningrad speak. The girl fascinated me with her vaguely familiar features. Or was it her coloring that was familiar? Flaxen hair, naturally wavy, short, with bangs, and those large, cornflower-blue eyes! Lida! Yes, my Dulovo friend, Lida! How the girl on the train resembled her! The girl at one point leaned on the shoulder of the woman she traveled with—a large-boned woman, in her late forties, with dark hair parted in the middle and arranged in a fat bun. Her kind, brown eyes regarded the girl with steady warmth.

The man, much older than his wife, was completely bald, his large head shining as if only shaved and scrubbed that day. And while his skull and chin were free of hair, he sported, as if to compensate, a thick, graying moustache and heavy, bushy eyebrows. The eyebrows seemed desperately trying to reach his steel-colored eyes and hide them from any onlookers, but could not. The man's eyes were not cold, but were sparkling with brownish specks, as if laughing at everything good-heartedly. He, like his wife, was exceptionally tall, and I wondered looking at both the parents, how very unlike them the girl was built— small, delicate, with the high-arched feet of a dancer.

It took not too many hours of traveling together before we knew that the girl's name was Zhenya—the diminutive for Eugenie. Her mother's name was Raisa Mikhailovna. She was a mathematics teacher who had worked with her husband, Boris Fyodorovich, a teacher of chemistry, in a Leningrad high school. The family was expelled from Riga when their passes, allowing them to visit distant relatives, expired.

A day and a half passed in travel. Night descended. With the arrival of the second dawn, our train began creaking to a stop. I opened the window, straining my eyes to see the large sign in the distance, trying to read the name of the town. I could barely distinguish the black letters in Latin alphabet—LITZMANSTADT. A very German-sounding name. Perhaps a town in Bavaria again? No, it must be some other spot in Germany. There were no mountains as in Bavaria. All open spaces, pretty meadows, woods. And something strange in the behavior, even in the looks of the people on the station platform. The women looked very different from the other German women I had seen. Slight, trim, long-legged, their small feet encased in high-heeled pumps, the women were dressed with a superb elegance that was peculiarly their own. And the men on the platform! Slender, medium height, with fine features, moustached, and all in elegant civilian clothing. Could those men be German? How they bowed to the women! All men kissed the hand of every woman they greeted, and they jumped to give way to a woman, or open a door for her, or hurried to lift her luggage. As if the female was some adored creature, no matter what her age. Actually, the older a woman was, the more adulation she appeared to receive. And not only from the male. A very old woman, walking with the help of a cane, was greeted by a group of people, and everyone in the group, including teenage girls and young women, kissed the old lady's hand!

There were many Germans in uniform, yet the civilians seemed not only to be indifferent to the presence of the military personnel, but as if by some unanimous, unspoken agreement, they ignored the soldiers, looking through them as though they were an empty space. Not one woman turned toward a German, or gave him a friendly look. I was practically falling out of the train window, straining to hear the native language, still expecting it to be German, only because we were told in Riga that we were being brought to Germany. And when the words began to fly toward me, I could understand them, although it was neither Russian nor German. I could understand most of the words I heard! And that constant *proshe pani*—that exceedingly polite form of address toward each other—*proshe pani*—only Poles used it! We were in Poland!

"Mother! Boris Fyodorovich!" I shouted. "We're in Litzmanstadt!"

While the others wondered where Litzmanstadt was, Boris Fyodorovich said calmly, "We're in Lodz. Yep! The Germans call it Litzmanstadt. A general named Litzman in the last war captured Lodz. So the town is his. It's a textile town. My! Where are the owners of all those textile factories?" He looked carefully around and then whispered, "The owners were mostly Jews."

Raisa Mikhailovna, round-eyed, asked, "What are we expected to do in a Polish textile town?"

Only Mother, due to glaucoma, was allowed to remain behind at our new camp, performing kitchen duties and attending to the cleanliness of the barracks. Slava and Boris Fyodorovich were sent to a fur factory, where they were put to work processing rabbit skins that were being turned into uniform linings or mittens and hats. Raisa Mikhailovna, Zhenya, and I were sent to repair worn clothes. The two-story U-shaped brick building, once a textile factory owned by a Jewish family, was now being used solely for clothing storage. Vast rooms, where hundreds of long, thick beams were attached horizontally to opposite walls, contained thousands upon thousands of neatly hung articles of clothing. In one room were only cloth coats, in another only furs. Shirts hung in still another, followed by dresses, skirts, blouses, jackets. What silk gowns, magnificent lace, the finest wools, the richest velvet! Where, where have all those clothes come from? And who wore them, we wondered?

Zhenya and I, when we first saw such riches, simply could not comprehend so much clothing concentrated under one roof. No factory could produce such abundance.

"Girls! Stop staring! Close your gaping mouths!" It was our new supervisor, clapping her hands to bring us out of our stupor. A short-legged, long-waisted, very efficient woman of about 30, with a thin, sandy blond bun at the nape of her neck, introduced herself to us. "I am Frau Emma, your main supervisor. My helpers are Ukrainian *Volks-deutsche*. We have only one Polish woman working here, our best mender, a genius." And Frau Emma pointed her finger at a graying, yet still young woman who did not even raise her eyes from her work. She was behaving toward the German Frau Emma as I had observed the Poles behave toward the uniformed Germans on the train platform. "You are from Latvia, Balts," Frau Emma then declared.

So, I thought, we are considered to be Latvians, not Soviet Russians.

Somehow, perhaps during the bureaucratic shuffling in the transport out of Riga, we became "Balts." And this building, and the work we were assigned to, was it perhaps "privileged" work?

Frau Emma came toward me, and asked my name. "Nina? Ninchen. All right, Ninchen. Can you sew? Not at all? What am I to do with you?" She turned to Zhenya. "What is your name? What?" She tried to repeat Zhenya's name, but, laughing at her pronunciation, waved her arm and said, "Gretchen, that's what I'll call you. Simpler that way. Why Gretchen? We call pretty girls Gretchen."

We two, and Raisa Mikhailovna, were directed toward a long, wide wooden table where several sewing machines were standing. Raisa Mikhailovna sat next to the Polish wonder-mender, while Zhenya and I were facing them. There were no sewing machines in front of our two places.

"Since you can't sew, I'll let you two undo the articles we can't use, like this skirt," and she threw a skirt with several holes in it to Zhenya. "Here, Gretchen. Rip it at the seams, and fold it neatly. We'll turn it into a child's skirt, or something. Ninchen, take this dress and start ripping it at the seams." She threw a dreary-looking piece to me. "Pack it all in this box." And Frau Emma pointed to a large cardboard carton, empty, waiting to be used. Raisa Mikhailovna was given the job of repairing hems and, where needed, going over seams with the sewing machine.

I was bored to death with my work. Week after week, the whole day long, I was bent at the neck, tearing out the seams of worn, unattractive clothes, while others were handling soft, luxurious high fashion dresses, suits, and coats. All articles reaching our work room were scrupulously clean. Everything was pressed, ironed, laundered, having no trace of perspiration or soiled spots. Yet most of the hems were ripped open, and required resewing. And on some articles, seams on the sides, or sleeves, were also undone, and undone crudely, as if by some impatient, uncaring hand. Where did all this clothing come from? A *Volksdeutsche* said that it all came from the Lodz ghetto, a huge enclave that resembled a city within a city, into which most of the former merchants of Lodz had been driven.

And then one day, the Polish seamstress, perhaps beginning to trust us after many weeks of working together, said that the newly arriving shipments came from Oswiecim. The name Oswiecim meant nothing to us. Even when the Pole told us that the Germans called that village, surrounded by birch forests, Auschwitz, it still meant nothing. She then pointed to the pile of shabby clothing lying in one corner, from which Zhenya and I were taking the articles to be completely ripped apart.

"Those things," she turned her head quickly in all directions, checking to see if Frau Emma was nearby, "those are here for months. Before you girls came, no one was assigned to undo them. Those things came from Tre-blin-ka." And the Pole fell abruptly silent, her fingers touching her lips, as if commanding us to silence.

Treblinka. My brain registered a certain pleasure at the sound of this name. While Auschwitz, neither in Polish nor in German attracted my ear, Treblinka was a juicy sort of word. It rhymed for instance with *malinka* (raspberry), and raspberries were always juicy. The bushes of tasty *malinka* immediately appeared in front of my mind's eye, surrounding the place called Treblinka. The name also rhymed with the word *Lesginka,* the Georgian tribal dance I performed in Feodosia. And there was another tribal dance, *Kabardinka,* a swirling, energy-filled routine. It, too, rhymed with the name of the mysterious town. Treblinka was a sound of music, of joy.

One late fall morning we arrived at work, taking our places, shivering from the dampness. One woman started a fire in the iron stove, and soon our fingers relaxed, performing the chores more easily. The Polish mending woman had sent word that she was ill with the flu, running a fever, and could not come to work that day. Frau Emma began to distribute the clothes to everyone, and quite absent-mindedly she handed me a stunning, sky-blue woolen crepe dress, its hem ripped open so crudely that the skirt was almost ruined. I squealed in delight when the soft, rich fabric of the dress touched my hands. Perhaps surprised to hear my squeal, Frau Emma took another look at what she had handed me and taking it back, she said in her ever good-humored tone, "My mistake, Ninchen. Ah! Our best mender is out with a cold. Well, then," and Frau Emma handed the dress to Zhenya's mother. "Try to repair it neatly, even if it's to be made shorter."

The supervisor went to the pile of ragged clothes, and picking up a dark dress, she tossed it to Zhenya. Then she dug up a mustard-colored, dreary-looking jumper, and threw it to me. "There, girls. Rip them open. We can make nice aprons out of those."

Aprons. . . . I felt grumpy, bending my neck over the jumper. Such a rag! And I was stuck with it, just because my fingers refused to learn how to handle a needle. Or was it up to my fingers? After all, the same fingers did astonishing things at the needlepoint sessions with Praskovia Ivanovna. In Riga, I had flabbergasted Aunt Natasha with what I could do with canvas and thread and needle. Yet to sew a button, to repair a seam threw me into a sweat. While needlepointing, I felt I was creating, beautifying, whereas sewing was a necessity, a tedious chore, and I could scream from boredom. The only good thing about the ragged jumper was that I could make a big blunder with the scissors and not be punished for it. At one point, a few minutes into the work, I whispered to Zhenya, "I hate this damned potato sack! Such junk." "I hate my crummy rag, too," Zhenya replied.

The women began to murmur melodies to themselves. Raisa Mikhailovna, too, hummed softly at first, then let her strong, pleasant contralto rise, while Zhenya added her perky young soprano to the swelling chorus. The women began to sing "Evening Bells," a song created by the old Russian émigrés who left their country after losing the Civil War to the Bolsheviks. Traveling the globe, trying to find an hospitable corner in which to settle down, to raise a family, they never forgot what they had left behind, expressing their longing for Russia in "Evening Bells." To perform the song, a deep bass was needed, which Boris Fyodorovich provided when it was sung at the camp. The deep voice was needed especially to suggest the sound of a powerful church bell—Bo-o-om! Bo-o-om! Bo-o-om! Bo-o-om! It fell upon me to provide those sounds in the sewing room, where no men were present, and, in the process, save the chorus from my periodic deaf-ear interventions. "Booming" on cue, I undid the hem, a bit surprised it was still intact. Then I began to work on the side seam, snipping unhurriedly toward the armpit. And I stopped! What was under my finger tips? Something unusual, something that my fingers had never encountered before. A piece of paper! Why was paper sewn into the seam? I was ready to call out to Frau Emma and inform her of the paper in the seam, when women's voices shouted, "Ninochka! Don't stop booming!" I tried to "boom" as before, but my attention was on the paper. I was sliding it out of the partially ripped seam—a long neatly folded pale green paper. A message? The greenish paper, as soon as it escaped the seam's restraint, seemed to straighten itself out, fan-like, exposing black words written in the Latin alphabet—THE UNITED STATES OF AMERICA—and on each corner the number 100 sprang out at me. A portly, older man stared out of the paper, a bit past me, and under his double chin I read—"One Hundred Dollars"!

I wanted to study other signs on the bill, but Zhenya, suddenly bending over the table past my chair, as if to reach a pair of scissors lying at the absent Polish woman's place, cautioned, "Keep booming. Frau Emma will notice."

I hardly moved my lips, asking, "What to do? I must turn it in to her."

Zhenya hissed back, "Don't be a fool. It's not hers! Stick it in your pantaloons."

Without changing either the position of my body or my head, or my arm, I raised my skirt slightly, and pushed the banknote under the elastic of my full pantaloons, elastic that served as stocking holders. That done, I began to relax a bit. A hundred American dollars! What could I buy with it? Could I buy a small house and move out of the camp? Perhaps I could buy a horse—my dream come true, to have a horse to race through the meadows. Might it only buy a chicken? Or just a loaf of bread?

The "Evening Bells" came to an end, no one needing my cooperation any longer. I continued to work on the side seam, my palms damp from excitement. And then . . . again! My fingers once more felt the now-familiar thickness, stiffness in the seam that preceded the first folded bill. What was it? Another paper bill? Another? God Almighty! Yes! A second number 100 was staring at me shamelessly, as if throwing me a challenge of some sort. I felt a need to run to the toilet room from the excitement—excitement that could not be shared openly with anyone else.

Zhenya hissed once again, "Stay put. Pull yourself together."

Raisa Mikhailovna, by that time noticing my flustered face, realized that something unusual was transpiring on our side of the table. Zhenya leaned toward the thread-filled box which was placed by her mother's elbow, and whispered only one word, "*Klad*" (Treasure). Raisa Mikhailovna understood instantly. There were persistent rumors that from time to time gold coins, watches, and jewelry were found in the clothing seams, but we took those rumors as exactly that, rumors, promoted by people's inflamed imaginations. Raisa Mikhailovna, seeing my distraught face, shouted to the seamstresses, "Girls! How about "Stenka Razin"? Let's sing it for Frau Emma. She likes that song." Raisa Mikhailovna led the willing chorus in the fabled Cossack ballad, which tells of the rebellious, cruel Stenka Razin, who only once in his life fell in love—with a captive Persian princess presented to him as a gift. At the end of the ballad, when his men began to make fun of their leader who, they felt, had turned "soft" because of "love for a wench," Stenka—heartbroken, but determined to prove to his men that he "did not turn into a wench himself"—throws the young girl overboard from the deck of his barge into the Volga, imploring the river to accept this ultimate gift from the Cossack.

While the chorus was thus entertaining Frau Emma, I returned once more to opening the seam, wishing for nothing more than to finish with the jumper, to throw the unripped pieces away. A scream froze in my throat. Another hundred dollar bill! Enough! Enough! My inflamed brain shouted, almost in panic. When will it stop?

I finished the seam, switching to the second side. And immediately, almost brutally, without giving me a moment of respite, my fingers found another paper bill. Ten dollars? Not 100? Then another ten. Then a number five appeared, and still another five, and a third. It no longer mattered what number appeared on the bills. I was becoming sort of numb to the findings, then almost annoyed by the whole thing, as if it was not a joyous event to find such treasure, but rather a sin, deserving punishment. And surely, would I not be punished if Frau Emma found out about it?

I reached the neck seam, and there, too, my fingers sensed something protruding slightly. Not the long, stiff papers, but something hard, round, small. The seam burst open, as if on its own, exposing a ring! Eight tiny diamonds were arranged in a circle, and in the middle of the circle was a sharp, upright pin, as if it was surmounted at one time with a pearl. Was the pearl also in the dress? But almost no seams were left undone. Only one small square at the shoulder, holding the two sides of the dress, was left to undo. Could the pearl be there? Something was there. A small package fell into my palm wrapped in thin, cigarette-like paper. And what was spilling out of it? Five, ten, twenty diamond chips!

"Hide it, dummy! Count it later," Zhenya directed, then adding, quickly, "Danger."

I just had time to clasp the chips in my left palm tightly, partially covering it with the mustard-colored dress, when Frau Emma's voice thundered right next to my ear. "Ninchen, what is with you?" She put her hand on my forehead. "Girlie, you're red as a beet, burning." She sounded concerned, her voice no longer thundering at all. It never did. It only sounded thunderous to me, to my extra alert ear and brain. "I don't want sick people here, infecting others. Now, Ninchen, if tomorrow you don't feel better, stay home."

And looking at the mustard-colored pieces of unripped jumper, Frau Emma said, "I don't know if I want to use it! Not even for an apron."

CHAPTER FORTY-EIGHT

*T**he year* 1944 was fast approaching. Mother, wanting to meet the New Year as clean as conditions allowed, scrubbed our Lodz barracks, with the others assigned to the upkeep of the camp. She splashed the wooden bunk bed frames with boiling water and kerosene to kill the bloodthirsty bed bugs. She aired the straw mattresses on the hard, deep snow, chasing the fleas away. Blankets were pressed with a red hot iron to get rid of possible lice and their eggs. The small, square barracks windows were washed and decorated with a new set of white curtains made out of cheap gauze. And lastly, the wood plank floors were scrubbed and again scrubbed. Once the floors were cleaned, the whole barracks sort of sparkled, if it was at all possible for that dreary place to sparkle.

The New Year's Eve table was loaded with sardines, cheese, smoked sausage, some pickled apples, tomatoes, cucumbers, and bottles of red wine. All became available because a one hundred dollar bill was successfully "exchanged" by Boris Fyodorovich with the help of one of the guards, who was neither unduly curious nor coy about his role, only business-like. "Fifty-fifty," he said, keeping half of the "take" for himself. It was again the guard who "sold" us the foodstuffs. No house, or racing horse, could be bought with a hundred dollar bill, but it fed our "corner" in the camp for a whole month.

On that New Year's Eve, while waiting for midnight to arrive, many in our barracks approached a fortuneteller, Madame Belovskaya, to predict their future. Madame Belovskaya was a refugee from Leningrad, a violinist by profession. In the camp, she exercised not her original talent, that of being a musician, but perfected another gift nature had bestowed upon her—predicting the future by laying cards. And this recently discovered gift, was keeping her better fed and clothed than anyone else, since her services were constantly sought after. Even without asking for any kind of payment, she always received a slice of bread, a teaspoon of marmalade, a handful of sunflower seeds, a cube of sugar, or maybe some articles of worn out, but still useable clothing, or a sliver of soap. And no one grudged to give part of his meager possessions to dear Madame Belovskaya, because she somehow always managed to send every client away filled with hope. To some, Madame Belovskaya appeared to be a bit dotty, but to many others she was a narcotic, a drug to mask the soul's pain, if only temporarily.

To live up to the image of a "professional" fortuneteller, Madame Belovskaya kept her hair black, somewhere acquiring dye to chase away the abundant gray. Her face was heavily covered in an almost chalk-white powder, her dark eyes staring out of that pale, aging face with an inquisitive, slightly mocking gaze.

On that New Year's Eve in 1943, Madame Belovskaya—already a bit tipsy after an unaccustomed glass of red wine, said to my mother, whose turn had come to sit at the card table, "There, Natalia Alex-androvna, see?" With her right hand she performed an all-embracing gesture involving the rows of cards. "See how good the diamonds and hearts are to you! The red cards are all over the place. Yes! Yes!" the fortuneteller exclaimed. "No spades, those black crows! Crows of death! None of them came out! This year of 1944 will see you united with your Mark. What?" she roared, her palm coming down on the table. "You don't believe me? But look! Here, you see? That's your Mark. Yes, he is a club. No, no, Natalia Alexandrovna. If he was a young man, then he would be a diamond." Mother apologized quickly, promising not to question the wisdom of the cards.

"See here, I swear it's your Mark!" Madame Belovskaya continued enthusiastically. "And here, that's you, and here—the two children, a boy and a girl, all together. What is it? You want to know how Mark's hand is? What hand? Left hand was wounded? Well, I see no wounds . . . nothing whatsoever. It must háve healed. He's all right now. Waiting for all of you." And, fully satisfied with her performance, Madame Belovskaya repeated, "Very good cards, Natalia Alex-androvna, very good year this 1944."

I listened with a certain envy and irritation to Madame Belovskaya—that she should know all about Father while we, his immediate family, were utterly in the dark concerning his whereabouts. Mother though, had a slightly faraway smile on her lips—a smile of hope, of promise. And that midnight, when Mother burned paper on the back of a plate, watching for the shadows to appear on the wall, she felt positive that she saw a tall, upright figure of a warrior—Father. But as hard as we wished, however long we stared, Slava and I could not turn the slightly uplifted end of a charred newspaper into Father's image.

CHAPTER FORTY-NINE

February of 1944 was whipping us with its frigid cold, the Lodz barracks never being warm enough to allow us to undress fully for the night's sleep. Sweaters and shawls wrapped women's and men's bodies to give some additional warmth during the night. One evening, quite late, the barracks door unexpectedly swung open and a grumpy camp commandant barked out an order to us:

"People! Pack for tomorrow! New orders just arrived! First thing in the morning you'll be shipped out to Germany!"

The next day we said our farewell to Lodz, and boarded an unheated third-class coach, its icy, wooden benches serving us as beds. On February 24, the train stopped in the station at Gotha, capital of the German state of Thuringia. Gloomy leaden skies reminded me of Dulovo's winters—gray, severe. These northern German people were more subdued than the Bavarians we met in 1942. One heard no congenial "*Grüss Gott,*" not even "Hello, there." Almost every adult, it seemed, now wore a band of black crepe on the left sleeve.

The railroad station was within walking distance to our new destination—an ammunition factory. The guard told us that this particular *muna* (slang for "ammunition plant"), where we were to work and live, was producing parts for airplanes, and that we would meet about five hundred other *Ost* already working there. On reaching the *muna,* our guard led us toward a small, isolated barracks near the entrance, quite separate from the rest of the buildings. He then pointed to the opposite end of the factory area.

"There," he said, indicating several long, wooden buildings. "That's where you'll go in a few days. Some *Ostarbeiter* are ill. They'll be removed and you'll take their places. Now, march to this small barracks and be ready for tomorrow's six o'clock shift!" And then, as if blaming us, he grumbled, "You were late arriving. The Hitler *Jugend* are replacing you today. But only for today."

We dragged ourselves and our bundles to the barracks. There, as was the custom in every camp, we immediately created an *ugol* (a corner)—an area occupied by people who felt most comfortable with one another. And every barracks usually was divided into five or six such corners. In our *ugol,* besides us three, were Zhenya with her parents, Madame Belovskaya, and another woman-musician from Leningrad. We quickly inspected the bunks and mattresses, and began to unpack, trying to get as much rest as possible before the factory work would begin the next morning.

At one o'clock in the afternoon, tin cans of kohlrabi soup were brought into the barracks, exuding a most unappetizing smell. Mother, curious on seeing our fortuneteller already laying out cards on her lower bunk bed, said pleadingly, "Madame Belovskaya, tell us, dear, what awaits us here? How will this camp treat us?"

"Do I need to make a forecast about it?" Madame Belovskaya laughed softly, and pointed to the neighboring corner where a woman with a weak bladder was arranging her damp bloomers by a small iron stove, trying to dry them out. A gray-haired, toothless man was hanging his dirty socks next to the bloomers, while arguing with the woman as to who should be entitled to how much time in that precious spot by the stove. But Mother repeated her plea and soon several others joined in urging the fortuneteller to lay out the cards.

"Come now, Madame Belovskaya. Don't be a prima donna! You're not on a Leningrad stage. What are you waiting for? Applause?"

Madame Belovskaya gave in. She began to lay out the cards on her mattress, surrounded by curious women. Zhenya and I climbed on the bunk above Madame Belovskaya, and with our heads hanging down, we observed as she worked her "magic."

Madame Belovskaya was not pleased with what the cards were telling her. "Hmm. Look here. So many spades! I don't like those black ravens." She slapped the offending cards with her palm, taking care not to disturb their order. "Today there will be a lot of commotion among us. Oh! Oh! Such commotion! And so-o soon! No, I don't like what I see. Fire. Death."

Boris Fyodorovich raised his voice in irritation, which was an unusual reaction for that even-tempered man.

"Now really, Madame!" he boomed. "No need to overdo it! Death! Fire! Why frighten people?"

But then, Boris Fyodorovich was quite skeptical when it came to fortunetellers. Someone in the group agreeing with him, bravely tried to express doubt concerning Madame Belovskaya's predictions.

"Are you sure there'll be fire? Death? Among us?"

Madame Belovskaya snapped back, "My cards are faithful. There will be commotion. Yes! But see here? No one of us will be hurt. Aha! Very good cards here." And Madame Belovskaya once more became the prognosticator of good tidings. "See here, people? A train! Yes. This card means another train is waiting for us. We won't be long here, thank God! All will end splendidly!" Then, she dismissed us all with a regal wave of the hand. "I must lay cards now for myself, just for me," she said.

It was exactly 1:30 in the afternoon. Hundreds of American bombers were approaching Gotha at that hour; their main target—the airplane factory—*muna*. We had returned to Germany during the so-called "Big Week," when the Americans and British decided to drop almost 10,000 tons of bombs on industrial targets, Gotha included. But when the alarm sirens began to wail, we were not unduly disturbed, because we never yet had experienced Allied bombing. Through the windows we watched the workers popping out of the factory building and running madly for the earthen bomb shelters, as the whistle sounded again and again. The workers began to scream to each other, "Twenty-five whistles! The Americans are aiming for Gotha!" That particular number warned the populace that the bombers were not heading for some neighboring town, but for theirs.

Zhenya and I continued to lie on our upper bunks, listening to some of our people who had run outside, shouting to us through the partially opened door, "Look! Look!" One woman pointed to the sky. "The Americans! The Americans are above us!" Excitedly, half smiling, she started to count the dots above her. "So many! One! Two! Three! Four! Oh! Look how they glow! Like silver butterflies! Nine! Ten! Eleven! Oh! I can't count. So many! Hundreds of them!"

All at once, our barracks began to shake violently, as if threatening to fall apart, to sink into the ground, dragging us under too. I could see people outside opening their mouths to scream, but I could not hear their screams. The thunderous explosions drowned out all other sounds, allowing only short, whistling noises to be heard—the noise of the air being cut by the weight of the falling bombs. All of us who were on the upper bunks, jumped down, dragging the mattresses with us as protection from flying debris and splintered glass.

Then . . . all was quiet. It was over. The heavy hum of the bombers faded from the sky. Or was it over? The hum! That death-laden hum! It again was reaching our ears. Boris Fyodorovich grabbed Zhenya and pushed her under one bunk bed on the floor, ordering his wife to do the same. Slava and I quickly crawled under another set of bunk beds, while Mother threw all our bundles, our down comforter and pillows on the mattresses that were covering us, creating a thick barrier. She then pressed herself close to us, covering her exposed side with a straw mattress. No one in the barracks was weeping, praying, or cursing. A strange, unnatural silence reigned, and a crucial question seemed to hang on everyone's lips—will it miss us? Will it? Will the Grim Reaper turn a blind eye toward us in this second wave of bombing? If only he would. I clung to the floor boards as if those pathetic, worn planks could provide the needed protection to avoid death. The barracks floor was dancing under my belly, echoing the explosions in my very gut.

And then, when the worst seemed to be inevitable, once again quiet descended. How good it felt, this quiet, this everyday, ordinary quiet that was not even noticed, unappreciated until the bombers inter-rupted its natural stillness. I felt as if heavy, crushing pliers had let go of my skull, let go of my rib cage, allowing me to relax a bit. How good it felt to escape sudden death! To escape being wounded, mutilated, blinded. Many did not escape. I knew, because the factory was ablaze, receiving a direct hit.

Poor, poor people! How many *Ost* died? And the boys in their early teens, how many of them died? They were filling in for us, because our train was late. But must I torture myself over the fate of others? I was alive! Slava was alive! Mother was alive! Should I not thank God for this?

All thanks froze on my lips, on everyone's lips, sinking the barracks in a deafening silence. The sky was again humming. The death-raining machines—the silver butterflies—were returning.

"The third wave? The final wave! We'll all perish in this wave!" Madame Belovskaya screamed, and ran toward the door. While run-ning, she still screamed, "They won't miss our barracks! I know! I know!" She had to cross about two hundred yards of open ground in order to reach the bomb shelter located in the middle of the factory yard. Pinned down by the bunk beds, I tried to watch her progress through the open door, uneasy in my mind that perhaps we all should do the same thing—crawl from under our flimsy cover that really could not protect anyone if a bomb fell on the barracks, and run with Madame Belovskaya. What if she, by some special power, knew that our barracks was predestined to be wiped out of existence by this third wave?

The fortuneteller was nearing the shelter, when a frightful thump deafened us temporarily, and a dense cloud of plaster dust from a blown-up building nearby swept over us, blinding, choking. The barracks roof collapsed, falling on the upper bunks, and glass from the windows flew like a hail of bullets.

Only seconds later, I raised my head and tried to see through the blown-away door opening if Madame Belovskaya was still there. She was. She had stopped running, and just stood there, swaying. Her back was to us, and she seemed to be looking down, her head so low that we saw only her shoulders. Her body appeared to lean forward, then backwards, as if the swirling air currents, intensified by the explosions, were literally holding her up. She seemed to act as if she could not decide what to do. Then she decided. She swayed once more and fell forward on a pile of rubble.

Boris Fyodorovich threw off his mattress, and raced out of the barracks, shouting to us, "She might be wounded! I must help her!" We watched Boris Fyodorovich reaching Madame Belovskaya, his head shaking incredulously, as if not believing what he saw. He seemed to be looking for something in the immediate vicinity where Madame Belovskaya fell, but apparently in vain. When Boris Fyodorovich stumbled back into the barracks, his face was ashen, sweat glistening on the forehead.

"Her head. . . . No head on her. Cut off, like with a sabre. And still she stood."

The toothless man, who was drying his socks earlier, said, matter-of-fact, "Like a chicken. No different. Chop off the head of a chicken and she'll still be on her feet."

I covered my ears with the down pillow, trying to stifle the man's words out of my consciousness, but the words pounded through the down, "Like a chicken. No different. Just like a chicken."

CHAPTER FIFTY

After the third wave of the air assault on that day in Gotha, we were rushed out of the crumbled barracks and put on a truck.

"You're not needed here!" the factory supervisor shouted angrily, as if we brought the curse of destruction with us. While we dragged our belongings to the waiting truck, the Germans around us were busy trying to salvage what was salvageable. Men were attempting to put out the fires, while fire trucks and ambulances raced to assist. Hundreds of civilians, mostly women, were hastening toward the factory, on their bicycles. Among those anxiety-filled women were mothers of the boys who were trapped under the burning rubble. With their bare hands, the women began clearing the debris, trying to get to their trapped children. Removing one piece of rubble at a time, they passed it to the nearest woman standing in line. No hysteria was apparent, no wringing of hands or soul-tearing shouts of complaint or accusation directed either to God or to the Americans. When a body was uncovered, and one of the mothers recognized it to be her son, she cleared the dirt and dust from his body, off his face, stroking his cheeks tenderly. Then, not waiting for any man's help, she herself carried the body of her son home, her strong legs making long strides as if to conserve energy, her feet—big, in thick-soled shoes—marching steadily, never stumbling or faltering, neck upright, adorned with that plain, no-nonsense, sausage-like bun of hair.

* * *

During the next few weeks we were tossed from one camp to another, from one *muna* to another. Some days, only a few hours after our arrival, or sometimes just before, the *muna* or the barracks meant to house us, was destroyed by the Allies' bombing.

In the beginning of April, a truck was racing to deliver us to a new location. It was nearing the time of day when dusk threatened to descend. Our driver was hurrying to drop us off at our new lodgings before the curfew time. The truck entered the pleasant, small town of Ohrdruf, about 15 to 18 kilometers south of Gotha. Neat, well-cared for gardens came into view, surrounded by wooden fences, all painted white, with no boards missing, as if the man of the house had never left to go fight in the war. The one and two story houses stood untouched by the bombing, brass doorknobs gleaming, window boxes filled with African violets. Many fences were intertwined with climbing roses, impatient to start blooming. The lilac bushes were puffing up with luxuriant clusters of purple blossoms. Such a darling town could not have a *muna*, could it?

Yet it had something that we were not prepared for at all—a concentration camp! And the truck was rushing us toward that concentration camp, toward the barbed wire, toward the guard towers bristling with machine guns. As soon as we realized where we were headed, someone cried out, "Why are we being brought to the concentration camp? We were told that another *muna* is waiting for us!"

"Don't worry, don't worry." Our guard waved his arm, as if tired of the whole procedure. "We can't find a place for you people. Many *munas* gone. Boom!" He threw his arms up high, his chin lifted to the sky. "Americans bomb like crazy! Looking for *munas*. No place to put you to work."

On reaching the guardhouse, after asking something of the heavily armed sentry, our soldier-escort pointed to one building near the gate, and said, "Go to this barracks. Maybe in a few days a place'll be found for you at a *muna* just eight kilometers south of here."

We had lived in dreadful shacks at times, but the barracks at Ohrdruf was the most wretched. No individual bunks existed. Instead, a single wooden platform ran the entire length of the barracks, and above it another one. No mattresses here, only damp, brown straw, thinly spread, to soften slightly the harshness of naked boards. Small squares of dirty glass served as windows, allowing very little light to reach the interior. Wooden plank floors, too, were strewn with dirty straw, and here and there, from under this meager mat, small holes peeked through, as if someone gouged out those holes with a specific purpose in mind, covering them later with straw, to hide them from the guard's eyes. Each hole was encrusted with dried feces sticking to its rim and giving forth a strong outhouse smell.

"Inmates," Boris Fyodorovich mused, trying to figure out the need for the holes. "They probably couldn't get to the latrine. Most likely locked up day and night, so they made the holes."

A few minutes later a new guard—an SS man—appeared, and announced that since we had not been expected, no food rations were allotted to us for that day, but would start arriving the next day. "All will straighten out tomorrow," the SS man promised. "But!" He lifted his leather-gloved index finger, "No communication with anyone in the camp! Understand?"

Boris Fyodorovich raised a question, booming out, "Are we prisoners, then?"

The SS man, as if disarmed by the richness of Boris Fyodorovich's voice, laughed out loud. "No. No! No prisoners. But the order is for you not to communicate with those who are prisoners. Understand? You are to remain in the barracks at all times. Food will be brought to you. Water will be allocated. The latrine will be emptied. But no leaving the barracks."

We were crestfallen. If to be locked up in the barracks did not make us prisoners, then what were we?

With a cruel jolt, the next morning brought the dark reality of Ohrdruf right into our lives. Peering out of the tiny windows, we saw columns of men being marched past our barracks, toward the gate. Marched? In their lightweight prison uniforms that protected them not at all from the still chilly morning air, their knees seemed to refuse to bend willingly, but were forced nevertheless to bend in order to move one foot in front of the other; their arms listless, those gray-faced, gray-clad men—all Jews—were being herded out to labor.

Only a few minutes after the column of Jews passed our windows, Mother suddenly uttered a stifled cry full of anguish.

"What is it, Natalia Alexandrovna?" Raisa Mikhailovna rushed to Mother's window. Slava and I clung to the next window, staring at the column of Soviet prisoners of war marching toward the gate. Mother, did she see, did she recognize one among those men? Father? Someone resembling him? But how could anyone resemble him? Those were no men. They were skeletons, and their bones were covered with filthy old Red Army greatcoats, full of holes and tears, not cleaned in one, two, or three years. Their feet were wrapped in rags. Some, not having rags, wrapped their feet in newspapers. All had wooden clogs for shoes. Their hands, long unprotected from frost, were red, sores bleeding, fingers unbending, like prongs on a rake. And among their faces—covered by black sores, those cadaverous faces—could there be that of my father?

Slava and I heard Mother whisper to Raisa Mikhailovna, "I must know if by some chance my Mark is here or was here. Maybe one of those men came across Mark somewhere."

Mother still hoped. Slava and I tried, but could not hope any longer. Father was past his fiftieth year, with a heart condition, and his left hand not healing even under our constant supervision back in Feodosia. The men who marched by our windows that morning looked to be over fifty also, but by calendar year they were in their 20s and early 30s. Could Father have lived through the brutal conditions allotted to the Russian prisoners of war?

Neither the Americans, nor the British, who fell into Hitler's hands, were abandoned by their respective governments, by their leaders, who fought tooth and nail through the International Red Cross to provide their men in captivity with the basic necessities for survival, even for comfort. Not only bread rations and fats and protein were supplied to those Westerners, but even such non-necessities as chocolate! Cigarettes! Even alcohol! Those Western nations insisted on inspecting the camps where their men were confined, holding Hitler strictly responsible for the well-being of their nationals, and threatening to retaliate in their treatment of German prisoners under their control, if Hitler did not abide by the international code of humane treatment of war prisoners. They forced Hitler to abide. Yet, the complete opposite occurred on the Soviet side. Stalin threatened to "mistreat" German prisoners under his control if Hitler were to provide any *humane* treatment whatsoever to the Soviet men! British Foreign Secretary Anthony Eden was baffled by Stalin's methods. "Well," he said one day, to concerned Russian émigrés living in England, "for some reason which we know nothing about, Stalin is determined that nothing be done for the Russian prisoners." And nothing was done.

Not many could possibly survive the internment. They were so crowded on the wooden plank pallets, or the naked floors of their barracks, that they could not find room to stretch out on their backs, but had to lie squeezed one against the other, on their sides. The dead among them often remained lying thus for days. Weak from starvation, many could not get up, could not reach the latrine, and not even feeling or smelling it any longer, they glued themselves to their adjacent neighbors with excrement. Almost no flesh covered their skeletons; instead, to replace the vanished cell tissue, water filled their skin, and their bellies and legs blew up with edema. Many lay comatose, not even feeling their frost-bitten feet or hands, or ears or noses fall off, while receiving no medication or doctor's attention. The men were covered with crawling vermin which spread devastating skin rashes and ulcers that could not heal. Tuberculosis, typhus, and cholera were rampant, attacking and exterminating entire barracks, whole camps, while the guards simply moved away, watching from a safe distance as the men died off. No clergy were allowed to visit the Russians, as was allowed for all other nationals. No right of correspondence applied to those men. They could not inform their families or friends of their whereabouts, and they could not receive a loving note, not a single word from anyone.

"We have no prisoners of war," Stalin kept saying, when questioned by foreign correspondents. "All our soldiers fight to the end." And he recognized no Soviet prisoners in German custody. Neither did the International Red Cross.

One day followed another with dreadful monotony. The utter isolation in the barracks bothered us more than the surrounding filth, or the stink of the kohlrabi soup; more than lice-infested blankets or the latrine pails. Daily, men-prisoners passed by our windows. And once, not men, but women walked past our barracks. They were not in striped prison uniforms, and their hair was not cropped or shaved. A column of about 20 women, all carrying small bundles as we used to do when going to the *banya,* trudged silently by one late afternoon, looking neither left nor right. Many were in their 20s or 30s, good-looking, well-built. The last two women held my attention especially, their profiles so similar that I was convinced they were related. One, nearer to my window, was about 35 years old. The other was much younger. Her sister? Her daughter? Both women had light-colored, crocheted shawls thrown loosely over their wavy, dark auburn hair. Nicely tailored camel-colored spring coats and long boots of soft, thin leather made the women stand out in the dreary Ohrdruf surroundings.

The two walked as if tied to each other. They did not walk as if they were physically ill, their bodies needing actual support. And yet, looking at the women, I somehow felt that if one let go of the arm of her companion, both would collapse and fall. And their eyes! They stared straight ahead, not at anything on either side, not at the heads or above the heads of the women in front of them, but somewhere just above the waists of those ahead. And this unmoving, unblinking, vacant stare seemed to shout to an indifferent world of their own indifference, of their own inner isolation.

One of the Ukrainian women in our barracks bent low next to Mother's ear, and said, "Whores. Camp prostitutes."

I waited by the window for the women to return from the baths, to see if the two at the back of the column would behave differently. The arrival of curfew time forced me to cover the window with a blanket and move away. Whores, I thought. They were selling their bodies. Selling? In the concentration camp at Ohrdruf? Or were they buying an extra day of life?

Mother bribed our guard with a ten dollar bill to try to find out if Mark Illarionovich, prisoner of war number 410 was now, or had been at sometime, in this camp. One morning, delivering to us ersatz coffee and slices of bread for breakfast, the guard quietly said to Mother, "Frau, no number 410. No Mark Illarionovich was ever here. I checked." And then, as if to comfort Mother he said, brutally honest, "Look, Frau, he must be dead by now. Face it! A fifty-year-old man. Not possibly could he survive. I sure as hell couldn't have survived if I were him."

I listened numbly, remembering that Christmas Eve of 1941, running after the cattle train that was rushing my father away. Rushing him to survival? To his death? How many times since then had we come upon camps where Russian war prisoners were held! And we never came upon anyone who knew of Father, of number 410. We followed Russian language newspapers, magazines, scanning them for Father's name. Nothing.

If only to know that he was alive! Or, if only to know that he was dead! To *know!*

And if he was dead, where did his body finally come to rest? In some mass grave? Or was it hidden by some caring hand, under a thin layer of Mother Earth? On Russian or German soil? Without a single marker to honor his eternal bed. Perhaps field flowers nourished by his secret grave, were appearing in spring—more luxuriant than their neighbors, longer lasting, and, pointing their bright blossoms to the mute, indifferent heaven, shouting exuberantly, "Mark Illarionovich, number 410, lies here! Eternally! Feeding us! Eternally!"

CHAPTER FIFTY-ONE

My fifteenth year of life passed at the end of April, and we still were in Ohrdruf concentration camp. The very first day of my sixteenth year on this earth began with the melancholy thought, how very old I was getting to be! Could it be that never, while I was still in my teens, would I go on a date with a boy? Would there be a time when I would sit in a movie theater and melt, while holding hands with him? Would I ever stand very close to a boy, feeling his arms on my waist, and move slowly to the music of a tango or waltz? How I wanted to dance, to laugh, to *be* a teenager!

That morning, kissing me tenderly, Mother said, "You're an adult now, Ninochka, an adult. You would have received a passport today, if we were home. And in old Russia you'd have 'come out' today."

My birthday was nevertheless marked by a very special event. A guard, while delivering our skimpy breakfast that morning, shouted brusquely, "Folks! Eat in a hurry, and march to the showers! Drag your belongings with you. Delousing. Off you go today!"

"Where? Where? Tell us where," people cried, running toward the bearer of good tidings.

"To Crawinkel, a town eight kilometers south of here. There is a *muna*. Living quarters have been found for you finally."

"Big camp?" we wanted to know.

The fellow laughed. "You'll see for yourself in a couple of hours."

A birthday present! Ohrdruf was letting go of me!

Scrubbed, disinfected, my braids still damp, face shining from soap and water, cheeks glowing, I climbed up on the truck, and not wanting to sit on the bundles as the rest of the people were doing, I stood holding on to Slava's shoulder. I was observing the passing villages with their placid, satisfied cows in the fields, school children with huge rucksacks full of books on their backs, housewives airing, shaking out their down pillows and comforters, while perky dachshunds—Germany's favored dogs—frisked about, and I realized that I was free. Free! Even with the armed guard seeing that no one would jump off the truck and run, I felt—after weeks at Ohrdruf—that I was free.

Quickly—too quickly for me—the truck reached the town of Crawinkel. Actually just a village, with only one road, from which several small streets and alleys branched off, constituting the entire settlement. Where possibly could the *muna* be located? Every *muna* that I had seen, was a huge factory, taking, in some towns, as much space as the whole of Crawinkel did! The guard, when I asked him where the *muna* was located, pointed to the north of the approaching village, "There, in the woods. All hidden from the bombers."

The truck stopped in front of the local tavern. My heart smiled—perhaps we'll be given some cool, sweet lemonade. I was naively certain that everyone in the world, including our guard, knew of my birthday and was anxious to reward me with a glass of lemonade or tea. A stout couple came out, their bellies thoroughly covered with oilcloth aprons. Were they welcoming us, welcoming me to their restaurant-tavern, perhaps with a waiting meal, perhaps with a glass of wine? After all, a sixteenth birthday is so special.

"Dump them there, in the courtyard. Go to the back entrance!" the woman proprietress instructed, showing the truck driver where to turn. Then she said to our guard, "Those filthy Italian prisoners of war! Such a mess they left behind! Let the newcomers scrub it themselves. I'm too busy running the tavern."

So! The tavern was our new "camp"! While half of the building was still functioning as a cabaret and restaurant for the locals, the other half—a much bigger part—formerly a dance hall, now was commandeered to house us, the foreign workers, and before us the Italian prisoners of war. The windows of the "free" part of the pub were sparkling with cleanliness, with red and white checkered curtains, with blooming geraniums, while the windows in the other part were barred with iron grill work.

The Italians did leave the place unbelievably filthy, so that we were forced to demand new straw mattresses; otherwise the room was much cozier than the standard, narrow, oblong barracks. Its ceiling was high, and the windows—even barred—were letting a lot of light and air into the square room. After Ohrdruf's accommodations this tavern's dance hall appeared palatial.

While several women, including Mother, were put in charge of the camp's housekeeping—we, the young and able-bodied, were immediately employed at the *muna*.

CHAPTER FIFTY-TWO

*T*he *summer* passed—a summer in which Count Claus von Stauffenberg had tried to assassinate Hitler. On November 14, 1944, General Vlasov—leader of the Russian Liberation Army—read a manifesto in Prague, calling for the liberation of Russia from Communist rule and the creation of a government that guaranteed private property, equality before the law, an independent judiciary, and freedom of speech, freedom of assembly, and freedom of religion. The text of Vlasov's Manifesto was read and reread by us all at the Crawinkel *muna*, where—since leaving Ohrdruf—we had worked ten hours a day, sometimes having no Sundays off. We all were losing weight, exhausted by the physical demands on our bodies. Even with rare additions of eggs and cheese or meat to our diets that the second $100 bill allowed us to have, we—the young and still growing—suffered more than adults. Zhenya and I became anemic. During the night, Slava often called to me in a whisper, so as not to disturb the others, and asked if I saw huge balloons when I shut my eyelids—blue, gold, and red—so bright that it almost hurt. I did not see the balloons, but Slava was tormented by them. And they were not just pretty balloons that children played with, but monstrously huge, each covering the whole horizon, taking up the entire visible earth, pushing at my brother as if chasing him out of his own skin. Mother was convinced that Slava suffered much more from anemia than we girls did, and tried to pass on to him any extra scrap of food that was available.

Yet some people suspected that our health was affected not only by diminishing food rations, but also, perhaps, by our work environment.

The very first time we entered the *muna*, we were enchanted with its park-like surroundings. The roofs of the buildings here and there peeked through the thick tree foliage. Some of the roofs were rectangular. Others were shaped like mounds, covered with grass and moss to camouflage them from the prying, searching eyes of American reconnaissance above. Beneath the mounds, in cave-like storage rooms, was a huge inventory of munitions in all shapes and sizes. And all day— from sunrise to sunset—men were loading crates of ammunition upon waiting trucks. Those workers were mostly Russian and Yugoslav prisoners of war, although there were a few anti-Mussolini Italian prisoners and some *Volksdeutsche* as well. No Jews were allowed on the premises of Crawinkel's *muna*.

After loading, each truck was driven quickly to a railroad station one and a half kilometers from the *muna*. The station was very small and unobtrusive. Not even a waiting room existed—only a few outdoor benches and a ticket booth. At the station, there always stood six to ten freight cars waiting to be loaded with ammunition. As soon as the cars were filled, the short train hurried off, immediately being replaced with an empty one. Allied airplanes never spotted Crawinkel's woodsy *muna*, never saw anything worth bombing at its small railroad station. Had they done otherwise, no Crawinkel would have remained on the map. Its *muna* was more of a gigantic ammunition storage depot than a factory where ammunition was produced.

But then we heard that something extraordinary was produced at that *muna*, and we, the newly arrived workers from Ohrdruf, were assigned to produce it. Entering the *muna* for the first time, we could see men struggling with crates that weighed an average of about 200 pounds, and happy we were to find out that this was not our assignment. Rather, we were to work in one of the long, wide barracks where on both sides stood armed sentries, guarding it as if something precious was kept inside. The barracks was divided lengthwise in two. We were led into the wider part, which was again divided into several cubicles. Every cubicle had a long, four foot wide table, seating six people on each side, working in pairs, making six teams in all at a table. In turn, each pair was separated from its neighbor by a low plywood divider. Miniature rails cut through the middle of the table were constantly loaded with crates, filled with something that we at first took to be grenades. We called those devices "toys." Slava and I were placed in one of the cubicles, facing Zhenya and Raisa Mikhailovna. The supervisor assigned me to a place at a wooden wheel about twenty inches in diameter with a slotted opening in the middle. My task followed Slava's closely. He had to dip a specially designed rubber ring into a thick, maroon-colored paint-like substance, and place it on the nose of the "toy," securing it with a small cap. At that point I took the "toy," and while constantly spinning the wheel with my right hand, I held the "toy," in the dead center of the wheel, thus screwing down tightly its detonator cap. Next to Slava on the plywood divider hung a sheet of paper, and each time one crate was filled with completed "toys," the supervisor inspected it very thoroughly and, if satisfied, allowed Slava to put a cross on the paper. We were required to fill a quota of 100 crosses a day, or work on our day off to make up the deficiency.

While women and youngsters were assigned to the long tables, our men were working in the other part of the barracks, together with Yugoslav prisoners, most of whom were Tito's partisans caught by the Germans. These men were supplying our tables through small, window-like openings in the wall that divided the barracks, with full boxes of "toys," straining to meet the constant, insatiable demand.

We did not know at first what it was we were working on, speculating that the "toys" were some sort of fancy-shaped grenades. But one day, at the supper table, Boris Fyodorovich, while gulping down the meatless kohlrabi stew, blurted out unexpectedly, "We're working on the goddamned 'Fau'!" "Fau" was how Germans pronounced the letter "V." "We're working on the cluster bombs for the V-1!"

"Fau! Us? *Ost* working on such a thing?" someone shouted, waving away Boris Fyodorovich's announcement.

"Who told you, dad?" Zhenya asked.

Boris Fyodorovich looked at the girl, his eyes probing, worried, but not unkind. "Your friend Kosta. He knows for sure, that fellow."

Zhenya blushed, quickly turning away in embarrassment. Kosta was a Yugoslav prisoner, nine years older than Zhenya, athletic, handsome, with dark, almond-shaped eyes, black hair always falling in unruly curls over his forehead, with long white teeth that often gleamed in an easy smile. We called him "Gypsy," and Zhenya called him her "Destiny." Kosta worked side by side with Boris Fyodorovich supplying our table with fresh crates, always staring at Zhenya through the small opening, while putting the crate on the rails.

Zhenya wanted it that way, wanted the tall, broad-shouldered Kosta to look at no one but her. Watching the girl at work, sitting across from Slava and me, I guessed before Boris Fyodorovich, that she was suffering her first serious love pangs. And it was suffering, because no dating, no dancing, no going to the occasional movie, no telephone conversations, no visiting was allowed between the Yugoslav prisoners and us. But Zhenya wrote letters, wrote poems to her Kosta, already his wife in those letters, loving him until death. During the lunch break, when many of us ran toward nearby raspberry bushes loaded with overripe berries—our dessert—Zhenya dropped her letters in one of the bushes that was serving as a mailbox for the two lovers.

Many weeks passed, stretching into months. Slava was feeling worse with each passing day. Always tired, weak, he was hardly able to reach his bunk in the evening and fall in. Even the ever present, gnawing, permanent sensation of hunger began to leave him. One morning, while marching to work in the brisk autumn air, surrounded on both sides of our route by trees glowing in their fall colors, Slava said, his voice dull, lifeless, "Sis, I feel queasy, like the earth is falling away from under me."

I quickly pushed my arm through his, while Zhenya offered hers on the opposite side, and Slava, leaning heavily on us, proceeded toward the *muna*. Once at our work table, I changed places with my brother, painting the rubber rings, and inhaling the foul-smelling fumes, while he was spinning the wooden wheel. But to work the wheel was not easy either. One had to spin it uninterruptedly, always making sure that the top part of the "toy" was tightly screwed on, always counting the finished 'toys,' always hurrying to reach the required norm. It was decided among Zhenya, Raisa Mikhailovna, and me that after returning from the lunch break, the three of us would have to manage the job four people were performing, allowing Slava just to sit on the stool, pretending to work, but actually resting as much as possible.

Then, only a few minutes before the midday whistle, Slava swayed and fell off his stool, trying to rise immediately on his elbows. I jumped off my stool and, bending over my brother, began to lift him up. The supervisor from the opposite end of the barracks, seeing our stools empty, hurried toward us yelling, "Get back to work! No lunch time yet!"

"My brother is not well!" I retorted. "Let me bring him out in the fresh air!" I started to drag Slava to the door. The supervisor lifted his rubber hose and hit me on the shoulders, trying to chase me away. Then he began to beat Slava, landing his rubber truncheon on the boy's neck, on the top of his head, on his face.

"Stop!" I screamed, trying to grasp the arm of the man. Slava lifted both hands to cover his head but, furious by now, the man was hitting Slava's fingers, aiming to get past those fingers to Slava's skull. My brother could not escape the violent blows, his hands falling at his sides listlessly. He was near unconsciousness, but the supervisor, gone berserk, did not stop hitting the boy.

Opening the small window in order to push a new supply of "toys" to us, Boris Fyodorovich saw what was taking place in our part of the barracks. "Stop! Stop! You have no right to hit us! No right!" he roared at the supervisor. To me he commanded, "Ninochka! Run to the Oberst! Report it!"

Hating to leave my brother—on the floor, bleeding, his eyes closed, not responding any longer to the pain—yet, helpless to stop the beating, I ran out of the workshop toward the *muna* entrance gate, where the offices of the German personnel were located, including that of the Colonel-Oberst, our general supervisor. Just then the long-awaited lunch whistle blew. Already half way to the Oberst's office, I looked back and noted with relief that the guard was heading for the German cafeteria. So, I thought, he stopped hitting Slava. He stopped. Then I saw Kosta and Boris Fyodorovich holding Slava up between them, half-carrying, half-dragging the unconscious boy to the dispensary, which was right next to the Oberst's office.

With the lunch whistle sounding, the Oberst too, left his office and was crossing the road, heading for the same cafeteria as the supervisor. I ran toward the Oberst and pointing to the brutal man said, sobbing, "Herr Oberst! That guard! He beat my brother!" I was not afraid to face the high-ranking officer who was in charge of the Crawinkel *muna*. People liked him because he was calm, patient, and took time to hear out the many complaints. He inspected our work barracks daily, insisting the windows be opened more often for better ventilation, to dissipate the ever-present paint smell. He also periodically checked our cafeteria, and even tasted the stew, making sure we were getting the full portion allotted us.

"Beat your brother? No corporal punishment is allowed on these premises!" The Oberst's eyebrows drew together in a frown. He whistled to the supervisor, with a sign ordering him to stop walking and wait for him. And to Kosta, he shouted, "Hurry the boy to the doctor!"

Slava lay all that afternoon in the waiting room after receiving a shot. "To stabilize his heart rhythm," the doctor said to me. He added, "Herr Oberst wants your brother to have two weeks rest, recuperation. But no longer. I have no power to excuse any one of you *Ost* from work for longer than two weeks."

Two weeks! I was sure Slava would recover in those two weeks.

* * *

Ironically, only a few days after Slava's ordeal, the workshop where we were apparently being slowly poisoned by the volatile, sickening fumes, was permanently and tightly shut down. It seemed that no shipments of rubber rings were reaching our *muna*, without which the assembly of cluster bombs could not continue. We were all put to work loading the empty trucks with the heavy crates of ammunition. The tempo quickened noticeably in transporting the needed material to the Eastern front, where the Germans were trying to stave off the onslaught of the Red Army. For the first time we began to see Jewish men brought to the railroad station on foot, all the way from Ohrdruf, and there put to work unloading the trucks. They still were not allowed to enter the premises of the *muna*.

Slava was not recovering quickly, suffering from devastating headaches. Two weeks of rest allowed by the doctor, had passed. He tried to walk one morning toward the *muna*, but his knees simply gave out under him, and I was given permission to help him back to the camp.

A few days later, the guard who came to fetch us each morning looked at my mother as if apologizing for the sorrow he knew awaited her, and said, "Frau, very sorry, but Herr Oberst wants to see you today, about your son. Please, walk with us now to the *muna*."

About her son! . . . Mother feared that separation, perhaps eternal, was impending.

She had become friendly with the woman who ran the tavern and was teaching her how to knit bootees for small children, something she had been taught by the nuns in the Riga monastery when she herself was no more than a child.

One day, with the knitting needles in her hands, relaxed after a refreshing glass of dark German beer, the woman blurted out to Mother, "Frau, your boy is not too well, is he? Well, be on the alert, Frau. If the officials say to you, 'Let's send him to a sanatorium,' don't believe it! Don't let him go there! Hide him, or do something."

"Why?"

"Because I know," the German said, her knitting needles stilled suddenly. "An old man here, in the neighborhood, went a bit nutty . . . you know?" She banged her forehead with a finger. "And pffft! To the sanatorium! So what d'you think happened three weeks later? His ashes arrived. The family was told he died. Died? Strong as an ox he was. Only a bit light in the head. Sure died quick in that sanatorium."

I walked toward the *muna*, not noticing the peaceful countryside, the fallen leaves under my feet. I was thinking of my poor brother. Not three years after leaving Feodosia as a healthy 16-year-old, he was turning into an invalid, having no strength to remain on his feet, plagued by devastating headaches after that merciless beating. And now the Oberst wanted to see Mother, to inform her of what? I stumbled, and Zhenya quickly caught me by the elbow. But no one needed to help Mother to walk that morning. She marched—her short, finely chiseled nose slightly lifted, chin up, lips pressed tightly—as if challenging someone, or everyone. Her eyes were staring straight ahead; the right, blind eye already was losing its coloration, but the left—sharp as an arrow—was piercing through everything in front of her. Mother was in a fighting mood, marching to defend her offspring. She had said earlier, before we left the camp, "Ninochka, if it'll be necessary, I'll try to bribe the Oberst, or the doctor, to give Slava more time to stay with us.

"Bribe?" I asked.

"We still have a hundred dollar bill—the last of the three. I have it ready in here, see?" And she opened her dress collar to show me where the small envelope was hidden, safely in her brassiere.

The Oberst was in his office, standing by the picture window as he did every morning, observing workers entering the compound. When he saw Mother walking toward the office, he opened the door and directed her to take a seat by a massive desk. Sinking into a swivel chair, he handed a certificate to Mother.

"Read it, Frau," he said, curtly.

Mother's eyes anxiously started to scan the certificate and she felt instant relief at not seeing the word "sanatorium." But then the word "Ohrdruf" leaped out of the text, throwing Mother into a panic.

"Herr Oberst, my son must be sent to Ohrdruf? To the concentration camp? But it will mean death to my sick boy! He won't survive there for long!"

The Oberst was very quiet, his face immobile, eyes veiled, as if he did not want to involve himself in the inner turmoil of this half-blind, middle-aged Russian woman who was about to lose her son.

"Then send me, too, to Ohrdruf!" Mother exclaimed. "I might be able to help my boy somehow."

How to approach this stern, unfeeling German officer and try to "buy" his good will with the hundred dollar bill hidden in her bosom? One hundred dollars! Slava's life to be bought with a hundred dollars?

Mother felt so crushed by her predicament that she sat staring wide-eyed at the German and dared not attempt to bribe him.

The Oberst was not looking at Mother at all. He spun his chair around, turning his back to her, and was observing a column of Soviet prisoners of war entering the gate, ending a march on foot all the way from Ohrdruf. And then as he watched, a column of Jews came through the gate and for the first time the *muna* at Crawinkel welcomed even those *untermenschen*. As long as the V-1 or parts of the V-1 were handled at Crawinkel *muna*, Jews were kept out because Albert Speer, the Armament Minister of the Third Reich, had to obey Hitler's directive that no Jews were to come in contact with *munas* that carried out 'special projects,' as the Crawinkel *muna* did until very recently.

"The war is coming to an end. Soon."

Was the Oberst speaking to himself? Was he sharing his thoughts with Mother? His back was still turned to her, when he suddenly blurted out, "Do you remember the 20th of July?"

What 20th of July? Mother was taken aback with the Oberst's question, and he gave her no time to respond.

Swinging his chair abruptly, he again faced her and said, "The war is ending, Frau. You know it, don't you?"

Mother remained silent. The 20th of July. The Stauffenberg attempt on Hitler's life!

"Why do you speak such good German, Frau?" the Oberst suddenly asked. He listened carefully to every word Mother was saying, explaining to him that she had learned Russian, German, and Latvian, because in Riga, where she was born, one was more or less forced to be trilingual in order to be able to communicate effectively in any situation.

Riga! What magic that word seemed to contain! Just as in a Bavarian town, two years earlier, Herr Ordnung seized on this word, helping Mother to get to an eye doctor and finally to reach the town of her birth, so now, in this Thuringian *muna*, the high-ranking officer was grasping at the same word—Riga.

"Riga! Frau! Listen! I have been given orders to send out of this *muna* about thirty people, all *Volksdeutsche* from the Ukraine. They'll go to a camp in the town of Triptis, fifty kilometers east of here. There is a large camp for *Volksdeutsche*."

Mother listened without comment, not understanding what all this had to do with poor Slava's fate. The Oberst leaned over the desk, closer to Mother, his face intent, and said conspiratorially, "In the Triptis camp, there are many Volga German families—infants, old people, half-invalids. I'll try to place you among the people going there. Your son won't call attention to himself. At least not for a while."

Mother could hardly believe her ears. But she still was uncertain, fearful that in the new camp Slava would not escape hard labor. "But what if the Triptis *muna* will need workers? My son won't be able. . . ."

"There's no *muna* in Triptis," the Oberst interrupted. "No war industry of any kind. Don't worry about that. I'll provide you with temporary papers, stating you are Balts. One more family from your barracks can go to Triptis also. And God be with you." The man rose. He had already spent much time. Other duties called him.

Mother, too, rose. She had come to the Oberst's office ready to beg, to bribe, to humiliate herself in order to try to save Slava. And this sober-faced man made none of it necessary. Suddenly seized by violent weeping, Mother, without a formal farewell, without formal words of thanks, ran out of the man's office. The hundred dollars! Still in her bodice. Tonight, when Boris Fyodorovich returns, he must get in touch with the guard. The same guard who exchanged the previous hundred dollars. Must get food. Food for Slava! Nourish him back to health.

She raced toward the *muna*'s gate, toward the road leading to Crawinkel, toward the tavern and the bunk where Slava lay, waiting.

CHAPTER FIFTY-THREE

The new camp we were sent to turned out to be an abandoned theater on the very outskirts of the utterly nondescript, small Thuringian town of Triptis. As in Crawinkel, meadows and woods surrounded it, and undernourished trees were near the building on the northern side.

Dragging our bundles and suitcases with us into the dim interior, we were greeted by rows of bunk beds where peasants were sprawled, mending, knitting, or repairing their footwear, or inspecting clothing and hair for lice. Some younger women held infants to their full breasts. They all spoke a Volga German dialect, almost incomprehensible to us. Most were women who left Russia with the retreating German army. Their men had either already perished in the Soviet Gulag, or on the road of retreat, or were perishing still, while trying to hold the advancing Red Army at bay.

No one rushed toward us as was customary in all the camps, to ask where we were from. As if knowing that we were not of their ethnic group, the Volga Germans let us pass their many rows of bunks without meeting our eyes. The camp had no guard. The camp supervisor led us past a raised platform, formerly a stage. It sported an old burgundy curtain of velvet, ripped in many places and mended with pieces of blankets. Behind this privacy drape lived a group of Latvian and Estonian refugees—all women. When our group came near the stage, a curtain parted and a middle-aged woman with a flat, boyish haircut popped her head out and shouted to us in German, "Anyone from Riga?"

Mother quickly responded, but as soon as the woman realized that Mother was not of Baltic German descent, she lost interest and disappeared behind the curtain. On both sides of the stage were long hallways leading to narrow, steep stairs. Those stairs, in turn, led to what had been the male and female dressing rooms. Our group of 12 was directed to the left, into a rectangular room brightly lit by a large window. Six double bunks crowded the narrow room mercilessly. I quickly ran toward one bunk located alongside a window. Although it was colder there, at night, when everyone would be asleep or dozing and I could remove the black-out blanket, that window would reward me with the fantastic spectacle of nature—leading my eye to spacious meadows, the horizon pierced by thin, tall firs, and to the moon!

Slava took the lower bunk, while I climbed to the one on top. Mother settled by the opposite wall where it was warmer, and Raisa Mikhailovna with Boris Fyodorovich became her immediate neighbors. But there was no Zhenya. She did not come with us. The girl had at first tried gently, patiently to make her parents understand that she was afraid to leave Crawinkel, afraid to be separated from Kosta while the actual fighting was coming closer and closer to us all. But seeing that the older people still expected her to remain with them, she blurted out, "I am married to Kosta! Yes, wedded!"

Boris Fyodorovich asked unbelievingly, "By whom?"

"By each other, like in the old days in Germany. It's sacred! Mother, Dad, please go without me. I'm Kosta's."

And Zhenya remained behind, receiving from our family the 20 minute diamond chips I found in Lodz—a wedding gift. "For your ring, Zhenichka," Mother said, pushing the tiny packet into the girl's palm.

The beginning of the year 1945 found us near starvation in the most desperately hungry camp we had experienced up to that time. It was a non-working camp, and we soon learned that rations were allotted accordingly. The last one hundred dollars—all that remained of the found dollar fortune—was swiftly eaten away. We were looking forward to spring, for spring would bring much life into the fields and meadows and many edible plants and grasses.

With the coming of February we began to hear from the Balts that a very important conference was to take place in Yalta among the three Allies, and the future fate of us all was to be decided at that time. Our fate? To be determined by three strangers? We told the Balts, who listened secretly to a shortwave radio kept carefully hidden, that with the ending of the war, when the Nazi regime would be destroyed, no one would command *our* fate. We would be free! Totally free! We of course would remain in Europe, since the Americans and British would make sure that Europe's freedom was to be nurtured and protected. Who would guarantee us this freedom if we returned to Stalin?

In conjunction with the approaching Yalta meeting, the Western Allies began to bomb Germany as never before. The Joint Intelligence Committee reported that there was a ". . . political value in demonstrating to the Russians, in the best way open to us, a desire on the part of the British and Americans to assist them in the present battle."

The Western Allies began to assist the Soviets early in February 1945 with an operation named "Clarion," which called for bombing very small towns, until then spared from American daytime air attack. Many of us on the ground considered the Americans to be "gallant" bombers. Even in attacking Triptis that first week in February, they tried to avoid hitting residential areas by aiming mainly at the railways. The British pilots on the other hand, under the command of Sir Arthur Harris, were called "the butchers," because they seemed to relish hitting the sleeping, defenseless population.

I stopped running into the cellars during the night bombing. I was tired, terribly tired of the whole procedure. Had hunger, or long work hours, exhausted me so thoroughly? Could I go on another year or longer, working at *munas,* lifting crates, eating watery kohlrabi stew? I could. But could I survive another year if every single night were to be interrupted by the air raid alarm chasing me, together with other tired, sleepy people, into crowded, dark cellars and earthen shelters? There, many became hysterical with fear; children screamed and cried, begging their mothers for protection; and mothers, in turn, screamed and cried, begging God for protection, begging fate to turn the trained, young air killers away from them—to turn them in any direction, but away from the cellar they were in.

So I stayed in my bunk. There I lay, stretched out, staring at the ceiling, almost nightly listening to the death-soaked hum, heavy, dull, blood-laden. I tried to visualize the faces of the pilots. They must be young—handsome perhaps. Caring about their wives, their girl-friends, their children. And caring about no one else? I could not for the life of me visualize a human face manipulating the death machines. I could not imagine a human voice saying, perhaps with a smile of satisfaction, "Good show! Right on target!"

And while lying on my bunk, listening to the hum approaching nearer and nearer, not one muscle in my body moved. Only beads of sweat appeared over my upper lip—even in the freezing room. Relaxation began soon after I heard the explosions erupting faintly, somewhere in the distance. Immediately the desire to sleep returned, lullabying me with the song of survival, "Aha, someone else was destined to get it this time. Now you may sleep, Ninochka. Sleep now. Not your turn yet. The sky-robots missed you. Missed you."

It was nearing two in the morning when on February 14, the sirens called us to the bomb shelters. Slava and I remained on our bunks. I moved the blanket from the window, and we both stared at the ink-like sky, at the snow-covered fields stretching all the way to the horizon. To the northeast the horizon was tinged with a rosy glow. Sunrise? The thought pierced through my still sleepy brain. But the sun couldn't rise at two in the morning, could it? Yet the eastern horizon looked as if the sun was struggling to escape the bonds of earth as it has to do eternally, every single morning. The palest salmon-pink streak—actually, a suggestion of a streak—was decorating the horizon to the east-northeast. At two in the morning this glowing, thread-like band of light was very pronounced and eye-catching for it was not put there by nature as the stars and moon and sun are put there, giving out a glow of their own, a natural glow.

Slava's melancholy voice reached my bunk, letting me know that he, too, was wondering about the strangely luminous horizon.

"Something is burning, far away. Probably a city, bombed to bits."

The air raid alarm produced no planes that night, and people began to return to their beds. I was still gazing out of the window, observing Boris Fyodorovich, who lingered on the steps of the bomb shelter, pointing out to the Latvian woman with the boyish haircut the puzzling salmon horizon.

When he returned to our quarters, his voice was soft with wonderment, or perhaps with empathy, as he spoke:

"That woman from Riga heard that Dresden was bombed. She swears it must be Dresden burning. That glow, so hard to believe. It's more than 150 kilometers from us as the crow flies. How could this light be Dresden?"

And Slava, half to himself remarked, "If it is Dresden, it must be hell on earth there now."

And it was, reportedly claiming many more lives in one night's bombing than were lost in the entire war from Hitler's bombing of England.

CHAPTER FIFTY-FOUR

The Americans reportedly were not far from Thuringia, from Triptis, signaling the end of the war. Nature itself seemed to want to
greet the end of human hostilities. Spring covered the meadows with a
fresh, young carpet of green, with field flowers, with edible, much
sought after sorrel. The month of April arrived promising so much!
However, our camp supervisor, who began to wear only civilian
clothing—no more the sharply creased uniform—could not promise
even the next day's food rations. He faced the hundreds of camp
inmates in the first days of April, and said apologetically, "Folks! I have
very little food reserves left. Nothing additional is arriving. Try to earn
some rations on the surrounding farms."

I stood on the steps of the former theater, looking in the direction of
the neighboring farmland, land damp with the earth's warmth, begging to be nurtured, cared for. Well, I thought, did I not help Father in
our Dulovo garden? Was that not, in a way, farming?

"Mother," I said quietly, "I'll scout around. There," I pointed in a
northerly direction. "If I don't come back tonight, it means I am hired."

"But, Ninochka, don't separate from us. The Americans are coming."

"When?" I snapped. "Tomorrow? Or a month from now? Or when?
Mama, I am starving. Maybe I'll be hired for a few hours and paid with
a meal." Boris Fyodorovich, standing next to Mother, overheard me.

"Ninochka, I'll go with you. My dear wife needs some nourishment

331

to perk her up." And, turning to Mother he said reassuringly, "Natalia Alexandrovna, we two will stick together. Don't worry."

And off we went. Reaching the very first village, no more than two kilometers from the camp, we encountered some familiar faces—Volga German women from our camp who got there before us and were quickly hired, for they promised to be good laborers, having been born into a life of agriculture. We marched on, being rejected in several more places until we reached a village six kilometers from Triptis, and began to knock on every gate. The Volga Germans seemed not to have been in this village as yet, and Boris Fyodorovich was hired at the very first farm.

"Ja! Ja! I need you," the wealthy farmer said, when Boris Fyodorovich asked for a job. "Four Russian prisoners of war were just taken away from us. I need someone to attend to the horses. Know anything about horses?"

Boris Fyodorovich said he knew a lot about horses. Leaving him, I went to the next farm gate. A woman waved me away. "No one needed here." At the next gate a fellow looked me over critically—too tall for field work; hands not raw enough. He waved me on.

A small farm was coming into view. Too small, I thought. No one will be needed there. Half-heartedly, I knocked on the gate and after waiting a while, opened it myself, stepping into a neat, cobblestoned yard. Cows mooed, as if in greeting from their stalls, directly opposite the gate. Pigs oinked on my left, chickens started to cluck—their territory, their kingdom having been invaded by a stranger. Spotting an entrance door on my right, I walked toward it. It was opened by a pale, sickly-looking woman in her early forties, with straight black hair and very large, dark blue eyes. The eyes looked at me questioningly. Through the wide open door I could see into a spacious, brightly lit kitchen. A generous pot of meat stew, reddish in color, was cooking on the top of the huge stove, while a deep tray of cabbage leaf rolls stuffed with meat, swimming in tomato sauce, had just been removed from the oven. All smelled so devastatingly good, mouth-watering. And it smelled so familiar. The woman observed my eyes fixed on the stove, and said quietly, her voice hoarse, as if suffering from a cold, "Hungry? Come in."

I was afraid she would ask me to leave, finding out that I was Russian, but instead, hearing my accent, she smiled.

"Well, no wonder you're surprised to see *golubtsy* in my kitchen. Our Russian prisoners of war taught me how to prepare the cabbage rolls. And borscht." She pointed to the stew pot. "Poor fellows. They were marched off the other day. Didn't want to go, but things are changing so rapidly. You know where the Americans are now?"

I said I did not.

"What're you doing here, girlie?" she finally wanted to know. When I said I was looking for a job in return for food, she asked, "Ever worked on a farm? Do you know how to milk cows? Worked with horses? What *can* you do?"

She did not really need me, and I could not mislead her, for I had never worked with farm animals. Before dismissing me though, she loaded a deep soup plate with thick, meaty borscht, and another plate with cabbage rolls.

"Eat," she said, seating herself opposite me. "Your name? Nina? Ninchen." She observed quietly for a while, as I more or less inhaled the heavenly tasting borscht, and began to devour the cabbage rolls. And all of a sudden, with a jolt, Slava's thin face appeared before me. A spasm closed my throat, as if forbidding it to make another swallow.

"May I save those cabbage rolls for my mother and brother?" I asked shyly, planning to wrap the food in paper, and run back to Triptis. The woman looked at me for a while, preoccupied with a thought. Then she said, "I can use you to help me in the kitchen and with housecleaning. I am ill—cancer. I tire easily." She held on to her lower abdomen, as if to emphasize to me where the illness was located. "My husband is in the fields now. I don't think he'd mind your staying and helping me a bit."

I was beside myself with joy at being hired. The farmer's wife immediately set me to cleaning her parlor. On my own initiative, I moved the sofa away from the wall, discovering a blanket of dust underneath. Then I moved, aired, and dusted all the overstuffed armchairs, every throw pillow, finally lifting the rugs, dragging them outside to air.

"Oh! All those things have become so heavy to handle," the farmer's wife sighed, openly pleased with my work. She even gave in to my suggestion that a few things in the parlor should be rearranged, repositioned, so as to make the room appear less crowded.

"Hungry?" she wanted to know after several hours of energetic work on my part. I *was* again hungry, but I asked if it would be all right for me to run to the camp and give my brother and mother the cabbage rolls I had saved from the previous meal. I would cover the six kilometers there and six kilometers back with the speed of a bullet. And what joy those meat rolls would bring to my family. The woman, very tired, her face deathly pale, sat on the sofa.

"I don't need you any more," she said hoarsely. My heart fell into my heels from the disappointment. She doesn't need me any more. Only for one day she needed me.

"For today a job is done," she continued. "Come back tomorrow morning. Bring a change of clothes. You'll stay here a while. We'll give a good scrubbing to the kitchen tomorrow." She put several cabbage rolls into a deep dish, filled a milk can with borscht, placing the container on the bottom of a burlap carrying bag. Then she tossed half a dozen thick slices of white bread and a chunk of hard cheese on top of the container and—as if to shock me even more with her generosity—the woman then added a huge slab of thin, sweet *kuchen*. Her face breaking out in a kind, melancholy smile, she commanded me out of my stupor. "Run, girlie. Run to your people. But, hurry back tomorrow."

I did hurry back the next morning, thrilled at having found a job that not only fed me, but allowed me every few days to carry a bag full of foodstuffs to my starving family.

The farmer's wife was unabashedly anti-Nazi, blasting Hitler's policies when she and I were alone at the kitchen table. Learning of Slava's brutal beating at the Crawinkel *muna*, she exclaimed, "Those bastards! Bringing ruin upon all of us. Not only upon you. They're dragging Germany into an abyss."

Yet her own husband was a Nazi. It was her second husband, whom she had married only two years earlier, when she became a war widow. As she was small, quiet-tempered, so he was bully-like, with a loud voice, coarse in manner. At the dinner table, he often belched loudly, as if on purpose, forcing out a repulsive, rolling sound. If a burp refused to come forth, the fellow farted instead, insisting that gases must leave the body in one way or another. A huge portrait of him in Nazi parade uniform hung over the parlor sofa, as though it were an icon demanding veneration and homage. It showed a man in his mid-fifties, with dark hair thinning at the top, brown eyes bulging. His nose was thick and short, with large, upturned nostrils.

The farmer was willing to tolerate my presence, only grumbling at times to his wife when I was out of the room, but close enough to hear him.

"The kid is useless. Helps you with the house cleaning, you say? Bah! Bakes good bread? Poppycock! Anyone could bake bread! We need laborers! Not some skinny kid like her."

I wondered, How long will they keep me? What will there be to eat if I am thrown out of the farm house? The last time I ran to the camp, everyone had received three slimy, cold, boiled potatoes and nothing else. One could eat those three potatoes all at once, or divide them into several meals through the day, receiving nothing additional. The camp supervisor actually did not appear some days at all. And when he did appear, he would only encourage the starving people by saying that the Americans were coming, and soon. But when? Soon.

On April 13, in the evening, my farmers gave a party. It was Friday. The radio that day had announced that on the previous day, April 12, the American President Roosevelt had died. The radio was appealing to the German population to continue to have faith in the greatness of the Führer, who would not allow the Reich to perish. And now that the Soviet sympathizer and appeaser Roosevelt was dead, a change in the Western Allies' policies and their relationship with the Soviet Union was bound to occur. The new President would surely recognize Stalin's true motive—that of world domination—and would break up with the menacing Soviets. The degrading ultimatum of unconditional surrender for Germany would surely be dropped by the Western Allies, leading to more acceptable terms for an honorable peace. All of this the radio broadcasts repeated persistently.

After the party, I climbed the stairs leading to the attic room where my cot was placed, and, not even undressing, sank into the soft, warm bed. I was very tired from all the cooking, serving, and cleaning I had done. Sleep came promptly, embracing me for hours. Then a nightmare began to haunt me—a large, ugly, immensely heavy toad was climbing on top of me, covering my body with its slimy cold skin. The toad's hideous, bulging eyes were staring at me, at my terror-stricken face. And the toad's eyes were mocking me, laughing, while its slimy body was rubbing against my belly. The toad knew that I was paralyzed with fear. It knew that when I was seven years old, on my very first day of elementary school, an older boy had thrown three frogs under my dress collar, and those slimy creatures crawled on my chest, and into my underwear, trying to find a way out. I stood surrounded by laughing boys, and screamed and screamed, until the frogs were removed by the teacher. Since that time I had been afraid of frogs and the toad in my nightmarish dream knew that I was afraid of him. And he enjoyed my fear, laughing. Or was the creature moaning? A strange, dull moan.

Finally, vaguely, I realized that the toad was appearing in a nightmare, and that I should try to wake up, to open my eyes, and chase the nightmare away. But when, with much effort, I succeeded in opening my eyes, the nightmare did not vanish. In the light of breaking dawn, the bulging eyes were still staring at me. The eyes of my farmer-employer! He was not lying on me, but standing up, buttoning his fly, his face hard, cold. He quickly reached the door, and ran down the stairs, not even trying to muffle his steps, banging the gate on his way out.

I lay rigid, wishing to scream, to weep, to hit someone, my fingers feeling something sticky covering my belly. The stairs squeaked again and the farmer's wife burst in, out of breath. Her pale face full of anguish, her eyes wide with a question.

"Did he hurt you? That swine! Did he hurt you?"

I did not know if he hurt me. Perhaps while I was deeply asleep, he had done something I did not even feel. She calmed when she saw that, although my abdomen and chest were exposed, my bloomers were still in place.

"Thank God! You survived," she sighed with relief.

How familiar this phrase sounded in that Thuringian attic room, the same phrase that was uttered all over Feodosia when women met one another after the Soviet descent of 1941.

The farmer's wife brought warm water in a wash basin, cleaning my abdomen and chest of her husband's semen. She made me dress in clean, dry underwear, and bringing my coat and boots from downstairs she said, tears wetting her sunken cheeks, "Go, Ninchen. Return to your mother. The Americans are reported near Triptis. Go quickly. And take this food parcel. God be with you!"

The good woman pushed me out of the farm gate, once more shouting when I was already far away, "God be with you!"

"Ninochka! Where are you running?" Boris Fyodorovich shouted, coming out of his farmer's gate.

"To Mother! To the camp! The Americans are coming!" I shouted back, not wishing to stop for a moment.

"I might as well leave too," he decided.

A few minutes later we came upon the highway, and stood there, gaping in amazement, trying to take in the picture opening to our eyes. The entire road, as far as one could see, was jammed with retreating Wehrmacht soldiers, ragged, tired, unshaven. And alongside were marched—still under guard—Russian prisoners of war. SS troops hurried by, overtaking the others, pushing forward, some running into the surrounding woods. What were they doing in the woods, we wondered? Suddenly we found reason of our own for seeking shelter among the trees, because American planes began to fly low over the area, firing sporadic bursts of machine gun fire into the empty fields. Huddled beneath the trees, we could see that the SS men were dropping their uniforms and changing into civilian clothes. Then they ran to their motor bikes, to their cars, and scurried away.

CHAPTER FIFTY-FIVE

The blackout blanket on the window by my bed was snatched away, sending a stream of sunlight into my still sleepy eyes.

"Look!" And into my still sleepy ears, the deep voice of Boris Fyodorovich boomed like a big, powerful church bell. "The Americans are here! Look at them marching into Triptis!"

Sleep chased away completely, I sprang up from my bed and chimed in with Boris Fyodorovich, "Look! Look, everybody! The Americans are here! The Americans came!"

Still in my nightclothes, forehead pressing against the window, I stared wide-eyed at the highway full of marching men, and men in tanks, in jeeps, and on their motorcycles. Planes flew low over our heads, and for the first time no bullets, no bombs were sent our way.

The end of the war? For us, in Triptis this Sunday morning, April 15, 1945, was a deliverance day. A deliverance from the slaughterous, merciless air attacks; deliverance from the fear of the Nazis sending Slava to a sanatorium; deliverance from the fear of being in an area occupied by the Red Army with its vodka-inflamed men, as revengeful upon their own women as they were upon the German women whom they not only raped to death, but sometimes even crucified. What a blessing to be liberated, truly liberated by no one but those wonderful, wondrous Americans! They would not rape us, would not torture us, would not exterminate us. We knew it! We knew it!

Dressing quickly, we all hurried toward the highway, shouting the only English words many of us knew, "Americans! Our friends! Thank God for you! For your help! Our liberators!"

I was running toward the approaching soldiers, my braids flying behind me, my drab, poorly fitting dress with the ugly *Ost* pinned to it—all set off by my wornout shoes that left one big toe protruding. The soldiers in olive-drab uniforms marched toward me, past me; tanks rolled by, jeeps, motorcycles tried to speed by, but were forced to follow the traffic. Trucks were passing me, moving at a crawl, with soldiers sitting alert, rifles in their hands. They seemed peculiarly unfriendly at first, but hearing me shout that I was Russian, their faces broke out in friendly grins, hands blowing kisses.

"Hey, Russky! Hey, there! War kaput!" their throaty, laughing voices responded in a chorus. And their way of speaking was so peculiar! As if they were rolling something hot in their mouths. I ran toward the foot soldiers and threw myself upon a smartly marching sergeant, striding along at the side of his platoon. He tried to keep his dignity, his commanding posture, but could not. Noticing the *Ost*, he looked at my tear-stained face, half-asking, half-stating, "Russky?"

"I love you! I love you, American soldiers! Thank you! Thank you!" I tried to keep pace with the marching man, not knowing how better to express my true feelings, and how to stop the tears rolling down my cheeks.

"Don't cry anymore, Russky," the sergeant kept repeating. "Don't cry. You're free. War kaput."

I turned to others in his platoon, trying to touch an arm, a shoulder, a hand of every soldier, repeating and repeating my few English phrases, "I love you. Thank you. I love you, American soldiers. Thank you. Thank you." As a freed puppy runs wild with joy after being caged up for a long time, so I felt and behaved toward the Americans, not being able to stop expressing my joy.

And how magnificent our liberators looked! And how they walked! Not rigid the way German soldiers walked, or undisciplined as Red Army men, but easy, free, yet self-controlled. Their uniforms, too, were so different from other uniforms already familiar to me. Especially their trousers! So tightly fitted! Each time a soldier made a step, his buttocks moved, exposed to my eyes by his snugly fitted seat. No German or Russian man—soldier or otherwise—would dare to wear such tight clothing.

And then! More men were marching toward us, wearing the same uniforms. But how different they looked! They were even taller than the ones that had just passed, and all had faces and hands the color of chocolate. Some were very dark chocolate, others looked as if some milk was added to the chocolate, and yet others were almost white, though their facial features were still not quite Caucasian.

"Negroes," a woman standing behind me said in awe. The men were marching past us as smartly as the white-skinned soldiers did before them, only their grins were even wider, their teeth like sugar cubes, their dark eyes sparkling with laughter and friendliness. At our welcoming shouts, they began to throw us chocolate, cigarettes, bars of soap. While the white soldiers marched past the Germans, even past the very young children as if those people did not exist, the black soldiers did not do so. They obviously were not going to follow very strictly the order on non-fraternization with the German population, and the youngsters were ecstatic at not being chased away, but given a chocolate bar or chewing gum instead.

That day we spent hours roaming the streets of Triptis, mingling with the Americans. "Come to our camp! Visit with us!" We kept inviting them. Reluctantly, with the coming of dusk, we returned to camp, accompanied by a cigarette-puffing Boris Fyodorovich.

"Heaven! Pure heaven, this tobacco." Boris Fyodorovich smacked his lips. "A Negro gave me a few cigarettes. I saw the package, with a camel pictured on it. A camel!"

We were near the entrance door to our camp, when Boris Fyodorovich stopped, turning toward the now quiet highway, and said solemnly, "Always we must remember this day, friends. The day of our liberation—not just from the camp life, but true, spiritual liberation."

While many enthusiastically agreed, a Ukrainian woman's voice rang out as if mocking Boris Fyodorovich. "Well, I remember the day the Germans came into my town, in Ukraine." Her laugh was filled with sarcasm. "We greeted them, too, as liberators, didn't we?" She stared quizzically at Mother. "How about you, Natalia Alexandrovna? In Crimea, didn't you, too, greet the Germans as true liberators, eh? I don't know a town in Occupied Russia that didn't."

My cheeks flushed, remembering that November day of 1941, when as a 13-year-old, I held the tray with bread and salt. And I remembered Slava's prophetic words, insisting that the Nazis were not—and could not be—true liberators; that the dawn they were promising would be a false dawn. Now Slava was leaning on Mother's arm, pale, a sickly boy of 19, to whom that dawn truly proved to be false. He turned to me, as if knowing what I was thinking, and said, "Today's dawn is *real*, sis. Real liberation."

"If only this liberation came earlier! Slavochka, Slavochka! If only it came in Crawinkel, before you were hurt," Mother said, her voice hoarse with choking tears.

But Slava was not in a self-pitying mood. "We survived, Mother, didn't we?"

Later that evening, when we all were ready to say good night to one another, Boris Fyodorovich, as if repeating the words of a newly composed prayer, solemnly intoned, "The dawn is real, thank God."

The Americans did come to visit us! They actually invaded our camp with boxes of food, soap, chocolate, cigarettes. Many pilots—all in their early twenties—visited us daily. Then, as they were ordered to push on, others replaced them. To my delight and surprise, they courted me as if I were a celebrity of a sort. And in a way perhaps I was, for I was the only girl nearing a seventeenth birthday in the whole population of the camp. Others were either much younger or already in their twenties. It was I who received the most motorcycle rides, the most jeep rides, and was constantly asked out for walks. And the lessons I received during those walks! Lessons in English. One young man after another tried to prove to me he was a better instructor in English than his comrades. For some reason the form of address—that all-embracing "you"—did not bother me as it did six years earlier, during our foreign language lessons in Feodosia with dear Dmitry Antonovich.

By my bunk, three names were scribbled in chalk on the wall, belonging to my American beaus. Bob, I reminded myself—while visualizing the slender, dark-haired young fellow, with a straight, sharp nose and bushy eyebrows over his blue, child-like eyes—must be pronounced "B-ah-b," and not the reasonable way, "B-oh-b," as it should have been if Americans pronounced their letters as they are written. And there was sandy-haired, rosy-cheeked Mike, who spoke good Polish. His name, too, should not be pronounced as written—"Me-kay." No. It must be turned into "M-eye-k." And Jack, the name of my favorite pilot who was always ready to burst into the "Volga Boatman" song, or "O Sole Mio," or any other melody Boris Fyodorovich chose to sing, helping the older man with his perky young tenor—his name, too, was not as it should be—"J-aa-k," but peculiarly unsure of its own sound—"Jee-ak!"

When my seventeenth birthday arrived at the end of April, the American soldiers gave me a surprise party. And it was a surprise, because I did not tell them of my coming birthday. But Jack saw Slava gathering field flowers in the meadow near our camp, for a bouquet to give me—the only thing he could present me with—and this is how the American found out that those flowers were to mark my birthday. On that day, right after lunch, I heard through the open window the sound of a jeep racing toward the camp entrance, then screeching to an abrupt halt.

"Ninochka!" Jack's familiar voice reached all the way to my bunk. "Come out! Hurry!"

When I flew downstairs toward him, he caught me in his arms and exclaimed, "Happy birthday, young lady!" Smacking me on the cheek, he pointed to his jeep, loaded with dresses, coats, hats, and shoes. "Select what you like! Whatever fits you. The rest pass on to others. Come on! Don't stare as if you're in shock or something!"

But I was in shock of a sort. I reached out my hand to a navy blue spring coat and touched its fine wool. I saw a dark red beret, a mocha dress, a powder blue dress. I saw a caracul hat and another hat made of white, fluffy felt with a mushroom-like floppy brim. And shoes! All shapes, all colors, high heels, low heels, medium heels. And most were displaying Paris labels. And there was a kimono of black-lined silk, with embroidered persimmon chrysanthemums. "Mine! Mine!" I registered silently, knowing that this kimono, no matter how short, or long, or wide it might be, was destined from now on to cover my body and no one else's.

"So beautiful, J-aa-k!" I squeezed out the words with difficulty. "Where did you get it all!"

Nonchalantly Jack said, "I plundered a few deserted Nazi houses."

My face must have expressed some apprehension, perhaps even fear—after all, just a few days earlier, a German bullet would have been put in my head for such looting.

"Don't worry, kid. No one will come for those clothes. The Nazis all ran. I don't know why they ran. We'll catch up with them anyhow."

Seeing that I was no longer afraid to help myself to some of the articles, Jack settled himself on the steps, and directed.

"Okay, Ninochka. Start modeling for me. That hat, there. The mushroom one. Very nice. And that black lamb hat looks real Russian. Grab it. The kimono? You like that Jap thing? Oh, well, take it then."

I selected three dresses, the navy blue coat, the magnificent kimono, and five hats! And I found a nice-fitting pair of leather boots, a pair of smart rubber boots, and shoes that had one, two, and three inch heels. One pair—black suede pumps, with rhinestone buckles—had almost four inch heels, and when I put them on, enchanted with the effect they had on my foot, Jack moaned, "Oh, no! No, Ninochka! Listen." He got up and came closer to me, touching his shoulder with mine. "Such a heel is no good for you. Look for lower heels. See! Your shoulder is higher than mine. It's not good for a girl to be so tall."

Well, I thought stubbornly, I must have those shoes, even if their heels make me taller than all the men on earth. "They're so beautiful, beautiful, those shoes, J-aa-k," I persisted. "Like in a fairy tale. I must have them."

"Well," the fellow waved his hand in disgust, "have them. But don't wear them while you're with me."

"I will wear them when sitting," I compromised, trying to be reasonable.

All the women in our room received some clothing. Mother found two nice dresses of gray and black wool, and a dark charcoal coat. She selected shoes strictly for comfort—not following my example. Raisa Mikhailovna was sporting a smart suit and fur hat, with matching muffler. We all were in a state of happy commotion, modeling dresses for each other, and coats, and hats, giggling as if intoxicated.

After Jack drove away, I put on a creamy white crepe dress with long sleeves and tightly fitted waist, its full skirt falling in rich, heavy folds. The dress made me look a bit rounder everywhere but the waist.

"My! My!" Raisa Mikhailovna's voice was full of surprise, examining me while I was swirling. "What a lovely figure you're developing, Ninochka! Such a nice waist. And you are filling out nicely here." She pointed to her chest.

True. I was filling out, but in shabby, shapeless clothes no one really noticed it. So! I was growing up, but those stupid braids! A child's hairdo. Such a nuisance. Yet Mother kept insisting that a Russian maiden—that is, a virgin—must wear her hair braided until her marriage. But I was 17! Seventeen! How much longer was I to put up with those "rat tails?" Weren't the girls in Old Russia allowed at the age of 16, when they "came out," to cut their braids? It seemed I had read that somewhere. I decided to approach Mother one day soon with those facts.

Late that afternoon, the whole band of our American friends arrived. Flowers, cookies, boxes of chocolate candy—some with real liqueurs—were given me. French perfume was sprinkled not only on our new clothes, but on straw mattresses, on old blankets, turning our room into a flower bouquet of sorts. Bob arrived with a genuine leather suitcase for me, which was filled with bottles of cognac, cartons of cigarettes, canned food, boxes of chewing gum. He climbed on the bunk opposite mine and offered me a pack of gum. I saw Americans chewing gum constantly, but never saw them removing it from their mouths. So I unwrapped one strip, and popped it in my mouth, chewing it for a while until all the sweet taste was sucked out of it. Then I swallowed it, convinced that it was the thing to do. I opened another strip, and after a few minutes was ready to swallow that piece, too.

"What are you doing, Ninochka?" an observant Mike shouted to me from the next bunk, where he was sitting with Bob. "Don't swallow! Just keep on chewing. It doesn't taste like anything? Well, spit it out. Get rid of it! But don't foul up your gut with it!" I decided then and there that chewing gum was not my cup of tea. "What next?" Jack coaxed, inviting my inspection of the overflowing suitcase. I regally pointed to a can with a picture of a pineapple on its label. Bob opened it, and handed it to me, saying—"It's not the whole fruit. It's just the juice squeezed out of it. Try it!"

What a novelty! To drink fruit juice! How many whole fruits were needed to fill each can? I drained the can without taking a breath. Delicious. Yet, some aftertaste remained in my mouth, not pleasing to my palate. A metallic aftertaste. I inspected the row of waiting jars and cans on top of the suitcase. Spotting one with a picture of white, fruit-like clusters, I decided to try it. Probably exotic large berries of some sort, I figured. Bob handed the can to me. I read aloud a word that meant nothing, absolutely nothing to me: po-ta-toes. Tasting the white, round stuff, I was indignant.

"It's *kartofel*! That's what it's called? Po-tah-toes?"

"Yeah, it's a delicacy—spring potatoes," Bob said.

Delicacy? I could not imagine anyone in the whole world who would consider canned spring potatoes a delicacy.

"And what would your much esteemed ladyship try next?" Bob inquired a bit sarcastically.

I pointed to a jar, its label proclaiming boldly—PEANUT BUT-TER. "What is this stuff, 'pe-ah-nuht'? 'Butter' is 'butter,' in German, but 'pe-ah-nuht'? What is it?"

The Americans could not translate the word peanut, so I took a spoon and tasted it. Terrific! So smooth, but still in no way would it remind one of plain butter. A bit sweet in taste, thick and toothsome.

"You mustn't eat it with a soup spoon, Ninochka. And don't swallow it so fast! It isn't ice cream!" Jack instructed me at my elbow, his eyes round in wonderment and rising concern. "You should spread it on bread and make sandwiches, not gulp it down!" He raised his voice as if to try to stop me. But he could not tear me away from this butter made of a "nut" called "pea"!

"My present," I insisted, "and I may eat and eat and finish it all."

The three Americans sat wide-eyed, hypnotized by my dogged persistence in emptying the one pound jar of rich, never-until-then tasted stuff.

Bob grabbed the remaining two jars of peanut butter and said to Slava, "Take it. Hide it from her."

I sat like a pasha of sorts on a bunk throne, in my magnificent kimono thrown over the creamy white dress, the four inch heeled pumps still on my feet, the rest of the presents strategically arranged on the pillows, on the mattress, on the bunk poles, on the wall.

At one point, Jack, climbing upon the opposite bunk, joining his two buddies, said to them, "Doesn't she look like Greta Garbo a bit?"

Mike quickly agreed. "You're right, Jack. Garbo playing 'Ninotchka' in the movie. Remember?"

But Bob disagreed, saying quite frankly, "Not with those braids, she doesn't."

I pricked up my ears. My braids! They were talking about my braids! And Greta Garbo! Wasn't she in her forties? An old lady! Bob took the white hat with the floppy brim, and set it on my hair, tucking it all neatly inside.

"Look! In that mushroom hat she *does* resemble Garbo!" And then, staring hard into my eyes, he blurted out a challenge, "How about chopping off your braids, Ninochka! Huh? How about it?"

Filled with sudden courage, I looked out of the window to see if Mother was still in the courtyard. She was still there, sitting on a bench with Raisa Mikhailovna. She was admiring her new shoes that had perfect heels, no holes in the soles, and no breaks in the leather top. If only she would remain sitting a while longer, I wished desperately.

Jumping off my bunk, and locating a pair of scissors in Mother's handbag, which she kept under her pillow, I climbed up again. Slava, watching me, shook his head in disapproval, while his lips were not able to suppress a smile.

"Mother'll whip you," he warned.

It was a figurative expression, not frightening me a bit, because Mother never whipped us. Several women gathered around my bunk. A small hand mirror was produced. I directed the waiting Bob, "Okay, B-ah-b. Cut!"

One braid fell quickly, making a slight tumbling noise; the second braid followed. A moan escaped from one woman, as if she mourned a part, a live part, of my anatomy being separated from me. My heart, too, it seemed, felt a momentary regret. The Americans appeared a bit crestfallen as well, staring at me silently. But soon Jack took the initiative directing the hair styling procedure.

"Now, Bob, try to scoop some hair over her forehead. Get rid of the part in the middle. She needs bangs. Yep! Cut just over the eyebrows. Now, trim a bit more over the ears. Look, fellows! Garbo is coming through! Definitely! But, of course, much younger—much, much younger!"

When all the necessary hairstyling seemed to be finished, Jack—pleased with my patient behavior—hastened to reward me with the final results. "Now, Ninochka! Look at yourself! At a new you!"

I glanced at the two braids, lying lifeless on the blanket next to me, and swallowing the lump in my throat, anxiously peeked into the mirror. The face of a stranger stared back at me, with a high forehead completely camouflaged by the bangs, nose suddenly quite prominent, eyes no longer wide open to the world, but sort of hidden. While the soldiers were holding their breath, waiting for my reaction, I barely could hide my tears, "A plucked duckling, that's what I look like! Just a duckling. You try to tell me that a movie star could look so ugly?" Crushed with disappointment, I lifted the braids, my two lifelong companions and pressed them to my chest. "I can't stick them back on, can I?"

The soldiers earnestly tried to convince me that I looked not in the least like a plucked duckling—only perhaps a bit older, more sophisticated.

Then Mother's shouts reached our room.

"My girl! They're telling me she's cutting off her braids!" Puffing, after running up the stairs, she stood in front of me, shaking her head in disbelief. Then she turned to Jack and said, more in sorrow than in anger, "And I left her in your custody. Shame on you."

Jack tried to explain timidly, "But, ma'am, in the United States, seven-year-olds have their braids cut. And Ninochka is seventeen."

"United States! United States!" Mother grumbled.

Sensing a slight softening in her mood, I interjected, "The soldiers say that I look like a movie star, mama. Like Greta Garbo!"

"Greta Garbo?" Mother once more was aroused, indignant. "What a fable! Garbo is fair-haired! How can you look like Garbo? Like a plucked duckling! That's how you look right now!"

"See!" I turned on my hairdressers. "What did I tell you? You ruined me! Ruined me!"

The dancing party that evening smoothed out most of the friction connected with my new hairdo. When I came down, many Volga Germans clicked their tongues in strong disapproval at my short hair, but the Balts all praised my first step into womanhood, saying that now I was truly "a European"! Mother, too, calmed down after drinking a few toasts with the Americans to my good health. She even laughed, half-amused, half-hopeful, when she repeated to others the soldiers' words, that they thought I resembled a movie star.

I looked impatiently forward to dancing with my Americans. I knew some quite intricate steps for the tango, taught to me in ballet school under the lessons entitled, "Western Salon Dances." I was prepared to make my dancing partners proud of me in the tango when I would, after swirling energetically, throw my leg out, reaching the level of my forehead in lightning quickness, and then bend my body backwards, practically touching the ground with my hair, while my partner held me at the waist. And the Boston Waltz! I'll flow like a swan in water.

And then I realized that Americans were very poor, uninterested partners when it came to "Western Salon" dances. Instead, they introduced us to their own dance, which they called the "Jitterbug." And truly, resembling gigantic jittering bugs, they flabbergasted us with their furious tempos, with the wild body movements. I would have given my front teeth to be able to dance the way the Americans did. But no matter how much I tried to resemble a "jittery bug," I looked stiff and ridiculous simulating the jungle-like rhythms, while they looked as if they were born to it.

CHAPTER FIFTY-SIX

On the day my braids were cut, Hitler married his long-time mistress, Eva Braun. The next day they both committed suicide. The war in Europe officially ended on May 9, 1945, and President Harry S. Truman hastened to send a congratulatory message to Stalin:

> "Now that the Nazi armies of aggression have been forced by the coordinated efforts of Soviet-Anglo-American forces to an unconditional surrender, I wish to express to you and through you to your heroic Army, the appreciation and congratulations of the United States government on its splendid contribution to the cause of civilization and liberty."

And *Pravda* at the time of V-E Day published Ilya Enrenburg's words:

> "We long fought single-handed against the colossal forces of Germany. . . . We saved not only our own country, but also human culture, the ancient foundations of Europe, its cradles, its workers, its museums, its books. . . ."

The Americans in Triptis truly tried to work at "saving civilization," if only at the very elementary level. In our camp they replaced straw mattresses with real ones; provided us with warm, clean blankets, sheets, and bath towels; and distributed new sets of underwear and night clothing. They groomed us, bathing us in unbelievably aromatic soaps and lotions, disinfecting our surroundings. Doctors and nurses appeared, examining our lungs, hearts, kidneys, eyes, teeth, hair. Medicine and vitamins were dispensed to the needy ones. Our diet improved a thousandfold. Instead of slimy potatoes and kohlrabi soup, wonderfully meaty, thick stew was served daily. Even chicken made a debut. Children had no shortage of milk, eggs, fats.

Our future was smiling at us. No one in the camp planned to return to the Soviet Union. All had decided to remain in Germany. True, the country lay in ruins, but now, with American help, Germany, we were convinced, would be on her way to a recovery. And would she not need us—the former *Ost*, the former prisoners of war, the former soldiers of Vlasov's Army—to help her recuperate, to stand on her feet once more? After all, there were by the conservative estimates of the Germans themselves, seven million of us, former Soviet citizens, roaming on German soil—three times the population of Latvia! How much we could do! We were not a lazy people, dependent on handouts, but anxious to earn a living by our own efforts, asking only that we be given the chance to remain on free soil and prove our worth.

All of us in the Triptis camp were prepared to do just that—to prove our worth. If Germany did not need us, other countries might. We were ready to go to black Africa, to the jungles of South America, to the vast, unpopulated territories of Australia, to the mines of Belgium—only not back to Stalin.

Were we not the luckiest people, truly, to fall into American hands? All of us knew that we were. About half of the seven million Soviet citizens fell into Stalin's hands when the Red Army overran German towns and cities. The other half had fallen into the hands of the Americans and British. We—the lucky—felt at ease, looking toward the future.

In our corner, only Raisa Mikhailovna and Boris Fyodorovich were apprehensive, not over their future, but over Zhenya's. Where was she? Did the Americans occupy Crawinkel too? Someone in the Baltic group informed them that Crawinkel was in American hands as well. Boris Fyodorovich, several times a day tried to comfort his wife.

"Raiska, dear, Kosta will protect Zhenya. I am sure of that. I sort of feel they'll knock on our door any time now!"

One day, in the beginning of June, a high-ranking American officer entered our camp, summoning us all into the cafeteria, saying that he brought very important news—good tidings. The officer was accompanied by a sergeant, a man in his mid-twenties with a handsome, pronouncedly Semitic face, with a hair line that promised very soon to recede, surmounting a rather high forehead. Large brown eyes were set wide apart—observing, inquiring eyes. The sergeant's name was Julius, and he was to translate the officer's words for us from English to German.

"Folks!" the officer said very business-like, but trying to put a spark of enthusiasm into his voice. "Tomorrow Soviet officers will arrive in your camp. They'll ask if there are any complaints on your part toward our treatment of you. We hope you'll let them know that all is well, and that we live up to our obligations toward displaced people."

We stood thunderstruck. Soviet officers—invading our camp, our sanctuary?

The American continued. "The Soviet officers will need to have your names, places of birth, and where your homes were before you came to Germany. They will interview each one of you, and proceed with the repatriation to your homeland."

Every new word brought a new shock.

"Why repatriation?" one very old man finally asked. "We're not Russian."

The officer flatly stated, "You are Soviet citizens nonetheless."

The old man tried to hold his ground. "I was, but I am not any longer. My daughter has a baby." The old man pointed to a young woman with a nursing child. "The child was born on German soil. He's not Soviet. She stays here, with him, and I stay with them."

The American was annoyed. "Damn! In every camp the same damn business." He more or less barked a command. "Tomorrow the SMERSH officers will be here! And you will all be here! That's an order!"

What a word—SMERSH! No one could understand the full meaning of this word unless one imbibed the Russian language together with one's mother's milk. The word is constructed of two shortened ones—*smert,* meaning death, and *spion,* meaning spy: "Death to spies." The word *smert,* has at its end a softening indicator. With this softening indicator the hard sound of "t" turns soft, as if to make the word "death" a bit more acceptable. During the war, someone in the Kremlin came upon an idea to eliminate the letter "t" and replace it with the first letter for the word *spion.* So, the new word was created—SMERSH—

and this harsh last sound of "sh" turned the whole word into a cobra's hiss, stabbing a native Russian as if with a dagger. Perhaps the mad genius who created the new word wanted to accomplish just that—to put a dread into every Soviet citizen's heart. The heretofore terror-inspiring name—NKVD—simply paled by comparison.

Stalin established the organization SMERSH in the late part of 1941, but it did not really deal with spies only. Its duty was to interrogate every single person in recaptured areas of the Soviet Union, and interrogate every person captured outside of the Soviet Union—be it a Russian prisoner of war who lost both limbs fighting the Germans, or an *Ost,* or a teenager, or an eighty-year-old—all Soviet citizens were questioned by SMERSH and questioned brutally.

And those hardened, trained thugs were to descend upon us in our safe haven, Triptis camp, for the purpose of registering us for repatriation! Bedlam broke loose after the old Volga German insisted that he was remaining in Germany.

"We're not going back!" people shouted, their voices angry, full of fear, of tears. "Drag us in iron chains, Mr. American Officer, but we won't go willingly!"

The American was offended, perhaps even hurt. "What's the matter with you people? What are you? Criminals or something? Are you afraid to be punished for war crimes? What the hell are you acting like this for?"

Boris Fyodorovich standing silent until then, suddenly dominated the whole building with his stentorian, indignant voice, "We're not the criminals! But Stalin is!" The people answered with a deafening ovation.

The officer shouted, his face stern. "I will not allow anyone to talk to me in such fashion about our ally!"

"Incredible!" Boris Fyodorovich shook his head. "This American would rather believe the criminal than us, the victims." I stared at the officer in wide-eyed disbelief. And how flat, detached his face truly was. Yet one could not hate such a face. It was a good-looking, open, clean face. Only his eyes had a peculiarly decided look about them—as if those eyes felt they knew all there was to know, and wanted to know no more. Good, honest eyes, yet so indifferent. If only his eyes would become more involved, I wished desperately.

And then I heard a voice more familiar to me than any other voice on earth, "Mr. American Officer! I beg! Beg! Don't send us back!" It was my mother, at the officer's boots, embracing his calves, persisting, imploring the American to be kind. When was it once before that I saw her do it? As if in a nightmarish dream repeating itself. But no, it was not a dream. It was at the Marktredwitz market place, beseeching the factory owner not to separate our family.

The officer was visibly embarrassed. "Up! Up!" he mumbled, while Mother persisted.

"I won't get up! Don't force us to return! It'll be our death! You're handing us a death warrant."

"Oh for godsake! Don't be so melodramatic." Turning to Julius, the officer said, "Lift her up."

Julius rushed to Mother's side trying to lift her off the floor. I ran to the other side and said to her quietly, "Mama. . . . Don't belittle yourself in front of this, this 'liberator.' It's one thing to lie at the feet of a Nazi, quite another at the feet of that great democrat." I said those words in German, wanting to sting the young interpreter, Julius.

While lifting Mother, my eyes met his, and with a jolt I realized that his eyes were not flat and uninterested. His eyes showed pain. He cared!

The next day, as promised, two SMERSH majors arrived—both tall, young, good-looking, smiling. They wore crisp uniforms, the tunics sporting oversized, Czar-type epaulets. Their energetic, friendly voices rang through the camp building, "*Sdravstwuyte, tovarishy!*" They greeted us as comrades. No response came from the people. The SMERSH officers registered no surprise, did not seem disturbed or annoyed. They must have gotten used to such stony encounters. The officers started to call out people's names, but not one person came forward. The American officer with Julius on his side, was frowning, perspiring, but not the SMERSH. After about thirty minutes of such a totally unproductive roll call, calmly they gathered up their papers, closed their briefcases and after some amiable conversation with the American officer, they jumped into their jeep and departed. The camp sighed in relief.

The American officer, on returning to the building after escorting the SMERSH outside, said to us, "Well, folks, we won't force you to go, if you don't want to."

Some cynics dared to doubt the officer. "You won't really force us? Word of honor?"

"Word of honor."

Julius returned that evening, knocking on the door but not entering, asking me if I would like to sit with him on the bench near the main camp entrance. The rules seemed to have changed in the last few weeks, not allowing the visiting Americans to enter our sleeping quarters. Perhaps those rules always existed, but were not obeyed strictly, as on the day of the cutting of my braids. I followed Julius to the bench, but was too keyed up to sit quietly, proposing instead to march around the camp once or twice. Then we sat on the bench, and Julius finally said what he had come to say. "Nina, you'll be in big trouble if you're so set against returning home."

"Why!" I looked straight into those warm, brown eyes of his. "Why in trouble? Your officer gave us his word of honor that he won't repatriate us by force."

Julius bent low as if to reach the laces on his sturdy boots, avoiding my gaze. "Don't you know?"

"Know what?" I demanded impatiently.

"Even if we don't send you back, it'll be all the same in the end. The Red Army will enter Thuringia and Triptis."

The Red Army in Triptis? What was he saying?

"But, Julius! The American army is in Triptis!"

"Yeah, but it was agreed that we'll pull back from here, giving Thuringia to the Soviets."

He finally straightened up from adjusting his boot laces, and looked at me while I shook my head in disbelief, even wanting to laugh at such a bizarre disclosure. And yet I did believe Julius.

"So," I said, "it was easy for your officer to promise not to force us back. He knew that if we didn't go, the SMERSH would get us soon anyhow. No wonder the SMERSH officers were so cordial. They have time on their side."

How I wanted to remain near Julius that evening. Somehow, the only safety from SMERSH seemed to be in Julius being near me. When Mother called me in, I regretfully left the bench, left Julius, and climbing to my bunk, slowly, deliberately wiped all the names that were scribbled on my bunk wall. The names of Jack and Bob and Mike had vanished as the men themselves vanished, replaced by Tom and Leo and Jimmy, these to vanish as well. And on the clean wall, I put three names, far apart, so that they would constantly be in front of my eyes—Julius, Julius, Julius.

Several days passed. Julius was visiting us daily—in his official capacity as an interpreter, and in an unofficial capacity. I waited impatiently for those visits. Raisa Mikhailovna, noticing me sitting by the open window one day, staring at the highway, listening for the sound of Julius' jeep, said to my mother, "Ninochka is bitten by the love bug."

I myself did not know if I was bitten or not, but the name Julius was pounding constantly upon my brain, almost annoying me. And when once I noticed a vivacious red-headed German nurse, brought to our camp to inspect children's mouths, giving Julius coy, teasing glances, I was awfully glad of the non-fraternization rule between Americans and Germans.

When the camp found out about the impending surrender of Thuringia to the Soviets, deep gloom enveloped all. What to do? Where to go? In order to leave the camp, one needed special permission with a pass from the Americans. No one was given such a pass because the Americans were required to deliver all inhabitants of the camp to the Soviets.

Early one evening, Julius came—his shirt crisply starched, its back sporting three pleats put there by the iron; his trousers stiff with knife-like creases, face exuding a pleasant, mild scent of aftershave. We sat on the same bench, his knee touching mine, his palms holding my hand, playing with my fingers. He looked at those fingers of mine and said, as if puzzled by something that he truly wanted to understand, "Ninochka, why? Why such fear on the part of your people to go home? Was it *so* bad?"

How to explain to an American how bad it was? To start telling him of *besprizhorniks*? Of hunger? Of never-ending fear of authorities? Of government-enforced isolation from the rest of the world? I began to feel irritated by Julius' naiveté, and looking into his intelligent, kind eyes, at his young caring face, I hissed:

"You! You great American democrats! Frauds! Hypocrites! That's what you are!"

Julius wrinkled his forehead as if I had hit him. I still fumed, my voice barely rising over a whisper. "In my town of Feodosia lived many Jews. One girl, Maya, was my schoolmate, a friend. The SS marched her to the outskirts of town and machine-gunned nine hundred people. Maya died quickly. Not much time was given her to be afraid, to think about death. But you! You give us plenty of time to think! To prepare ourselves! For what? For Siberia? For physical abuse? For gang rape? What are you, but sadists! I hate you! Hear? I hate you!"

I banged my fists at Julius's broad chest, the chest that I actually longed to bury my face in and weep. Instead, I sprang up from the bench, and ran to our room.

Climbing upon my bunk, I shouted to no one in particular, "Lock that door! Don't let that . . . that Julius enter our room!"

I turned to the wall and, seeing the three Juliuses, was wracked with bitter sobs.

CHAPTER FIFTY-SEVEN

*A*fter half an hour of unrestrained weeping, I very much wanted for Julius to enter our room, to comfort me. But he did not come. That night, dark scenes of approaching doom hounded me mercilessly. I thought of being crucified on a barn door, as the Soviets did to so many Silesian women after gang-raping them; or of being shipped to Kolyma, to dig for gold, where every guard would use me. We must try to escape the Soviets. But how? I lay wide-eyed, staring through the open window at the night sky, pinpointing a small, far-away star. If only to escape to that star. But the star just winked, twinkled, as though laughing at my unattainable wishes. When was it that I used to stare at the night sky, and "wish upon a star"? In Feodosia! On Praskovia Ivanovna's patio, sleeping in the old silk hammock.

And there she was, still remembered by me with so much warmth. Dear Praskovia Ivanovna, trotting toward us at the railroad station on the day of our arrival from Dulovo. She was prancing toward me, her finger pointing at me as though trying to say something. And the leather harness over her chest, sort of glowing, as if to catch my special attention. And what was the harness for? To help in dragging the two-wheeler for our baggage.

The two-wheel cart! Praskovia Ivanovna was still trotting toward me, but somehow a bit more removed, and instead of pointing her finger, she nodded her head, seeming to praise me for interpreting her message correctly. My trance-like, half-sleeping state vanished.

"Mother!" I jumped down, tiptoeing to her bunk. "Mother, Praskovia Ivanovna just visited me. I was sort of dozing." Mother was visibly distraught. "But *dochenka*, it's a bad sign, the dead visiting in a dream."

"Nonsense!" I energetically dismissed Mother's superstitions. "We need a two-wheeler—a cart, or even a wheelbarrow."

Mother instantly understood. "Yes, yes! Like Praskovia Ivanovna had strapped to her chest. It'll be our salvation. We need it for Slava."

Actually, if Slava was in better physical shape, we would have all three left Triptis on foot, getting along without a cart. But Slava could walk only a couple of kilometers at a stretch before needing to rest. It would take us a long time to walk to safety. If we had a cart, he could sit in it while Mother and I pulled him along. Mother would speak German for us all, because she spoke it with a Riga accent, and we could pass for Baltic refugees. The next morning I started to hunt for a two-wheeler, but did not locate one. No one had a cart to spare, not even when American cigarettes were offered. Many Thuringians, learning of the impending American withdrawal, were getting ready to leave too.

That evening, exhausted from a day-long hunt, I lay on my bunk, planning for the next day. Perhaps, I thought, I should go to the farmer's wife I had worked for. Maybe she could help me get a cart. It was then that a knock was heard at our door.

Julius! My heart sort of leaped and my lips tried to repress a smile. He returned. I abused him, demeaned him that evening on the bench, downright accused him of being a sadist, but he came. He understood.

The door opened. The figure appearing on the threshold was not that of Julius. But the first instant of utter disappointment was immediately replaced by joy. "Kosta!" He stood dusty, tired, and very sad. His eyes searched for Raisa Mikhailovna's and Boris Fyodorovich's corner and, finding it, he hurried to them. The couple embraced him in greeting, while still looking at the entrance door.

"Zhenya? Where is our little Zhenichka?" Raisa Mikhailovna asked, a bit apprehensive, but smiling, her voice full of joy at seeing the young man.

Kosta was not smiling, and I knew then that he was bringing sad tidings.

"I don't know where Zhenya is," Kosta finally said. Dropping heavily on an empty bunk, he sat, not speaking, not moving, face hidden in his palms. Boris Fyodorovich reached under his bunk, and locating a small bottle of brandy left over from my birthday, poured some into a glass, offering it to Kosta. When Kosta finished telling us what had happened to Zhenya, I knew—knew!—that I must find the cart the very next day. Must!

The Americans entered Crawinkel a couple of days before Triptis. General Patton occupied the neighboring Ohrdruf camp on April 12— on the day of President Roosevelt's death. Patton recorded that several ordinary citizens of that little town had committed suicide after he had forced them to examine for themselves what had been taking place at the camp.

Just a few weeks before the Americans arrived, the *muna*'s Oberst allowed Kosta and Zhenya to be married by the local justice of the peace. Kosta, finding a skilled silversmith among the Germans he knew, had had the diamond chips worked into a magnificent engagement-wedding ring for Zhenya. When the Americans arrived, Zhenya wanted to remain in Thuringia, especially because she was having spells of queasiness in the morning. Kosta, realizing that she was probably pregnant, persuaded her that she should go with him to Yugoslavia before her condition became too advanced. Kosta's plan was to reach the Soviet Zone by walking along the railroad tracks until they would come to a main assembly point, where returnees were loaded on trains and delivered to their native countries.

The whole of Germany seemed to be on the move, like a giant, stirred-up ant hill. Although a few homesick individuals among the Poles, Yugoslavs, Hungarians, and Czechs hurried to their pre-war homes, hoping to reunite with their families—the vast majority of people hastened west. About ten million Germans were leaving Pomerania, Brandenburg, Breslau, Silesia, and East Prussia, not only because the Red Army was there, but because they were being forced out of their ancestral lands due to agreements reached at the Yalta Conference in February 1945.

Against all that sea of marching, crawling, trotting humanity heading west, Kosta kept pulling Zhenya toward the east, toward the Soviet army. Before leaving Crawinkel, Zhenya for a while felt apprehensive about facing the Soviets, but Kosta convinced her that she no longer was the property of the Soviet government—she was his wife, the wife of a Tito partisan. And Tito was a friend of the Kremlin. Kosta was certain no one would dare to harm his bride. Never would he allow anyone to harm her!

And so, Zhenya followed her husband. They crossed into the Soviet-occupied Zone, and headed in the direction of a main assemblage of freight, cattle, and passenger cars—all waiting for their human cargo of repatriates.

Kosta pointed to one of the freight cars with fresh straw on the floor, and said, "Zhenichka, we'll sleep and rest up in this car. Tomorrow, we'll find someone in authority and show our documents. Perhaps we could get a train ride to Yugoslavia."

Zhenya felt listless, spent, wanting nothing so much as to stretch out on the soft straw and doze off. Army cars, trucks, and jeeps were zipping through on the road parallel with the railroad tracks, but Kosta felt no fear. Evening was approaching—a warm, May evening. Kosta saw several people, mostly women and children with their refugee bundles in hand, clambering into nearby empty boxcars, and settling there for the night. Where else in that war-torn country could a more convenient roof be found?

The Soviet jeeps began to appear more often. The soldiers knew that refugees were inevitably tempted to spend the approaching night in the cars. At dusk they grew loud—singing, waving vodka bottles, cursing in their terribly vile, angry way. Kosta felt uneasy, but did not disturb the dozing Zhenya. Just in case, he took out his identification papers and his marriage license.

Then, a few cars away, Kosta heard a woman scream, pleading, "No! No!" There was a drunken, challenging, "No? Yeah, Frau!" Zhenya, immediately awake, crawled to Kosta, clinging to him, just as a jeep stopped right in front of their car. Four bottle-waving Soviet soldiers jumped like agile wildcats over the ditch separating the highway from the railway car.

Kosta tried not to appear anxious, and greeted the Soviets with extended hand. They accepted no hand. He produced the documents, repeating several times that he was a Tito Partisan, hoping to establish a common link with the Soviets. But they were only interested in Zhenya.

"She's my wife! My wife!" Kosta shouted, suddenly becoming panic-stricken. "Our marriage license, look! My wife is pregnant. Baby." Kosta spoke in his native language, trying to use as many Russian words as he had learned from Zhenya, although they spoke German with each other as a rule.

But now Zhenya, frightened, began to speak Russian to Kosta and to the four soldiers. "I am his wife! His lawful wife! I am Russian! From Leningrad! I am not German!"

One short-legged fellow with Mongol features said in slightly accented Russian, "So! That whore is ours! Not a German frau, but our own Soviet whore! Hitler's mattress! Collaborator!" A second soldier, turning to Kosta, spat out, "She's not your wife! She's ours, ain't she, fellows?"

The short-legged one, nearest to Zhenya, tossing his vodka bottle aside, began to unbutton his fly, pushing Zhenya to the floor. Kosta sprang at the fellow, reaching for his throat, but the other three gave him no chance to free Zhenya. The attacker snatched a knife from inside his boot, and cut Zhenya's dress and underwear with one precise stroke—from collar to hem. And then Zhenya's desperate, helpless scream to her husband, while six fists were pounding him totally senseless—pounding at his mouth, nose, ears, groin.

Hours later, when he came to himself in a nearby ditch—perhaps left for dead by the four assailants—Kosta saw no train, no car where he had settled with Zhenya the night before. And there was no Zhenya. Nowhere could he find her. Robbed of all his possessions—watch, ring, wallet—Kosta nevertheless was left with one thing connecting him to Zhenya—the crumpled marriage certificate, still clutched in his hand.

Our room was quiet that night. No one slept. Neither snores, nor talking, nor moaning in one's sleep was heard. Not long before dawn, Slava called out in a whisper:

"Sis? You're awake? Listen to me." I knew what he was going to say. He was going to tell me to try to save myself, to run from Triptis alone.

"Don't let me hold you here. They might spare Mother, but they won't spare you. If today you don't find a cart, walk away from here—alone."

I had my answer ready, because ever since Kosta left, I had thought of nothing but of what we must do. I whispered back, "If I don't find a cart tomorrow, then the three of us are leaving the day after tomorrow. Yes! All three, Slava! We carry nothing, hear me? Nothing. No suitcase, no bundles, nothing in our hands. We put on two, three changes of clothes, shoes best for walking. Stuff our pockets with American cigarettes." My whisper was hoarse, bossy.

"But, Ninochka, how far do you think we'll get before I give out?"

"That's why we won't carry a thing. Mother will hold you up on one side. I'll support you on the other. You can walk that way for three or four kilometers. Then if your legs give out, I'll carry you. Don't give me this 'Oh, sis' business! I'll carry you on my back. You're just a midget next to me, anyhow."

I heard Mother quietly blowing her nose. She must have overheard us, and was crying. When the light pierced through an open window, people began to stir, and sigh, and moan. Many began to weep silently.

Mother fixed some bread and sausage for breakfast, and tea. We sat by our suitcases—serving as a table—and ate, but not truly tasting the food. Raisa Mikhailovna and Boris Fyodorovich did not want to stir, to eat, to talk. When it was nearing eight o'clock, I decided to march straight to my former employer, the farmer's wife, and beg her for a cart.

Just as I was leaving, Mother said, her voice unfamiliarly soft and hesitant, "Ninochka, *dochenka*, forgive me for disciplining you that day, for cutting your braids. I wanted to see you remain a child a bit longer. And now, you're all of a sudden our *opóra*."

Opóra! One called a father or a husband an *opóra*—a strong person in a family unit, one on whom others could lean for support. *Opóra* literally means "a leaning stock." And according to Mother, I had become our family's leaning stock.

"Don't despair if no cart will come your way," Mother said, her voice once again very matter of fact. "We'll do what you proposed to your · brother during the night. Tomorrow, we'll leave Triptis. I'll help you carry Slava."

I had walked about one-third of the distance toward the kind farm-wife's place when I heard a motorcar behind me, coming fast, catching up with me, and Julius' voice shouting, "Come, Ninochka! Come back! Hop in! Your mother told me where you were going! Come for a ride!"

"No ride!" I announced sternly, continuing to walk toward my goal. "No time for a ride, Julius. Thank you very much. I must find a cart. We're leaving Triptis tomorrow. At the latest, the day after."

"That's it!" Julius shouted at the top of his voice. "You *are* leaving Triptis tomorrow. Jump in! I have to tell you!"

I jumped in.

"There are several Jewish survivors in Triptis. They want to get to their former homes, southwest of here, in the Rhineland. An old bus is being repaired right now to transport them out of here. Ninochka! There'll be several seats available. About nine of you could go with those people to Frankfurt or Mainz."

* * *

That evening, Mother did not call me to come in when darkness fell, allowing me to sit with Julius on the bench. I was parting with someone who seemed to have reached my very soul, touching it gently, but was being torn away from me by circumstances that were not allowing any strong ties to develop.

Julius handed me three passes that he himself had issued, without superior authorization. One pass entitled Mother, Slava, and me to leave Triptis unharassed, and to receive at any American field kitchen a hot meal daily. The second pass I gave to Raisa Mikhailovna and Boris Fyodorovich. And the third I gave to a family of Ukrainians—all women. The youngest had borne the child of a Wehrmacht soldier back in the Ukraine. Were she to fall once more into Soviet hands, it could spell death.

Putting the passes in my skirt pocket, I did not want to lift my eyes, did not want Julius to see how happy I was when near him. I did not want him to see in my eyes what I felt for him—a sergeant—going against the orders of his superiors, trying to help us survive.

Julius was quiet for a long time. Then, as if reaching a decision, he lifted my face to his, and gently—hardly touching my lips—kissed me. And abruptly, as if not wishing to allow himself any deep emotional involvement, he got up and hurried to the jeep.

"Be good!" he said. Half way to his jeep, as if in afterthought, he added, "Good luck. Good luck, Ninochka!"

I could not rise from the bench, doubled up in silent sobs as Julius' jeep roared away and disappeared.

"*Proshaiy. Proshaiy,* Julius," I kept whispering. Farewell. Forgive, and be forgiven, but not forgotten, never forgotten.

CHAPTER FIFTY-EIGHT

riptis was retreating as the bus rushed us to safety. Mother crossed herself repeatedly, whispering prayers of thanks. We were all still in a state of disbelief for only one day earlier we were hunting for a cart or a wheelbarrow, planning to walk to safety on our own two feet, while begging for food in exchange for cigarettes. And there we were, reclining in leather upholstered seats, lifting our feet from time to time for even greater comfort, and scheduled to stop at an American base to be fed!

"A lucky star hangs over you, Ninochka," Mother suddenly said, patting my cheek. She had been saying those words, from time to time, for as long as I could remember, and I always wondered why she was so convinced of this. But this bus trip, was it not another proof that a lucky star did indeed hang over my head, sending Julius to our rescue?

Boris Fyodorovich, seeing a man light a cigarette, excused himself and went to join the passenger in a smoke. The two men sat silently for a while, looking out of the window. The countryside showed little evidence of heavy war damage. We were still in the midst of Thuringia's villages, woods, and meadows. The men began to converse quietly, amiably at first. But slowly, Boris Fyodorovich's bass began to reach us, making us wonder why he was so upset when he said, "Can't be! Impossible! The Americans and British wouldn't do that!"

His companion continued to speak softly, and again Boris Fyodorovich's voice boomed through the bus. "But children? Women? They were never in uniform. Are you sure?" He lit another cigarette and sat puffing, puffing, trying to get a grip on himself before returning to us.

"The hunt is on," he said, after leaving his smoking companion and taking the seat by his wife's side. "We were all sold out at Yalta. Americans. Liberators? Their orders are to catch us all, just because we're Russian. Catch us and turn us over to Stalin. Yes!" He persisted, as we cried out in disbelief, "That man knows about the Yalta agreement. All Soviet citizens—children, women, all! To be returned *by force if necessary,* to Stalin!"

While millions of our countrymen were being repatriated by force to the Soviet Union, we were sitting in a bus, hoping desperately to escape this unenviable fate. More than 400 kilometers now separated us from Triptis.

Our bus driver stopped at a railroad station—as he had several times during the trip—and asked us, "Want to get off here?" Most of our traveling companions were already gone. We looked at the nightmarish picture—at black, contorted, snake-like rails writhing in the air; at several trains caught in the station by an air raid, their cars climbing one atop the other, helter-skelter; at the crystal carpet of shattered glass covering the area; at the sign almost hidden in the rubble, informing us that we were at the FRANKFURT BAHNHOF. Across from the station, mounds of rubble stared at us challengingly, as if to say, "Go ahead! Try! Just try to make a home amidst all this!"

The bus driver looked at our crestfallen faces and did not ask again if we wanted to remain there. But he had to drop us off somewhere. Faced with the novelty of decision-making, we felt lost. Until then, we were always given directions, instructions, commands, and given lodging and food. No matter how poor the camp's accommodations were, we were organized and looked after. And now for the first time in years we were on our own. How to start? Where to go? While the cushioned seats of our bus were so comfortable, its roof solidly protecting us from the rain, its walls protecting us from the scavengers, where was there protection to be found in the towns and cities we had passed? Hills of rubble, followed us all the way from Thuringia. From time to time an individual wall of a multi-storied building showed off its strength amidst the debris, its dark squares—previously windows—observing us blindly. Our bus had to make countless detours in order to get through the center of some towns, where once universities, churches, and museums were flourishing. Everything was in ruins. And in those ruins a flower would appear, stuck between the fallen stones of a rubble mound, marking a spot where a perished human being found a grave beneath a crumbled building. And those flowers, carefully placed by the caring, mourning survivors, were even more disturbing and heartrending to see than the black armbands during the war.

After leaving Frankfurt, our bus covered about 40 kilometers, going southwest, paralleling the Rhine River, coming upon a small railroad station, right on the banks of the river. Its small sign said: MAINZ-KASTELL. Mainz? The 2,000-year-old city of the Romans, the city famed for its cathedral, its world-renowned university, the city of Gutenberg—and the railroad station no bigger than the one in Crawinkel?

The bus driver then pointed to a long, war-damaged bridge—freshly and crudely repaired in several places—crossing the Rhine. "There! See? Mainz is across the river."

And there, about a kilometer away—on the opposite bank of the River Rhine and at the mouth of the River Main—stood the ancient city of Mainz. Stood? Eighty-five percent of the city was in ruins and much of it lay flat. After witnessing the passing of two millennia, Mainz did not wish to stand up, as if it was forever finished with the role of a live city. But the steeples of the famed Dom—erected almost 1,000 years earlier—stood proudly, as if shouting to the British Air Marshall, 'Butcher' Harris, "You can't get all of the cathedrals! You can't kill history!"

The sight of this dead city should have thrown us into even deeper depression than the sight of Frankfurt. Yet, there was the river separating Mainz from the place where we stood. To our minds—frightened, insecure, and petrified by Yalta—the river seemed to offer an extra protection, an extra barrier in case the Red Army decided to march into this part of Germany.

The driver queried us once more, this time with a tone of finality. "Folks, I ask you for the last time. Do you want to cross the bridge that will bring you to the Mainz main railroad station? If not, I'll drop you off here, in Kastell." Then, as if to help us make up our minds, he added, "I must warn you, though. I heard that Mainz, and all the land across the Rhine, will be given to the French. On this side of the river, everything will remain in American hands."

"French? Were they at Yalta?" Boris Fyodorovich asked anxiously.

"I . . . I don't believe they were. Why?" the driver was puzzled by the question. To us, it was a sign of Providence. If the French were not at the Yalta Conference, they made no deals with Stalin about returning us by force to the Soviet Union.

"To the Mainz main railroad station!" Boris Fyodorovich directed.

The Mainz Bahnhof stared at us sadly—lonely, forlorn—only its long, broad steps, some walls, and the floor still intact. Much of the roof lay sprawled comfortably on the station floor, joined by many demolished side walls. Although ten times the target of Allied bombing, the station stubbornly refused to crumble completely.

No people were visible anywhere. Mainz was so devastated that our driver had to make a very long detour after crossing the bridge, driving first to a neighboring village, and from there approaching the railroad station. Directly opposite the station stood one multi-storied building, a hotel displaying a sign—AMERICAN MILITARY HEADQUARTERS—and on all sides of this building, as far as the eye could see, lay rubble, its mounds rising and falling, and rising again.

We dragged our belongings out of the bus and sat still for a while, trying to adjust to the new surroundings. The driver, as soon as the bus was emptied, waved to us, shouting, "Good luck!" Then he disappeared. The weather was warm, and we took comfort in knowing that we could spend the night on our bundles right there, on the steps of the Mainz railroad station, if we had to. But only a few minutes after our driver left, a German policeman appeared from inside the station, hurrying to us and shouting in great agitation, "People! People! You can't sit here! No! No!" His face was flushed from excitement. He pointed to the American headquarters. As if to back up his words, a jeep zoomed toward us carrying two American MPs.

One MP shouted in German, trying to chase us away, "*Raus! Raus!*" Mother quickly showed the pass issued by Julius. "Okay! But no stay here," the soldier said in broken German. "Go away! Help you? No help here. Go to camp. Not far from here. What? Don't want to go to camp? Why?" Then, as if not truly interested in why we did not want to go to a camp, the American said, looking at his watch, "Twenty minutes. You have twenty minutes. Then, ffsssst," and he whistled, his arm sweeping in a motion to indicate our complete disappearance.

After the jeep sped away, the policeman looked at us with a certain compassion, his aging face sad. "You are from the Baltic, aren't you," he said to Mother, who had been the only one speaking German. She nodded her head, not really being untruthful. "Ja, ja," the man said, sorrowfully, "so many of our people now are homeless. They come here and beg for help. What can I do? Some try to crawl into the rubble, but they run out the next morning. Too many rats, you know. There are still human remains. Rats must smell them. So, the refugees come to the railroad cars. They try to spend a few nights there; then they move on to the villages, begging for employment on the farms, or they go to the nearby towns. Some towns weren't heavily devastated. People help if they can."

There he was, this utter stranger whom we did not know until fifteen minutes earlier, planning for us the very next step to make. And we had to hurry and make it, since very little time was left before the Americans were scheduled to return. What if they lost their patience, and packed us on a truck, delivering us to the neighboring camp and then to SMERSH? Mother dug into her dress pocket and took out a pack of American cigarettes. She counted ten and handing them to the policeman, said, "Please lead us to an empty train car. Just for a few nights."

The policeman, delighted with the gift, brought us to a cattle car standing all by itself, separated from the rest of the bleak, battered vehicles. Before housing us, the car already had served hundreds of refugees. Because there were no toilet facilities, all the surrounding area—the railroad tracks, the strips between, even under the car itself—had been turned into an open sewer.

The policeman was full of helpful suggestions about where one could get some water, where one could get a bowl of soup. "You are Catholics, aren't you?" We did not contradict him. "Well, the nuns are running a soup kitchen just a few blocks behind the American headquarters, in a basement. A ladle of hot soup for each refugee." Then he said, "Good night!" and walked away. "Wait! I forgot to tell you." He hurried back. "The railroad is operational. Don't be taken by surprise. From time to time you'll hear trains passing, not stopping. Mainly, the Soviet nationals are being shipped east. What a sight! Portraits, placards, bayans, balalaikas! A real circus."

We spent several days in the cattle car, still disoriented and depressed, watching several trains pass us daily—all decorated with red banners. Through the train windows, tense, pale faces were visible, women hugging children on their laps, men staring vacantly, while old people openly wept, some crossing themselves repeatedly as if in a funeral cortege. But always several drunken voices were heard shouting patriotic Soviet songs—"Wide Is My Country" or "Beloved Moscow." The trains inside and out were decorated with red ribbons, red placards, red stars, and the four famed profiles on a red background—those of Marx, Engels, Lenin, and Stalin—Stalin's grinning face outnumbering all others.

At the end of the fifth day, our cattle car sojourn came to a forced end. The policeman arrived at our door and, shaking his head sadly, said, "You must go, people. The inspection commission is coming in a few days. We must clear these cars and tracks."

Mother offered the German a cigarette as a parting gesture, and while smoking together with Boris Fyodorovich, the policeman offered some advice. "Go to Gonzenheim, about four kilometers from here. A small town, not bombed out. There is a canning plant for fruit. The owner lost all of his *Ost* workers. He is short of laborers."

And so, with bundles on our backs, suitcases in hand, we marched toward Gonzenheim. The farther we walked from Mainz, the less depressing the surroundings became, with fruit tree orchards lining one side of the road, hiding the railroad tracks, while on the other, pretty, dacha-like houses nestled amidst neat fenced-in gardens. As soon as we reached the outskirts of Gonzenheim, a cluster of two-story, red brick barracks greeted us—all intact, but neglected looking. They had been reserved for the occupation forces, but because the Americans were in the process of withdrawing and the French still had not arrived, there was a deserted, dark look about them. Not far from the barracks, the main road separated, creating an island-like square occupied by a chapel, forcing the traffic to go around on either side. Block after block of the small town stood intact, its main street, Breite Strasse, laced with black steel rails for trolley cars, looking deserted, not having any trolleys to accommodate.

Then, a pleasant, rectangular park greeted us, with lovely villas nestled in the forest on our right. At the City Hall we turned left, toward the canning plant, and there, bomb crater after bomb crater appeared, swallowing a two-story brick factory, leaving only a wall and a stairway standing, as if inviting one to climb up and observe the scene below. We asked a German pedestrian where the canning plant was and he pointed to a group of barracks-type buildings just across the road. The owner, a man in his late 50s, was a grumpy, crafty-looking fellow, openly hostile to us foreigners. But he needed us nevertheless, and he knew that we needed him, because we would not be given a ration card without being employed. When asked where we would be quartered, the man pointed to the bombed-out factory we had just passed and said, "There! You can spend the summer there. In one corner you'll see a room still intact. No doors or windows, but what's the difference? The weather is warm and you won't die of cold." Then he barked out an order, "Tomorrow morning, be here at eight! On the dot!"

Trudging to the destroyed building, we located in one corner of the debris the room our new employer was offering us, and not being able to act stoic any longer, exhausted by our travels, we just sat on our bundles and howled. Boris Fyodorovich placed his arm comfortingly around his wife and said, as my father so often said to Mother, "*Nichevo, nichevo,*" ("It's nothing, nothing"). He looked at the twisted ceiling beams lying on the glass and brick-littered floor, looked at the gaping, empty window frames, at the sagging opening where once a door had hung, and said, "Okay, folks. Let's clean up the floors a bit and make some room to stretch out for a while and rest. Then, let's start looking for wood under the rubble. We'll fix up this hovel. We'll turn it into a palace before the cold weather comes!"

The first priority of the French troops who marched into Mainz in July, replacing the Americans, seemed to be to rob and plunder their newly acquired domain of all its available foodstuffs. Only what remained after satisfying their voracious appetites, was distributed to the population. Our rations were drastically reduced after the withdrawal of the Americans, who had been wonderfully self-sufficient, providing not only ample food for their troops—food imported from the United States—but allowing their surplus to spill over to the civilian population. After the Americans crossed the Rhine, leaving Mainz to the French, we began to starve. While under the Americans we received up to 1,200 calories a day, under the French we received 600 to 800 calories, and at times only 400. The only place we could look for help came from the cherry, plum, and apple trees that we harvested for our employer, of necessity helping ourselves before stuffing the fruit in the cans.

Then a real silver lining appeared in the French takeover of Gonzenheim. The brick barracks were quickly occupied by soldiers of the French army, the majority of whom were dark-skinned Algerians. The French administrators needed scrub women to keep the barracks clean, offering, as payment, a daily portion of meat stew—the same thick, nourishing meat stew that the soldiers were eating! No one needed to ask me twice to offer my services as a scrubwoman.

Mother and Raisa Mikhailovna both went with me to apply for the job, but Mother was rejected out of hand because of her glaucoma. I was immediately hired, and Raisa Mikhailovna, after insisting vigorously that she, too, was very strong, was also given the chance to earn a daily portion of meat stew. We quickly found out that the French were not stingy with the precious stew, giving seconds and even thirds on some days. All this we saved, stored in containers, and in the evening, Mother, Slava, Boris Fyodorovich, Raisa Mikhailovna, and I had a feast.

The French were quite strict with us scrubwomen, checking us monthly for venereal diseases. Every month I climbed on the examining table, as I did in Feodosia, and every month the French army doctor exclaimed in English, "Ah! Still a baby!" He appeared a bit owl-eyed in surprise, undoubtedly because of the collapse of sexual morality in occupied Germany. While under Hitler's rule, German women behaved proudly, even haughtily, faithfully waiting for their men to return from the war, now the same women, with very few exceptions, were welcoming the attention of occupation soldiers—be they French, American, or British—as long as their *Schatzies* paid them with food. These women had to feed not only themselves, but aging parents, relatives invalided in the bombings, and fatherless children. They were not true prostitutes, but women deserted, deprived of their menfolk. They provided genuinely warm, steady relationships for their multinational *Schatzies*, and a wave of marriages swept occupied Germany soon after the non-fraternization rule was lifted at the end of 1945.

As for me, perhaps due to my preoccupation with trying to escape the forced repatriation, no serious prospect of love had appeared so far. Several Frenchmen at the barracks had made cheap, casual "sleep with me" passes. One hit me in the jaw with all his strength, when I said simply, "No." There was one French officer who daily roared into the barracks compound in his jeep, delivering papers from the main French headquarters, where he was assigned. He asked me repeatedly to Saturday evening dances that were held in the ballroom of a vacant castle, the dancers often spilling out into the magnificent gardens. I did long to be with young people, to listen to the lively music, to dance. But looking at this fellow's pale, long, acne-covered face, at his narrow shoulders, at his head which was several inches below mine, noticing his walk, toes in, I wondered, how would he dance with those toes going in? Yet, he did have large, open eyes, bright as a child's eyes. If only I could like the rest of him as I liked his eyes, I thought, feeling miserable while saying no to his persistent dance invitations.

In addition to receiving a daily generous portion of stew, the French rewarded us scrubwomen with another highly prized privilege—that of having a decent lodging. Mother, Slava, and I received one room in the home of a former minor Nazi official. It was a large, bright, well-furnished bedroom, with an additional small alcove where an iron stove stood beside a table and divan—our dining area. The new quarters were right smack on the main street, a three to four minute walk from the barracks, and almost next to the lovely little church that stood in the middle of the main road. Raisa Mikhailovna and Boris Fyodorovich were by then very satisfied with their original room, bringing it to such good condition, that to leave it was pointless. And besides, Boris Fyodorovich figured there was a greater margin of safety in those surrounding ruins, away from the center of town.

Life was indeed beginning once again to smile upon us. And according to one German fortuneteller, who lived right across from the church, life was about to shower us with unprecedented riches! The old lady, trying to gain a slice of bread from me as a reward, looked at my raw, broken-nailed, scrubwoman hand, and said with perfect sincerity, while tracing the lines in my red palm, "Mark my word, girlie. You'll walk in silks and velvets one day!"

"When?" I wanted to know, already not putting much value on the old woman's words, deciding that Germans made poor fortunetellers. To live in silk and velvet meant to be wealthy. And what was wealth to me just then? I already had a clean, spacious room and a daily portion of meat stew. We had all that life could offer to the inhabitants of war-ravaged Germany. And yet, not even one night since leaving Triptis, could we go to sleep without our last thought being—would we survive the forced repatriation in the coming day? On awakening, our very first thought was again—would we survive until the night? If only the kindly fortuneteller, instead of promising me silk and velvet would have promised me that I would find inner and outer security—find it soon! How wealthy I would have felt!

CHAPTER FIFTY-NINE

W/*ithin a* year of the day when we stood by the Mainz bridge hoping that the French would not betray us but would give us asylum on their territory, they signed a separate agreement with Stalin to hand us over, in return receiving grain supplied by the Soviet Union. SMERSH promptly occupied one of the most luxurious villas in Gonzenheim, and began to hunt down Soviet nationals. They soon found us.

On June 7, 1946, a German policeman knocked on our door, handing Mother an official document. "Read it," he commanded. "I must see to it that you understand its meaning."

Mother read it in German:

> Natalie Alexandrovna, Slava, Nina, of Gonzenheim, Breite Strasse—The German Police, together with the French and Soviet Repatriation Authorities, hereby inform you that you must allow yourselves to be sent back to the Soviet Union. You will have until Monday, 10 June 1946, to appear before Captain Rasdobudko, who will instruct you on the future procedure concerning your return to your Fatherland.
>
> This order of the French Military Occupation Authorities must be obeyed and carried out.
>
> /s/ (by the French Commander)
> /s/ (by the German Police Head)

When the policeman was leaving our apartment, Mother heard him say in a half-whisper to the landlady in the hallway, "Not long now. Tell your husband, the room'll soon be yours once again."

We did not really have the three days as stated in the document. SMERSH knew how their nationals ran from them whenever they got the chance. And they gave us no chance to run. On the 8th, shortly after nine in the morning, a jeep with two SMERSH men in the company of a French officer, stopped in front of our building. A small truck with a machine gun-armed French soldier parked right behind the jeep.

We were having breakfast in the alcove-dining area. Hearing the motor stop at our gate, I jumped up from my chair, clad in a nightdress and the black kimono with persimmon chrysanthemums, and ran toward the window. There they were. The hunters had caught us! And one of the party was my little acne-faced French officer who had not once succeeded in taking me to a Saturday dance! He was the hunting party's leader! We were caught! Unprepared, unprotected. Where to run? Where to hide? To jump from the window and crawl behind the lilac bushes? But the French soldier, weapon ready, was sitting alert, observing our apartment.

I ran back to the alcove, "Mama, SMERSH," I whispered. Mother almost dropped the glass of hot tea she was handing to Slava. "Speak only German," I kept whispering, beside myself with fear. "No matter what, speak only German. Not one word in Russian."

"I know, I know," she agreed, her hands shaking, face ashen. "They won't want Slava. I'll turn Latvian. But you! Crawl under the bed!"

Under the bed? Steps were already echoing in the narrow hallway and we heard our landlady's honey-like voice, "Welcome! Welcome!"

A knock! I sprang toward the mirrored wardrobe, and climbed deep into it, doors tightly shut, with my knees to my chin, not stirring. The Frenchman's voice cut through the stillness of the room like a whip, as he said to Mother in broken German—"Madame, you, two children, back to Soviet Union. Order!"

"Why?" mother's voice was calm, strong. "I no Soviet. See here!" She carefully, unhurriedly spread before the officer her birth certificate, pointing with a finger for the Frenchman to study the word—RIGA. "See, Monsieur. It says Riga. I born in Riga, no Soviet Union."

At that moment she noticed part of my kimono hem caught outside the mirrored wardrobe door, its persimmon chrysanthemum glowing like a flashlight in the dark. God! She tried to position her body so as to block it from view, and not allow the SMERSH officers to notice the telltale scrap of silk.

The French officer, meanwhile, after inspecting Mother's birth certificate, walked toward a round side table on which stood a lamp and a picture of me taken only weeks earlier by a Mainz photographer. The

Frenchman gasped in consternation, recognizing the girl he for so long had invited to dances and who had always refused him.

He turned to Mother, "This girl in the photograph, your daughter?" Mother nodded. "Daughter not home now. Away."

The man took the frame in his hands, and held it for a few seconds, as if studying the picture. Then his glance drifted to the mirrored doors of the wardrobe, and my mother knew that we were all in mortal danger. The officer's gaze turned to her, eyes wide with a silent question. And Mother's eyes, boring into his, into his conscience, imploring, shaming, demanding—Don't betray us. Be humane. Spare us.

He seemed to be undecided. Would he end up marching to the mirrored door, pull it open, and say triumphantly to the SMERSH officers, savoring the feeling of getting even with the haughty Russian girl, "There, comrades! Take her! Take them all!"

He did march toward the wardrobe, and I covered my ears with my palms, pressing on them until they hurt, not wanting to hear his approaching steps. The door will be flung open any moment. And then, SMERSH.

The door was not flung open. It was closing even tighter. The French officer was leaning with his elbows on the mirror. Holding the repatriation order against the wardrobe door, he wrote slowly, deliberately, in illiterate German:

"NO GO TO SOVIET UNION. LATVIAN."

When the SMERSH men and the Frenchmen left and we all calmed down a bit, Mother said to us in a half-whisper, as if afraid she would be overheard by those earlier intruders, "I'll rush to Raisa Mikhailovna and warn them. Perhaps SMERSH will be after them too."

And she hurried off to our friends. By then, Boris Fyodorovich had so improved the condition of their dwelling that his German neighbors congratulated him on his labors. Not only windows and doors were made operational, but Boris Fyodorovich dug out enough bricks from under the rubble to erect a fireplace, taking up one wall of the room, and out of the rest of the found bricks he built an outdoor grill, where most of their cooking was done. Out of salvaged pieces of wood he fashioned a picnic table with benches and a large coffee table. Making up for the lack of curtains and drapes, he provided the windows with handsomely designed shutters.

While most Germans wholeheartedly complimented Boris Fyodorovich on his unceasing efforts to better his surroundings, one woman—a refugee from the eastern part of Germany—decided that our friends' lodging should be hers. In her early thirties, with wide hips, and heavy bosom, the brassy-voiced woman was seen often in the company of an older German policeman. But in the late evenings, Algerian soldiers were seen entering and leaving her basement apartment.

When Mother reached our friends' place, it was this woman who opened the familiar door, and stood at the threshold, arms folded across her chest. Mother saw several chairs overturned, beds in disarray, boxes lying on the floor as if a whirlwind had swept the room.

"Where is the couple who live here?" Mother asked, and wished not to hear the answer, because she knew what it would be.

"You're late, Frau. Too late! They're gone back to Russia. The room is mine now."

The same jeep with the same French lieutenant and two SMERSH officers, and the same truck with the machine gun-armed guard that had earlier stopped at our doorstep, had next raced to the dwelling of our friends, who had no birth certificate displaying the name of a European city to come to their rescue, no pretty face of a teenage girl to soften the heart of the French officer. So, they perished.

Until that day I felt no hate toward the German people as a whole, but after the SMERSH raid upon us and the capture of Boris Fyodorovich and Raisa Mikhailovna, I began to develop a violent bitterness toward the Germans. To think that one would call the attention of the authorities to the Soviet refugees, and betray them into forced repatriation in order to receive their room! I knew then that we had to fear not only the military occupation forces who were obliged to send us back, and not only SMERSH and the German police, but also we had to fear our German neighbors. I began to look at every German with hidden fear and deep suspicion. Will he run to the police; will she start shouting, "That girl is Soviet! Take her!"

I hated Germans even more when I looked at my dear brother, injured by the brutal Nazi at the *muna*. Poor Slava! How he had changed physically and was deteriorating still. His body had shrunk and his face was gray, with dull eyes, his forehead—once marking him as the "philosopher"—was cut by deep horizontal folds, turning him into an aging man. And yet, he was only twenty. He began to get bald, and his tongue seemed to move slowly, slurring his speech. Slava's hands that had been so agile, constantly trying to form something new out of clay, were now helpless, awkward, not able to rinse out a sock or handkerchief. And he suffered from periodic attacks, when he felt as if he was falling through the floor.

One mid-morning, looking at Slava's still figure by the window, I said to Mother, "I hate those Germans! How I hate them. Every time I look at Slavka, I hate them—all of them!"

And Slava, listening to my torrent of rancor and bitterness, said without even turning his head away from the window, "Don't hate them, sis. They suffer as much as we do. Their country is torn apart. And how many Germans are rotting in Soviet camps right now?"

Mother, seeming to agree with Slava, took my hand into hers, and said quietly, "Ninochka, *dochenka*, that hate will eat at your soul like acid. It'll blind you for the rest of your life if you let it. You truly can't afford hating."

"But I want to hate Germans! Why shouldn't I?"

"Because Germany might become your adopted country. It might be your children's country of birth. What are you going to teach them—to hate their native land? Hate its people?"

Children? I was not looking that far into the future. "I don't care what you two say. I still hate them," I persisted, although a bit calmer.

"So, you hate a whole people because a few are brutal and cruel."

"Well!" I still did not wish to part with that all-encompassing, self-excusing feeling of hate. "You won't forbid me to hate that bloody German who beat Slava into a pulp, will you?" and I slammed the door on my way out.

Where did I want to go? Nowhere, really. Just to run out into the fields that were spread like emerald rugs right behind our house, separated from one another by brown patches of earth. I wanted to pass those fields and walk toward the highway that would lead me out of Gonzenheim. The highway was bordered on both sides by yet more fields growing tomatoes, cucumbers, scallions, onions, and rhubarb—all ripening, ready for harvest. I was not so much aiming at those fields to harvest them, as to walk off my frustration, to get away for a while from the overpopulated town I lived in, from our tiny apartment, to lose myself in the open country.

I was about two kilometers from home. A lush cucumber patch invited me, more or less, to come in and help myself to some crunchy, aromatic gherkins. I ate several right then and there, and began to stuff my pockets with all the cucumbers I could find. They were not available to buy.

Someone was approaching the patch. I dropped to my knees trying to blend with the earth. A girl's voice, humming "Lili Marlene" came closer and closer. I berated the low foliage that could not effectively camouflage me. Would this girl turn me over to the police for pilfering? Would the officials then find out that I was a Soviet and deport me? The French officer had taken pity upon us and had led the SMERSH men away. Yet, were they to return with a Latvian translator, I would be lost, since I understood not a word of Latvian. No birth certificate of Mother's would help me buy more time.

The approaching girl was carrying her tied-together shoes over her shoulder, striding barefoot along the highway. Probably trying to save her shoe soles, I figured. She walked tall, straight, unafraid, her head up high.

The girl turned off the road to the cucumber patch I had just stripped. She found a cucumber and crunched it with relish. She was utterly preoccupied for a while, lifting the vines and not finding many cucumbers underneath, because I had just "harvested" them. Then she saw me.

"Good morning," the German said. When she heard my reply she looked at me closely and said, "Ah! You're the Russian girl, aren't you?"

"What do you mean?" I was instantly alert for possible danger.

"Sure. Gonzenheim is a small place. We all know you." The girl continued to pick cucumbers, filling her pockets, even as I did earlier. "My name is Ursula," she said, her face friendly, open. "And yours?"

"Nina."

"Ni-NOCH-ka."

"No!" I barked. "Not Ni-NOCH-ka! It's NIN-och-ka, accent on the first syllable!"

Never had I corrected anyone previously about the universal mispronunciation of my name's diminutive. In fact, I had grown accustomed to being called "Ni-NOCH-ka." But there, in that cucumber patch, it became somehow all important that my name be pronounced correctly. I must have surprised Ursula with my vehement insistence. She straightened out her bent back, her eyes searching mine. Then she again bent over the green foliage, saying, "My fiancé was in Russia. Lost one arm. He doesn't want to get married soon. He's awfully bitter." She hurried toward the road all at once. "Want to go to the next patch? Scallions." I followed her, silent. "I've got my aunt from East Prussia living with me now, temporarily. She was gang raped by the Soviet soldiers." The girl once again looked at me with a wide-eyed, questioning look. "Well," she continued, "I guess the Wehrmacht did even worse atrocities in Russia, huh?"

"Like what?" I countered, thinking of Maya, of special SS units.

Somehow, I never could associate the Wehrmacht men I knew with Maya's death.

"Oh, like raping the women in occupied Russia."

I again felt an unreasoning anger at that Ursula. What did she know of German soldiers' behavior in Russia? Did she live there as I did? Did she see the 200 corpses of Russian women in the Feodosia prison basement, killed not by her soldiers but by mine, for giving "solace" to the enemy? And solace they did give. As much solace as German women were giving to the occupying forces of Americans and British and French. Only more. Just in the first twelve months of war, the women of Russia conceived over one million offspring by Wehrmacht soldiers. Hitler was flabbergasted when the news was delivered to him by Himmler, but quickly directed that all youngsters who looked Aryan should be brought up by the Reich. One million and more on the way!

But with the war not progressing as the children's mothers envisioned, many tried to leave the Soviet Union with the retreating Germans. Even more were forced to remain behind.

Since many Russian mothers of half-German children were being forcibly repatriated, they—in order to earn the Communist Party's forgiveness—willingly gave voice to the fable that they were all raped. And on that scallion patch in little Gonzenheim, a 19-year-old German girl was naively parroting this fable.

I poured out all this and more to the dumbfounded Ursula who was chewing vigorously all the while on the juicy, crisp scallions.

"There. Take it!" She handed me a bunch of them. "Good for your gums." Then she stopped walking, and stood still. "You know, Ninchen," she said softly. "I am awfully glad to hear it—about our men. After all, you were there, and we were your enemy—invaders. What reason would you have to defend German soldiers' behavior? My fiancé swore up and down that they behaved decently toward women in Russia. But I didn't believe him."

We reached a plot of rhubarb. I started to break a stalk, wanting to chew on it, but Ursula stopped me. "Rhubarb is tricky. It must be fully ripened." And then, glancing at her wrist watch, she exclaimed, "I must hurry!"

I wanted to remain with her. I craved the companionship of a girl my age.

"Why are you walking barefoot?" I asked, following Ursula to the highway.

She laughed. "I bet I do look strange. But our ballet master insists that we should walk barefoot at every opportunity. Healthy for the instep."

I gaped at the girl. She was in ballet? The word ballet instantly brought before my mind's eye a tutu and hard-toed shoes. And that girl—who was about five feet, eight inches—on her toes?

"You're in ballet?" I was incredulous. "You're too tall for ballet!"

Ursula laughed again. "Not classical, of course. We dance barefoot. Expressionistic."

Oh, that crazy stuff. Like Isadora Duncan, who married the Soviet poet Esenin. That woman came to our Soviet paradise in the 1920s to teach children her method of dancing. Not for long though. She didn't like our spartan diet, and left in a huff. So, Ursula was doing the same kind of thing. Tramping barefoot on the stage, grimacing like a clown.

"I used to dance as a child, back in Russia," I heard my own voice saying wistfully, regretfully. "I used to love it. But war came . . . camps. I guess it wasn't meant for me to dance."

Ursula grabbed my arm. "Ninchen! Listen! Come with me! Herr Raymonda is looking desperately for dancers. He's just starting to put a troupe together. He's planning to travel to the American and British Zones. We'll be paid with food! Hear me?"

Yes, I heard. Food. With the meat stew eliminated from our daily fare because I was afraid to show myself to the French, I needed help. And I did not dare register for a ration card after the SMERSH visit. My black suede pumps with the rhinestone buckles were first to go in exchange for food. All hats were eaten away. Most of the Triptis birthday presents were just a memory. Would I be forced soon to part with my kimono?

"But, Ursula." I looked at the girl, not quite able to believe her words, and yet wishing for her to insist that I follow her. "I am stiff as an old lady! No dancing, no barre exercises since. . . ."

Ursula would not let go of my arm. "Just come with me, Ninchen. Herr Raymonda is very nice. He's, you know. . . ." Ursula seemed to think that I knew what she meant. But I did not.

"He's . . . he doesn't fall in love with women, you know. But it's even better for us girls. We feel pretty free around him."

We walked in silence for a while. "There! You see the two-story villa on the right?" Ursula pointed to a large, neat house untouched by war, with a fenced-in back yard. "We sunbathe in that yard—in the nude. Need less makeup that way. Besides, it's healthy for you."

How health-oriented the girl was! Scallions are healthy for one's gums, walking barefoot is healthy for the instep, suntanning is healthy too.

We reached the front of the house where a large sign hung over the entrance—BALLET RAYMONDA. Ursula caught my arm again when I was just ready to turn back, intimidated by the sign. She said proudly, trying to impress me, but intimidating me even more, "Herr Raymonda even had his troupe perform in New York City, just before the war broke out. Then he had to give up ballet. Hitler sent people like him to the camps."

To be able to travel, to escape Gonzenheim for days at a time, to get away from the SMERSH headquarters located only a few short blocks from my bed!

"Ursula, what about some job with the troupe? Any chores to do? In case Herr Raymonda won't want me as a dancer?"

"Sure! We need a seamstress. Our wardrobe is a mess. The costumes need so much repair. Maybe you could do that! Sewing is easy. You do sew, don't you?"

I wanted to say—"No! Anything but sewing! I loathe it!"—but, I held my tongue.

Opening the heavy double entrance door, we stepped into a small vestibule, serving also as an office for the ballet master. A light-colored leather sofa and armchair stood at one side, with a large desk opposite. Framed photographs, portraits of dancers covered the walls. Many photos showed a slender, long-legged blond woman in a tutu, with a wholesome, heavily made up face, on her toes, posing in all different positions.

"Who is that?" I asked Ursula.

"Oh, it's our ballet master. Looks good, doesn't he? Well, that was years ago. He's changed, of course."

A portly, medium-height man with graying blond hair hurried toward us, clapping his hands, "Ursula, sweetie, hurry! Hurry! To the barre!" The man's very bright blue eyes sparkled, his full mouth half-grinning while giving commands.

Ursula said to the man, "Herr Ballettmeister, I brought a Russian girl, Nina. She used to dance back in Russia."

The man let his grin spread wider. "Nina! Aha, Ni-NOCH-ka! Ah, those Russian dancers! What passion! What dedication!" And then, his grin disappearing, he asked, his voice grumpy, "Why are you so darned tall? Taking after whom?"

"I am taking after my father's people, Herr Ballettmeister, after the Streltsy!"

"Streltsy! I know all about them. I love Russian history. Those giants! How they hated Peter."

"And loved Russia," I interjected.

Herr Raymonda nodded vigorously. "True! True! Proud people. Well! Listen, Ninochka. We must hurry with the barre exercises. Our pianist is hired by the hour. Come some other time . . . perhaps in a day or two. We'll talk."

He was dismissing me. Streltsy or no Streltsy, he had no time for me. And Ursula, that naive girl, hoped for me to be hired. Back to Gonzenheim. How long could I rob Mother and Slava of their part of the food rations after all my clothes were "eaten" away? They both received invalid rations, because they were unemployed. I would be forced to register sooner or later for a ration card. And bang! The trap would spring shut, as my papers stated that I was a Soviet national. My face must have expressed my inner helplessness and defeat. I was already opening the door, ready to hit the road back to Gonzenheim, when the ballet master's eyes were suddenly in front of me.

"What's the trouble, Ninchen? You remind me of a cornered rabbit. Nowhere to run, to hide, is that it?"

He knew! Perhaps because he himself, not long ago, had been hunted? Instinctively he knew when another human being was in mortal danger. Touched by his probing, caring words, I tried to hold back tears. "I must survive the repatriation, Herr Raymonda. Must! Perhaps it won't last much longer. But now I am a hunted rabbit."

Ursula standing next to me, broke out in a moan. "Oh, Ninchen, Ninchen, poor girl. I had no idea things were so bad for you." She put her arms around my neck, hiding her face in my hair. Herr Raymonda blew his nose a couple of times and said finally to the girl, "Now, Ursula, try to find a leotard for Ninochka. God! Is she long, that Streltsy girl. To the barre, everybody! To the barre!"

I was awestruck by the agility of the girls at the barre. Many were professional dancers already. About one-third of the girls were quite tall. I could not imagine such tall women to be in ballet of any kind in Russia. And how they bent and unbent, and stretched and split their legs in scissor-like fashion, and bent their spines in a "bridge." Like gymnasts they leaped high, fell immediately on the floor and rolled like rubber balls through their own legs. Were I to do so, my spine would have cracked. I certainly was not about to set anyone's mind aflame with my abilities.

Then a roar reached my ears, the roar of the ballet master's voice, perhaps to ridicule me, to dismiss me, to send me packing?

"Now, girls! Truly! You disgust me! Don't butcher your arm movements! Look at that Ninochka! No training for three or four years! But look at her arms! They sing. Her legs are heavy, but her arms dance! Follow her on the arm movements!"

Could I hope? When all the others had left, including Ursula, who promised to stop at our place and tell my mother where I was, Herr Raymonda, keeping the pianist overtime, said to me in the empty exercise room, "Ninochka, dear, much, much work you'll need. I would like to try to give you individual numbers, so that you won't appear so tall. Ah!" He shook his head, quite unhappy with me. "In the group numbers I would have to stick you in the back, to minimize your height. I can't break up the group's visual harmony. But there is a dance I want to create. It's still only in my head—brewing, sort of. You know, while I was in the camp, I remember the Jews, their walk, the way they moved. The dance could be called 'The Death March,' to the Chopin 'Funeral March,' or perhaps to Bach's music, to his *'Komm Süsser Tod.'* About seven women come on stage, all in black. No hands, no neck, no feet visible, only their faces. All in black, like a shroud. See?"

He snatched a dark piece of cloth from a pile of costumes and threw it over my head, wrapping me in it. The pianist started to play the "Funeral March," slowly, not following the notes, but interpreting the ballet master's mood, remaining for the most part in the low register—heavy, oppressive. Herr Raymonds continued to instruct.

"The dancers will do no especially difficult steps. Much will depend on their facial expressions . . . and posture. They'll cross the stage slowly, stopping at times for a fleeting moment. All as if bound together like one mass—a whole people. One will carry an infant. One will hold a small bundle. The seven figures will just sort of float across the stage, expressing utter, abject, total sorrow—sorrow at being forced to part with life so prematurely, so abruptly."

He took my arm, directing me to stretch it out toward him, and began to walk backwards to the pianist, while I was facing him. His eyes were constantly observing while he was coaching me—how to walk, to look, to stop walking. At first I was stiff, wooden, truly intimidated by his watching eyes. And then I stopped looking at him, seeing no longer his bright, intense gaze. Instead, Ohrdruf reappeared as it was on the day I watched the group of women with bundles marching past our barracks. I remembered the two in the rear of the column clinging to each other, as if each was helping the other to stay alive—their inner despair spilling out, enveloping them wholly. Was I turning into one of those women propelling myself forward with extreme effort? And the man in front of me with his arms outstretched, as if trying to show me the way, his huge blue eyes full of tears was whispering "Yes, yes, that's it. Don't stop now. A bit more, a few steps, very slow steps. Steps to oblivion . . . to a finale."

A wail escaped the pianist's fingers—a muted, soul-tearing wail for all those who perished; and my own wail at trying to survive, trying not to perish.

The pianist was dismissed. I put on my street clothes, anxious to hurry home and tell my mother that I had a job—dancing!

Herr Raymonda called me to his desk. "Let's talk business," he said, briskly. "The pay will be only 180 marks a month. You'll be entitled to a 'Working Ration Card.' Then, when we will start traveling, then we'll start to live! We'll be paid with meals!"

I sat listening, and not really listening, realizing with a jolt that all my efforts that day were for nothing, because I could not register for the ration card without giving myself away. When I explained to Herr Raymonda about my difficulty in even getting a ration card, he was for a while as crestfallen as I was.

"Not only is it dangerous for you to register, Ninochka, but you also couldn't travel out of the French Zone with us. Travel between the occupied zones is very strictly supervised. What are you to do, dear girl? Hmm? You need new papers."

He stared at me for a while, his eyes not really seeing me, but figuring, calculating, conniving. A sudden slap on his knee signaled to me that salvation was at hand.

"The document forger! And a first-rate forger at that! He was the best in the whole camp! Jewish fellow. Lives now in Mainz." Herr Raymonda's face lighted up, but only for a moment. Then, as abruptly, a preoccupied look settled in his eyes. "But how to reward him? How to pay him for his work?" he asked, not really expecting me to answer.

Yet I had an answer! I knew how to pay the forger, the would-be creator of my lifesaving birth certificate! The diamond ring that I had found in Lodz! It was pinned to my bra. Doing nothing, just lying there. Mother planned to fix it one day soon, putting something in the empty middle, some semi-precious stone so that I could wear it. But I kept calling that ring "a ring of death"; and all the diamonds, with bluish, fiery life of their own, became "stones of death." To get rid of the ring! To receive in exchange a forged paper that would protect me from the repatriation! To receive a license to *live!*

"I've got it! Got it! Herr Ballettmeister! I have something! I'll give it to you!"

I turned away and unpinned from the bra a small linen case Mother had made for the ring.

"Here! See? Give it to the man in Mainz. Ask him to make me a Latvian. Born in Riga, like my mother. No more Russian. I can't be Russian. I hate it! I just dread being Russian!" Bitter and frustrated, I could not restrain the sobs.

"Oh, Ninchen, Ninchen. Poor, frightened child. One day you'll be proud to be a Russian. Be proud of your thousand-year-old past. Of your culture and customs."

The ballet master stroked my hair, touching my cheek. "There, a clean hanky. Now, wipe your nose."

Hiding my face in the handkerchief, I kept insisting vehemently that never, never, would I again call myself Russian, because to admit to being Russian amounted to the same as during Hitler's time it was for a Jew in hiding to admit to being Jewish.

"Ninchen," the good man kept reassuring me, "one day the hunt will stop and the hunters will be ashamed. Go to your mother now. Comfort her. Tell her I'll do everything possible to make you a 'non-Soviet.' I wish we had American cigarettes to give to the forger, instead of the ring. Cigarettes move mountains. Relax now, girlie. And here. Take this goose leg. One of the girls lives with a farm family. She keeps me well fed. Take it! Take it! Here's some sauerkraut. Here, some stewed apples. Take the whole pot. Return it tomorrow at barre time."

CHAPTER SIXTY

A *nd so* my life with the Raymonda Troupe began. I met the approaching year of 1947 secure in the knowledge that my newly obtained birth certificate made me Latvian-born, exempting me from the forced repatriation to the Soviet Union.

Our ballet troupe at first traveled only in the French Zone, where after the performance we were always given plenty of hot meat stew that was left over from the soldiers' mess. The British, too, began to invite us, but soon Herr Raymonda discontinued traveling to the British Zone, because we returned from the performances there famished, not once being offered even some tea and biscuits. On the other hand, the Americans were very generous, stuffing us with doughnuts, all kinds of sandwiches, milkshakes, and gallons of terrific coffee. I filled my pockets with all available doughnuts, discovering that when dried out, they turned into excellent *suhary*, lasting a month at least in that state. And how those doughnuts enchanted Mother and Slava, when they dipped them in tea to soften them a bit, savoring the delicious taste. During the very first tasting, Mother exclaimed, "That is the best *suhar* I ever hoped to taste! What is it called? Doughnut? Nut of dough! Very interesting."

One day in early spring of 1947, I hurried from the tour to Gonzenheim, lugging a suitcase full of American goodies—dried doughnuts and loaves of stale bread that Americans were in the habit of tossing out in the garbage pail; many cigarette butts collected from the floor of American clubs, with much tobacco still salvageable. And the fragrant smelling soap pieces in my coat pockets! They were only used slivers, but still such a treasure, and absolutely unavailable to the population.

Mother did not open the door to our room when I knocked. Neither she nor Slava answered when I shouted, "Mama! Slava! It's me! Back from the tour!"

Silence.

I felt panicky, my knees buckling under me, forcing me to sit on the steps in the foyer. Could it be? Snatched? My dear mother and Slava snatched by the SMERSH? Dragged like potato sacks and tossed into the trucks, with no reprieve, no mercy from their machine gun-armed abductors. Mother, probably praying loudly, screaming to God for help.

How long will my poor brother last? He will probably perish in transport to the Gulag. And Mother's eye—"Use glaucoma drops religiously"—the Riga eye surgeon had instructed her years earlier. Glaucoma drops for the returnees in the Soviet Gulag?

I looked at the polished parquet floor, lovingly cared for by our landlady, visualizing Slava's and mother's last shoe imprints on its unfeeling surface. And the walls surrounding me, were they still echoing Mother's fierce, protesting cries? Slava's words of comfort—"Mama, Mamochka, *nichevo, nichevo*"—"It's nothing, nothing"—the way Father used to comfort her.

Listless, crushed by the sorrow that had befallen me, I sat on the steps, leaning against the door that so often in the past was opened by Mother's impatient hand, her always smiling face welcoming me with that strong, clear, almost singing, "*Dochenka*! Ninochka! You're back!" And a juicy smack on both cheeks.

How long did I sit? An hour? A minute? Twenty seconds? The door started to open slowly, but only part way.

A hand was pushing a piece of paper toward me, and the landlady's voice said indifferently, "Here. Your mother asked me to give it to you."

Her last words, her farewell. Probably imploring God to keep me. I snatched the paper and opened it. But what was it? No farewell words, no cry of anguish at separation was expressed in Mother's handwriting. Only the words—KLEIN WINTERNHEIM-WALD STRASSE.

The landlady's impersonal voice again explained. "Your family was moved to that small village. We're entitled to our own apartment after keeping you for two years. We've paid enough."

I jumped up and ran to the trolley car, which brought me back to the Mainz railroad station, where I boarded another train, and was soon banging on that Waldstrasse gate, in the village only a few kilometers from Mainz. An old peasant woman unlatched the high wooden gate, and I entered a neat cobblestoned yard. Cows, horses, chickens—all were tucked away in their living quarters for the night. But where was my family?

"There," the old woman pointed to the attic. "That's all I could spare."

The attic was heaven to Mother and Slava, since they had expected to be deported when they saw the truck coming to move them. This "heaven" was a rectangular, narrow room, very small. Two cots took up one long side of the room while against the other wall stood a small table with two chairs, and the wall itself was covered with hooks, holding articles of clothing. A little window looked out on neighboring roofs and a church steeple. The glass had been partially removed to make room for a thick pipe going outside, which ran from a squat iron stove.

No SMERSH men were going to turn this tiny heaven into a hell.

CHAPTER SIXTY-ONE

*T*_*he summer* of 1947 arrived, but Germany still lay as though paralyzed under heaps of rubble. Yet in living day to day among those ruins one noticed certain changes. The country began to breathe more steadily, a slow recuperation taking place. German communities began to ask Herr Raymonda to perform for them. Yet, every time "The Death March" was performed, our German audiences—almost to a person—stood up and walked out.

It was during this summer of 1947 that we arrived in Bad-Nauheim, a famed resort about 90 kilometers from Mainz by train. At the railroad station we were met by an American bus that delivered us to the town's Kuhrhaus, which had been taken over by the Americans and turned into a Red Cross club for servicemen. The club was surrounded by magnificent parks with large ponds where white and black swans glided in a stately dance. The park benches were occupied by American servicemen in the company of pretty girls.

We were told by Herr Raymonda to rest up a bit in the dressing room. Then, after a brief warmup, we were ready for the afternoon performance. The hall was overflowing with soldiers, officers, and American civilians. Snack bar waitresses, clerical workers, club staff members were lining the walls. It was somehow more pleasant to perform when not enough seats were available for the spectators and many had to stand. We must have been in good form, because the applause meeting each number was quite generous, accompanied by, what was still disturbing to us, loud, piercing whistles as an American sign of approval. But no whistles came after the "The Death March"—

only silence. Then, while we stood on the stage, our heads lowered, the audience began to clap slowly, in unison. They clapped for a long time. A girl in waitress uniform was wiping tears from her cheeks with her palms.

The Kuhrhaus snack room was set with round tables, ready to treat us to a hearty meal. It was a cozy, alcove-like room, separated from the rest of the club, and out of its French double doors lining two walls, the ponds and park seemed almost to enter the building. How lovely this Bad-Nauheim was! I recalled hearing once that Tolstoy, in his novel *Anna Karenina*, used the Bad-Nauheim Kurhaus setting as the scene of young Kitty's "taking the cure" while dying of her love for Vronsky, who—the scoundrel!—chose a married woman, Anna Karenina instead.

No longer were Russian nobility coming for the cure, walking along the gravel paths, sitting on the wooden benches, observing the swans. Neither, I thought, were there any Russians of lesser standing. But still, I stared out through the French doors and dared to imagine hearing Kitty's voice.

"Eat, Fraulein, eat," the waitresses kept urging. They were young, good-looking girls in their early twenties, efficient and eager. After I could no longer eat, one waitress—with black, button-like eyes—came to my table. Her dark, curly hair was neatly held by a white crown, her mouth very red with lipstick, open in a wide smile, exposing healthy upper teeth so white they looked unreal, and directing that smile at me, she said, "More coffee?"

I could not accept any more coffee, could not accept more of anything. A second waitress who also was no longer busy, joined my girl and they both—leaning against the wall, with their empty trays— began to chat, right behind my chair.

"That crane," my waitress's voice announced, and I knew she meant me, "she stuffed her pockets full of doughnuts."

The second girl said compassionately—"What do you expect? On their ration card, one could starve to death. Funny, though, that 'kraut' jumped off her seat like a bee stung her when I brought the peanut butter sandwiches to that table there. She moved to your table and sits all alone."

"If you ask me," the first girl observed, "she's too tall. Sticks out on the stage like a lamp post. Should be a fashion model maybe, but not dancing."

"Well," the other protested, "she sure made me weep in that dance— all in black, death-like."

The girls stirred, coming over to once more offer some coffee. I sat with my throat in spasms, tears rolling down my heavily made-up cheeks, rolling into my mouth, down my neck, under my dress collar. And I could not stop this salty deluge, because the tears welled up the minute those girls started to talk. They were speaking in Russian! The purest Russian! They spoke the language I dared not use anywhere except with my family, and then often in a whisper. Since Boris Fyodorovich and Raisa Mikhailovna had vanished, I knew no one who spoke Russian. And there they were, those two unafraid Russian girls, chattering in the forbidden language, as if they were living on another planet where neither SMERSH, nor German civilians, nor American military authorities could grab them and deport them just because they were Russian. They even were as bold as to make their living working for the Americans. How could it be?

With her coffee carafe ready to pour, the girl with the button-like eyes said to the other girl, "Lida! Look! That girl is crying like a waterfall." And then to me, in German, "What's the matter, Fraulein? Can we help you? Something hurts?" Then the girl—in a peculiarly Russian gesture, erasing national boundaries—embraced my shoulders, and taking a paper napkin began to wipe away the tears.

"Something hurts?" she again asked, and stroked my hair. I still could not utter a sound, my throat refusing to open.

"Lena," the second girl, bending over me on the opposite side, said, quite concerned, "we have to find out what's the matter with her. She just doesn't say a word."

Getting myself under control, I finally said, still choking, "I am Russian, too. Russian. I cry because I'm happy!"

The girls screamed, forgetting they were still on duty. "Ours! You're ours! Oh! Our girl! What's your name? NEEN-och-kaa!"

The girls sat at my table, eyeing me with open delight, joy, petting my cheeks, my hands, wiping tears off my face, repeatedly saying, "Ours! Ours!" And this "ours" was so dear to me. They behaved as if they had found a long-lost relative, a sister. Their oft-repeated "ours" made me feel as if I *belonged,* and was no longer a refugee, a fugitive from SMERSH.

"But how can you work here? Not afraid of repatriation?" I finally asked my compatriots.

"Oh! That's no problem! We all have fake birth certificates. Some of us are Latvians, some Estonians, some even Germans. Ha! Ha! Ha!" They laughed because to be German was least desirable in the war-ruined country, but still preferable to repatriation. "Without those documents, krrrr," and Lena made a cutting-like gesture across her throat.

We three were chatting away, when a middle-aged man, very thin, with a prominent Greek nose, huge hazel eyes, burst into the snack room, and crisply commanded, "Girls! Hurry! Miss Lee needs you in the dance room to rearrange the tables. The Hawaiian Hula Dancers will need more room tonight!"

God in Heaven! This man was talking in the purest Soviet Russian! No Latvian or Estonian accent, but Soviet, which was slightly different even from the Russian that was spoken before the revolution. I was aghast.

"Oh, that's Nikolai Alexseyevich, our assistant manager. Miss Lee is the manager. She is from England. Cockney. We can hardly understand her. She's really strict. We've got to run!"

While they were getting up, another man, portly, short, about 40, all teeth missing, lisped as loud as he could, "Nikolai Alexseyevich! I need you in the office!" And this bookkeeper, too, was speaking Russian!

Before running off to their chores, the girls kissed me warmly and Lena said, "Ninochka, come to our 'Russian house' tonight. We have a whole colony here. Church too." And Lida chimed in, "How about working here at the club? Miss Lee is looking for a cashier. She canned a German woman the other day for stealing."

Finally, before leaving me, while they both tried to convince me to stay, Lena said conspiratorially, "If you don't have good fake papers, we'll get them for you."

I left the ballet troupe with much regret, and with the deepest, sincerest gratitude to its founder, Herr Raymonda. Now, instead of earning food with dancing, I began to earn it by being a cashier in the Bad-Nauheim Red Cross Club. The pay was 200 marks a month, and several thousand marks in cigarettes alone, for never did I say I did not smoke when offered a cigarette. And those cigarettes were feeding my mother, so that she began finally to gain weight, not reminding me of a skeleton when I embraced her. Slava, too, gained weight, and was receiving medical help from a German doctor who could be reached day or night—paid with tobacco.

I began to receive many invitations from Americans to evening dances in the club, to concerts, to movies. One fellow, named Henry, was particularly attentive, trying to invite me every single Saturday to the dance. He was a nice young man, with an auburn tint to his hair, and a kind smile, his eyes open, not devious.

New Year's Eve was approaching, and I loaded my suitcase with doughnuts, biscuits, and hot dog rolls, ready to cart it all to Mother. What she did not need, she passed on to her landlady, who still was living with the rest of the German population on very skimpy rations. Finding out about my impending trip by train, Henry offered to drive me in his jeep.

"I am driving to Frankfurt tomorrow. I can give you a lift," he said eagerly. The train ride took several hours, because I had to transfer three times to reach Klein Winternheim, sometimes waiting hours for my connections.

"But I have to go beyond Frankfurt—to Mainz," I said, regretting already having to miss the comfort a jeep would provide.

"That's okay! If you don't mind waiting a half hour for me in the jeep at Frankfurt Headquarters, I'll bring you to your mother and back!"

The next morning, bright and early, Henry's jeep was honking at the door of my efficiency apartment. Loaded with food parcels I climbed aboard, and two hours later I stood at the door to the attic room, anxious to surprise Mother, who was not expecting me that early.

On opening the door, and seeing the stranger with me, Mother said hurriedly, "Ninochka, wait a while. Slava has an attack." But it was too late to keep Henry from witnessing the situation. He stood at the threshold, looking at pale, shaking Slava, whose forehead was covered with vinegar compresses, imploring Mother to stay near him, "Mamochka, don't let me fall. Don't let me fall through the floor." Slava knew that the floors were not opening to swallow him, but in those moments it seemed so to him, and no amount of reasoning could completely reassure my brother until the attack was over.

While Mother held Slava's head in her lap, I hurried to a basin containing a vinegar and water solution, refreshing the compress, as the German doctor prescribed. The seizures only lasted three to four minutes, an eternity to the stricken Slava. And then, quickly, he came around, but remained pale and weak.

Henry stood shaken, observing us three in the grip of unexpected chaos, the onset of sudden illness, and Slava's need for a chamber pot during the attack. He gazed about at the narrow, pathetic garret with two cots and a table with two chairs; looked at the puny iron stove and the wall with hooks holding our shabby clothing—and he felt terribly sorry for us.

After Slava needed the vinegar compresses no longer, I turned to Henry, still standing in the doorway and said to him, "Please wait a few minutes in the courtyard. I'll call you." Pushing him away, I threw myself at the task of setting the room in order. The chamber pot disappeared, a curtain made of sheets was drawn over the hooks holding clothing, presenting now an entire wall of white; against it stood the small table covered with a crisp, fresh, linen tablecloth, hand embroidered by Mother. The bed linens were changed, the down pillows in lace-trimmed cases rose high and proud. Slava's face was quickly sponged, his hair combed, a cotton Russian-type shirt was produced out of one of the suitcases serving as a chest of drawers, while the small window flew open, letting in the crisp, winter air to chase away the sour smell of vinegar and illness. Soon a tea kettle was puffing, and as I had known instantly on entering the room earlier—even through the smell of Slava's compresses—*lepeshky* dough was rising, waiting for my arrival.

When Henry returned from his exile in the farm courtyard, our room had undergone a transformation. To us, that is. Not to Henry. He put his arm on my shoulder and said, voice full of pity, "How hard it is for you folks. To live in such poverty!"

Yet, were we truly living in poverty? I looked into Henry's eyes, and did not know how to convince him that we were actually very well off. Were we in the Soviet Union now, this attic room, with its individual cots, with the iron stove heating the tea kettle and frying the mouth-watering *lepeshky,* would have seemed a horn of plenty.

At that moment, Russia—victorious in war—was going through a frightful period with a famine of 1930s proportions engulfing the whole land. Cannibalism had once again raised its ugly head. And Stalin and SMERSH continued their terror, tightening the clamps that had been loosened during the war, uprooting the people, further centralizing farming, stocking the Gulags.

Were church bells ringing through the whole land, reaching even remote *kolkhozes,* as they were allowed to do during the war? Not any longer. Churches once again began to be boarded up or literally destroyed by the Party activists. The word "Russia" became once more a curse word. Stalin felt no limits on his power.

And here was my American friend Henry, pitying me and my family in that heavenly warm attic room, our table loaded with hot *lepeshky* and steaming tea with sugar cubes! Besides *lepeshky,* a glass bowl was overflowing with doughnuts. A paper bag full of cigarette butts stood under the table—that tobacco capable of buying comforts gold could not buy. No lice, no bed bugs plagued our abode. No paralyzing frosty winds kept us shivering. Still, the young fellow's face continued to reflect the initial shock, perhaps even revulsion, on seeing how we lived. There was a flatness, a shallowness in his eyes. They were not unkind but they had some sort of inner barrier, as if they needed, wanted to know only so much, nothing more. Yes! The eyes of that Triptis officer for whom Julius translated!

Not able to hide the slight irritation in my voice, I asked, "What is that saying, Henry, about the pessimist and the optimist?"

"Oh, you mean, 'The pessimist sees his glass half-empty, while the optimist sees his glass half-full'?"

"Yes, that's it! Our glass is not half-empty at all, Henry."

But the fellow shook his head. "Don't try to act brave and tell me it's half-full."

I knew at that moment, that the next time I came to visit my family, I would not be enjoying the comforts of a jeep, delivering me to the door as if it were a taxi, but rather I would come by train. By three trains.

Raising my tea glass and clinking it with Mother's and Slava's, I proposed a toast, "To our survival!"

Henry raised his glass, too. "I'll drink to that. After all, you survived the war, survived the Nazis."

"And Yalta!" I added.

"Yalta?" Henry did not understand.

Yet so many of my people who did not escape the forced repatriation, how well they would have understood this toast! Among them Zhenya, Raisa Mikhailovna, Boris Fyodorovich. And for the few lucky ones who did survive as we had done—the glass was not half-empty by any means.

Having survived Yalta, our cup runneth over.

While Henry seemed not to understand Yalta's far-reaching consequences, another young American serviceman did. He entered Bad-Nauheim's Red Cross Club soon after I parted with Henry—and he entered my life as well. It was his child I was carrying within me as a war bride, hurrying across the Atlantic, to give birth to a new American.

Perhaps my story will one day serve not only this child of mine, but his children also, as a bridge of understanding, uniting two great peoples—both my Russian predecessors and my American descendants. Had I not succeeded in escaping the forced repatriation, those descendants of mine would have been born—as I was—in the Soviet

Union. They would have been condemned to relive all that I had lived through in my own childhood.

May they know of the tumultuous routes I have traveled, before Fate led me into the country destined to become their native land—to the blessed shores of America.

Epilogue

Operation Keelhaul

*M*_any years_ were destined to pass before I could calmly, if still sadly, think and speak of certain events out of my past, especially of Yalta. It hurts to think of Yalta, hurts because atrocities committed against a helpless people were committed not by Nazis, or Fascists, or Communists, but by democracies. It hurts even more upon learning that no documents were signed, not even oral agreements were reached between Stalin and the Western Allies on using force during our repatriation. Stalin did ask for our return, including the return of prisoners of war, whose existence all through the war he refused to acknowledge. Yet he, himself, did not use the word "force." The initiative came from the British government of Prime Minister Churchill. Sir Winston succeeded in persuading an at first very reluctant President Roosevelt to follow the British example in using force. Within the American High Command in Europe at that time no general protested or questioned the orders. Except one—General George Patton. He questioned and protested, but to no avail.

Neither the Americans nor the French were carrying out the command to use force against the unwilling returnees as relentlessly as did the British. Not only men in the uniform of General Vlasov's Russian Liberation Army and other anti-Stalin units, but toddlers, expectant mothers, and crippled, invalided old folk were often treated with great inhumaneness by the British, and, in one instance, even shot at and massacred during a religious service. So many years later, the government of Prime Minister Thatcher found it fitting to dedicate a memorial to the victims of forced repatriation. Britain's historian-writer, Nikolai Tolstoy, spent years researching and documenting the Western

Allies' actions in many of his books, and particularly in *The Secret Betrayal*. American journalist Julius Epstein also recorded these events in his book *Operation Keelhaul*—a name given in 1947 to the program of forced repatriation. (Until then it was known as "Operation East-bound.") The later version was a fitting name, borrowed from times long past, when a sailor in the Dutch or British navy, having been adjudged guilty of some crime, was tied with ropes at the wrists and ankles and, after being thrown into the water, was dragged by two sailors leisurely walking from one end of the deck to the other, pulling the victim under the ship's hull. When they reached the opposite end of the deck, they hauled the sailor out. More often than not, by then the man would be dead from drowning, unable to breathe during this prolonged submersion. In exceptional cases, even if the man escaped drowning, he was brutally lacerated and scraped by the sharp shells and barnacles covering the bottom of the ship, dying of the infections. Keelhauling was tantamount to receiving a death sentence, only more sadistic than being shot or hanged.

The 20th century keelhauling lasted for four full years. Only in 1949 were the last SMERSH officers asked to leave the American Occupation Zone, and "Operation Keelhaul" came to a halt. The hunt had finally ended. But for many, it was too late.